Stephen N. Haynes

C. Chrisman Wilson

# *Behavioral Assessment*

## Recent Advances in Methods, Concepts, and Applications

Jossey-Bass Publishers

San Francisco • Washington • London • 1979

BEHAVIORAL ASSESSMENT
*Recent Advances in Methods, Concepts, and Applications*
by Stephen N. Haynes and C. Chrisman Wilson

Copyright © 1979 by: Jossey-Bass Inc., Publishers
433 California Street
San Francisco, California 94104
&
Jossey-Bass Limited
28 Banner Street
London EC1Y 8QE

**Library of Congress Cataloging in Publication Data**
Haynes, Stephen N
        Behavioral assessment.

        (The Jossey-Bass social and behavioral science series)
        Bibliography: p.
        1. Psychological tests. I. Wilson, C. Chrisman,
joint author. II. Title.
BF176.H39        155.2′8        79-88775
ISBN 0-87589-439-9

Manufactured in the United States of America


JACKET DESIGN BY WILLI BAUM




FIRST EDITION

*Code 7937*

The Jossey-Bass
Social and Behavioral Science Series

# Preface

Perhaps the most significant developments in psychological assessment have resulted from applying a behavioral construct system to enhance the functioning of individuals, families, institutions, and social systems. The increasing use of behavioral intervention strategies has fostered the need for preintervention assessment instruments and procedures that are methodologically sound and congruent with the theoretical assumptions underlying a behavioral construct system. As a result, there has been a dramatic increase in research on and clinical application of behavioral assessment instruments and procedures. In any of the behavior therapy journals, one can find a high percentage of articles with direct implications for behavioral assessment. The increasing importance of behavioral assessment is also indicated by the recent publication of books in the area and of two journals devoted to assessment.

The research activity, clinical application, and general interest in the field of behavioral assessment have suggested the need for a publication presenting recent advances in the field. This book is intended to fill that need by providing an integrated overview of recent advances in behavioral assessment. Included are presentations of recent research in the fields of structured observation procedures, observation in the natural environment, interviewing, questionnaires, self-monitoring, and psychophysiology. Also included are discussions on statistics, reliability and validity assessment, diagnosis, assessment of cognitive variables, computer assessment, environmental and community assessment, the use of participant observers, social validity, product-of-behavior measures, new methods of coding observation data, and new behavioral assessment instruments.

The format of this volume differs significantly from that of other books with a "recent advances" or "annual review" focus (for example, *Annual Review of Behavior Therapy*) in that the material is an *integration* of each specific area of behavioral assessment. As a result, each chapter provides an overview of a great many articles, which would be a difficult task if another format were adopted.

*Behavioral Assessment* focuses on recent advances in the field of behavioral assessment and does not attempt to present basic principles. Basic issues such as underlying assumptions, function, generalizability, reliability, content validity, criterion validity, construct validity, sensitivity, reactivity, and interobserver agreement have been presented in Cone and Hawkins (1977) and Haynes (1978) and are only briefly reiterated here. This book, therefore, is probably most suited for individuals who are actively engaged and knowledgeable in behavioral assessment research and clinical application. It is also suitable for use as an adjunct text in courses dealing with behavioral assessment and behavioral interventions.

Our intent was to include every recently published article with significant implications for issues, procedures, or principles of behavioral assessment. Although omissions are undoubtedly unavoidable, we feel that the chapters accurately represent current research trends in each particular field. This book is an overview of articles published in 1977 and 1978. Articles published prior to 1977 are not included unless they have direct relevance to recently published material.

The book is organized according to assessment strategy (for example, interviews, questionnaires) rather than target population (for example, social skills assessment, assessment of parent-child interaction). However, a comprehensive and detailed subject index will assist researchers and clinicians to locate research on particular target populations.

We would like to express our appreciation to Joseph Durlak, Linda Gannon, Bernard Jensen, Donald Shoemaker, and Gail Wilson for helpful comments on earlier versions of this book, and to Amy, Andy, Buffy, Burrhus, Felix, Harold, Maud, and Nicholas for supplying a high rate of noncontingent reinforcement during the preparation of this book.

*September 1979*                                         STEPHEN N. HAYNES
                                                        *Carbondale, Illinois*


                                                        C. CHRISMAN WILSON
                                                        *Austin, Texas*

# Contents

# Tables

# The Authors

STEPHEN N. HAYNES is professor of psychology at Southern Illinois University at Carbondale and previously was associate professor of psychology at the University of South Carolina. He was awarded the B.A. degree in psychology from Western Michigan University (1966), the M.A. degree in psychology from the University of Colorado (1969), and the Ph.D. degree in psychology from the University of Colorado (1971).

Haynes is the author of *Principles of Behavioral Assessment* (1978) and is co-editor with Linda Gannon of *Psychosomatic Disorders: A Psychophysiological Approach to Etiology and Treatment* (in press). His research and numerous journal publications in the fields of behavioral assessment and behavior analysis and therapy have included assessment and intervention with a variety of psychophysiological disorders, including headaches and sleep disturbances, and analysis and intervention with marital dysfunction.

C. CHRISMAN WILSON is assistant professor on the graduate faculty of the Department of Educational Psychology, University of

Texas at Austin. Previously he was visiting assistant professor in the Department of Psychology, University of South Carolina. He was awarded the B.S. degree in psychology from Western Carolina University (1965), the M.S. degree in psychology from Radford College (1968), and the Ph.D. degree in psychology from the University of South Carolina (1976).

Wilson's research in behavioral assessment and behavior analysis has involved investigations of social learning influences on children's prosocial behavior, the vicarious effects of intervention programs with children, the development of behavior coding and management procedures in speech therapy settings, and interventions with psychophysiological disorders including atopic dermatitis and essential hypertension.

# *Behavioral Assessment*

## Recent Advances in Methods, Concepts, and Applications

# CHAPTER ONE

# *Current Issues in Behavioral Assessment*

The behavioral construct system has continued to generate a large number of diverse intervention strategies and has been applied to an expanding number of personal and social problems. The implementation of these intervention strategies has occurred in a milieu emphasizing rigorous evaluation of theoretical assumptions and intervention procedures. The constructs and empirical orientation inherent in a behavioral model also have served to emphasize the importance of preintervention assessment. Assumptions of individual differences in topography and causative or maintaining factors of behavior, an emphasis upon the intensive study of one person or a few individuals, and the application of intervention strategies specifically designed for individual target subjects have underscored the importance of assessment in behavioral intervention. Preintervention assessment is a necessary antecedent of behavior therapy and serves a variety of functions, including the identification of idiosyncratic behavior patterns and maintenance factors as well as providing data with which to evaluate the effects of intervention.

The growing importance of behavioral assessment is evidenced by the number of recently published books on this topic (Ciminero, Calhoun, and Adams, 1977; Cone and Hawkins, 1977; Haynes, 1978; Hersen and Bellack, 1976a), the number of published articles dealing with issues and procedures in behavioral assessment, and the development of a new journal, *Behavioral Assessment*, under the auspices of the Association for the Advancement of Behavior Therapy. To illustrate, during a search of the literature in preparation for this book, over 400 articles published in 1977 were identified in which behavioral assessment instruments were used. In the same year, over 100 articles reported using observation in the natural environment (schools, homes, institutions, or the community) as an assessment instrument. These data dramatically illustrate the expanding applicability and growing importance of behavioral assessment. This volume is in response to the increasing application and importance of behavioral assessment and is meant to fill the gap between the intermittently published survey books and the ever-growing literature on behavioral assessment. The function of this volume is to present to the reader an integrated overview of recently published (1977-1978) articles and new developments in the field of behavioral assessment. An integrated review format, rather than a reprint format, was selected to facilitate coverage of the large number of relevant articles. For example, several hundred recently published articles are presented in the chapters on psychophysiology, interviewing, and naturalistic observation. Other methods of presentation would severely limit the number and scope of articles that could be included.

The book is organized around major behavioral assessment instruments: observation in the natural environment, observation in analogue environments, self-monitoring, questionnaires, interviewing, and psychophysiological assessment. The recently published research in each of these areas will be reviewed in terms of its applicability, function, reliability, validity, errors, innovative applications, and technological advancements; particular attention will be paid to articles presenting criterion-related validity data. It is not the function of this volume to present the conceptual foundations of the individual assessment instruments or of the assumptions, principles, and methods underlying behavioral assessment. These are important topics but have been adequately presented in the recently published volumes already noted. There is also no attempt to introduce the reader to the principles and assumptions of the behavioral construct systems upon which behavioral assessment strategies are based; these have been covered in books on behavior therapy (Leitenberg, 1976; Bandura, 1969). In addition, standard measurement theory concepts (reliability and criterion-related validity) are only briefly introduced. For example, in discussing recent advances in naturalistic observation (Chapter Three), it is assumed that the reader is familiar with issues of observer drift, time-sampling procedures, observer training methods, reactivity, and reliability. Instead of reiterating issues that have been satisfactorily presented elsewhere, this volume emphasizes *recent advances* in applicability, development, evaluation, and instrumentation in behavioral assessment.

## Individual Differences

The idiographic nature of human behavior and its determinants is perhaps the factor most responsible for the increasingly pivotal role of behavioral assessment within a behavioral construct system. Because of significant between-subject differences, some of the most important functions of behavioral assessment are the identification and specification of target behaviors and their characteristics and the specification of antecedent and consequent events. These functions of behavioral assessment are based upon the assumption that between-subject differences in response topography, maintaining and eliciting events, expectancies, historical factors, and social factors have a significant impact upon behavioral intervention development and outcome. Although it is certainly not a new concept, recent behavioral assessment articles have further emphasized this notion of individual differences and its importance in an assessment and intervention program.

Although individual differences will be discussed within the context of individual assessment instruments in subsequent chapters (see especially Chapter Eight), the concept also has implications for the general field of behavioral assessment. An article by Emery and Marholin (1977), for example, emphasized the importance of identifying individualized target behaviors in intervention programs with delinquents. In a survey of the literature from 1968 to 1977, however, the authors found that only 9.1 percent of the studies used individually tailored intervention strategies as a result of preintervention assessment findings. Most of the studies (twenty to twenty-two) selected the same target behavior as a dependent variable for all subjects and disregarded between-subject differences. Emery and Marholin illustrated the importance of preintervention behavioral assessment by noting the history of intervention with children in ghetto schools. It was assumed that the poor academic performance of many ghetto children could be attributed to the lack of adequate stimulation in the preschool home environment. Based on this untested assumption, many preschool programs, such as Head Start, were initiated. The initial disappointing effects of these programs may be attributed, in part, to inadequate assessment of determinants of poor academic performance prior to intervention. Later analyses suggested that inadequate school environments and poor teaching also contributed significantly to the underachievement of these children.

The importance of preintervention assessment and of the concept of individual differences in behavior determinants and topography was also emphasized in an article by Mischel (1977). He stressed the need for more "person-centered" functional analyses that recognize individual differences and focus upon the client's rather than the assessor's construct systems. Along the same lines, Evans (1977) stressed the importance of between-subject differences in biofeedback intervention. The author noted that a variety of etiological factors might be involved in psychosomatic disorders and suggested preintervention assessment of (1) operant consequences of targeted behavior, (2) specific skill deficits, (3) stress responses in specific situations, (4) stress responses to high-pressure situations, and (5) cognitive components. Emphasis upon preintervention assessment of individual differences in factors that maintain behavior problems is also found in the writings of Carr (1977), Goldfried and Goldfried (1977), Marziller and Winter (1978), Harris and Ersner-Hershfield (1978), Norton and Nielson (1977), Runyan (1977), and Klaus, Hersen, and Bellack (1977). Wolpe (1977), in particular, has stressed the importance of preintervention identification of maintaining factors in the selection of intervention strategies. He noted that similar behavior patterns may have different etiologies and that, as a result, differences in outcome could be expected from the application of one treatment method across a number of subjects with the same problem.

Wolpe's assertion that between-subject differences in the outcome of behavioral intervention may be a function of variation in the determinants of targeted behaviors has been reiterated in several recently published articles (D. Carroll, 1977; Caster and Parsons, 1977; Ciminero and Drabman, 1977; Leiblum and Kopel, 1977; Marziller and Winter, 1978; Runyan, 1977). Vogler and others (1977) and Vogler, Weissbach, and Compton (1977), for example, noted that whether controlled drinking or abstinence training is a more appropriate intervention goal with an alcoholic may be a function of preintervention drinking rates and such other characteristics as social and physical deterioration. Harris and Ersner-Hershfield (1978) reviewed studies on the suppression of seriously disruptive behavior with psychotic and retarded patients. The authors stressed the importance of individual differences in etiology and maintaining factors and argued that intervention strategies should be congruent with the assessment of these factors. The authors suggested that different intervention strategies would be indicated depending upon whether the seriously disruptive behavior was organically determined, maintained by positive reinforcement, maintained by negative reinforcement, or maintained by the need for stimulation.

Curran (1977) noted considerable evidence for individual differences in the etiology and maintenance of heterosexual social anxiety. He suggested that this behavioral syndrome may be a function of conditioned social anxiety, social skills deficits, or faulty cognitive appraisal of social stimuli. Therefore, the outcome of any one intervention modality, such as systematic desensitization or role playing, would be expected to vary as a function of the etiological and maintaining factors operating with individual target subjects. The clinical implication of these hypotheses is that preintervention assessment of controlling factors might facilitate selection of the potentially most effective intervention strategy. These contentions were supported in a recent study by Marziller and Winter (1978), who utilized within-subject designs to assess the effects of social skills training on four psychiatric outpatients. The authors noted important differences among patients—differences that affected the choice of treatment components (relaxation training, videotaped feedback, directive advice, and traditional social skills training) and the outcome of the intervention programs.

It is evident from these recent studies that the concept of individual differences in topography of behavior, in antecedent and maintaining factors, and in behavioral correlates (behaviors covarying or associated with the main target behavior) is receiving increasing emphasis by behavior analysts and is being increasingly integrated into behavioral construct systems and behavioral assessment. Most published behavioral intervention studies, however, still apply a single intervention strategy across a number of subjects. This can be attributed to several factors: (1) to adequately evaluate the interaction between intervention strategies and the individual differences of subjects, fairly complex experimented designs are necessary; (2) a large number of subjects is necessary for adequate analysis of the effect of individual differences; (3) there is an insufficient basis for selecting a few subject variables to study from the multitude available; (4) research on the overall effects of an intervention is prerequisite to a fine-grained analysis of the role of individual differences; and (5) there is little empirical foundation for the matching of intervention strategies to subject characteristics.

The assertion that individual differences are important in selecting and evaluating behavioral interventions is based upon rational rather than empirical analysis. Although there is a substantial body of research supporting between-subject variation in topography, etiological factors, and response to treatment, the relative importance of that variation has not been evaluated empirically. Because formal incorporation of the concept of individual differences into intervention methodology would significantly complicate assessment and intervention strategies, it is important to ascertain the proportion of variance ($R^2$) in treatment outcome that is attributable to individual differences. For example, in the treatment of muscle-contraction headache, relaxation training and frontal electromyographic (EMG) biofeedback are quite effective in reducing the frequency of headaches (approximately 80 to 100 percent reduction in frequency for most subjects) without taking into consideration individual differences in etiology (Beaty and Haynes, in press). In this case, the proportion of unexplained variance is small, and only a portion of that residual variance could be explained by an analysis of individual differences. With interventions that are very effective across subjects, the effort required to assess individual differences (such as psychophysiological assessment in the case of headaches) may not be warranted by the expected degree of increased effectiveness. With muscle-contraction headache, for example, it may be more cost efficient to expose each subject to relaxation instructions or frontal EMG feedback without considering individual differences in etiology.

The previous discussion was meant to emphasize the concept of *explained variance* in treatment outcome, and we are not recommending that research on individual differences in etiology be abandoned. We are simply recommending closer examination of the a priori assumption that assessment of individual differences will, in all cases, result in a significant increase in the applicability and effectiveness of intervention. Ultimately, a cost-benefit analysis (cost of assessing individual differences and benefits in improved effectiveness) will dictate the utility of emphasizing individual differences. The increased benefits accruing to an evaluation of individual differences will be a function of the amount of additional variance accounted for, along with the clinical importance of that variance.

## Evaluation of Behavioral
## Assessment Instruments

Until recently, the evaluation of behavioral assessment instruments (such as naturalistic observation or self-monitoring) has been relatively unsystematic, partially as a result of behavior analysts' tendencies to reject traditional, nonbehavioral assessment instruments. Unfortunately, the rejection of these instruments was accompanied by a rejection of such traditional psychometric concepts as reliability and validity, and evaluation of behavioral assessment instruments was pursued with concepts more specific to the idiosyncratic characteristics of behavioral assessment instruments. Thus, naturalistic observation of a family in its home has been most frequently evaluated on issues of observer accuracy, the particular codes utilized, observer drift, sampling parameters, and reactivity. Concepts such as between-session reliability, content validity, and criterion validity were seldom invoked when discussing a particular assessment instrument.

A major recent development in the field of behavioral assessment is the use of traditional psychometric concepts to complement those evaluative concepts idiosyncratic to behavioral assessment. As a result, there is less of a tendency than formerly to consider data derived from trained observers to be indicative of "real behavior" and a more appropriate tendency to consider them as simply information from one assessment instrument that may or may not be reliable or correlate with data from other assessment instruments. This incorporation of traditional psychometric concepts has greatly increased the sophistication of behavioral assessment, and major portions of subsequent chapters will focus on the reliability and validity of various assessment instruments. This section will briefly discuss these psychometric concepts, but readers unfamiliar with them should consult Cone and Hawkins (1977), Mischel (1977), Maloney and Ward (1976), or Haynes (1978).

*Applicability and utility* refer to the amenability of an instrument to the assessment of particular populations, target problems, questions, and environments, and the degree of training necessary for its application. The behavioral interview, for example, may not be applicable with some severely retarded subjects or in the assessment of the relationship between heart-rate and pressure. Similarly, it is often difficult to utilize psychophysiological assessment in the natural environment or in the assessment of such social interactions as marital dysfunction. Inferences about the applicability and utility of an assessment instrument are based upon a rational analysis of the instrument, of the target responses, and of the validity of derived data for particular targets. For example, since data on child abuse gathered from home interviews may not be valid (it may not correlate with data from other assessment procedures, such as inspection of police files), interviews with this target population may not be applicable. Amenability of an assessment instrument to use by *mediators* is another important consideration. Self-monitoring and naturalistic observation, for example, have been effectively used by children, parents, teachers, and institutionalized individuals, thus greatly enhancing their applicability and utility.

*Sensitivity* refers to the degree to which an assessment instrument reflects changes in the target population or behaviors and the latency between behavior change and its reflection in assessment data. Some questionnaires, for example, are more sensitive than others to day-by-day changes in feelings of depression; others reflect only long-term or more extensive changes. Direct observation of an aggressive child in the classroom may be more sensitive than teachers' subjective perceptions of aggression to modifications in the rate of aggressive behavior associated with a behavioral intervention program. When an instrument is considered insensitive, this implies that changes in the target constructs, such as hyperactivity or marital dissatisfaction, have occurred but are not reflected in changes in the data derived from the measurement instrument. Sensitivity may vary as a function of the measures derived from an assessment instrument. For example, several recent articles (see Chapter Eight) noted that heart-rate variability may be more sensitive than mean heart rate to the presentation of feared stimuli. A measurement instrument may be *too* sensitive if it registers maximal response to small changes in stimulus levels. Skin conductance, for example, often demonstrates maximal increases to mild pain stimuli, and increases in pain levels are not accompanied by increases in skin conductance.

*Reliability* is a complex concept that is often used inconsistently. Reliability generally refers to the consistency or stability of behavior or of inferences that can be derived from one administration of an assessment instrument (one administration of a questionnaire or one observation session), or to the consistency within portions of an instrument (consistency between time samples within an observation session or agreement between questionnaire or interview items). Mischel (1977) and Cone and Hawkins (1977) have recently discussed reliability and also noted the complexity of the concept.

Reliability of a measurement instrument most frequently refers to the consistency or stability of data derived from a series of administrations—the degree to which one datum can be predicted from previous data. Inconsistency may be a reflection of true variability of the target behavior or may be a function of error in the measurement instrument (Nelson and others, 1977). *Internal consistency* most frequently involves the relationship among elements of an assessment instrument (such as behavior codes, time samples, or questions) or the relationship between these elements and the overall score derived from the instrument. Internal consistency can be measured by numerous procedures, including interitem correlations, split-half reliabilities, cluster analyses, and factor analyses. All measures of internal consistency help the researcher evaluate the homogeneity of an instrument (the degree to which its elements measure the same construct) and to identify factors or concepts that may be embodied in it.

The consistency in resultant data between separate administrations of an assessment instrument (sometimes referred to as *external reliability*) is most frequently evaluated by *test-retest reliability* procedures in which scores or other data, such as behavior rates derived from one administration, are compared to scores or rates from a subsequent or previous administration. In utilizing observation procedures, the concept of reliability is frequently confused with the concept of *interobserver agreement*. Interobserver agreement is evaluated by having more than one observer observe the same target subject at the same time and by calculating a coefficient of agreement among observers. Interobserver agreement does not provide a measure of consistency over time. *Criterion agreement* usually refers to the degree of agreement between an observer and a criterion observation protocol carefully scored by several highly trained observers. Both procedures are meant to estimate the accuracy of the observers. All forms of reliability are important because they suggest the maximum degree of confidence that can be placed in the data derived from an assessment instrument. Thus, reliability is a prerequisite to, and sets maximum limits on, validity.

*Content validity* refers to the degree to which the content of a measurement instrument reflects concepts inherent in the target constructs being assessed. For example, analogue observation situations for assessing assertive behavior should include a variety of situations, such as turning down an unreasonable request, expressing positive feelings toward a friend, or disagreeing with an opinion. Similarly, the assessment instrument should sample behavioral, cognitive, and subjective components. These situational and response elements of the analogue assessment instrument reflect current conceptualizations of assertive behavior. Also, to reflect current conceptualizations of depression, a behavioral questionnaire on depression should contain questions on recent loss of reinforcement, attitudes of helplessness, and response of others to depressive behaviors. Content validity is most often a subjectively evaluated characteristic of an assessment instrument and is usually reflected in criterion-validity coefficients.

A recently published article by Foster (1978) has implications for the content validity of most assessment procedures. Foster noted a failure in applied behavioral research to evaluate adjunctive or schedule-induced behavior changes that might be associated with behavioral intervention programs. Many behaviors, he noted, may be indirectly affected by changes in controlling stimuli of other behaviors (for example, contingent punishment for spitting might increase aggression). It is important that the assessment procedures implemented be sensitive to the occurrences of these behaviors. Examples of adjunctive behavior changes might include modification of teacher-child social interactions associated with time-out programs for disruptive classroom behavior or changes in the rate of enuretic behavior associated with a contingency program for noncompliance. Despite indications in the literature on experimental analysis of behavior that changes in adjunctive behavior are a frequent occurrence, applied behavior analysts have been too narrow in their assessment focus and have not attempted to evaluate adjunctive behavior changes that might be associated with behavioral intervention programs.

*Criterion-related validity,* another complex and inconsistently applied concept, refers to the degree to which the outcome of a measurement instrument correlates with the outcome of other measurement instruments or with the naturally defined status of target subjects. Criterion validity may be internal or external. As Tunnell (1977) noted, internal validity is concerned with ascertaining the degree to which the obtained results are a function of the concepts under study rather than of some other factors. Internal validity of an assessment device is reflected by the degree of correlation between two simultaneous but different measures of the same target constructs. Thus, the internal validity of a subject's self-monitoring may be assessed by utilizing an external observer who concurrently monitors the same behavior. External validity is the degree to which data from one assessment instrument correlates with data from other instruments administered in different situations or at different times; or, as Tunnell (1977) noted, external validity is the degree to which findings from one assessment instrument can be generalized to other situations or instruments. External validity may involve the same or different elements of target constructs. For example, the external validity of an interview with parents regarding their child's aggressive behavior may be evaluated by home observations, self-monitoring, or interviews with other family members.

Criterion-related validity may be either predictive or concurrent. *Predictive validity* is the degree to which the results from an assessment instrument correlate with data from other assessment instruments administered at a later time (such as the association of a pretreatment questionnaire with the effectiveness of parents as behavior modifiers). *Concurrent validity* is the correlation between two assessment instruments administered at the same time. Other types of external validity include *discriminant validity*—the degree to which an instrument can identify subjects who are classified in groups on the basis of naturally occurring phenomena (examples might include hospitalized and nonhospitalized patients, divorced and married couples). One cautionary note in interpreting validity coefficients was offered in a recent article by Green (1978). Although focusing particularly upon selection tests such as the Scholastic Aptitude Test (SAT), B. F. Green (1978) noted that the coefficient between any questionnaire score and behavior emitted in specific situations would probably be low. Tests tend to measure

aggregates of behavior across time and situations, and their predictive validity for one specific situation may not be high. Low-validity coefficients, therefore, are not necessarily indicative of invalidity; to interpret a validity coefficient, it is imperative to examine the comparative contents of the two assessment instruments.

Inherent in evaluation of assessment instruments is an evaluation of the targeted constructs that they are designed to measure. Low criterion-validity coefficients may be indicative of an invalid assessment instrument, an invalid construct, or both. For example, a marital satisfaction questionnaire must reflect the behavioral conceptualizations of marital satisfaction. Indices of the validity of the questionnaire (such as effectiveness in identifying couples seeking marital counseling from those not seeking marital counseling) also support the *construct validity* of the concepts incorporated in the questionnaire. All validity assessment has implications for the construct validity of an assessment instrument. Indices of invalidity may reflect on the assessment instrument or upon the construct.

The classic (Campbell and Fiske, 1959) model of construct validation involves the use of divergent and convergent validation assessment (multimethod, multitrait approach). In essence, several constructs are evaluated with several assessment instruments. Construct validity would be indicated by high correlations among instruments assessing the same construct and low correlations when assessing different constructs. One powerful method of construct validation in behavioral analysis is manipulation. All behavioral construct systems involve assumptions about the degree of control over behavior exerted by various behavioral, cognitive, physiological, and environmental factors. If these conceptualizations are valid, manipulation of the hypothesized controlling factors should be associated with modifications of the dependent behaviors. The fields of experimental analysis of behavior and applied behavior analysis can be conceptualized as attempts to assess the validity of a behavioral and environmental construct system and to refine that construct system through manipulation studies. However, manipulation is only an indirect method of construct validation. Without supporting evidence, it cannot be assumed that behavior changes that accompany manipulation of hypothesized controlling variables are actually attributable to those variables rather than to some other mediational event.

A concept closely tied to that of reliability and validity but perhaps involving a more systematic approach is *generalizability theory* (Cone and Hawkins, 1977; Cronbach and others, 1972). The concepts of reliability and validity may be reinterpreted as determining the dimensions across which the data derived from one assessment administration are generalizable. External validity, for example, reflects the degree to which inferences from an assessment instrument can be generalized to other situations. Cone (1977) noted six aspects of generalization: (1) scorer (interobserver agreement), (2) item, (3) time, (4) setting, (5) method, and (6) dimension. Coates and Thoresen (1978) presented a well-conceptualized discussion of the implications of generalizability theory in behavioral observation. The authors noted that the primary contribution of generalizability theory is that it identifies variance proportions associated with various factors in an assessment program (such as variance between observation sessions, between observers, and between situations) and thus assists the behavior analyst in determining procedures necessary for generating reliable estimates of behavior. For example, analysis of the variance in behavior rates between successive observation periods (assuming other factors remain constant) allows the behavior analyst to determine the number of observation sessions necessary to generate reliable estimates of behavior rate and also to estimate the confidence that can be placed in the reliability of data derived from any one observation session.

Coates and Thoresen (1978) also noted several characteristics and benefits associated with the application of generalizability theory: (1) it is an extension of the concept of reliability and emphasizes the relativity of inferences; (2) it emphasizes the multiple sources of error in any assessment instrument; (3) it allows evaluation of the proportion of variance accounted for by various sources of variation (between subjects, within subjects, between observers, and between situations); and (4) it has important implications for the cost effectiveness of various intervention strategies. Coates and Thoresen's article exemplifies current trends within the field of measurement—and specifically in behavioral assessment—to form more consistent and meaningful conceptualizations of assessment instrument characteristics than were formerly available. Such efforts should result in more fine-grained evaluations of assessment instruments, facilitate the development of assessment instruments with a higher degree of empirical validity, and focus attention upon the cost effectiveness of various assessment strategies.

The issue of *reactivity* is particularly important in behavioral assessment. Reactivity refers to immediate or long-term changes in the target behavior or target subjects as a function of the assessment procedures. Self-monitoring of smoking, for example, may be associated with modifications in the rate of smoking by the target subject. To further illustrate, long-term effects on marital interaction or satisfaction may result from the assessment of the communication skills of a couple in an analogue situation. The analogue assessment experience may stimulate further discussion and analysis of marital interaction by the couple and therefore affect overall marital satisfaction. Reactivity is partially a function of the obtrusiveness of an assessment procedure and is a threat to the external validity of assessment data. Thus, if an assessment procedure is associated with a modification in the topography or rate of the target behavior, the degree to which the data reflect the behavior of the target subject outside the assessment situation is minimized. Less novel or less obtrusive assessment procedures may result in data with a greater degree of external validity. A variety of factors may control reactivity, including knowledge of the assessment procedures, expectancy factors, obtrusiveness, novelty, and previous exposure to similar assessment situations. Because determinants and degree of reactivity vary among assessment instruments, reactivity will be considered in greater detail in subsequent chapters.

As noted, there has been an increasing recognition of the importance of psychometric and conceptual evaluation of assessment instruments. Too often, behavior analysts have assumed that data derived from behavioral assessment instruments, particularly direct observation, were valid without sufficient empirical foundations upon which to base those assumptions. An increasing number of researchers, such as Nelson, Cone, Coates, and Mischel, are emphasizing the importance of reliability and validity assessment and are calling for a more thorough assessment of sources of error in assessment instruments. This methodological approach is bound to produce an increasing sophistication in behavior assessment instruments and procedures.

There are many other factors that can affect the validity of an assessment instrument—for example, credibility of the instrument (Kirsch and Henry, 1977), expectancies by subjects (Briddell and Wilson, 1976; Wilson, 1977), response bias, cultural bias, experimenter errors (Barber, 1976), and demand factors (Lick and Unger, 1977). These factors are all capable of decreasing the degree of confidence that can be placed in the data derived from a measurement instrument. One frequent source of error is the response bias sometimes associated with socially sensitive targets. For example, self-report information regarding sexual behavior, antisocial behavior, or illicit drug intake is often suspect because of the social values associated with these behaviors. Subjects sometimes provide inaccurate information about these topics in a questionnaire or an interview.

Fidler and Kleinknecht (1977) presented an interesting and potentially useful randomized response procedure for obtaining information about socially sensitive topics (in their study, sexual behavior and sexual values). Each subject is placed alone in a room. Before answering each question from a questionnaire, the subject turns a wheel containing pellets indicating that the response to be provided should be either the "real" response or one indicated by the pellets. In the Fidler and Kleinknecht study, there were ten red pellets, three nonred pellets with "yes" printed on them, and three nonred pellets with "no" printed on them. If the subject selected a nonred pellet, the answer printed on the pellet was to be entered as the answer to the question. If a red pellet was selected, the subject was to answer honestly. This procedure thus assures the anonymity of each subject's response. With a large number of subjects and with a prior knowledge of the probabilities of red and nonred pellets, the assessor can ascertain the "true" rate of a particular answer, and data with a higher degree of validity on socially sensitive issues can be derived than would otherwise be possible. When Fidler and Kleinknecht compared data derived from this randomized response procedure to other questionnaire procedures

where anonymity of responses was stressed to the subjects but where the randomized procedure was not used, they obtained results suggesting that the data from the randomized response procedure were more valid. This assessment method obviously is limited to rather large groups of subjects but is a highly ingenious method of assessing targets for which valid information is difficult to gather because of the socially sensitive nature of the material.

## Response Fractionation and
## Multimodal Assessment

The term *response fractionation* refers to the assumption that behavioral constructs such as aggression, social skills, or fear are composed of many elements that frequently do not covary in their response to external stimuli or to behavioral intervention. For example, sexual dysfunctions may involve interfering cognitive stimuli, sympathetically mediated physiological arousal, behavioral avoidance, and skill deficits. These components are likely to vary in their occurrence and role among individuals with sexual dysfunctions and to be differentially affected by any one intervention strategy. Response fractionation is not a new concept, but it has recently received increasing emphasis within behavior construct systems. The importance of response fractionation and its impact upon behavioral assessment have been stressed in several recent articles (Adams and Sturgis, 1977; Hartmann, Roper, and Gelfand, 1977; Marziller and Winter, 1978; Sartory, Rachman, and Grey, 1977). As noted in Chapter Eight, fractionation may be observed within a response system as well as between systems (May, 1977a, 1977b; G. E. Schwartz, 1977). For example, within a physiological response system, heart rate may react differently from skin conductancy to systematic desensitization. Similarly, some behavior codes used in naturalistic observation may reflect changes as a function of behavioral intervention, others may not.

The concept of response fractionation (sometimes referred to as response desynchronization) has significant implications for behavioral assessment. The major impact is an emphasis upon broad-spectrum (multimodal) assessment. Assumptions of low levels of covariance between response modes and variability in

these measures in response to behavioral intervention suggest that multimodal assessment is necessary for a comprehensive evaluation of a target construct and for evaluation of treatment outcome. Because a particular target problem such as autism or depression may involve idiosyncratic combinations of a number of response systems and elements for individual subjects, assessment of cognitive, overt behavioral, subjective perception, and physiological modes is necessary to delineate adequately its characteristics and maintaining factors.

The concept of response fractionation also complicates the evaluation of intervention outcomes. If interventions can be expected to have differential impact upon various response modes, multimodal assessment is necessary to identify adequately the effects of an intervention or to compare two or more interventions. As Wolpe (1977) noted, desensitization would be expected to be more effective with physiological than with cognitive components of fear or anxiety. Comparing desensitization with a cognitive restructuring approach and using a cognitive dependent variable would not result in a sufficiently valid or comprehensive evaluation of the comparative effectiveness of the two interventions and would introduce bias into inferences of effectiveness. Care must be exercised in the selection of dependent variables when assessing intervention outcome because various dependent variables will be differentially sensitive to different interventions. Response fractionation also complicates the task of criterion-related validation. Criterion-related validation procedures are based on the assumption that the criterion and target measures should demonstrate a high degree of correlation; low correlation suggests low validity. The concept of response fractionation, however, qualifies the assumption of covariation and makes interpretation of negative findings more difficult.

A number of recent studies have utilized multimodal assessment techniques and noted low correlations among dependent measures. Bronwell, Hayes, and Barlow (1977), for example, utilized physiological, self-report card-sort, self-monitoring, and interview measures with several cases of sexual behavior disorders. Some measures were highly correlated, others were not. Burchardt and Levis (1977) noted low correlations between self-report and

overt behavioral measures of fear. Cohen (1977) compared a variety of self-report and overt behavior measures of acrophobia and found significant variation in correlation coefficients among an acrophobia questionnaire, structured observation, the Fear Survey Schedule, and self-report measures. B. Martin (1977) found significant differences between interview- and telephone-derived information about family problems. Mathews and Rezin (1977) exposed subjects with dental fear to several behavioral interventions and found variability in outcome depending upon whether questionnaire responses or observation measures were evaluated. Moss and Arend (1977) noted variable but generally high correlations among analogue observation, Fear Survey Schedule, and Fear Thermometer measures of the effects of self-directed contact desensitization on snake avoidance. Nelson and others (1977) reported generally low correlations between teachers' self-monitoring data and data from external observers. Thomas and Rapp (1977) reported the case of a forty-year-old woman with eyepatch phobia treated with flooding. These authors found the greatest treatment effects evidenced in an analogue observation assessment; there was also significant change in physiological measures, but no change in self-reported anxiety.

The finding of response fractionation in some but not other studies suggests that the occurrence or extent of this phenomenon is a function of subject, response, or methodology variables and should be subjected to empirical evaluation. Factors affecting the degree of correlation among response modalities are complex and probably include:

1. Random error within each assessment modality. Each response modality has its own source of measurement error (such as sixty-cycle interference in physiological measures and reactivity in analogue observation situations). These idiosyncratic sources of error increase error variance in the obtained data and reduce the correlations among modes (Mintz and others, 1973).
2. Response intensity or variability. Subjects who demonstrate more intense or variable responses may demonstrate higher correlation coefficients among dependent measures than do other subjects. Consistent with this assumption, Rachman (1976)

suggested that correlations among responses should be higher before than after treatment because treatment can decrease intensity or variability of responses. This hypothesis has also been supported by Sartory, Rachman, and Grey (1977), who found that correlations among measures increased with increases in fear intensities. The relationship between response fractionation and intensity may represent a statistical property because of a greater range in variables or may accurately state the relationship between variables as a function of the subject's "state."

3. Other sources of error. Hartmann, Roper, and Gelfand (1977) have noted that several other factors serve to minimize the degree of covariation among response modalities. They noted that response measures differ in their domains, degree of specificity, manner of data collection, sources of vantage points (behavior analyst or client), setting, and sampling procedures.

In summary, response fractionation is an increasingly important concept in behavioral assessment. It emphasizes the importance of multimodal assessment in facilitating valid analyses of targeted behaviors and in the comprehensive evaluation of intervention outcomes. Because of response fractionation, however, considerable care must be given to interpreting the results of criterion-related validity studies. Response fractionation is inconsistently observed, and its occurrence and extent should be the subject of empirical examination.

Based on the assumptions that response fractionation exists, that behavior has multiple and complex components and determinants, that individual differences are important, and that criterion and generalization assessment is also important (Angle and others, 1977; Haynes, 1978; Ketterer and Smith, 1977; Klorman, Weissberg, and Wiesenfeld, 1977; LeBow, Goldberg, and Collins, 1977; May, 1977a, 1977b; Mischel, 1977; Valle and DeGood, 1977), *multimodal assessment* has received increasing emphasis within behavioral construct systems. Such broad-spectrum assessment stresses the utilization of a variety of measurement procedures as well as the assessment of a variety of components of target problems. But, although numerous authors have recently encouraged the utilization of multimodal behavioral assessment (Epstein and Abel, 1977; Hartmann, Roper, and Gelfand, 1977; Lazarus, 1976;

Lineham and others, 1978; Reynolds, 1977; and Stuart, 1970), Angle and others (1977) have suggested that its efficacy may be a function of the particular targets being assessed and may not always be appropriate. These authors have suggested that the appropriateness of broad- or narrow-spectrum assessment will vary with the particular target behavior, applicable assessment procedures, financial and time considerations, social significance of the targeted problems, and client concerns.

Although multimodal assessment offers obvious benefits to the behavior analyst, the cautions noted by Angle and others (1977) are well taken. The utility of multimodal assessment should be the subject of substantial empirical evaluation. Ultimately, a cost-benefit analysis will be necessary before an empirically based recommendation can be offered concerning its appropriateness with specific targets. As will be evident from subsequent chapters, multimodal assessment is being pursued in an increasing proportion of studies in the behavioral intervention literature. However, as Angle and associates pointed out, even if a philosophy of multimodal assessment is adopted, there are currently no procedural guidelines to assist the behavior analyst in the selection of measures or of targets to be assessed.

## Behavioral Diagnosis

Like response fractionation and multimodal assessment, diagnosis has been the focus of increasing discussion in recent behavioral assessment literature. Behavioral assessment procedures are being used to classify individuals into diagnostic categories, and numerous behavioral researchers have stressed the importance of developing an alternative to the Diagnostic and Statistical Manual (DSM) of the American Psychiatric Association. Although Eysenck (1977) and Guilford (1975) focused on personality traits such as "impulsiveness," they noted that the goal of diagnostic efforts may be delineation of personality or behavioral factors, better understanding of the etiology of behavior, and better understanding of socially significant behavior. The most recent emphasis upon behavioral diagnosis has been due, in part, to the methodological and conceptual inadequacies of the DSM. Limitations of the DSM have been frequently noted and may be summarized as (1) insufficient interjudge reliability (Achenbach, 1974; Ciminero and Drabman, 1977; Hobbs, 1975a, 1975b, 1975c; Hogan, DeSoto, and Solano, 1977; Spitzer and Fleiss, 1974; Strasburger and Jackson, 1977); (2) an overemphasis upon "trait" conceptualizations of human behavior (Hogan, DeSoto, and Solano, 1977); (3) adoption of a disease model for behavior disorders (Achenbach, 1974); (4) vague and ambiguous categorical concepts and excessive symptom variance within categories (O'Farrell and Upper, 1977; Philips and Draguns, 1971); (5) inefficiency of the standard assessment procedures (Clavelle and Butcher, 1977); (6) insufficient criterion-related validity assessment, whether predictive or concurrent (Achenbach, 1974; Ciminero and Drabman, 1977; Hobbs, 1975a, 1975b, 1975c; Ross, 1974); and (7) limited applicability and utility (Achenbach, 1974; Ciminero and Drabman, 1977; Hobbs, 1975a, 1975b, 1975c; Ross, 1974).

The "trait" concept has been a prime target of behavior analysts' attacks upon the traditional diagnostic approaches. Inherent in trait concepts is the assumption that behavior occurs in clusters or syndromes and that these clusters tend to occur reliably across situations. Individuals who manifest traits such as "aggressiveness," "dependency," or "impulsiveness" will tend to emit behaviors within those categories across a broad range of situations. Hogan, DeSoto, and Solano (1977) addressed the issue of traits in personality theory and suggested that the criticism of trait theorists is, in part, inappropriate. They reviewed the major criticisms of personality research (use of trait concept, insufficient concurrent and predictive validity, primary function of personality theory being the assignment of subjects to categories, and generation of "mindless" research). They noted that traits refer only to stylistic consistencies of subjects and that there is no assumption of cross-situation invariability inherent in trait theory. They also noted that the "trait" concept does not imply an explanatory function; that is, "impulsiveness" or "hostility" may be descriptive of behavior patterns, and such terms do not necessarily imply mediational or causative factors. Attacks upon "traits," they noted, might better be directed at the behavioral scientists who misuse them in the assessment process.

Hogan and his associates suggested that disagreements about the utility of traits may arise from variability in their use, interpretation, and role as descriptive concepts (for example, compare the utility of traits such as "fingernail biting" and "egoism"). They noted that the most consistent traits tend to be "goals" of individuals rather than "means." They also took issue with the idea that traits are totally constructed in the "mind of the beholder"; they cited cross-cultural research indicating that some traits are fairly universal. The primary test of the utility of a trait, they suggested, is its predictive efficacy; some traits may be capable of explaining a significant proportion of behavioral variance. Mischel (1977) noted that *some* people probably demonstrate stability in *some* traits, a point that suggests the need for research on the determinants of trait stability. In essence, Hogan and associates and Mischel are suggesting that the potential utility of traits should not be prematurely rejected and that their utility will vary as a function of their application and the behavioral types they are describing.

Mellstrom, Zuckerman, and Cicala (1978) reported a study on the predictive validity of specific and general anxiety traits. One hundred and fourteen subjects were pretested with general measures—State-Trait Anxiety Inventory (STAI) A-Trait and Neuroticism Scale of Eysenck Personality Inventory—or specific measures—Fear Survey Schedule III and Zuckerman Inventory of Personal Reactions—and exposed to three situations involving a rat, a test, and social anxiety. Specific but not general trait measures of anxiety predicted subjects' behavioral and subjective responses in these situations; thus, the predictive validity of the specific measures was significantly greater than that of the general measures in seven of thirty-two comparisons, but the reverse was never true. This study serves to emphasize that the utility of a trait is a function of various factors—in this case, degree of specificity.

The assumptions underlying behavioral diagnosis are similar to those underlying traditional diagnostic efforts. The primary assumption is that behaviors can be grouped into meaningful clusters, classes, or factors and that some behaviors will tend to covary together or to demonstrate similar changes across situations. This assumption has been recently emphasized by Eysenck (1977), Achenbach (1978), Achenbach and Edelbrock (1978), Newmark

and others (1976), Mischel (1977), and Morf, Syrotuik, and
Krznaric (1977). Mischel has noted, more specifically, that the degree to which behaviors covary or the stability of traits will vary
among individuals and as a function of the cluster under study.
Like other researchers, Mischel stressed that some traits, for some
individuals or across some situations, are useful concepts.

The significance of trait theory lies not just in assumptions
of cross-situation stability but in the implications of this concept for
etiological inferences and treatment. It is assumed that, if a behavior cluster can be reliably identified, the determinants of behaviors
within that cluster will be similar and similar determinants will be
operating across individuals manifesting that cluster. For example,
with a trait or cluster of behaviors labeled "depression" (behaviors
such as low rates of social interaction, decreased mobility, high rate
of depressive statements, cognitive self-deprecatory thoughts, and
unassertiveness), trait theory would suggest that individuals labeled
"depressed" would have been affected by similar determinants and
would be amenable to similar interventions (Eysenck, 1977; Morf,
Syrotuik, and Krznaric, 1977). In some cases, the treatment implications associated with various diagnostic categories are readily apparent. For example, diagnosis of a headache subject as having
migraine or muscle-contraction headaches would have significant
implications for the selection of the most potentially efficacious
treatment (Feuerstein and Adams, 1977). Similarly, diagnosis of
erectile failure as functional or organic (Fisher and others, 1975)
might not only identify etiology but also suggest the most efficacious treatment. In a similar vein, Buskirk (1977) noted that
between-study differences in the outcome of behavioral intervention with anorexia nervosa may be a function of the lack of reliable
diagnostic procedures and of variation in symptoms within that
classification.

The treatment implications of diagnostic efforts have also
been illustrated in other recently published articles. Cairns and
Pasino (1977), for example, discussed the use of sodium pentothal
to diagnose pain as organic or functional in origin. Unfortunately,
although this approach seems useful, the outcome of behavioral
intervention in their research was not associated with differential

diagnosis of a sample of nine patients. Carlin and Stauss (1977) described a diagnostic procedure to classify youthful drug abusers as either "streetwise" or "straight." Such information might have implications for the most appropriate intervention, although this was not tested in their study. Fisher and others (1975) discussed measures of nocturnal penile erections as diagnostic criteria for organic or functional erectile failure. Decreased nocturnal erective responses would be indicative of organic erectile failure and presumably indicate nonbehavioral intervention. Morf, Syrotuik, and Krznaric (1977) discussed the utility and methodology of a two-stage diagnostic system based upon a Baysean model. Although approaching diagnosis from a nonbehavioral paradigm, the authors noted the great potential reward for generating reliable and homogeneous behavior categories. They also noted, however, that a set of categories that is useful for one population is rarely useful for others. Of the many procedures available for determining diagnostic categories, the authors recommended the use of a formal-empirical method involving cluster analysis and Q-factor analysis.

The issue of the cross-situational stability of behavior is central to diagnostic efforts and has been a thorny one for behavior analysts. There is little doubt that behavior is significantly affected by transient environmental stimuli, but there is also little doubt that there are differences among individuals in the probability that a class of behaviors will be emitted across situations. Thus, an "unassertive" individual will demonstrate significant variability in assertive behaviors across situations but is probably more likely to emit unassertive behaviors across situations than one who is labeled "assertive." Inherent in any attempt to categorize or diagnose individuals is an assumption that the targeted behaviors are relatively stable across situations. As indicated previously, however, stability of categorical constructs (such as "aggression" or "dependency") probably varies among categories. Diagnostic efforts may be useful only with stable constructs; furthermore, effective categorization of behavior that demonstrates a high degree of situational specificity would necessitate an excessive number of categories. To be useful, a diagnostic category must be homogeneous (Morf, Syrotuik, and

Krznaric, 1977) with a minimum of within-category and between-situation variance. With highly variable behaviors, homogeneity can only be attained if the categories reflect situational factors.

If it is assumed, for example, that "aggression" in children is not a stable trait and aggressive behavior varies as a function of the environmental contexts, useful diagnostic schemes must encompass factors controlling variability in order to produce homogeneous groups. Separate diagnostic classifications might include: (1) physical aggression toward peers in school, (2) physical aggression toward adults in school, (3) verbal aggression toward peers, and (4) verbal aggression toward parents. If "aggressive" children tend to emit aggressive behaviors across methods (verbal and physical) and across situations (school and home), these subcategories would not be necessary to ensure homogeneity and predictive validity. The primary factor determining the efficacy of diagnostic efforts, then, is that of explained variance. If variance in behavior can be sufficiently explained by knowledge of a behavioral trait without reference to situational factors, diagnosis may have utility. If situational factors are necessary to adequately explain variance in behavior, diagnostic categories must include those factors to ensure homogeneity. In such a case the utility of diagnostic efforts may be reduced.

The most likely outcome of the analysis of cross-situational stability is that some behavioral traits will be relatively stable across situations but others will not. Some individuals may evidence cross-situational stability for a particular behavioral trait, but others may demonstrate considerable variation for the same trait as a function of situational factors. Although research efforts in this area are insufficiently advanced to warrant recommendations, generating a coefficient of stability for a particular behavioral trait—a coefficient representing the relationship between variance in the environment and response—and for a particular individual would assist the behavior analyst in interpreting the generalizability of a particular trait for a subject.

In addition to the diagnostic efforts with headaches and erectile dysfunction noted previously, several other recently published articles have involved diagnostic efforts in behavioral assessment. A chemical analysis of blood serum to diagnose cigarette smoking was discussed by Brockway (1978). Achenbach (1978) discussed the child behavior profile for the diagnosis and classification of child behavior problems. Atsaides, Neuringer, and Davis (1977), for example, attempted to differentially diagnose chronic alcoholics and neurotics by using a Minnesota Multiphasic Personality Inventory (MMPI). Although nonbehavioral in theoretical orientation, their research serves to illustrate some procedures for assessing diagnostic efficacy. The authors compared the frequencies of items on MMPI long forms from thirty-five inpatient alcoholics and thirty-five neurotics. Responses from the two groups were compared by using a chi-square or Fisher's exact test to generate an initial set of items at the .05 level of confidence. These items were then readministered to a second set of patients (thirty-five in each group) to select items that demonstrated discriminant validity for both samples. The final set of items was then administered to the previously tested 140 patients to establish a maximum efficiency cut-off score, or the score that would correctly diagnose the greatest number of patients while minimizing the rate of false diagnoses. The final eight-item scale was approximately 87 percent accurate in diagnosing each group. Although this questionnaire is both short and effective, inferences about its utility and generality are hindered because of the use of nonindependent samples, insufficiently validated criterion measures, and limits on generality resulting from an all-male sample.

Chesney and Tasto (1975) developed a Menstrual Symptom Questionnaire to diagnose two types of primary dysmenorrhea—spasmodic (distress during flow apparently associated with excessive muscle tension) and congestive (premenstrual tension apparently associated with fluid retention). Rekers (1977) used analogue observation situations to diagnose boys with and without "gender identity" difficulties or "pretranssexual" behavior patterns. Observation of amount of play with "masculine" and "feminine" toys and observation of "masculine" and "feminine" mannerisms have been used by Rekers and others (1977) as diagnostic indicators and as outcome measures for behavioral intervention.

Noting the lack of a useful diagnostic system for children, Achenbach (1978) reported on an ambitious research program for the development of a descriptive classification system with children. Achenbach attempted to develop a system that would be useful for both researchers and practitioners and one that would reflect a child's strengths as well as behavior problems. The system involves a series of Child Behavior Profiles standardized for three age groups (four to five, six to eleven, and twelve to sixteen) and scored on a checklist. In this article the scales of six-year-old to eleven-year-old boys with behavior problems were factor analyzed. Based on parent report, nine first-order factors (schizoid, depressed, uncommunicative, obsessive-compulsive, somatic complaints, social withdrawal, hyperactive, aggressive, and delinquent) and two second-order factors (internalizing and externalizing) were identified. Three social competency factors (activities, social, and school) were also constructed. Normative data were based on a sample of 300 boys. Achenbach indicated significant differences among the three age groups on all first- and second-order factors and an eight-day test-retest correlation of .89. Achenbach recommended increased use of multivariate statistical techniques in devising classificatory systems, noted that broad-band (second-order) factors are more reliable and robust than first-order, and recommended increased attempts at standardization of instruments (with particular emphasis upon the Behavior Problem Checklist developed by Quay).

O'Farrell and Upper (1977) assessed the interjudge reliability of Cautela and Upper's (1975) Behavioral Coding System (BCS). The BCS has been proposed as an alternative to the DSM framework but has not been readily adopted by most researchers. In O'Farrell and Upper's study, four raters independently examined case materials for twenty male psychiatric patients and then completed a checklist for the 365 specific BCS categories. Interjudge agreement for the 21 general categories ranged from 78.7 to 88.4 percent; the mean overall agreement rate was 85.4 percent. For all 365 specific categories, the overall agreement rate was 66.2 percent. Although the authors noted that their interjudge agreement rates were significantly higher than those typically reported for traditional diagnostic systems, there remained a significant proportion of error variance in ratings, and the possibility of erroneous diagnosis is sufficient to warrant cautious application.

Achenbach and Edelbrock (1978) reviewed articles involving

the classification of child behavior problems. The authors distinguished between broad-band and narrow-band syndromes (second-order and first-order factors). Two broad-band factors (overcontrolled and undercontrolled) and a number of narrow-band factors (aggressive, delinquent, hyperactive, schizoid, anxious, depressed, somatic, and withdrawn) were identified across numerous studies, thus suggesting that they may be reliable classificatory types. These categories tended to occur across raters (parents and teachers), and the authors noted that interrater reliabilities varied with the similarities between the types of raters.

Although attempts to develop and evaluate behavioral diagnostic procedures have been increasing in recent years, several limitations of this endeavor have already been noted, and adoption of a classificatory philosophy in a behavioral construct system should be approached cautiously. Some of the limitations inherent to classification schemes are summarized below.

1. The generalizability of classification schemes may be limited by characteristics of the target sample (socioeconomic status, race, sex, inpatient or outpatient).
2. Diagnosis and categorization are based upon the unproven assumption that subjects within categories will demonstrate similar etiological factors and similar responses to specific treatments.
3 Diagnostic efforts are based upon assumptions of cross-situational stability, and diagnostic schemes that account for situational factors may be unwieldly.
4. The amount of variance accounted for by situational factors probably differs among individuals, populations, and behavior categories.
5. Diagnostic models or emphasis on categorization of behavior may be incompatible with a behavioral construct system that emphasizes individual differences in behavior topography, etiology, and response to treatment.
6. Classification procedures must be based upon normative data. Such data, particularly with observational and psychophysiological assessment methodologies, are unavailable in most cases.
7. As noted by Ciminero and Drabman (1977) and Achenbach and

Edelbrock (1978), diagnosis implies that subjects will be labeled, and the behavior of significant mediators (parents, teachers, spouses, and friends) can be adversely affected by labels.

In sum, behavior analysts are becoming increasingly involved in issues of diagnosis. Although it is obvious that such efforts are worthwhile with many behavior problems, the premature adoption of diagnostic construct systems should be avoided. Issues of explained variance, utility, situational specificity, and generality must be closely examined.

A further cautionary note has been added by Blum (1978) in his study of psychiatric hospital admissions to one institution in 1954, 1964, and 1974. Blum noted a significant variation in the classifications of patients entering the hospital in the years sampled and suggested that changes in admission rates could not be accounted for by changes in the population. He suggested that diagnoses reflect current states of psychological conceptualization more than the condition of the people being classified and that caution should be exercised in using psychiatric diagnoses as independent variables in research. More relevant research targets, he suggested, would be the ways people become identified as patients, the factors leading to hospitalization, and patients' experiences during therapy. Finally, current efforts at developing behaviorally oriented diagnostic systems are characterized by errors analogous to those committed by the developers of the DSM. In essence, except for work by Achenbach, behaviorally oriented diagnostic systems are being designed on a rational rather than an empirical basis. Thus, while the concepts of proposed behavioral diagnostic systems are more specific, less inferential, and perhaps more homogeneous than their traditional counterparts, the trait categories are based on the developers' conceptualizations of meaningful behavioral classes rather than on an empirical identification of covarying behaviors.

## Computer-Assisted Assessment

Clinical applications of preintervention assessment usually involve interviews or questionnaires to help the behavior analyst identify problem areas and etiological factors. These initial evaluations are particularly important in university counseling centers, child guidance centers, and outpatient mental health centers. Several recent articles have discussed the use of computer-assisted assessments to help identify patient concerns, possible causative factors, collateral behaviors, and historical factors (Angle and others, 1977; Clavelle and Butcher, 1977; Giannetti and others, 1976; Johnson, Giannetti, and Williams, 1976; Klingler and others, 1977; Lucas and others, 1977; Mayne, Weksel, and Sholtz, 1968; Slack and Van Cura, 1968; Shure and Meeker, 1978). Although not developed within behavioral, methodological, or construct systems, these assessment procedures are discussed here because of their potential interest to behavior analysts.

Computer-assisted assessment systems usually involve interactive procedures in which the subject is seated in front of a console with a screen upon which stimuli are presented by a computer. The subject responds to the stimuli on a keyboard (usually with a yes/no or multiple-choice format), and subsequent stimuli are presented as a function of each subject's responses (Clavelle and Butcher, 1977). The computer system involves an interactive decision tree with paths selected according to the responses of individual subjects. For example, an initial presentation on the projection screen might be a listing of twenty-five different problem areas. If the subject indicates "anxiety in the presence of other people" as one problem area, the next stimulus might be a list of social situations in which the subject might experience anxiety. If the subject indicates feeling anxious "around strangers," the next presentation might inquire whether anxiety occurs with men and/or women or with large or small groups. This process continues for each problem area. Following the completion of intake, the computer could furnish the behavior analyst with a summary of problem areas, hypothesized causative factors, potential treatment strategies, hypothesized diagnostic categories, and other information of interest.

Several benefits may result from computer-assisted assessment. First, the system may produce a substantial saving in professional time. This may be a particularly important asset in busy psychiatric facilities. Second, the system offers the possibility of providing a massive amount of information on a broad range of topics of potential interest to behavior analysts. Such information may prove useful for treatment design and implementation and in the detection of additional areas that need attention. A third and very important attribute of computer-assisted assessment is that it may reduce the error variance associated with clinical interviews. Because the method of presentation is constant across subjects, variance attributable to interviewer fatigue, nonverbal cues, reactions to the subjects' responses, or interviewer bias might be reduced. Another major advantage is that analysis of data would be facilitated by utilizing software to summarize and analyze the subjects' responses. A computer-assisted assessment procedure may also involve both interview (interactive) and questionnaire formats. For example, for a subject who indicates sexual concerns, the Sexual Interaction Inventory (Chapter Six) might be administered, in addition to items specifically related to the respondent's problem areas.

Although there are obvious benefits to the use of computer-assisted assessment, there are several issues that need to be evaluated prior to widespread adoption. Perhaps most importantly, additional information is needed about the validity of data derived from computer assessment. This information can be gathered from internal reliability checks during assessment as well as by comparing derived data with data from other measurement instruments. Because it would probably be more amenable to some than to other populations (college students rather than hospitalized psychiatric patients), the applicability of computer-assisted assessment also needs to be evaluated. Another important issue is its acceptability to clients; the issue of validity becomes unimportant if clients are reluctant to indicate their personal problems to a computer. Several recently published studies have focused on some of these issues and are presented below.

Lucas and others (1977) evaluated the reliability and criterion validity of computer interviews with alcoholics. Thirty-six volunteer male alcoholic patients were administered a computer interview three times by two psychiatrists and then filled out attitudinal and behavioral questionnaires. The authors reported high agreement coefficients between information elicited in the computer interviews and information elicited during psychiatric interviews and questionnaires. During the computer interview, however, alcoholics reported significantly greater alcoholic ingestion than during the psychiatric interview. This would suggest that, compared to personal interviews, computer interviews might provide more valid assessment data on such sensitive areas as antisocial and sexual behavior. The authors also noted that the subjects rated the computer interview as highly acceptable. Angle and others (1977) presented a general discussion of computer-assisted and broad-spectrum assessment. The authors noted that, although broad-spectrum assessment has been urged by many behavior analysts, other authors have more recently questioned the parsimony of comprehensive assessment. They also noted that procedures for engaging in broad-spectrum assessment have not been delineated. Angle and others described their own interactive computer set-up, which is based on the PDP 11/40 (Digital Equipment Corporation) with sixteen keyboard terminals. Following completion of the assessment sessions, the computer provides a print-out of fear hierarchies, areas of unassertiveness, appearance concerns, and other material of interest.

Several potential limitations of computer-assisted assessment should be noted. As pointed out by Klingler and others (1977), the system may have to be abbreviated or bypassed in crisis cases, and the determination of a crisis situation would most likely have to be made by an intake interviewer. The system is also probably not very amenable to assessment of individuals with lower levels of cognitive functioning—for example, young children, the mentally retarded, or long-term psychiatric residents—although it is possible to modify the format of stimulus presentation (presenting simple questions auditorally or in picture format) to extend its generalizability. To make computer assessment sufficiently flexible to handle most of the intake problems of psychiatric facilities would require tremendous programming efforts, complex interactive designs, and extensive time commitments on the part of subjects. Another possible limitation is cost. Most computer assessment thus far has used scientific interactive computer systems whose cost can run to many thousands of dollars. A cost-benefit analysis would have to determine if such financial outlays are warranted. Another major drawback is that the stimuli of any computer system would reflect the conceptual biases of the developer. The types of responses elicited would be constrained by the stimuli presented, and bias in the system would be difficult to detect and overcome. (It is likely, however, that computer systems could be programmed to be less biased than typical interviewers.) Another drawback is the difficulty in constructing systems that are sufficiently flexible to detect the myriad of concerns held by individuals seeking psychiatric assistance. Rare but important target behavior such as bizarre ideations, delusions, fetishes, or phobias would be difficult to detect without making the system unmanageably cumbersome.

In summary, some evidence suggests that computer-assisted assessment can result in data that are reliable and valid and that the system is not objectionable to users. This assessment procedure is highly promising as an efficient method of diagnosis, problem identification, treatment planning, and outcome evaluation. However, substantial research is still needed on validity and sources of error, and there are many possible difficulties with the system that need to be evaluated.

## Behavioral Assessment of Cognitive Events

It is unnecessary to document the growing role of cognitive factors in behavioral theory and intervention. The significance of cognitive elements has been adequately illustrated by the works of Beck, Bandura, Meichenbaum, Mahoney, and Ellis, by the publication of a new journal (*Cognitive Behavior Therapy*), and by a BMA audiotape series by Meichenbaum. Behavioral theorists who stress the importance of cognition emphasize its role as a dependent, mediational, or explanatory factor. Cognitive factors such as the ruminative presleep thinking of insomniacs or obsessive thought patterns may be the main targets of behavioral intervention (a dependent variable). They may also be conceptualized as mediational factors and used to account for individual differences in response to environmental stimuli—for example, differences among people in reaction to loss of reinforcement. Similarly, cognitive events such as attribution, self-reinforcement, or self-punishment may be conceptualized as etiological factors affecting such other behaviors as assertiveness, aggression, or response to intervention.

Recently published articles have further emphasized the role of cognition in behavioral theory and intervention. Evans (1977) stressed the importance of cognitive factors as possible determinants of headaches. Mahoney (1977) reflected on the role of cognitive factors in psychotherapy and noted their impact on assessment: an increasingly cognitive orientation in psychology is exemplified by less reliance on intrapsychic instruments and more emphasis upon self-monitoring, electrophysiological, and questionnaire instruments. Mischel (1977) has also noted the importance of integrating assessment procedures with cognitive psychology and has emphasized differences in the manner in which individuals interpret or organize events and how these idiosyncratic interpretations function as significant determinants of behavior and behavior problems. Kenny, Mowbray, and Lalani (1978) focused upon obsessive ideation in the treatment of a case of obsessive-compulsive neurosis. Fiedler and Beach (1978) noted the importance of cognitive factors in determining whether assertive behavior will be emitted or not. In their study, the best predictor of assertive behavior was the subject's perception of the expected probability of various positive and negative contingencies for the assertive act. Wade, Malloy, and Proctor (1977) stressed the importance of cognitions in fear behavior. These researchers found differences between high- and low-avoidance subjects in the degree and frequency of aversive imagery. Dash and Brown (1977) developed a scale to measure cognitive factors associated with dieting. Evans and Kazarian (1977) reported on the development of a scale to identify obsessional thoughts that interfere with daily activities. Forehand and King (1977) utilized a scale of parental attitudes toward children as a measure of the outcome of a parent-training program. Their adoption of attitudes as dependent variables was based on previous work (Lobitz and Johnson, 1973) that suggested that parental attitudes are better predictors of referrals for behavioral treatment than is the behavior of the child. Kendall and Finch (1978) presented a cognitive-behavioral treatment approach for impulsive children. There was a tendency for the group of children exposed to verbal self-instructions through modeling to demonstrate greater improvement than a group receiving only response-cost contingencies. Weisenberg (1977) stressed the importance of cognitive factors in response to pain, the need for assessment of cognitive factors in pain, and the importance of including cognitive interventions in pain therapy.

Other researchers (Bandura, 1977; Briddell and Wilson, 1976; Sullivan and Denny, 1977; Wilson, 1977) have suggested that subject or client expectancies are significant determinants of behavior in assessment situations and of subjects' responses to intervention. Expectancy has been systematically manipulated by Borkovec in a number of behavioral intervention studies utilizing demand and counterdemand instructions to subjects. His research has suggested that, for some target behaviors, a significant proportion of the variance in treatment outcome can be accounted for by subjects' preintervention expectancies of benefits or by perceived therapy credibility. If client expectancies can in fact mediate or directly affect intervention outcome, behavior analysts should attempt to evaluate carefully this factor in clinical and research applications of behavior therapy.

Although recognizing the importance of cognitive factors, Nisbett and Wilson (1977) emphasized the difficulties in assessing cognitive processes. They suggested that subjects are frequently unaware of the existence of their cognitions or of the stimuli that elicit them. The authors further noted that self-reports of cognitive activity may reflect the beliefs or implicitly held theories surrounding the events in question and may not be valid reflections of cognitive processes. Presumably, some cognitive processes are more amenable than others to introspective reporting, and one major area of research in cognitive assessment is the identification of factors controlling the validity of cognitive introspection. As Beck noted in his 1978 Association for Advancement of Behavior Therapy workshop, it is also necessary to assume that there are individual differences in the role of cognitive factors in behavior disorders. Depression, for example, may be primarily a function of cognitive misinterpretation of existing reinforcers or social relationships, or it may be a function of actual decreases in reinforcement rate or of disruption in social relationships. The task of the behavior analysts, therefore, is to evaluate the role of cognitive factors in behavioral disorders so that a cognitive intervention strategy can be selected when appropriate.

As Nisbett and Wilson (1977) noted, the assessment of cognitive factors presents some particularly difficult issues, primarily because of the private and covert nature of the target events. With most overt and psychophysiological target behaviors, it is possible to generate confidence estimates in the resultant data through the use of criterion-related validity evaluations. For example, the validity of self-monitoring of food intake can be estimated by simultaneously using measures of weight, analogue observation, and observation by participant observers. With current technology, the assessment of cognitive factors is limited to self-report instruments. Criterion-validity evaluation of such factors is difficult and, in most cases, relies on indirect inferences. Regardless of the importance of cognitive events, inferences that measures of them are valid must remain indirect. The occurrence and sources of error in cognitive assessment, compared to the assessment of noncognitive events, will be more difficult to detect; hence, data on cognitive factors must be interpreted with caution.

The function of this section has been to underscore the growing role of cognitive factors in behavioral construct systems, in behavioral intervention, and in behavioral assessment. Regardless of the difficulties involved in the assessment of cognitive events, recent behavioral literature has increasingly focused upon cognitive factors. Cognitive processes are particularly amenable to assessment via self-monitoring, questionnaires, and interviews. Each of the chapters devoted to those assessment instruments will more closely consider the issue of assessment of cognitive events.

## Social Validity

Several recent articles have addressed the issue of the clinical significance and relevance of intervention goals and outcomes and the appropriateness of methods used to achieve those goals (Kazdin, 1977b; Wolfe, 1978). The term *social validity* has been used to identify these issues. Concern with social validity underscores the interest of behavior analysts in the social impact and relevance of their activities and the reactions of consumers of their services. Kazdin (1977b) discussed the issue of social validity or the clinical significance of behavior change and noted that there are two methods of social validation. In social comparison procedures, the target client, after participating in a behavioral intervention program, is compared to normative levels of functioning. For example, this method would evaluate the degree to which the social skills of a withdrawn child approximate those of his or her classmates following behavioral intervention. The second method of social validation is through *subjective evaluation* in which behavior change is evaluated by the client or by people who have contact with the client. Both methods assist the behavior analyst in evaluating the social significance of behavior change and reduce dependence upon statistical criteria or the behavior analyst's subjective appraisal.

The concept of social validity has special relevance for the types of data collected in behavioral assessment. It suggests that the goals of behavioral intervention (target behaviors) should be selected after consultation with the target subjects and that inferences about the outcome of a behavioral intervention program should take into account the judgments of the target subjects. Caution would be advised, for example, in focusing on target behaviors that are inconsistent with the etiological hypotheses and concepts held by the subjects. Instituting treatments that seem invalid to the consumers or without their explicit cooperation would probably have little chance of success. It is important, therefore, in preintervention assessment to evaluate the subjective perceptions of the target subjects about their problems and the intervention procedures that might be used. Questionnaires or interviews could be used to collect this information, and it should have an impact on the intervention procedures utilized and on therapist-client interaction. Attributions about causation of behavior problems that are at variance with those held by the behavior analyst, for example, suggest the need for an insight-oriented approach using discussions with the client or readings. The behavior analyst should also give careful consideration to the subjective impressions of the target subjects about which target behaviors are the most important. It might be inappropriate, for example, to initiate communication training with a marital couple based upon analogue observation of their communication skills if they state that they are more concerned with the rate of aversive behaviors emitted in the home.

Similarly, in evaluating the outcome of behavioral intervention, it is highly desirable to evaluate the subjective impressions of the target subjects. The factors responsible for most referrals are subjective perceptions, and modification of those perceptions should be considered a necessary, although insufficient, criterion for success. Parents, for example, usually seek assistance because of feelings of discomfort with or about their child, not because of high rates of noncompliant behavior. Marital couples seek therapy when they feel dissatisfied, frustrated, or angry, not because their rate of mutually shared activities is lower than desired. It is insufficient, then, to evaluate the outcome of behavioral intervention by monitoring only those factors targeted by the behavior analyst without reference to the perceptions of the target subject. Intervention with a marital couple that results in increased communication, problem-solving abilities, positive exchanges, and decreased rates of aversive behaviors cannot be assumed to be successful unless the couple also reports feeling more satisfied with their marriage and each other.

Social validity is also tied to the concept of content validity. A measurement instrument with a high degree of content validity may also have a high degree of social validity. Role-playing situations, for example, would have greater social validity if they reflected commonly encountered situations in the natural environment. Deitz (1978) discussed the importance of social validity in applied behavior analysis and its impact upon the direction of that field. Deitz cautioned that excessive reliance upon consumer reactions to determine focuses and directions in behavioral research and therapy may have disadvantages. For example, consumer or social reactions may be in error, and excessively close reliance on these reactions may dissuade behavior analysts from fruitful areas of research. The main thrust of Deitz's discussion is that concern with consumer reactions must be tempered with professional insight. Achenbach (1978) focused upon the issue of social validity in diagnostic systems with children. In reviewing published research involving classification of children's behavior problems, Achenbach noted that increased efforts should be directed toward generating diagnostic categories that are useful to practitioners as well as researchers. He further noted that children would benefit only if such efforts were tied to the existing mental health systems.

Interest in social validity has meant a greater emphasis upon subjective measures in behavioral assessments. Behavior analysts have traditionally avoided subjective measurement because the determinants of subjective responses are often unknown, validity assessments are difficult, and subjective measures have been assumed to be sensitive to a wide range of error. While these considerations are valid, subjective measurement can be useful in the context of a multimodal assessment approach. Although it is never sufficient to judge therapy outcome or design intervention programs on the basis of subjective measures alone, subjective data viewed within the context of other information can greatly help the behavior analyst in planning treatment strategies, selecting target behaviors, and evaluating the outcome of treatment.

## Statistical Analysis of Time-Series Designs

As noted in Hersen and Barlow (1976), intervention procedures based upon a behavioral construct system emphasize single-subject designs and often utilize repeated measures of the same subject(s) over time (time-series designs). Although such experimental designs facilitate a fine-grained analysis of behavior as a function of time and environmental manipulations, they are not readily amenable to traditional statistical analysis procedures. The rationale and difficulties in applying traditional statistical procedures to time-series designs have been discussed by Kazdin (1976) and revolve primarily around the serial dependency of the data: data points within each phase or condition are not independent because they tend to be related to (can be predicted from) previous data points. To surmount this difficulty, a series of alternative analyses have been proposed (Kazdin, 1976); perhaps the most salient of these is time-series analysis (Glass, Wilson, and Gottman, 1975). *Time-series analysis* is based upon assumptions of serial dependency of data and provides information about the actual and comparative means, slope, variability, and initial levels of two sets of serially dependent data.

Several authors have recently addressed the issue of time-series analysis in behavioral research. Jones, Vaught, and Weinrott

(1977) presented a nontechnical discussion of the use of time-series analysis in behavioral research. They suggested that time-series analysis can be used to supplement visual inspection of data in operant time-series designs (traditional A-B-A-B replication designs). The authors noted the ability of time-series analysis, particularly in single-subject designs, to identify slope and serial dependency in the data. In a later article, Jones, Weinrott, and Vaught (1978) examined the relationship between the experimenter-inferred and the statistically determined significance of behavior changes in time-series designs. These authors examined twenty-four different articles from the *Journal of Applied Behavior Analysis* in which the original authors had suggested significant changes between treatment phases but where visual inspection of the data was ambiguous as to actual significance. Fifty-eight graphs were furnished to eleven judges; they were to determine whether a meaningful change in level had occurred between treatment phases. The data was also subjected to time-series analysis (.05 level of confidence), and analysis of variance was conducted on statistical-inferential agreement indices (factors were significance level from time-series analysis and degree of serial dependency of data). The authors noted that (1) interrater agreement coefficients were low, (2) agreement between judges and time-series analysis was low, and (3) agreement was best when serial dependency was low and when time-series analysis suggested no significant changes across phases. The authors interpreted the data to mean that, because of low interrater reliability, time-series analysis is the preferable method of determining significance of changes across phases of an intervention program.

Bernstein (1977) noted the applicability of time-series analysis to behavioral research but also noted some issues in its utilization. He first briefly outlined the procedures for utilizing time-series analysis: (1) identification of the appropriate model for the various conditions, (2) transformation of the defined models into standard regression models, (3) defining estimates of the model parameters, and (4) testing for significance. He then noted that, in some cases, fifty data points per condition may be necessary to identify the appropriate model and effectively utilize time-series analysis. He also pointed out other issues that remain to be addressed: (1) the effect of the various interventions on the model, (2) the minimum number of data points necessary to identify a model, and (3) the applicability of time-series analysis to studies involving several data points per day.

Simonton (1977) also discussed the use of time-series analysis but with designs involving large sample sizes. In the past, time-series analyses have most frequently been applied to single-subject research, but Simonton suggested the utilization of cross-sectional time-series experiments. *Cross-sectional time-series* experiments involve repeated measures over time on a large number of subjects under various conditions. Simonton noted that three types of time-series experiments (cross-sectional time-series, interrupted time-series, and equivalent time-series) are all based upon a multiple-regression model. He offered a least-squares estimation procedure (generating regression equations with minimal residual error) and suggested that it is a suitable alternative to the Box and Jenkins approach. Simonton argued that cross-sectional designs offer greater generalizability of results than do single-subject designs.

In sum, time-series designs appear to be gaining favor among behavior analysts who utilize a large number of serially dependent observations within several conditions with few or many subjects. It should be noted, however, that time-series analyses are utilized in only a handful of behavioral studies each year. Unfortunately, the assumptions underlying time-series models have not been thoroughly explored, and the necessary conditions for their application have not been adequately defined. Nevertheless, time-series analysis offers a potentially powerful method of evaluating changes in the behavior of subjects over time and as a function of environmental manipulations.

Many behavioral intervention studies utilize traditional group factorial designs. Kratochwill and Brody (1978) surveyed the use of inferential statistics in four behavior therapy journals up through 1974. They noted that, at that time, very few single-subject studies utilized statistical procedures but that all studies using group designs did use such procedures. Kaplan and Litrownik (1977) discussed the use of multivariate analysis and discriminant analysis of variance (MANOVA) procedures for studies employing traditional factorial designs with several dependent variables. The authors noted that the adoption of multivariate procedures is a direct outgrowth of the utilization of multiple dependent measures in behavioral research. The utilization of a series of univariate analyses with several dependent measures can lead to erroneous inferences because the dependent measures are usually intercorrelated. In MANOVA procedures, the alpha level (the probability of achieving particular results by chance) is not influenced by the addition of dependent variables. Not only do MONOVA procedures prevent unwarranted rejection of null hypotheses, but they may be more sensitive to marginal effects on a number of dependent variables. In MANOVA procedures, the dependent variable is a weighted composite of all outcome variables, which are combined to maximize the discriminant qualities of the variables (maximum variance accounted for by knowledge of intervention groups). Kaplan and Litrownik noted two major difficulties in the application of MANOVA procedures: (1) they are sometimes used by individuals insufficiently informed about their bases, and (2) there is disagreement about how to interpret results from MANOVA and the types of analyses that should be conducted following significant MANOVAs. Kaplan and Litrownik recommend the use of step-down F-statistics following significant MANOVAs to identify which dependent variables demonstrated significant between-group differences. Unlike traditional univariate F-tests, the step-down F-statistic indicates the effect of a treatment upon a dependent variable after partialling out the common variance of that variable with a previously analyzed variable. The authors provide a list of statistical packages for MANOVA and suggest avoiding the biomedical data (BMD) MANOVA package.

Kaplan and Litrownik also suggested that discriminant function analysis is a powerful method of interpreting multivariate effects. Using this statistical procedure, it is possible to identify the functions or composites of variables that best discriminate among groups. In a way similar to factor analysis, meanings of the functions are evaluated by the loadings of the dependent variables upon them. The significance of a discriminant function can be tested with an $X^2$. Because discriminant function analysis evaluates the manner in which variables change in relation to one another, results are more difficult to interpret when the dependent variables are highly intercorrelated. The 1977 article by Kaplan and Litrownik called forth a reply by O'Grady (1978) and a subsequent reply by Kaplan and Litrownik (1978). The major areas of contention in the two papers included: (1) the distinction made between MANOVA and discriminant analysis, (2) the appropriateness of univariate analysis following significant MANOVA effects, (3) the applicability of the step-down F-statistic, and (4) the applicability of $X^2$ to test discriminant functional analysis.

One statistical model that has not been explicitly discussed in the behavioral literature but that is also being increasingly used is multiple regression, particularly in the generation of regression or predictor equations. The multiple-regression model underlies many other statistical procedures, is based upon least-squares analysis, and can be applied to questions traditionally answered by analysis-of-variance procedures. Multiple regression has the positive attribute of allowing the user to estimate the amount of variance in one variable that can be accounted for by knowledge of variance in one variable or a combination of other variables. For example, instead of simply indicating whether there is a significant difference between satisfied and dissatisfied marital couples in level of depression, a multiple-regression analysis will also allow the researcher to ascertain the proportion of variance in depression that can be accounted for by knowledge of marital satisfaction or marital satisfaction along with sex-role stereotyping. In other words, the questions that can be answered with a multiple-regression model are often more powerful and of greater utility to the behavior analyst than those answered by other statistical models. Multiple-regression analyses are appearing more frequently in the behavioral literature and, it is hoped, will facilitate a more comprehensive understanding of behavior interrelationships.

Darlington (1978) focused upon difficulties in the application of multiple regression when the number of predictors is large in relation to sample size. Such ratios reduce the reliability and generalizability of the results. The author offered a reduced-variance regression technique (Stein-type regression and ridge regression). This method does not provide unbiased estimates of regression weights because rational knowledge of the variables is synthesized with regression theory. The authors outlined the attributes of reduced-variance regression: (1) it makes use of prior or rational weights; (2) it is relevant to cases in which there are more predictors than subjects; (3) it can be performed in stepwise fashion; (4) it is robust against deviations in linearity, homoscedasticity, and normality; (5) it is based upon a Baysean model because of the incorporation of prior estimates of parameters; (6) it is particularly useful when validity of a set of regressor variables is concentrated in the first few components; (7) it is useful when the predictors are highly correlated; and (8) it is easy to use procedurally.

## Summary

The primary purpose of this chapter was to present an overview of conceptual and methodological advances in behavioral assessment. One major factor in the growing emphasis upon behavioral assessment is the recognition of the importance of individual differences in behavior topography, in maintaining factors, and in response to intervention. These between-subject differences underscore the need for preintervention assessment to identify etiological factors and select the most appropriate intervention strategies.

The increasing application of traditional psychometric concepts in behavioral assessment was also noted. Behavioral assessment instruments are increasingly being evaluated on issues of applicability and utility, sensitivity, reliability, content validity, criterion-related validity, construct validity, generalizability, and sources of error. This emphasis upon the evaluation of behavioral assessment instruments is congruent with the empirical orientation of a behavioral construct system and has fostered the study of factors such as reactivity that affect the validity of assessment instruments. The concept of response fractionation has also become an integral part of behavioral construct systems and behavioral assessment. Numerous studies have provided support for the hypothesis that behavior has multiple components that may differ in mechanism of control or in response to treatment. Lack of covariation has been noted not only among cognitive, subjective, overt behavioral, and physiological elements but also within those response systems. With the growing realization of the importance of response fractionation, behavior analysts have more and more frequently been using multiple measures in preintervention assessment and in the evaluation of behavior therapy outcomes.

Recent discussions of behavioral diagnosis were also reviewed. Partly in response to the inadequacies of the traditional Diagnostic and Statistical Manual (DSM) formulations, behavior analysts have been devising behaviorally oriented diagnostic systems. The concept of traits is crucial to diagnostic efforts, and the utility of any system is partly a function of the cross-situation stability of behavior. The issue of behavioral stability, along with other concepts underlying behavioral diagnosis, was discussed. One innovation that has been receiving increasing attention is computer-assisted assessment. Programmed for questionnaire or interview-interactive formats, computer systems may provide an efficient and valid method of identifying and evaluating a variety of behavior problems. Although there have been some recent indications that such assessment systems may be valid and acceptable to clients, additional research is needed on a variety of psychometric and qualitative issues. The increasing focus upon cognitive processes and statistical procedures was also briefly noted in this chapter. Cognitive factors have become increasingly important conceptual elements in behavior and behavior disorders. Similarly, increased sophistication in the use of time-series designs has necessitated the adoption of statistical procedures to supplement traditional tests of significance. Since time-series designs are useful in some of these analyses, recent discussions of their application were reviewed.

# CHAPTER TWO

# *Conceptual and Methodological Advances*

Behavioral observation has achieved the status of a major assessment instrument. Its importance is illustrated by the several hundred published studies devoted to it and by its applicability to a wide variety of target populations and behavior problems in numerous assessment settings. The central role of observation—particularly observation in the natural environment—as a behavioral assessment instrument is a function of its congruence with the assumptions underlying a behavioral construct system—the importance of observable behavior, specificity of target variables, the derivation of quantitative data, the focus upon the natural environment, and minimization of the inferential qualities of concepts. The frequent use and increasing importance of observation in behavioral assessment account for its allocation of three chapters in this volume. Because procedures, issues, and sources of error in observation vary as a function of setting, Chapter Three focuses on observation in naturalistic environments and Chapter Four on observation in analogue settings. This chapter will present recent developments in concepts and procedures of behavioral observations that are relevant across assessment settings. Included in this chapter will be discussions of coding systems, methods of recording behavioral observations, interobserver agreement, sources of error, the use of participant observers, and advances in instrumentation.

## Behavioral Coding Systems
## and Checklists

Regardless of the method of recording observation data (paper-and-pencil forms, automated data-recording systems, digitek coding sheets, or event recorders), observers employ *behavioral coding systems* that define the universe of recordable events. Coding systems are composed of a number of antecedent events, target behavior events, and consequent events to which an observer must attend. Their selection is most often based on previously used coding systems, logical inferences about the events of interest, and the goals of the assessment (such as diagnosis or outcome evaluation). This structure is necessary to limit to a manageable number the thousands of potentially observable events. Behavioral codes are one component of observation systems; other components include time-sampling parameters, instructions to subjects, observer training procedures, observation environments, and observer reliability assessment. The entire observation system can be conceptualized as an assessment instrument and, as such, is subject to evaluation on dimensions of reliability and validity. Table 1 presents an overview of coding systems that have been used in recently published behavioral intervention research, along with those previously noted by Haynes (1978).

Several recently developed coding systems will be briefly introduced here and considered in greater detail in subsequent chapters. Abikoff, Gittelman-Klein, and Klein (1977) modified a previously used coding system to include elements relevant to the

**Table 1. Recently Published Behavior Observation Coding Systems**

| Reference | Comments |
|---|---|
| *Coding Systems for Monitoring Behaviors of Children and Adolescents* | |
| Abikoff, Gittelman-Klein, and Klein (1977) | Fourteen-category observation code for measuring the classroom behavior of children; primarily aimed at assessment of hyperactivity |
| Anderson, Vietze, and Dokecki (1977) | Mother-infant behaviors in the home |
| Becker and others (1967) | Classroom behaviors; teacher and child behaviors |
| Buell and others (1968) | Social and nonsocial behaviors of preschool children |
| Clark and others (1977) | Child behaviors in the supermarket |
| Fagot (1977a) | Thirty child behaviors and ten consequences; some elements designed to observe cross-gender behavior |
| Frankosky and Sulzer-Azaroff (1978) | Sixteen-item coding system for peer interaction among retarded individuals; categories of positive verbal, positive nonverbal, negative verbal, negative nonverbal, and isolate neutral |
| Glennon and Weisz (1978) | A scale for measuring anxiety in preschool children; used as a questionnaire but applicable as an observation form with slight modification; good content validity, interrater reliability, and external validity |
| Gottman (1977b) | Social interaction and isolation in children |
| Kaufman and O'Leary (1972) | Behavior of children and teachers in psychiatric hospital school |
| Kirby and Toler (1970) | Social and nonsocial behaviors of isolated children |
| Koegel and Rincover (1974) | Psychotic children in academic behaviors appropriate to classroom (limitation, attending, and reading) |
| Koegel, Clahn, and Nieminen (1978) | Behavior coding system for parents or trainers teaching skills to autistic children (such as consistent and uninterrupted discriminative stimuli and effective prompts) |

**Table 1. Recently Published Behavior Observation Coding Systems (Continued)**

| Reference | Comments |
|---|---|
| Kogen, Wimberger, and Bobbitt (1969) | Social and nonsocial child behaviors |
| O'Leary and Becker (1967) | Classroom behaviors |
| O'Leary and O'Leary (1972) | Classroom behaviors; a refinement of code used by O'Leary and Becker (1967) |
| Patterson and others (1969) | Family interaction (applicable to parent-child and marital interactions) |
| Patterson and others (1975) | A refinement of the coding system used by Patterson and others (1969); family and marital interactions |
| Patterson (1977a) | Modified original coding system to include fourteen topographically different categories for measuring interactions in homes of socially aggressive children |
| Peed, Roberts, and Forehand (1977) | Parent-child interaction measured in analogue and naturalistic settings; based on Hanf and Kling (1973) |
| Russo and Koegel (1977) | Verbal and nonverbal behavior of autistic children in a classroom |
| Sherman and Cormier (1974) | Classroom behaviors |
| Wahler (1975) | Adult-child interactions, home and school |
| Wahler, House, and Stambaugh (1976) | Child behaviors and adult-child interaction in home and school |
| *Coding Systems for Monitoring Behavior in Institutions* | |
| Alevizos and others (1978) | Coding system useful for program evaluation in several institutional settings and with different populations; contains mutually exclusive and concomitant behaviors; good interobserver reliability, sensitivity to program effects, and discriminant validity |
| Ayllon and Haughton (1964) | Observation codes for psychiatric inpatients; includes undesirable behaviors and behaviors incompatible with problem behaviors |
| Ayllon and Azrin (1968) | Behaviors of institutionalized psychiatric patients; includes self-help, work, and symptomatic behaviors |

| | |
|---|---|
| Browning (1971) | General functional and dysfunctional behaviors of autistic children |
| Johnson and Bailey (1977) | Leisure behavior of retarded women in halfway house; similar to that used by McClannahan and Risley (1975) |
| Koegel and Rincover (1974) | Psychotic children in academic behaviors appropriate to classroom (imitation, attending, and reading) |
| Liberman and others (1974) | Staff and patient behaviors in mental health and psychiatric institutions |
| Mariotto and Paul (1974) | Includes problem behaviors and appropriate behaviors of psychiatric inpatients |
| Matson and Stephens (1978) | Coding system for psychiatric inpatients; good content validity development |
| Peterson and others (1977) | Fourteen-behavior code for institutional geriatric behaviors (sitting, locomotion, and lying down) |
| Silvestri (1977) | The Nurses Observational Scale for Inpatient Evaluation (NOSIE)-30; thirty items relating to institutional ward behavior; typically used as checklist but elements could be modified for use as behavioral observation instrument |
| Strain and Ezzell (1978) | Eleven-category observation code for measuring disruptive and inappropriate behavior of behavioral disordered adolescents in a psychiatric facility; good content validity, development, and reliability |
| Wood and Flynn (1978) | Fifteen-item coding system for room cleanliness for inpatients |

*Coding Systems for Monitoring Family or Marital Interaction*

| | |
|---|---|
| Anderson, Vietze, and Dokecki (1977) | Mother-infant interaction in the home |
| Carter and Thomas (1973a) | Dyadic marital interchanges |
| Hops and others (1972) | Marital interaction |
| Patterson and others (1969) | Family interaction (applicable to parent-child and marital interaction) |
| Patterson and others (1975) | A refinement of the coding system used by Patterson and others (1969); family and marital interactions |
| Patterson (1977a) | Modified original coding system to include fourteen topographically different categories for measuring interactions in homes of socially aggressive children |

**Table 1. Recently Published Behavior Observation Coding Systems (Continued)**

| Reference | Comments |
|---|---|
| Peed, Roberts, and Forehand (1977) | Parent-child interaction measured in analogue and naturalistic settings; based on Hanf and Kling (1973) |
| Wahler (1975) | Adult-child behaviors and interactions, home and school |
| Wahler, House, and Stambaugh (1976) | Child behaviors and adult-child interaction in home and school |

*Coding Systems for Monitoring Anxiety and Social and Depressive Behaviors*

| Reference | Comments |
|---|---|
| Barlow and others (1977a) | Seventeen-item code or checklist for heterosexual skills; four categories: voice, affect, masculine/feminine sitting behaviors, and form of conversation |
| Bersoff and Moyer (1973) | Reinforcing social behaviors (such as praise) |
| Glennon and Weisz (1978) | A scale for measuring anxiety in preschool children; used as a questionnaire but applicable as an observation form with slight modification; good content validity, interrater reliability, and external validity. |
| Goldfried and Goldfried (1977) | Numerous anxiety behaviors (tremor, facial twitching); used for speech anxiety |
| Lewinsohn and Shaffer (1971) | Social interaction among adults, specifically applied to depression |
| Rathus (1973) | Assertive behaviors; college sample but generally applicable |

*Miscellaneous*

| Reference | Comments |
|---|---|
| Adams and others (1978) | Coding system for eating behaviors (such as active eating time, meal duration, frequency of bites, and drink frequency) did not discriminate between obese and nonobese subjects in current study |
| Bailey, Deardorff, and Nay (1977) | Behaviors of therapist during interview with client |

assessment of hyperactive children. The final sample of codes included events such as "gross motor movements," "out of chair," and "extended verbalization." Using standard time-sampling procedures, the authors observed children in a classroom setting who were diagnosed as either hyperactive or nonhyperactive and found that several of the behavioral codes discriminated between these two groups of children. Barlow and others (1977a) developed a heterosocial skills checklist. Initial target behaviors were derived from observing social interactions of several socially competent males. The behavioral items were then validated on a new sample of socially adequate and socially inadequate males. Using thirty-second time samples of videotaped interactions scored by trained raters, three of the four "behavioral categories" (there were a total of seventeen behaviors coded) discriminated between groups. Measures of "voice," "form," and "affect"—but not "sitting"—were found to discriminate between socially adequate and socially inadequate males in structured interactions.

Alevizos and others (1978) discussed the Behavior Observation Instrument, which is a behavioral observation system useful for program evaluation across a variety of settings. The coding system involves five mutually exclusive behaviors (such as walking and running) and twenty-one concomitant behaviors (such as drinking and group behavior) and is applicable in settings such as community mental health centers or inpatient psychiatric facilities. Commendably, the authors utilized empirical analyses to select five-second time samples and a sampling frequency of once per hour. These sampling parameters were shown to result in data that were highly correlated with continuous measures of the targeted behaviors. The authors also noted that satisfactory interobserver agreement (93 percent mean) could be achieved with a moderate amount of training and that there was no evidence for reactivity, that is, no evidence of habituation over observation sessions. Significant differences were noted between behavior rates derived from two divergent settings (discriminant validity) and as a function of changes in programs (sensitivity). Because this observation system was especially designed for program evaluation, the authors addressed the issue of cost-benefit ratios and suggested that the Behavior Observation Instrument was reasonable in time and financial costs.

These studies by Barlow and others, Abikoff and others, and Alevizos and others illustrate some of the empirical procedures that can be used in the development and evaluation of coding systems. But except for these coding systems and those developed by Wahler, House, and Stambaugh (1976), Patterson and others (1975), and O'Leary and O'Leary (1972), coding systems continue to be developed from logical or inferential rather than empirical analysis. Behavioral codes are most frequently selected for inclusion on the basis of a high face validity for the targeted behaviors or populations without regard to their discriminant validity. These codes are then applied as measures of intervention outcome without sufficient indications that the codes are valid measures of the constructs being assessed. Inadequate validation procedures complicate interpretation of insignificant results because it is impossible to ascertain if the results are attributable to ineffective interventions or to an assessment instrument that is not a sensitive measure of the targeted construct.

As noted by Haynes and Kerns (in press) in their comment on the study by Abikoff, Gittelman-Klein, and Klein (1977), caution must be exercised in the procedures used in validating coding systems. Inferences from a validation study may be biased because of errors in time-sampling procedures, the content validity of the codes, the method of interobserver agreement assessment, or the selection of subjects. Haynes and Kerns noted that, although Abikoff, Gittelman-Klein, and Klein carefully controlled many potentially biasing factors in their validity study, they neglected to control other potential sources of error such as (1) sampling the behavior of hyperactive children but not using matched controls at peak activity times, and (2) selecting as subjects some children who were referred for "behavior problems" and including some codes that reflected behavior problems, thus making it unclear whether the construct measured by the coding system was "hyperactivity" or "behavior problems." In addition, some of the interobserver agreement coefficients were sufficiently low to suggest that a substantial portion of the variability may be attributable to error rather than "real" change.

*Behavioral checklists* do not necessarily differ from behavioral coding systems but are sometimes used differently. Checklists are often composed of a larger number of items than are coding systems, sometimes in a questionnaire format, and are marked periodically on a point-time sampling basis (such as every hour) by an observer or rater. Typically, an observer will indicate the presence or absence (occurrence or nonoccurrence) of particular elements on the checklist on a fixed-interval schedule. Thus checklists and coding systems frequently differ only with respect to the time-sampling procedure employed. Also, some checklists, although behaviorally oriented, tend to target more global constructs and may be less precisely defined than coding systems. Again, this difference is one of practice rather than necessity, and behavioral checklists may be identical to coding systems in almost every way.

Several recent articles have used behavioral checklists (the checklist by Barlow and others, 1977a, was already mentioned). Derivations of Paul's (1966) speech anxiety behavioral checklist have been employed by several authors. Gautheir and Marshall (1977) used a twenty-item behavioral checklist derived from Paul for observing snake-phobic subjects during a behavioral avoidance test. Weissberg (1977) used a timed behavior checklist (Paul, 1966) for performance anxiety during speech anxiety assessment; the measure revealed significant changes across, but not between, intervention groups. Peck (1977) used a behavioral avoidance test, but the checklist was not sensitive to intervention effects. Quay (1977) employed the Behavior Problem Checklist composed of three-point scales for rating problem behaviors occurring in children and adolescents. This checklist is probably the least specifically behavioral of those mentioned but may provide the basis for additional refinement.

An examination of checklists and coding systems developed over the past several years suggests improvements in content validity, comprehensiveness, evaluation, and criterion validity. Coding systems and behavior checklists are more frequently developed from empirical than from rational bases (Barlow and others, 1977a), and there is also increasing recognition by behavior analysts of psychometric issues of criterion validity, reliability, and sensitivity, as well as of other issues relevant to the development and evaluation of coding systems. Issues in behavioral coding systems and checklists that necessitate additional attention include: (1) a continuing examination of factors affecting validity (time samples, observer accuracy examination); (2) closer examination of the content validity of coding systems (Ciminero and Drabman, 1977); (3) the development of empirically rather than logically based systems; (4) an examination of the validity, reliability, and sensitivity of coding systems prior to their application as outcome measures; (5) application of generalization theory (Chapter One) to the evaluation of coding systems; and (6) inclusion of adjunctive behavior (Chapter One) in coding systems.

## Automated Data-Recording Systems

Methods of recording targeted behaviors during observation have included paper-and-pencil recording, electromechanical event recorders, digitek optical scanning systems, and recording signals on audiotape. Most methods of recording observation data require excessive time for data transcription and analysis before meaningful information can be derived. Methods such as transcription onto high-speed recorders and use of electromechanical recorders do not remove the necessity for manipulation of data prior to analysis. The extensive data handling necessitated by these recording procedures increases the probability of error.

Recently, a series of pocket, computer-type storage devices have been marketed that function to automate the storage, retrieval, and analysis of observation data. Fitzpatrick (1977a) presented an overview of these automated data collection procedures and noted two basic modes of operation: parallel and serial input. Each emphasizes different aspects of the observation process and results in a different classification of data. In parallel systems, more than one event can be recorded at a time. Typically, an event key is depressed at the onset of an event and released upon termination. These data are stored in real time to facilitate the retrieval of duration data, and multiple events can be recorded easily from videotapes—for example, by viewing the tape several times. In serial systems, only one character can be recorded at a time. This system is particularly useful in the natural environment when the observer wishes to record the sequential occurrence of a large number of events. Fitzpatrick also presented criteria useful in the evaluation of the many automated systems now available. These include: (1) completeness of information provided, (2) type of memory, (3) storage capabilities, (4) availability of paper copy, (5) portability, (6) provisions for synchronization of separate data records, (7) method used to transmit data, and (8) speed of transmission.

In a second article Fitzpatrick (1977b) discussed a statistical package for the analysis of behavioral data collected and transmitted to computers through automated data collection systems and provided an example of the analysis of parent-child interaction to demonstrate the operation and characteristics of the program. The system contains several functions: (1) a sorting function that combines and selects events and portions of records; (2) a counting and summing function that tabulates frequencies of selected events, durations, rates, and histographs; and (3) an organizational description function that computes temporal relationships and histographs (computer data print-outs) between pairs of selected events and detects nonrandom occurrences of selected events. In the same article, Fitzpatrick provided a table on the characteristics and capabilities of eight automated data collection systems—a table that should be useful to potential purchasers of these data-recording systems. Information is included on the type of information provided and the capabilities of various instruments.

Several recently published articles have described one of the more commonly used automated data collection systems—the Datamyte 900 (Anderson, Vietze, and Dokecki, 1977; Sawin, Langlois, and Leitner, 1977; Sykes, 1977; Torgerson, 1977). The Datamyte 900 sorts between 16,000 and 32,000 characters in computer code to facilitate immediate transmission to a computer. The system includes fourteen character keys, ten numeric keys, and four alpha keys and can be used with a software system (programs for data analysis). Sawin, Langlois, and Leitner (1977) utilized the Datamyte in a study of parent-child interactions. Their coding system involved sixty child and sixty parent codes, and they reported that it required four to six weeks of careful training before observers could accurately utilize the system. They also noted that it required about three hours of careful editing for each observation session and that four types of data were available: (1) frequencies,

(2) durations, (3) event sequences, and (4) conditional probabilities. The authors also noted some difficulties with the system, including data loss when the battery runs down and difficulties with large coding systems.

Celhoffer, Boukydis, and Minde (1977) presented another system for automated collection of observation data. Their system involved a portable digital cassette system for recording single or simultaneous events. Data are entered through a keyboard that can handle sixty-four event channels, and the system is designed for direct computer access. The recorder can also provide a supplementary verbal record on a separate channel. Two recently published articles have also presented methods for automated data recording. Noting that computerized systems such as those mentioned above are expensive, Edleson (1978) suggested the use of a portable electronic calculator with a paper print-out. This recording procedure provides a permanent record, is easily transportable, can record up to ten figures per line, and is very flexible. The author noted that Texas Instruments and Sharp produce models that are relatively inexpensive and adaptable for use in behavioral observation. Frankel and Weber (1978) described a device mounted on a clipboard and composed of four integrated calculator circuits that can be used to measure duration of behavioral events. The device is powered by a nine-volt battery and lasts six hours under continuous use; its estimated cost is approximately forty dollars.

The development of automated data collection instruments represents a significant advance in the technology of behavioral observation. They can facilitate the storage, retrieval, presentation, and statistical analysis of observation data. However, there has been insufficient investigation of sources of error that may be idiosyncratic to these systems. Recording errors, for example, may be more likely with automated systems than with direct written coding systems. Also, automated data collection systems are limited in the manner in which data can be classified. It may be difficult to code subject groupings, subject characteristics, several concomitant behaviors, or the behavior of more than one subject. Additional evaluation will be needed to define more carefully the applicability and utility of these instruments.

## Assessing Interobserver Agreement

Interobserver agreement—the agreement between two observers independently recording the same target behaviors—has served as a method of estimating the accuracy of the observers and the maximum degree of confidence that can be placed in data derived from behavioral observation. It has been assumed that low coefficients of agreement between two or more observers are indicative of erroneous or insufficient specification of target events, faulty construction of the coding system, insufficient training of observers, errors in the time-sampling parameters, or other sources of error associated with the observation instrument. Interobserver agreement is therefore a necessary component in a valid behavioral observation system.

Because of the importance of the interobserver agreement coefficient in determining confidence in the derived data, considerable attention has been placed on methods of deriving that coefficient, the interaction between these methods, the coefficients derived, and the characteristics of the behavior. Commonly used methods include Pearson correlation, percent agreement for total frequencies, interval-by-interval agreement for occurrences, and interval-by-interval agreement for nonoccurrences. One issue that has continually concerned investigators of observation methodology is that the agreement coefficient derived from any one method is dependent upon the characteristics (primarily frequency and duration) of the target behavior. Rates of the targeted behaviors drastically affect chance agreement coefficients. For example, in observing a behavior with a probability of occurrence for each sampling interval of .8, two observers would be expected to agree by chance on the occurrence of the behavior in 60 percent of the sampling intervals. In working out actual agreement coefficients, researchers must consider the chance agreement level. The interaction between behavior characteristics and agreement coefficients complicates the assessment and interpretation of interobserver agreement.

In 1977, the *Journal of Applied Behavior Analysis (JABA)* published a series of articles that addressed the issue of interobserver agreement and procedures for its calculation (Baer, 1977a, 1977b; Hartmann, 1977a, 1977b; Hopkins and Hermann, 1977; Kazdin, 1977a; Kelly, 1977; Kratochwill and Wetzel, 1977; Yelton, Wildman, and Erickson, 1977). The primary emphasis of the series was upon the interaction among behavior rate, chance agreement coefficients, methods of assessing interobserver agreement, and procedures for comparing obtained agreement coefficients with chance agreement coefficients. Although containing some redundancies and variability in recommendations, the series provided an excellent overview of current thinking about these issues.

Hartmann (1977a, 1977b) addressed three issues affecting the nature of interobserver agreement: (1) the score unit (focus should be placed on the unit subjected to visual or statistical analysis), (2) the time span over which the data is compiled for analysis, and (3) the type of statistic used to assess agreement. Focusing on the third of these issues, Hartmann pointed out the benefits accruing from the use of correlational methods of estimating interobserver agreement. Hartmann noted that the correlation coefficient of agreement between two observers has well-known mathematical properties, can be used to generate confidence intervals that indicate the smallest differences between scores that can be interpreted meaningfully, can be used to estimate variance proportion attributable to error, provides an estimate of linear dependency, and can be used to estimate both the number of observation sessions required to detect significant effects and the necessary magnitude of change, given a constant number of observation sessions. Correlational procedures have disadvantages when there is little variability in scores for one or both observers, when the observer errors are correlated or nonlinear, or in cases of heteroscedasticity (when ratings differ markedly across sampling intervals). The phi statistic is the product-moment correlation between two sets of dichotomous data. Hartmann (1977a, 1977b) also discussed the use of the kappa statistic (Cohen, 1960) to generate an index of interobserver agreement for categorical data. The formula

$$(p_o - p_c) / (1 - p_c)$$

where $p_o$ = proportion of observed agreements and $p_c$ = proportion of agreement expected by chance provides a measure of agreement after correcting for chance agreement. The main thrust of Hartmann's articles was that correlational analysis might be preferable to other methods of assessing agreement because of its versatile properties and known mathematical characteristics.

In the same *JABA* series, Hopkins and Hermann (1977) discussed the procedures for comparing results obtained with expected interobserver agreement when both observers score approximately the same percent of intervals. Their formula for calculating chance agreement coefficients (for occurrences and nonoccurrences) is:

$$\frac{(O_1 \times O_2) + (N_1 \times N_2)}{(T)^2} \times 100$$

where $O_1$ is the number of intervals in which observer 1 records occurrences, $N_1$ is the number of intervals in which observer 1 records nonoccurrences, and $T$ is the number of intervals for which the two observers' records are compared. The chance agreement statistic derived from this formula is then compared to obtained agreement coefficients through the use of inferential statistics. Hopkins and Hermann recommended use of Cohen's $k$ or kappa statistic as a measure of interjudge agreement corrected for chance. They also noted that Fisher's exact test or chi-square can be used to compare obtained with expected agreement coefficients but that there is no currently satisfactory method of comparing obtained with expected agreement coefficients.

In addition to addressing the issues of chance agreement, Kratochwill and Wetzel (1977) discussed methods of presenting interobserver agreement data. They suggested that graphical plotting of calibrator and observer data may help readers interpret the agreement coefficients and facilitate detection of nonrandom error. They also noted, however, that such graphical presentation is expensive and may be misrepresentative when viewed independently of statistical analyses. Kratochwill and Wetzel also presented alternatives to assessment through conventional percent agreement; these included reporting special agreement estimates (such as percent agreement of occurrences and nonoccurrences) and correlational statistics. Like Kazdin (1977a) these authors also mentioned sources of error in observer accuracy—for example, feedback and drift.

Kazdin (1977a) reviewed various sources of error affecting observer accuracy and interobserver agreement coefficients (observer bias, reactivity to agreement assessment, observer drift, code complexity, and feedback) and differentiated between observer accuracy and agreement, with accuracy typically assessed by comparing the observer to a previously evaluated protocol. (In this book accuracy has been considered an index of validity of the observers' records and is *inferred* from observer agreement coefficients. Agreement with other data sources has been referred to as criterion agreement.) M. Kelly (1977) provided survey data on the type of interobserver agreement evaluation procedures utilized by *JABA* authors. In a review of 222 manuscripts published between 1968 and 1975, Kelly noted that 29 percent utilized event recording. He provided a table of reliability procedures utilized and the percent of published articles utilizing them, as well as those using product-of-behavior (8 percent) and duration (9 percent) measures. Kent and others (1977a) discussed characteristics of interobserver agreement in typical field settings in which the observer has knowledge of the calibrator, the experimenter is absent, and agreement coefficients are calculated in groups. In a controlled study, these researchers found that the factors noted above combined to provide an inflated index of interobserver agreement. To minimize inflation of agreement coefficients, the authors suggested the adoption of either continuous or covert interobserver agreement assessments, with particular care paid to definitional properties of the codes.

Like Kratochwill and Wetzel (1977), Meighan (1977) also discussed how best to present information on interobserver agreement. Meighan suggested that presentation of only mean interobserver agreement coefficients ignores statistical rules. Meighan recommended the presentation of sample size and variability as well. In addition, because the distribution of reliability coefficients tends to be toward higher coefficients, he recommended the use of nonparametric confidence intervals to estimate median. Meighan also suggested use of binomial statistical tables as a means of judging size of sample coefficients to be drawn to satisfy a reliability criterion of 95 to 99 percent.

In a follow-up on the 1977 *JABA* articles, Harris and Lahey (1978) reviewed some of the issues addressed in that series and presented methodology for assessing interobserver agreement based upon a model provided by Clement (1976). Their formula provides a mean of indices of occurrences and nonoccurrences weighted according to the rate of the targeted behavior. Thus, when relatively few intervals are scored, greater emphasis is placed upon occurrence agreement; but when a relatively large number of intervals are scored, greater emphasis is placed on nonoccurrence agreement. The formula presented by the authors was: Interobserver Agreement $= (A \times B) + (C \times D)$, where $A =$ number of agreements for occurrences divided by the number of time samples marked by the standard observer; $B = 1.00 -$ (occurrences marked by the standard observer divided by the total number of time samples); $C =$ number of agreements for nonoccurrences divided by the number of time samples marked by the standard observer; and $D = 1.00 -$ (nonoccurrences marked by the standard observer divided by the total number of time samples).

The excellent series of *JABA* articles and other articles in this area facilitate the integration and clarification of issues affecting estimates of observer accuracy and offer some alternative methods of calculating interobserver agreement. Perhaps the most useful suggestions involve the use of formulas that take into account expected chance agreement coefficients as a function of behavior frequency and provide the researcher with a coefficient indicative of agreement above chance levels. However, as indicated in several of the papers reviewed, there is still no satisfactory criterion for judging whether obtained interobserver agreement coefficients are significantly beyond levels that would be expected to occur by chance. Furthermore, substantial investigation will be needed before the strengths and weaknesses of the various formulas for assessing interobserver agreement can be ascertained. One negative impact of the articles cited in this review is that they may increase the types of calculation procedures used to assess interobserver agreement. Instead of the common interval-by-interval percent agreement calculations, a variety of correlational and noncorrelational methods may come to be utilized. While they may provide valid and sensitive indices. of observer accuracy, they will make comparisons among studies more difficult.

## Reactivity and Other Sources of Error
## in Behavioral Observation

The validity of behavioral observation is influenced by many factors that nonspecifically influence all assessment instruments (such as subject expectancy and reactivity) and by factors that are idiosyncratic to behavioral observation. Kazdin (1977a) and Kratochwill and Wetzel (1977), in discussing issues of observer agreement, have reemphasized several sources of error, including the method of assessing interobserver agreement, training of observers, observer drift, feedback to observers, observer bias, complexity of observation codes, observer expectancies, and predictability of behavior.

Although reactive effects vary in format and extent as a function of the setting (naturalistic versus analogue) and will be addressed in subsequent chapters, there have been several recently published studies that are of general relevance to this issue. G. D. White (1977), for example, investigated the effects of observer presence on the activity level of families. Utilizing a laboratory situation resembling a family living room, White monitored the location and activity level of family members through a one-way mirror while systematically manipulating the presence or absence of observers. He found that there was a marked reduction in activity level in the presence of observers for all five families participating in the study. Reisinger and Ora (1977) utilized a small recorder and transmitter system about the size of a package of cigarettes to record mother-child interaction in the home. Mothers wore the transmitters for two hours during an assessment stage of a behavioral intervention program. The transmitters were worn in the presence and absence of an observer, and Reisinger and Ora reported that the presence of live observers apparently served as a stimulus for parents to engage in special activities and was associated with higher rates of parent-child interactions.

Dubey and others (1977) investigated the effects of observers in a laboratory classroom. In each of several studies, observers were systematically introduced and removed while the behavior of children and their teacher was covertly observed. The children were observed during "independent math work," and the authors found no significant behavioral or subjective effects attributable to the presence of the observers. In a separate experiment, however, the authors found that the presence of observers was associated with an increase in disruptive behavior during baseline but a decrease during intervention; however, this finding was not replicated in a subsequent study. As part of a study on reducing sibling conflict in the home, Leitenberg and others (1977) used assessment instruments that included outside observers, participant monitoring by parents, and tape recordings of interactions in the home. Reactivity associated with the presence of outside observers was suggested by the finding that the rate of sibling conflict was lower on the first than the second assessment night. There was also less sibling conflict and less overall interaction on nights when the observer was present. These findings suggest that reactive effects were manifested in reduced rates of interaction rather than in a higher rate or proportion of appropriate interaction.

Melnick and Stocker (1977) assessed the reactive effects of tape-recording social interaction in a structured observation situation with unassertive students. The authors hypothesized that knowledge that one's responses were being recorded might trigger "self-monitoring" and influence the rate or types of behavior emitted. As it turned out, the subjects' behavior was not significantly affected. Alevizos and others (1978) assessed reactive effects of their Behavior Observation Instrument by assessing habituation across a series of observation sessions and found no significant indices of reactivity. In observing mother-child interactions in a laboratory setting, however, Zegiob and Forehand (1978) noted that knowledge of observation was associated with an increase in the frequency of mothers' behaviors and "good" parental behaviors, as defined by the observational code.

These recently published studies suggest that observation procedures can affect the behavior of targeted subjects but that reactive effects do not always occur. Numerous factors may affect the occurrence and degree of reactivity and should be the object of additional investigation. Variables influencing reactivity might include: (1) the obtrusiveness of the observation procedure, (2) the social sensitivity of the target behaviors (sexual or antisocial behaviors may be more reactive), (3) biases or expectancies of the targeted subjects, (4) the behavior or characteristics of the observers or recording apparatus, (5) previous experience of the target subjects with observation procedures, (6) age of target subjects, and (7) preassessment instructions provided to target subjects. As noted in Chapter One, reactivity in assessment is particularly important because it affects the external validity or generalizability of observation data. If observation procedures significantly affect the behavior of target subjects, the data obtained may not be indicative of the behavior of the subject in more naturalistic situations—situations in which the observer is not present. Reactive effects are less of a threat to validity if their occurrence, extent, and direction can be predicted, but our current state of assessment sophistication is insufficient to allow such predictions. The implications of the findings noted above is that caution should be exercised in interpreting data where reactive effects are possible or suspected.

In addition to reactivity, there are other potential sources of error in behavioral observation procedures. Horn (1978) addressed one of those sources—opposite-sex bias by observers when recording disruptive behavior of children. Male and female observers were trained on a four-item behavior coding system for use with children in classroom settings. From a videotape, the observers recorded disruptive behavior of male and female children in a simulated classroom setting and also provided subjective estimates of the target children's degree of "disruptiveness" and "normalcy." The behavior observation data did not vary as a function of the interaction between sex of the observer and the sex of the target child. On subjective ratings of normalcy, however, observers differed significantly, with male observers reporting higher subjective indices of deviation.

Another factor influencing the content and criterion validity of behavioral observation systems is time-sampling parameters. In a recently published article, Powell and others (1977) extended earlier work on the effects that varying sampling periods have on the validity of derived data. Previous work by Powell, Martindale, and Kulp (1975) suggested that, when using interval scoring (scoring the occurrence or nonoccurrence of a behavior within each sampling interval), the degree to which the derived estimates approximated a continuous measure of the same behavior varied with the method of scoring the occurrence of behavior during an interval (scoring an occurrence whenever a behavior occurred during an interval, scoring an occurrence if behavior lasted throughout the entire interval, or scoring an occurrence if behavior was occurring at the end of the interval). The results of the later study suggested that the accuracy of time-sampling methods was a complex function of the interaction between duration of the sampling interval and duration and frequency of the behavior.

In a further extension, Powell and Rockinson (1978) evaluated the relationship between the frequency and duration characteristics of a behavior on the one hand and the validity of time samples on the other. Using a computer simulation in which response duration and frequency were varied, the authors assessed the effects of various time-sampling parameters by comparing derived estimates with actual data derived from continuous measures. Although difficult to interpret, overall results suggested that there are many conditions under which interval-by-interval time sampling cannot yield valid measurement. Green and Alverson (1978) investigated the validity of four data collection procedures for sampling long-duration behaviors. In a computer simulation experiment, four sampling methods—whole-interval, partial-interval, momentary time-sampling, and continuous—were compared. Relative to the continuous measure, only momentary time sampling (point-time sampling) yielded unbiased results. The authors noted that the degree of bias for the other methods was affected by the interval recording length, the mean duration of the behavior, and the mean interresponse time. Because these factors cannot usually be estimated in applied research, the authors suggested that momentary time sampling be utilized.

These studies further underscore the assertion that data derived from behavioral observations cannot be assumed to be indicative of "true" behavior. The frequency and duration estimates derived from an observation system will be a function of the type of sampling procedures utilized, the sampling parameters of those procedures, and such characteristics of the responses as frequency, duration, and interresponse durations.

Another potential source of error in observation data—observing consequences on targeted behaviors—was reported by Harris and Ciminero (1978). In three experiments the authors found that observable consequences on subjects' targeted behavior (eye contact and face touching) were associated with increases in the frequency with which those behaviors were reported by observers but that the reported rate of collateral behaviors remained the same. The authors suggested that such effects might pose threats to the internal validity of observation procedures and that they may not be identifiable through interobserver accuracy checks.

## Participant Observers in
## Behavioral Assessment

Observation in the natural environment has been the assessment procedure most congruent with behavioral construct systems. Observing behavior change in the natural environment has been presumed to be the least biased, least inferential, and most valid method of assessing intervention effects. Observation in the natural environment, however, is expensive in time and money when external observers are used. Also, as noted in the previous section, there can be an unacceptable degree of reactivity associated with the introduction of external observers into a natural environment.

One method of possibly minimizing the expense and reactive effects of gathering data in the natural environment is to use participant observers—individuals who are normally part of the natural environment of the target subject—to observe and record the behavior of that subject. Table 2 presents an overview of recently published studies that have utilized participant observers. It is obvious from inspection of this table that participant observers have been used in a variety of settings and for a variety of target problems and populations. Since participant observers are thus assuming an increasingly important role in behavioral assessment, this assessment procedure warrants closer scrutiny.

Table 2. Recently Published Studies
Utilizing Participant Observers

| Reference | Participant Observer | Target Behavior, Population, and Situation |
|---|---|---|
| Arnold, Sturgis, and Forehand (1977) | Parents | Talk by fifteen-year-old mentally retarded female |
| Barnard, Christophersen, and Wolf (1977) | Mothers | Shopping behavior of boys in super-market |
| Broden, Beasley, and Hall (1978) | Parents | Spelling by chil-dren during home-tutoring sessions |
| Colletti and Harris (1977) | Parents | Behavior of autis-tic child's sibling in the home |
| Doleys and others (1977a) | Parents | Bladder capacity of enuretic children in the home |
| Elliott and Denny (1978) | Relatives, friends | Smoking behavior of subjects under-going intervention program |
| Epstein and Martin (1977) | Individuals in subject's eating environment | Food intake at mealtime of subject in weight control program |
| Finley, Wansley, and Blenkarn (1977) | Parents | Bed-wetting of enuretic children at home |
| Finley and Wansley (1977) | Parents | Bed-wetting of enuretic children at home |
| Garlington and Dericco (1977) | Bartender | Drinking behavior of alcoholics at simulated tavern |
| Greene and others (1978) | Ward supervisor | Training behaviors of hospital staff at institution for mul-tiply handicapped patients |

Table 2. Recently Published Studies
Utilizing Participant Observers (Continued)

| Reference | Participant Observer | Target Behavior, Population, and Situation |
|---|---|---|
| Hanson and Deysach (1977) | Nurses | Visit to infirmary by children at therapeutic summer camp |
| Harris and Purohit (1977) | Parents | Children's bed-wetting at home |
| Hay, Nelson, and Hay (1977) | Teachers | Behavior of elementary school children in the classroom |
| Karoly and Rosenthal (1977) | Parents | Appropriate and inappropriate child behaviors at home |
| Kauffman, Hallahan, and Ianna (1977) | Teacher | Tongue protrusions of retarded child during class |
| Kent and O'Leary (1977) | Teachers | Appropriate and inappropriate behaviors of children with conduct problems in class and sibling conflict in the home |
| Komaki and Barnett (1977) | Coaches | Play execution for football team composed of nine- and ten-year-olds |
| Leitenberg and others (1977) | Mother | Sibling conflict in the home |
| Loos, Williams, and Bailey (1977) | Teachers | Academic units completed by third-grade children at school |
| Matson and Ollendick (1977) | Mothers | Bed-wetting of children at home |

### Table 2. Recently Published Studies
### Utilizing Participant Observers (Continued)

| Reference | Participant Observer | Target Behavior, Population, and Situation |
|---|---|---|
| Matson and Stephens (1977) | Hospital staff | Aggressive behavior of schizophrenic woman in psychiatric hospital |
| Meyers, Nathan, and Kopel (1977) | Library staff | Book reshelving at library |
| Milby and others (1977) | Nursing staff | Behaviors and token transfers of psychiatric inpatients |
| Miller (1978) | Friends, relatives | Drinking behavior of problem drinkers |
| Nunes, Murphy, and Ruprecht (1977) | Teacher and teacher aide | Self-injurious behavior of mentally retarded male in institution |
| Reid and Hurlbut (1977) | Staff person | Nonvocal communication behavior of mentally retarded in institution |
| Rekers (1977b) | Parents | Sex-typed play of gender-disturbed boys at home |
| Rekers and others (1977) and Rekers, Amaro-Plotkin, and Low (1977) | Parents | Sex-typed play of gender-disturbed boys at home |
| Resick, Forehand, and McWhorter (1976) | Mothers | Desirable and undesirable behaviors of children at home |
| Sacks and De Leon (1978) | Parents | Enuretic children in the home |

Table 2. Recently Published Studies
Utilizing Participant Observers (Continued)

| Reference | Participant Observer | Target Behavior, Population, and Situation |
|---|---|---|
| G. J. Schwartz (1977) | Tutor | Reading skills of seventh grader with reading deficiencies |
| Switzer, Deal, and Bailey (1977) | Teachers | Stealing in second-grade classroom |
| Upper, Lochman, and Aveni (1977) | Foster parents | Problem behavior of former psychiatric patients (male) in foster homes |
| Van Houten and Van Houten (1977) | Teachers | Number of lessons completed by child at school |
| Wright and Bunch (1977) | Parents | Chronic constipation in children at home |
| Wulbert and Dries (1977) | Mother | Appropriate and inappropriate behavior of hyperactive child in the home |
| Żeiss (1977) | Spouse | Premature ejaculation at home |
| Zeiss (1978) | Wife | Ejaculatory latency of males with premature ejaculation |

Several characteristics of the current application of participant observers can be summarized. First, participant observers are used primarily to gather outcome data in program evaluation. Participant observation is seldom used as an intervention procedure to modify the behavior of the participant observer (as in self-monitoring) or in preintervention assessment and diagnosis. Second, participant observation is usually used as a secondary measure of program outcome to supplement data derived from such other sources as external observers or questionnaires. Third, the observation systems utilized by participant observers are typically less complex than those utilized by trained external observers. Participant observers tend to observe fewer and simpler behaviors, use longer time samples, and observe fewer times than external observers. Fourth, assessments of the reliability, validity, sensitivity, applicability, or other psychometric qualities of participant observation are infrequently undertaken. Finally, participant observers are most frequently utilized with children or institutionalized individuals as target subjects. They are seldom used with normal adult populations (see exceptions by Elliott and Denny, 1978; Epstein and Martin, 1977; Garlington and Dericco, 1977; Greene and others, 1978; Miller, 1978; Zeiss, 1977).

Participant observation does not appear to be used as an independent assessment instrument or as a substitute for observation by external observers; it usually serves as a supplementary measure and then only with limited populations and behaviors. It is unclear whether the selective and limited utilization of participant observers is a function of limitations of this assessment procedure or of bias on the part of the behavior analysts who utilize it. The degree of complexity of an observation system that can be utilized validly by a participant observer and its applicability to various target subjects are probably determined by many factors, such as level of intellectual functioning and motivation of the observer, constraints imposed by the natural environment, and degree of training of the observer.

Criterion or external validity is particularly important with participant observation because it may be excessively susceptible to such idiosyncratic sources of error as observer bias. Several recently published studies have evaluated the reliability or criterion-related validity of participant observation by including an external observer who observed the target subject simultaneously with the participant observer. Except for a study by Miller (1978), all recently published studies that employed external observers or self-monitoring concurrent with participant observation (Broden, Beasley, and Hall, 1978; Colletti and Harris, 1977; Elliott and Denny, 1978; Garlington and Dericco, 1977; Hay, Nelson, and Hay, 1977; Kauffman, Hallahan, and Ianna, 1977; Leitenberg and others, 1977; Meyers, Nathan, and Kopel, 1977; Reid and Hurlbut, 1977;

Switzer, Deal, and Bailey, 1977; Van Houten and Van Houten, 1977) reported satisfactory coefficients of agreement (above .80). These coefficients can be considered criterion-related measures of internal validity, but it should be reiterated that inferences of validity are confined to the specific populations, behaviors, and observation parameters utilized in each study.

Because the presumed reactivity associated with external observers in the natural environment is a primary rationale for the use of participant observers, the degree of reactivity associated with participant observation is an important consideration. A recently published article by Hay, Nelson, and Hay (1977) addressed the issue of reactivity associated with participant observation. These authors evaluated the use of teachers as behavioral observers of elementary school students in their classes. During the first phase of the study, external observers monitored the behavior of teachers and target students for five days; in the second phase, teachers also monitored student behavior. The authors noted that the initiation of participant observation by teachers was associated with a significant modification in the behavior of the students and teachers. Thus, their study suggested that, at least under some conditions, systematic observation in the natural environment by individuals normally in that environment may affect the behavior of target subjects and observers. It is still unclear, however, what factors affect the degree or direction of reactivity.

Although participant observers are being increasingly used in behavioral assessment, research is needed in several areas before the utility and validity of participant observation can be ascertained:

1. Additional research is needed on types and degree of reactivity associated with participant observation, including subjective responses of target individuals and observers, specific behaviors affected, duration of reactive effects, and factors influencing reactivity.
2. Further evaluation is needed of the complexity of observation systems usable by participant observers. For example, what factors affect the level of sophistication that can be expected from a particular participant observer?

3. Further research is required on the applicability of participant observation to particular target behaviors and target
populations.
4. The sensitivity to intervention effects of data derived from participant observers requires additional evaluation.
5. The reliability (session-by-session agreement) of participant observation and factors affecting it need further evaluation.
6. Additional research on the criterion-related validity of participant observation is needed. Coefficients of agreement between
participant and external observers are likely to be inflated estimates of overall accuracy because of observers' knowledge of
reliability assessment. It is also likely that validity of derived data
will vary among target behaviors, target subjects, participant
observers, and observation settings.

In summary, a number of recent articles have utilized participant observers with a variety of target populations and behaviors.
The observation systems utilized by participant observers tend not
to be as complex as those used by trained external observers. Several studies have suggested that data derived from participant observers have agreed with data derived from simultaneous observation by external observers. However, there is some reason to
suspect that participant observation may be associated with reactive effects on the behavior of the target subject and observer, and
there are additional areas that need research.

## Recent Advances in
## Observation Instrumentation

The reliability and validity of data derived from behavioral
observation are influenced by its associated technology. Thus, observers can attend more consistently to the target subjects, and the
probability of error due to variance in length of time samples is
reduced in time sampling by use of cassette tape recorders, tapes
with demarcated time samples, and earplugs. Similarly, video-
recording of target subjects has facilitated interobserver agreement assessment and the coding of a larger number of behaviors.

Several recently published studies have utilized or discussed other technological advances that can serve to improve the reliability and validity of behavioral observation. Barkley and Jackson (1977) described the use of actometers (Timex motion recorders attached at the wrist and ankle) for measuring activity levels and movement. The instrument was used to monitor activity levels of hyperactive and nonhyperactive children and provided information on the duration of activity during a sampling period. In the same study, the authors utilized a stabilimeter chair (from Lafayette instruments) that measured movement of the individual when sitting. Activity measures were taken during five different experimental periods (free-play, movie, testing, restricted play, and lab-recording periods), and significant differences between hyperactive and nonhyperactive children were noted on all activity measures. Barkley (1977a) also used the stabilimeter chair and actometer to evaluate the effects of methylphenidate on activity levels of hyperactive children. Actometer but not stabilimeter measures were found to be affected by the medication.

Schulman, Stevens, and Kupst (1977) described the use of a biomotometer—a small electronic package worn on the waist. This instrument measures activity levels by monitoring angular displacement of internal mercury switches. Composed of the biomotometer, read-out box unit, and display unit, the instrument can tabulate total activity counts and activity levels exceeding a designated criterion, as well as provide a biofeedback signal to the user when the activity level exceeds a criterion. The instrument was tested on several young children in a classroom setting and, in comparison with an actometer, agreement coefficients ranged from .38 to .86. Test-retest reliability coefficient across four sessions was .84. The range of coefficients between biomotometer and actometer may be a function of the type of activity in which coefficients were calculated (playroom versus woodshop) because each instrument is differentially sensitive to various movements. The authors also noted differences in activity levels between measurement sessions; these differences may represent an initial reactive effect to wearing the unit.

Brabyn and Strelow (1977) described a device for measuring locomotion within a large enclosed room. Lightweight wires are attached to the subject and to take-up drums in different parts of the room. The position of the subject is then monitored by a photocell arrangement that produces a stream of digital impulses suitable for direct computer analysis. Hay (1977) monitored the exploratory behavior of infants by monitoring their entry into testing rooms. The degree to which infants would follow a familiar figure into unfamiliar environments was measured by photocells that monitored entry into rooms. Farran and Ramey (1977) described a procedure for measuring movement and location of subjects with a videotape. The authors measured a child's proximity to adults by use of an acetate overlay that divided the observation room into four quadrants. This allowed calculation of the frequency and duration of proximity in each quadrant and of the total amount of time spent in each quadrant.

Instrumentation for monitoring body movements was described by Karoly and Dirks (1977) and Murphy and Doughty (1977). Karoly and Dirks presented a timing device (Hunter Model 120A Klockounter) that automatically monitored arm raising in children. The device provided a measure of duration of arm movements above the shoulder (twenty-degree angle). Murphy and Doughty described an automated device for monitoring head angle. This device is particularly useful in teaching mentally retarded or other physically disabled children head control. Other advances in instrumentation with potential use to behavior analysts include a polygraph print-out of pitch and amplitude traces for speech assessment (MacWhinney and Osser, 1977), monitoring of visual scanning and fixation of infants through use of superimposed infrared light on videotapes of an infant's eye (Pipp and Gaith, 1977), measurement of light and sound level in an infant assessment environment (Lawson, Daum, and Turkewitz, 1977), and an inexpensive cumulative counter useful in recording rapidly occurring speech (Guitar and Andrews, 1977).

Several investigators have utilized audiotaping or videotaping to facilitate observation methodology. M. Greenwald (1977) described an audiotaping system for social skills measures that employs an automatic switching mechanism so that the response but not the stimuli can be recorded. Stephenson and Roberts (1977) described a device that records multiple events in real time on audiotape and allows for high-speed transcription into a computer. Collis and Sharp (1977) described a method for superimposing visual stimuli, such as clock timers, on videotapes. The system utilizes a series of mirrors that reflect back into the camera a clock face that is in the same room as the camera. Field (1977) utilized a split-screen video technique for simultaneously recording the bodies and faces of mothers and infants while they were interacting. Reisinger and Ora (1977) utilized a method to reduce the reactive effects of home observation of parent-child interaction. Mothers wore a small FM transmitter (the size of a cigarette pack), and an FM receiver was placed in an adjacent room in the house. The packet was worn about the chest, and an elastic band that held it in place also contained an antenna. The receiver was connected to an audiotape recorder for recording the verbal interactions of the mother.

Hansen (1977) provided a schematic diagram and described a simple interval timer to demarcate sampling intervals. The system utilizes an unobtrusive light and auditory signal that is adjustable so that intervals can be monitored through a visual or auditory monitor. Although not providing reliability data, the author suggested a slight but unimportant variation in the timing intervals over a one-year period. The estimated cost of the instrument (at the time of publication) was ten dollars. Knapp (1978) described a portable observation apparatus constructed from plywood and one-way glass. The unit can be quickly assembled and disassembled, weighs less than fifty pounds, and costs approximately fifty dollars.

## Summary

Presented in this chapter were recent developments in the conceptualization and methodology of behavioral observation. Several new coding systems have been developed, and it was noted that recently developed observation systems were more likely to involve psychometric evaluation. Recently developed coding systems by Barlow and others, Abikoff, Gittelman-Klein, and Klein, and Alevizos and others appear particularly promising. Automated data-recording systems are another recent development that may increase the efficiency, data analysis capabilities, and overall sophistication of behavioral observation. These systems may shorten the time normally required for data transcription and analysis and facilitate a more sophisticated analysis of behavioral data. Various systems for automated data recording differ in their characteristics and capabilities, and a more comprehensive evaluation is still needed of their idiosyncratic sources of error.

Several recent articles have discussed methods of evaluating interobserver agreement and have stressed the interdependence among obtained agreement coefficients, methods of calculating the coefficient, and characteristics of the targeted behavior. Several authors suggested methods of comparing obtained agreement coefficients with coefficients expected by chance, but the interpretation of this ratio is still unclear. The issue of reactivity and other sources of error has also been addressed in several recent articles. Some studies have found evidence for the reactive effects of behavioral observation while others have not. A number of recently published articles have described the use of participant observers. Participant observers have been most frequently used to monitor the behavior of children and have typically been used in conjunction with other assessment procedures. Despite the use of this method with a variety of subjects and across a variety of situations, there is insufficient information on its sources of error, as well as its reliability, applicability, and criterion validity. Finally, a number of recent technological advances were noted. These included instrumentation for the measurement of movement, monitoring of other discrete behaviors, and the use of audiotape and videotape recording, radio transmitters, and automated time-sampling apparatus.

# CHAPTER THREE

# *Observation in Natural Environments*

As an assessment procedure, naturalistic observation is congruent with the framework of a behavioral construct system and associated assumptions regarding the environmental determinants of behavior. While assessment procedures such as observation in analogue environments may have utility for certain behaviors and populations and may offer some savings in time and cost (see Chapter Four), naturalistic observation is not only a desirable approach to assessment because of its greater content validity, but it also may be the least inferential method of assessing the effects of treatment programs carried out in naturalistic settings. For example, targeted behaviors such as interactions between staff and patients in institutions, the adherence of teachers to classroom behavior intervention strategies, or the driving habits of individuals participating in fuel conservation programs are not readily amenable to assessment in analogue settings.

In recent studies, naturalistic observation has been utilized as an assessment procedure in a variety of environmental settings—home and family, institutions and schools, and restaurants and other community areas. Various targeted behaviors, including parent-child interactions, ingestive and eliminative behaviors, stereotypic responses, aggressive and noncompliant behaviors, social skills, and academic behaviors, have been the focus of naturalistic observation. Observational data have been collected by external observers in some assessment formats and by participant observers (parents, teacher aides, and hospital staff) in others. Data collection techniques likewise vary considerably. While the most common format has involved observation of single or multiple behaviors through behavioral codes of varying complexity, product-of-behavior measures have also been utilized. The particular assessment procedure selected is typically a function of the particular behaviors targeted. Accordingly, subsequent sections of this chapter address the typical settings in which naturalistic observation has been employed and the specific behaviors targeted for observation within those settings. Issues related to observation in the natural environment are also presented; and, since a principal aim of this chapter is to evaluate issues of reliability and validity, studies having implications for those topics will be emphasized.

## Family Settings

Naturalistic observation has been extensively applied in family and home settings to collect information regarding social interactions among family members. Most frequently, the function of these assessment efforts has been to assess the effects of various behavioral intervention procedures. Applications in family settings are summarized in Table 3.

In the naturalistic assessment of family social interaction, including parent and caregiver interactions with children, behaviors targeted for observation have included "attachment responses" (Bakeman and Brown, 1977; Durfee and others, 1977; Lamb,

**Table 3. Recent Applications of Naturalistic Observation in Family Settings**

| Reference | Subjects | Setting | Behaviors Monitored |
|---|---|---|---|
| Anderson, Vietze, and Dokecki (1977) | Mothers and three-month-old infants | Home observation | Frequency, sequence, duration, proximity, and caregiving activities; the reciprocal influence of vocal interactions |
| Arnold, Sturgis, and Forehand | Mothers and children | Home observation | Frequencies of communication skills used, compared with total number of verbalizations |
| Bakeman and Brown (1977) | Mothers and infants | Hospital room | Mother-child interactions |
| Becker (1977) | Nine-month-old infants | Home observation | Narrative recordings of target, antecedent, and consequence |
| Blehar, Lieberman, and Ainsworth (1977) | Mothers and infants | Home observation | Coded maternal behaviors |
| Bollard and Woodroffe (1977) | Children | Home observation | Eliminative (enuretic) behavior |
| Camras (1977) | Children | Home observation | Coded facial expressions in conflict situations |
| Cochran (1977) | Children and caretakers | Home; day home; center | Semistructured separation situation to assess affectional ties; also two observation scales |

| | | |
|---|---|---|
| Cohen and Beckwith (1977) | Preterm infants | Home observation | Thirty-five caregiver and sixteen infant behaviors |
| Colletti and Harris (1977) | Children (sisters) | Home observation | Effectiveness of normal sibling as behavior modifier for autistic sister; effectiveness of parents as observers |
| Doleys and others (1977a) | Children (enuretic) | Home observation | Urine volume as a product-of-behavior measure of enuresis control training |
| Durfee and others (1977) | Infants | Home and lab | Social attachment between infant and primary caregiver with a coding system during free play |
| Finley and Wansley (1977) | Children (enuretic) | Home observation | Parents monitored bed-wetting, bedtime, time up next morning |
| Finley, Wansley, and Blenkarn (1977) | Children (enuretic) | Home observation | Parents monitored enuretic activity |
| Glennon and Weisz (1978) | Nursery school children | Mothers present and absent | Twenty-item scale to assess anxiety through observation under stress situations |
| Glogower and Sloop (1976) | Children | Home | Parents assessed temporal generality |
| Harris and Purohit (1977) | Children (enuretic) | Home observation | Bladder capacity via "water-load test"; participant observers monitored number of wet nights per week |

Table 3. Recent Applications of Naturalistic Observation in Family Settings (Continued)

| Reference | Subjects | Setting | Behaviors Monitored |
|---|---|---|---|
| Johnson and Bolstad (1975) | Children and parents | Home observation | Reactivity of observations in home by audio recordings with observers present or absent |
| Kandel, Ayllon, and Rosenbaum (1977) | Children (withdrawn) | Home observation | Flooding versus systematic exposure in treatment of social withdrawal |
| Karoly and Rosenthal (1977) | Families and children | Home observation | Parents monitored children's behavior as part of management training; utilized Patterson's coding system |
| Kilbride, Johnson, and Streissguth (1977) | Two-week-old infants | | Utilized eight-category code to assess type and quantity of caretaker interaction |
| Lamb (1977a) | Infants | Home observation | Mother-child interactions including affiliative and attachment behavior |
| Lamb (1977b) | Infants | Home observation | Interactions of infants with mothers, fathers, and strangers; tracked five affiliative and six attachment behaviors coded from taped narratives |

| Source | Subjects | Setting | Description |
|---|---|---|---|
| Leitenberg and others (1977) | Siblings | Home observation | Reductions in sibling conflicts |
| Lieberman (1977) | Children | Home observation | Mother-child interactions recorded on narrative tapes; willingness or resistance on specific tasks |
| Lovaas and others (1977) | Children (autistic) | Home and lab | Verbal behavior under three categories as compared with normal children's verbalizations |
| Lytton (1977) | Parents | Home observation | Differential treatment by parents of monozygotic and dizygotic twins |
| B. Martin (1977) | Mothers and children | Telephone assessment in home | Parent-child interactions; coded three child and three parent behaviors as means of preintervention assessment |
| Matson and Ollendick (1977) | Children (enuretic) | Home observation | Mothers as participant observers of bed-wetting frequencies |
| Nucci and Turiel (1978) | Preschool children | | Interactions under two domains of events: social-conventional and moral |
| Patterson (1977a) | Children (aggressive) | Home observation | Application of codes for observing problem family interactions |

**Table 3. Recent Applications of Naturalistic Observation in Family Settings (Continued)**

| Reference | Subjects | Setting | Behaviors Monitored |
|---|---|---|---|
| Patterson (1977b) | Children (aggressive) | Home observation | Discussion of behavioral coding system to assess family interactions |
| Peed, Roberts, and Forehand (1977) | Children and parents | Home and lab | Recorded sequences of parent-child behaviors (seven classes of parent behavior) to assess effectiveness of parent-training program |
| Rekers and others (1977) and Rekers, Amaro-Plotkin, and Low (1977) | Male child | Home and lab | Mother maintained checklist in home to record categories of cross-gender behaviors |
| Resick, Forehand, and McWhorter (1976) | Children | Home observation | Assessed sibling generality of a treatment program |
| Roper and Hinde (1978) | Preschool children | Village play group | Assessed social behaviors |
| Russell and Bernal (1977) | Parents of male children | Home observation | Systematic variation in rates of desirable or undesirable behavior as a function of temporal and climatic variables |
| Skarin (1977) | Infants | Home and lab | Infant fear responses to strangers; included behavioral ratings of facial expressions |
| Smith and Daglish (1977) | Families (English) | Home observation | Describes observation system with thirty-two child behavior categories and sixteen parent reactions |

| Stimbert, Minor, and McCoy (1977) | Children (mentally retarded) | Home observation | Mentally retarded feeding training in home; frequencies of correct/incorrect/inappropriate eating responses; continuous recording for rates of eating |
| Taplin and Reid (1977) | Parents and children | Home observation | Assessed changes in parent consequences with sequential codes for twenty-nine behavioral categories |
| Wulbert and Dries (1977) | Male child (hyperactive) | Home and lab | Mother recorded ritualistic behavior and task accuracy to assess drug effects upon hyperactivity |
| Zivin (1977) | Children | Home observation | Monitored face-making frequencies as related to social rank, along with hierarchy rankings by peers |

1977a, 1977b; Lieberman, 1977) and caregiver behaviors (Blehar, Lieberman, and Ainsworth, 1977; Cochran, 1977; Cohen and Beckwith, 1977; Kilbride, Johnson, and Streissguth, 1977), as well as reciprocal influences of parent-child vocalizations (Anderson, Vietze, and Dokecki, 1977), parental influences on language development (Elardo, Bradley, and Caldwell, 1977), parent reactions to children's sex-typed behaviors (Smith and Daglish, 1977), and differential responsiveness of parents to monozygotic and dizygotic twins (Lytton, 1977). While these could more appropriately be classified as developmental than as behavioral assessment or intervention studies, all employed naturalistic observation procedures and have implications for the evaluation of this assessment instrument. Parent-child problem interactions have also been the subject of observation, as, for example, in the assessment of parental interactions with aggressive children (Karoly and Rosenthal, 1977; Patterson, 1977a, 1977b; Taplin and Reid, 1977) and noncompliant children (B. Martin, 1977; Peed, Roberts, and Forehand, 1977).

With the exception of those studies of problem behaviors just mentioned, most studies using naturalistic observation of parent-child and child-peer interactions in family settings have basically involved developmental or child psychology research. However, naturalistic observation procedures have also been used to assess child behaviors and parent behaviors in the context of behavioral intervention programs. For example, children's behaviors targeted for assessment have included ingestive responses (Stimbert, Minor, and McCoy, 1977), enuretic responses (Bollard and Woodroffe, 1977; Doleys and others, 1977a; Harris and Purohit, 1977; Matson and Ollendick, 1977), and the effect of drug treatment on hyperactivity (Wulbert and Dries, 1977). As mentioned previously, problem behaviors such as aggression and noncompliance have been the subject of family assessment in natural settings, as have fear responses (Skarin, 1977), verbalizations by autistic children (Lovaas and others, 1977), social withdrawal (Kandel, Ayllon, and Rosenbaum, 1977), disturbances in gender-role behaviors (Rekers and others, 1977; Rekers, Amaro-Plotkin, and Low, 1977), and other undesirable behaviors (Glogower and Sloop, 1976; Russell and Bernal, 1977). Other targets for naturalistic observation have included effects upon a sibling of treatment of a target child (Resick, Forehand, and McWhorter, 1976), the effectiveness of parents as observers of their children (Colletti and Harris, 1977), and the effectiveness of parents as behavior change agents (Arnold, Sturgis, and Forehand, 1977) and of siblings (Colletti and Harris, 1977) as behavior change agents.

A majority of these studies reported that the observation procedures employed were sensitive to the effects of intervention; that is, the measures derived from naturalistic observation have been relatively quick in reflecting real changes in the target behaviors—an encouraging finding in that sensitivity represents one aspect of an instrument's validity. However, these observation formats have varied from simple frequency counts of target behavior occurrences to extremely sophisticated observational codes involving targeted behaviors and associated antecedent and consequent events (see Patterson, 1977b). It is to be expected that sensitivity would vary as a function of the setting, the particular observation procedure selected, and the behavior to which it is applied, but parameters affecting sensitivity of naturalistic observation have not been sufficiently investigated. Researchers have also reported reactive effects associated with observation in family settings (Johnson and Bolstad, 1975; Leitenberg and others, 1977). For example, Leitenberg and others (1977) noted less sibling conflict on nights when an outside observer was present in the home than on nights when the mother was recording alone. However, this differential outcome might reflect bias in parent reporting as well as reactive effects of the observation procedures. Reactive effects, nevertheless, constitute a threat to validity and thus are of concern in naturalistic observation, as they are in other assessment procedures and settings.

While there has been extensive application of observation procedures to assess social interactions and parental and child behaviors in family settings, few of these studies have reported evidence, other than sensitivity, for the validity of the instruments employed. In this regard, many researchers substitute measures of sensitivity for measures of criterion-related validity (Haynes, 1978); researchers are simply assuming that an observation procedure that reflects changes as a function of intervention is a valid assessment instrument. Again, observation codes frequently have been

employed to assess attachment and caregiving behavior in the context of parent-child interactions (Table 3), but we found no recently
published article in which the issue of content or criterion-related
validity of the observation system employed for this purpose was
addressed. This was also the case for a number of studies employing observation procedures to assess the effects of intervention.
Consistent with the suggestion of Patterson (1977b), the content
validity of observation procedures apparently is assumed to be high
owing to the considerable face validity of the behaviors selected for
inclusion in observation codes. Thus, the adequacy of instruments
to measure elements of the particular construct often seems to be
determined by judgments of individual researchers rather than by
empirical procedures.

A notable exception to this trend, however, has been the
systematic development of the Behavior Coding System (Patterson
and others, 1975), recently reported on by Patterson (1977b) and
extensively reviewed by Reid (1977). As a coding system for
naturalistic observation of children's aggressive interactions within
the family setting, the Behavior Coding System (BCS) has been
subjected to systematic evaluation and modification over a period
of approximately nine years. The coding system itself uses a time-
sampling procedure to reflect behavioral interactions among family members and provides for analysis of the temporal sequence of
behaviors as they occur. Operationally defined behavior categories
are subsumed under six classifications; that is, targeted behaviors
are coded by type as either verbal or nonverbal and are further
coded as first order or second order—a priority procedure for
coding multiple behaviors. Patterson (1977b) provided references
to data indirectly supporting the content validity of the code
categories in the form of comparisons between parents' ratings of
the aversiveness of deviant behaviors defined in the scale and a
priori clinical judgments (see also Johnson and Bolstad, 1973;
Jones, Reid, and Patterson, 1975; Patterson and others, 1975).

Along with the issue of content validity, another area of
concern relative to assessment procedures in naturalistic family settings is that of criterion-related validity, that is, the degree to which
observation measures correlate with another measure of the construct at similar points in time (concurrent validity), the degree to

which an assessment instrument discriminates between subjects classified on the basis of another variable (discriminant validity), or the degree to which the instrument predicts (correlates with) performance on assessment instruments administered at some point in the future (predictive validity). Evidence for the concurrent validity of the BCS has been reported previously (Patterson, 1977b). Similarly, employing Patterson's code, Karoly and Rosenthal (1977) reported results supportive of concurrent validity in a parent behavior modification training program; parents' reports of decreased problem behaviors were corroborated by home observation data. Only one additional recent study reported on the concurrent validity of observation procedures. In that study, Skarin (1977) videotaped facial expressions of infants in the home setting as each was approached by a stranger. Tapes were subsequently scored in the three categories (previously employed by Waters, Matas, and Sroufe, 1975) of positive responses, neutral responses, and negative responses. Heart-rate data was concurrently collected and scored at half-second intervals and then averaged for each of the five-second segments of the approach sequence. Scores for each segment were calculated by subtracting the mean heart rate of the five-second baseline immediately preceding the approach sequence from the mean for each of the six five-second steps in the approach sequence. Results indicated parallel effects for both dependent measures. Although a large number of the studies reviewed in this section have employed observation codes of one sort or another, the only code for which discriminant validity was reported was the Behavior Coding System; see Patterson (1977b) for research supportive of the discriminant validity of the BCS.

The small number of studies reporting criterion-related validity is significant when one considers the large number of studies that have utilized naturalistic observation in family and home settings. Also of note is the fact that, with the exception of applications reported by Patterson (1977a, 1977b) and Peed, Roberts, and Forehand (1977), observation procedures in the natural environment are apparently not being utilized as preintervention procedures to identify target behaviors for intervention. Rather, naturalistic observation procedures in family settings currently seem to be used only for basic developmental research and as outcome measures for behavior intervention strategies. It should additionally be emphasized that in the recent literature, and particularly in the case of research applications in family settings, naturalistic observation procedures apparently are often utilized on the basis of their face validity without sufficient consideration of their content or criterion-related validity.

Another issue deserving comment involves the effectiveness of parent observers in home settings. Colletti and Harris (1977) reported adequate agreement coefficients between parents and outside observers, suggesting the utility of parents in monitoring target behaviors. Certainly, the use of participant observers (such as parents or siblings) could significantly reduce time and cost constraints for assessment in family settings. Participant observers in the family might also reduce the potential reactive effects created through observation by outside observers (see discussion later in this chapter). As noted in the preceding chapter, the efficacy of participant observers in the family setting deserves further investigation since the validity and sources of error of this assessment instrument have not been sufficiently investigated. Finally, in another design having implications for the reduction of reactive effects of observation in family and home settings, Arnold, Sturgis, and Forehand (1977) utilized tape recordings made by the mother of a fifteen-year-old retarded female as a data collection procedure. Results indicated the procedure to yield data similar to those obtained from live observers—a finding also reported earlier by Johnson and Bolstad (1975). The efficacy of participant observers in family settings would also appear to vary as a function of task demands. For instance, B. Martin (1977) noted increasing resistance on the part of mothers to monitoring behaviors during seven continuous days of baseline recording, a factor that could represent an increasing threat to the validity of measures obtained.

In summary, naturalistic observation has been extensively applied in family settings for developmental and child psychology research and as a means of assessing the effects of behavioral intervention, although only limited use has been made of naturalistic observation for preintervention assessment to identify target behaviors for subsequent treatment. While a majority of studies cited have reported that the observation procedures employed were sensitive to the effects of intervention, observation formats have varied considerably, and it is to be expected that sensitivity would vary as a function of the setting, the observation procedure selected, and the behavior to which it is applied. But parameters such as these, which can affect the sensitivity and thus the validity of naturalistic observation, have not been sufficiently investigated. Likewise, additional research is needed on the content validity and criterion-related validity of the instrument. Also deserving of further investigation is the utility of participant observers. While some evidence attests to their usefulness, the validity and sources of error of this assessment instrument have not been sufficiently evaluated. And it should be emphasized again that the validity of assessment procedures also will vary depending upon the intended function of the assessment and, accordingly, the behavior targeted for observation.

## Institutions

Inspection of Table 4 reveals applications of naturalistic observation as an assessment instrument in a wide variety of institutional settings: treatment and residential centers, hospital wards and infirmaries, and institutional dining rooms, classrooms, and bathrooms, as well as prisons, daycare centers, halfway houses, and summer camps.

Within these settings, the function of assessment and the range of behaviors selected for observation have also been extensive. Observation has been employed to assess ingestive behaviors—for example, the effects of family-style dining structures on adolescent eating behavior (Doke, Geaster, and Predmore, 1977), adherence to dietary programs by children in hemodialysis wards (Magrab and Papadopoulou, 1977), alcohol ingestion (Griffiths, Bigelow, and Liebson, 1977), and food consumption related to nutritional problems (Herbert-Jackson and Risley, 1977). In addition to ingestive behaviors, eliminative behaviors such as enuresis (Jehu and others, 1977) and misdirected urinations (Siegel, 1977) have been the focus of observation. Naturalistic observation has also been employed to assess the effects of treatment on stereotypic and other inappropriate behaviors of mentally retarded subjects, including aversive behaviors (Burleigh and Marholin, 1977),

**Table 4. Recent Applications of Naturalistic Observation in Institutions**

| Reference | Subjects | Setting | Behaviors Monitored |
|---|---|---|---|
| Alevizos and others (1978) | Psychiatric patients | Inpatient and day-treatment areas | Described development of a behavioral observation code containing categories for mutually exclusive behaviors, concomitant behaviors, and locations |
| Anderson and Standley (1977) | Pregnant women | Hospital labor room | Physical state; social interaction and medical intervention; verbal communication |
| Andrasik and McNamara (1977) | Staff members | Forensic psychiatry unit, department of corrections | Performance in awarding proper points in behavior management program |
| Barrett and Yarrow (1977) | Boys and girls | Summer day camp | Relationship of assertiveness and prosocial behavior; monitored assertions, aggressions, and prosocial behaviors |
| Bassett and Blanchard (1977) | Staff members | Prison | Effects upon token economy of removal or reinstatement of direct supervision |
| Becker, Turner, and Sajwaj (1978) | Mentally retarded children | Hospital | Inappropriate behaviors, including ruminations, mannerisms, and crying |

| | | | |
|---|---|---|---|
| Burleigh and Marholin (1977) | Mentally retarded adults | Mental retardation facility | Eye orientation, on-task behavior, and number of blocks correctly placed to assess side effects of verbal prompts in terminating aversive behaviors |
| Carr and others (1978) | Autistic children | Psychiatric hospital | Correct and incorrect use of sign language responses |
| Cuvo, Leaf, and Borakove (1978) | Mentally retarded adults | Men's bathroom | Janitorial skills training with respect to six behaviors: cleaning of mirrors, sinks, urinals, toilets, mopping floors, and replacing cleaning supplies |
| Doke, Geaster, and Predmore (1977) | Adolescent psychiatric patients | Dining room in psychiatric center | Adults in dining room, youths dining cafeteria-style and family-style, with respect to "eat-and-run" behavior |
| Drabman and others (1978) | Blind child (mentally retarded) | Treatment center | Accuracy of scoring of occurrence or nonoccurrence of sucking and chewing behaviors by mentally retarded peer observers |
| Eisler and others (1978) | Adult male psychiatric patients | Psychiatric ward | Verbal and nonverbal behaviors (eye contact, smiles, duration and latency of responses, and loudness of speech) to evaluate social skills training |

Table 4. Recent Applications of Naturalistic Observation in Institutions (Continued)

| Reference | Subjects | Setting | Behaviors Monitored |
|---|---|---|---|
| Fabry and Reid (1978) | Female foster grandparent (institutional employee) | Institution | Scored three categories of foster grandparent behavior and three categories of teacher behavior |
| Farb and Throne (1978) | Six-year-old female (Down's syndrome) | Institution | Evaluated training to improve mnemonic performance (digit-span task) through recording of the occurrence or nonoccurrence of correct responses |
| Frankosky and Sulzer-Azaroff (1978) | Mentally retarded adult males | Institution | Frequency of appropriate and inappropriate verbal and nonverbal behavior; responses on block-sorting task |
| Gladstone and Spencer (1977) | Mentally retarded children | Bathroom | Effects of praise statements for correct responses on hand and face washing and toothbrushing |
| Greene and others (1978) | Treatment staff | Institution for mentally retarded | Evaluated effects of staff training to implement toilet training through observation of client participation (being placed on toilet or bedpan) |

| Griffiths, Bigelow, and Liebson (1977) | Adult alcoholics | Treatment ward | Drinking assessed through monitoring by ward personnel |
| Hanson and Deysach (1977) | Emotionally handicapped children | Therapeutic camp infirmary | Frequencies of infirmary visits, presenting symptoms, and tokens allotted |
| Herbert-Jackson and Risley (1977) | Three-year-old children | Daycare center | Behavioral measures of food consumption, including group-weighing procedures and observation of food tasting |
| Jehu and others (1977) | Enuretic children | Residential homes | Staff-monitored enuretic episodes |
| Jenkins and others (1977) | Elderly adults | Old persons' home | Use or nonuse of recreational materials; mobility, interactions, and activities |
| Johnson and Bailey (1977) | Female adolescents (mentally retarded) | Halfway house | Location, position, verbal conversations, and engagements in any specified activities observed to assess leisure behaviors |
| Koegel, Clahn, and Nieminen (1978) | Mothers and autistic children | Experimental classroom | Monitored five categories of parent behavior (providing discriminable cues, prompts, consequences, proper shaping, and assuring discrete trials) |

**Table 4. Recent Applications of Naturalistic Observation in Institutions (Continued)**

| Reference | Subjects | Setting | Behaviors Monitored |
|---|---|---|---|
| Koegel and Rincover (1977) | Autistic children | Institutional outdoor area | Extratherapy responding by monitoring previously trained responses to task demands from unfamiliar adults |
| Lawson, Daum, and Turkewitz (1977) | Premature infants | Hospital "grower" and intensive care units | Light levels, frequencies of handling, and occurrences of sound stimulation |
| Magrab and Papadopoulou (1977) | Male and female adolescents | Hospital hemodialysis unit | Weight, blood-urine-nitrogen, and potassium as measures of adherence to dietary program |
| Marholin and Townsend (1978) | Autistic child | Mentally retarded residential center | Frequencies of stereotypic hand movements |
| Matson and Stephens (1977) | Adult female schizophrenic | Dayroom of hospital ward | Frequencies of throwing objects at others' faces; to determine effects of an over-correction procedure |
| Matson and Stephens (1978) | Psychotic females | Psychiatric institution | Behavioral excesses and deficits in social skills |
| Milby and others (1977) | Adult inpatients | Ward | Whining, complaining, inappropriate demands or requests, and verbally aggressive behavior |

| Reference | Subjects | Setting | Behaviors |
|---|---|---|---|
| Montegar and others (1977) | Supervisors and attendants | Institution | Observation system for attendant and supervisor behaviors |
| Nunes, Murphy, and Ruprecht (1977) | Mentally retarded children | Mentally retarded facility gym and classroom; home | Occurrences of self-injurious behavior |
| Nutter and Reid (1978) | Female adult (mentally retarded) | Developmental disabilities center | Assessed appropriate selection of clothing with respect to pattern and color combinations |
| Peacock, Lyman, and Rickard (1978) | Disturbed male children | Therapeutic camp | Cabin-cleaning behaviors |
| Peterson and others (1977) | Geriatric patients | Institution | Institutional geriatric behaviors (nonsocial, non-active) including sitting, standing, locomotion, and lying down |
| Reid and Hurlbut (1977) | Mentally retarded adults | State retardation center | Correct or incorrect pointing behaviors |
| Rogers-Warren, Warren, and Baer (1977) | Four-year-old children | Daycare center playroom | Recorded verbal offers to share, verbal acceptances, refusals of offers, reports of sharing, actual sharing |
| Rollings, Baumeister, and Baumeister (1977) | Mentally retarded subjects | Mental retardation center ward | Assessed generalization of training in overcorrection for headweaving and rocking through use of proximity test (inhibition effects) |

**Table 4. Recent Applications of Naturalistic Observation in Institutions (Continued)**

| Reference | Subjects | Setting | Behaviors Monitored |
|---|---|---|---|
| Siegel (1977) | Mentally retarded children | Ward bathroom | Assessed misdirected urinations using code for target locations, frequencies, and duration |
| Strain and Ezzell (1978) | Behaviorally disordered adolescents | Residential psychiatric center | Frequencies of disruptive and aggressive behavior; eleven-category observation code |
| Wood and others (1977) | | | Reports a logbook for recording low-frequency unusual behaviors and aggressive behaviors, as well as ward operation information |
| Wood and Flynn (1978) | Predelinquent youths | Residential center | Monitored fifteen categories of cleaning behaviors |

ruminative behaviors (Becker, Turner, and Sajwaj, 1978), head weaving (Rollings, Baumeister, and Baumeister, 1977), sucking (Drabman and others, 1978), and hand moving (Marholin and Townsend, 1978). Physical aggression (Matson and Stephens, 1977), verbal aggression (Milby and others, 1977), self-injurious behaviors (Nunes, Murphy, and Ruprecht, 1977), disruptive behaviors (Strain and Ezzell, 1978), and inappropriate infirmary visits by children in therapeutic camps (Hanson and Deysach, 1977) have also been the subject of naturalistic observation. Additionally, observation has been employed to assess the effectiveness of training of parents of autistic children (Koegel, Clahn, and Nieminen, 1978).

Also targeted for observation have been social and communicative skills, including children's sharing behaviors (Rogers-Warren, Warren, and Baer, 1977), pointing behaviors of mentally retarded adults (Reid and Hurlbut, 1977), mnemonic performance on digit-span tasks by Down's syndrome children (Farb and Throne, 1978), assertive and prosocial behaviors (Barrett and Yarrow, 1977), youth-preferred social behaviors of child care personnel (Willner and others, 1977), and autistic children's responses to task demands (Koegel and Rincover, 1977) and their utilization of sign language responses (Carr and others, 1978). Applications of naturalistic observation have also included assessments of social skills training with male psychiatric patients (Eisler and others, 1978) and female psychiatric patients (Matson and Stephens, 1978), as well as the evaluation of leisure activities of mentally retarded women in halfway houses (Johnson and Bailey, 1977) and of elderly individuals in retirement homes (Jenkins and others, 1977). Additional targets of observation have been mentally retarded females' clothing selections (Nutter and Reid, 1978) and the cleaning behaviors of disturbed adolescents (Wood and Flynn, 1978; Peacock, Lyman, and Rickard, 1978). Staff compliance to treatment programs in prisons (Andrasik and McNamara, 1977; Bassett and Blanchard, 1977) and institutions (Fabry and Reid, 1978; Greene and others, 1978; Wood and others, 1977) has also been the subject of naturalistic observation, as have the effects of training on the janitorial skills of young mentally retarded adults (Cuvo, Leaf, and Borakove, 1978). And, finally, the influence of hospital environments on premature infants (Lawson, Daum, and Turkewitz, 1977) and of the physical characteristics of geriatric wards on elderly persons (Peterson and others, 1977), has also been assessed.

Two innovative applications of naturalistic observation in institutional settings should be noted. To assess diet-related (nutrition) problems with three-year-old children, Herbert-Jackson and Risley (1977) combined observations of food consumption and tasting by children with nutrient analysis of foods served in daycare centers to determine whether children would accept nonfat dry milk and textured vegetable protein, as well as other sources of protein. Mealtime observers independently recorded each child's tasting of foods and tallied each additional serving given each child. Comparisons were then made of amounts of food eaten in normal situations to identify foods eaten in sufficient quantity to produce adequate nutrient intake, while producing desired dietary changes. By means of group food-weighing procedures (Twardosz, Cataldo, and Risley, 1975), the total amount of prepared food was weighed on a gram scale before serving; following that, individual portions were weighed and placed in children's dishes. At the end of each meal, the amount not served was weighed, along with remains from plates, bibs, tables, and the floor. All these amounts were subtracted from the total weight of food prepared. The mean grams consumed by each child (a product-of-behavior measure) were then calculated by dividing the total weight consumed by the number of children served. Food tables were used to estimate amounts of nutrient, protein, and calcium supplied in 100 grams of each ingredient; calculations were then made of the amount of nutrient supplied in standard (100-gram) portions of each dish. Both the behavioral and nutritional measures used were reported by the authors to be sensitive in assessing eating behavior.

An innovative methodology for environmental assessment was reported by Lawson, Daum, and Turkewitz (1977) in two studies involving investigation of environmental stimulation levels in neonatal intensive care units (ICUs). In the first study, observations were confined to "grower" rooms (premature infant wards for infants not requiring intensive care); observers measured light levels with Gossen Lunasix light meters and additionally observed the frequencies with which children were handled by the ward staff. Observations were also made of sounds occurring in the environment (separate recordings of speech and nonspeech sounds were classified according to their occurrence inside or outside the nursing room). Sounds were also tape-recorded by means of microphones in each infant's isolette, with the recording levels adjusted to observers' auditory sensitivity for subsequent comparison with observers' recordings just described. In the second study, comparable information was obtained from ICU units, with the additional dependent measure of sound pressure level (generated with Bruel and Kjaer Precision Sound Level Meters) being obtained in both "grower" rooms and ICUs. Data reported by the authors suggested that these measures were sensitive to gross differences between the two settings. However, since specifics as to the criterion-related and discriminant validity of the measures obtained were not reported, only assumptions about gross differences can be made. Nevertheless, this assessment procedure suggests an interesting methodology for environmental assessment of stimulation levels in neonatal hospital environments.

With respect to institutional settings, a number of authors have reported observation procedures to be sensitive indicators of behavior change (Becker, Turner, and Sajwaj, 1978; Burleigh and Marholin, 1977; Carr and others, 1978; Drabman and others, 1978; Eisler and others, 1978; Fabry and Reid, 1978; Farb and Throne, 1978; Frankosky and Sulzer-Azaroff, 1978; Greene and others, 1978; Herbert-Jackson and Risley, 1977; Jenkins and others, 1977; Koegel and Rincover, 1977; Magrab and Papadopoulou, 1977; Marholin and Townsend, 1978; Matson and Stephens, 1978; Nutter and Reid, 1978; Peacock, Lyman, and Rickard, 1978; Reid and Hurlbut, 1977; Strain and Ezzell, 1978; Wood and Flynn, 1978). Peterson and others (1977), however, reported a behavior coding system employed with geriatric patients to be insensitive to intervention effects. This evidence serves once more to highlight the fact that, owing to the uniqueness of settings, purposes, and behaviors targeted, general assumptions about the sensitivity, reliability, and validity of instruments employed must be made with caution.

As mentioned previously, one method of assessing the validity of observation procedures is through comparison of the outcome of such procedures with independent measures. A procedure employed by Andrasik and McNamara (1977) is of interest in assessing the concurrent validity of observation measures in an institutional setting. In a department of corrections forensic psychiatry unit, the performance of thirty-three staff members in awarding proper point values in an employment rehabilitation program for residents was assessed. Dependent measures involved the percentage of resident point cards (stamped by staff in nine center employment areas) containing one or more errors per week; errors involved the staff's awarding of points for times not appearing on the resident's contract or marking for periods during which the resident did not work. Validity checks of these measures were made by comparing permissible stamping times (according to each resident's contract) to the times actually stamped on the card.

Willner and others (1977) described a validation procedure for the development and assessment of youth-preferred social behaviors by child care personnel. In a residential treatment setting, youths' preferences for a set of social interaction behaviors were assessed by having subjects first watch a series of twenty-six short interactions between teaching parents and youths and then write down specific parent behaviors they liked and disliked in each. Four observers then independently sorted these into categories; a category was established if three fourths of the observers placed youth comments into a category. The resultant twenty-nine categories were then rated by youths on a five-point scale to validate their importance. Next, staff members (trainees) were trained to use the preferred behaviors, and videotapes of pretraining and posttraining behavioral interactions with youth were analyzed for the presence of youth-preferred behaviors. In an analysis of youth preferences for the teaching parent behaviors depicted in seventy videotaped interaction segments, youth ratings on the five-point scale and trainee social interaction behaviors were employed to develop a scoring code (a complete set of response definitions is available from Willner). These definitions were then applied to the analysis of videotape segments for the presence or absence of each of the twenty-nine categories (thirteen liked; sixteen disliked). Additionally, the extent to which youth ratings of trainer behavior correlated with occurrences of youth-preferred trainee behavior was assessed by means of a Pearson correlation coefficient. The "social validity" of these measures was supported by corresponding changes in youth ratings and by comparison with normative behaviors.

Also of note is the recent development of an observational instrument for evaluating treatment programs in various settings. Alevizos and others (1978) reported on the background and development of the Behavior Observation Instrument (BOI), a multicategory, direct observation system. The scale itself contains two basic behavioral categories: (1) mutually exclusive behaviors (motor behaviors that, by definition, cannot occur concurrently), and (2) concomitant behaviors that occur in conjunction with mutually exclusive behaviors and include all other social or individual activities. Observers also record the location or setting in which the targeted behaviors are emitted. The primary function of the code, according to the authors, is to provide a behavioral index of the effects of treatment programs on individuals or groups of clients.

With reference to the development of the scale, several methodological procedures are of interest. Coding procedures were first evaluated by using a sequential observation format with patients in a daytreatment program and also with patients in a state hospital. Subjects who could not be located during observation sessions were scored as absent, with a later attempt at verification. Training of observers (members of a neighborhood youth corps) involved instructions and rehearsal in a classroom and in a variety of community environments. Interestingly, once in the treatment settings, an interobserver agreement criterion of 85 percent was reportedly reached within the first hour of practice. Observer agreement calculations (ratio of mutually agreed upon occurrences) yielded effective agreement coefficients ranging from 84.6 percent to 100 percent in the daytreatment center and coefficients ranging from 84 percent to 97 percent in the state hospital, with mean agreement coefficients of 94.9 percent and 93 percent, respectively. Kappa coefficients obtained for the state hospital data ranged between .72 and .87 across two weeks of observations. With respect to generalizability of data samples (representativeness of BOI observations), the authors alternated five observers, two at a time, to record and to tabulate data. Additionally, observation intervals of five, fifteen, and thirty seconds were initially employed to determine the most efficient (brief) observation interval that could be employed without sacrificing the representativeness of the data obtained. Findings indicated that, across days, five-second intervals were efficient. One observation per hour was adopted as a standard for evaluating program change; this was determined empirically. The question of reactivity of the scale was also addressed by the authors, although evidence thus far is inconclusive.

Finally, the utility of the BOI was examined in two studies (Alevizos and others, 1978). In the first, two inpatient treatment programs were compared to test the BOI's discriminative properties. In the second, the sensitivity of the BOI in detecting changes in a daytreatment program was examined. Results reported by the authors indicated that the BOI discriminated between inpatient programs (Study I) and was sensitive to changes in daytreatment programs (Study II), although, since the scale employs a time-sampling procedure, the BOI was reported relatively insensitive to low base-rate behaviors. While evidence for the validity of this instrument is limited, the investigations thus far reported suggest that the BOI has potential utility in providing program effectiveness data from direct observation and that the scale has generalizability.

To summarize, in recently published articles naturalistic observation has been applied in a wide range of institutional settings, with a variety of target behaviors and observation systems. The primary applications of these observation procedures in institutions have been as outcome measures of treatment manipulations and for the analysis of problem behaviors. There is little evidence in recent articles to suggest that observation instruments are being employed in the selection of target behaviors for intervention. Thus, in many cases where observation procedures are used in the context of intervention, the programs have been designed independently of the outcome of preintervention assessment. While a number of investigations have suggested that observation procedures are sensitive to treatment effects in institutional settings, the failure in other cases to demonstrate the sensitivity of an observation instrument once again highlights the fact that, because of the variations in institutional settings and behaviors targeted for assessment, general assumptions as to the sensitivity, reliability, and validity of instruments employed must be approached with caution. Since few of the applications of naturalistic observation in institutional settings have evaluated the criterion-related or content validity of the respective instruments employed, further research with respect to these issues would be desirable.

## Schools

Naturalistic observation procedures in school settings have been applied with a variety of behaviors in recent articles, as illustrated in Table 5. These applications have included assessments of social behaviors and play activities, language and speech behaviors, school-related activities (such as academic productivity, attention, and attendance), and children's problem behaviors. Also included in these applications have been assessments of targeted teacher behaviors.

Typically, the assessment of social behaviors of children in school and preschool classes has included the use of external observers and behavioral codes. For example, codes have been employed to assess caretaker-child interactions (Inoff and Galverson, 1977) and referential communications (Wellman and Lempers, 1977), as well as interactional behaviors of socially withdrawn children (Gottman, 1977a, 1977b; Oden and Asher, 1977; Strain, 1977). Naturalistic observation has also been used to assess the relationship between classroom structure and social behavior with disadvantaged children (Huston-Stein, Friedrick-Coffer, and Susman, 1977), interactions among preschool children (Leiter, 1977; Melahan and O'Donnell, 1978), children's sharing behaviors (Barton and Osborne, 1978), and the effect of training generalized improvisation of tools on preschool children (Parsonson and Baer, 1978). These behavioral observations have primarily served a basic child research function, although the function of observation in one case (Oden and Asher, 1977) was to assess treatment outcome.

Several authors have employed observation of preschool-children's play activities to assess cross-sex cooperative play (Serbin, Tonick, and Sternglanz, 1977) and sex-typed behaviors (Fagot, 1977a), to validate rating scales of strength of sex typing (Connor and Serbin, 1977), and to assess the effects of classroom population

**Table 5. Recent Applications of Naturalistic Observation in School Settings**

| Reference | Subjects | Setting | Behaviors Monitored |
|---|---|---|---|
| Abikoff, Gittelman-Klein, and Klein (1977) | Hyperactive children | Classroom | Fourteen-category observational code for classroom behaviors |
| Azrin, Azrin, and Armstrong (1977) | Children | Experimental classroom | Monitored obeying versus not obeying classroom rules |
| Baer, Ascione, and Casto (1977) | Mentally retarded children | Experimental room in school | Disruptive behaviors including feet on chair and speaking out of turn |
| Barber and Kagey (1977) | Elementary students | Elementary school classroom | Employed classroom attendance charts to assess attendance treatment program; provided attendance formula |
| Barton and Osborne (1978) | Deaf kindergarten children | Elementary school classroom | Frequencies of sharing behaviors (both physical and verbal) |
| Bolstad and Johnston (1977) | Teachers and children | Classroom | Employed coding system to compare retrospective teacher ratings with data from immediate observations |
| Bornstein, Hamilton, and Quevillon (1977) | Children | Classroom | Assessed out-of-seat behaviors |

| Study | Subjects | Setting | Description |
|---|---|---|---|
| Broden, Beasley, and Hall (1978) | Teachers and children | Classroom spelling period | Monitored teachers' verbalizations to children, teacher proximity, attending behaviors, and spelling accuracy |
| Broden and others (1977) | Teachers and children | Classroom | Monitored number and type of teacher questions, students called upon, and student responses to assess effects on student verbal behavior |
| Campbell, Endman, and Bernfeld (1977) | Teachers and children | Regular classroom | Three categories of teacher behavior (feedback) and six categories of child behavior (disrupting and distracting) |
| Connor and Serbin (1977) | Preschool children | Classroom | Male and female activity rates (four categories) to validate rating scales for strength of sex typing |
| Deitz and others (1978) | Male student (learning disabled) | Special classroom | Monitored inappropriate behaviors, including pushing, jumping, and hitting |
| Epstein and Goss (1978) | Disruptive male child | Classroom | Monitored talking out, out-of-seat behaviors, and on-task behaviors |
| Fagot (1977a) | Preschool children | Preschool class | Employed Fagot-Patterson code with four additional behaviors to assess peer and teacher reactions to sex-typed behaviors |

Table 5. Recent Applications of Naturalistic Observation in School Settings (Continued)

| Reference | Subjects | Setting | Behaviors Monitored |
|---|---|---|---|
| Fagot (1977b) | Preschool children | Preschool class | Coded four types of (1) child behavior, (2) social consequences, and (3) consequences of teacher behavior to assess effects of population density in preschools |
| Fagot (1978) | Teachers | Classroom | Frequencies of teacher-initiated activities among experienced and inexperienced teachers |
| Foxx and Shapiro (1978) | Mentally retarded male children | Cottage classroom | Effect of time-out procedure in reducing frequencies of disruptive behaviors |
| Garcia, Bullet, and Rust (1977) | Mentally retarded children | Tutoring booth in school | Monitored number of five-word sentences to assess generalization of speech therapy across home and school |
| Ginsburg, Pollman, and Wauson (1977) | Children | Playground | Videotape assessment of aggressive behavior and effects on height of recipient; measured in |

| Study | Subjects | Setting | Description |
|---|---|---|---|
| | | | inches from ground to top of head during fight sequence |
| Gottman (1977a) | Socially withdrawn (Head Start) children | Classroom | Observational category system for interactional behaviors |
| Gottman (1977b) | Children (Head Start) | Classroom | Employed two coding systems: (1) frequency of peer interactions (six categories) and (2) anecdotal observations (six categories of hovering behavior) |
| Greenwood, Hops, and Walker (1977) | Schoolchildren | Classroom | Classroom observational system |
| Hay, Hay, and Nelson (1977a) | Schoolchildren | Classroom | Effects of contingencies for on-task behavior on rate and accuracy; employed product-of-behavior measure |
| Hay, Nelson, and Hay (1977) | Teachers and children | Classroom | Monitored student behavior (appropriate/passive/disruptive) and teacher behavior (praises/prompts/criticizes) |

**Table 5. Recent Applications of Naturalistic Observation in School Settings (Continued)**

| Reference | Subjects | Setting | Behaviors Monitored |
|---|---|---|---|
| Humphrey, Karoly, and Kirschenbaum (1978) | Elementary school children | Classroom reading periods | Effects of response cost on rate of appropriate behavior (papers attempted and accuracy of responses) |
| Inoff and Galverson (1977) | Nursery school children | Nursery school | Monitored caretaker-child interactions (six types) and child behaviors (twenty-five) |
| Jones, Fremouw, and Carples (1977) | Children | Ghetto schools | Recorded talking to neighbors in class and out-of-seat behavior, along with classroom productivity, to assess disruptive student behavior |
| Kauffman, Hallahan, and Ianna (1977) | Mentally retarded children | Classroom | Continuous recording of rates of tongue protrusions |
| Kazdin (1977c) | Mentally retarded children | Classroom | Influences of preceding behaviors (attentive or inattentive) on increases in attention resulting from reinforcement |

| Reference | Population | Setting | Description |
|---|---|---|---|
| Kazdin (1977d) | Mentally retarded children | Classroom | Monitored teacher approval and child behaviors (attention or nonattention) |
| Kazdin and Geesey (1977) | Children | Classroom | Describes an observation system for child and teacher behaviors |
| Kelly and Drabman (1977b) | | | Illustration of observation procedures |
| Kent and O'Leary (1977) | Children manifesting conduct problems | Classroom | Monitored conduct-problem behaviors |
| Kent and others (1977a) | Children | Classroom | Reliability assessments employing nine categories of disruptive behavior |
| Koegel, Clahn, and Nieminen (1978) | Teachers of autistic children | Classroom | Teachers' use of behavior modification techniques; teachers scored on aspects of instructions, prompts, shaping, and consequences |
| Lahey and others (1977a) | Children | School and treatment center | Monitored letter legibility and left-right orientation to assess effect of reinforcement and corrective feedback on perceptual and motor handwriting differences |

Table 5. Recent Applications of Naturalistic Observation in School Settings (Continued)

| Reference | Subjects | Setting | Behaviors Monitored |
|---|---|---|---|
| Lahey and others (1977b) | Kindergarten children | Kindergarten class | Assessed effects of daily report cards through monitoring of resting, sleep, and distracting behavior |
| Leiter (1977) | Preschool children | Preschool class play period | Describes observational code for dyadic social imitations and responses; "Social Interaction Profile" |
| Litow (1977) | Children | Classroom | Provides a glossary of operationally defined classroom behaviors for pupils and teachers |
| Loos, Williams, and Bailey (1977) | Children | Classroom | Monitored changes in elementary classroom productivity through recordings of academic performance and off-task behaviors |
| McCullough, Huntsinger, and Nay (1977) | Adolescent | Home and school | Monitored verbally violent outbursts employing teachers and parents as observers |

| | | | |
|---|---|---|---|
| Marholin and Steinman (1977) | Male and female children manifesting conduct problems | Classroom | Monitored on-task and disruptive behaviors to assess the effects of teacher presence or absence; also recorded rates and accuracy of academic performance |
| Marlowe and others (1978) | Seventh-grade males | Classroom | Monitored effect of teacher behavior (academic approval or disapproval, social approval or disapproval, inappropriate responses, and no response) on off- and on-task behaviors |
| Melahan and O'Donnell (1978) | Children (Head Start) | School | Monitored child interactions: proximity, orientation, alone or with others, consequences and prompts, and verbal behavior |
| Meyers, Nathan, and Kopel (1977) | Library personnel | University library | Recorded the number of books and journals reshelved in library by staff |
| Moore and Stern (1978) | Teachers, aides, and undergraduates | School workshop program | Rates of verbalization |
| Murdock, Garcia, and Hardman (1977) | Mentally retarded children | Classroom | Scored correct work articulations from tape recordings to assess generalization of articulation training |

**Table 5. Recent Applications of Naturalistic Observation in School Settings (Continued)**

| Reference | Subjects | Setting | Behaviors Monitored |
|---|---|---|---|
| Neville and Shemberg (1978) | Children (Head Start) | Classroom | Frequencies of occurrence of adjectives and color nouns in conversation |
| Oden and Asher (1977) | Children (social isolates) | Classroom | Task participation and social orientation |
| Parsonson and Baer (1978) | Preschool children | Classroom | Improvisational use of objects as tools (hammer, container, and shoelaces) as a function of generalization training; scored pick-ups, attempts; improvisations |
| Plummer, Baer, and Leblanc (1977) | Preschool autistic female (mentally retarded) | Classroom in child development lab and mentally retarded class | Provides behavior codes for child and teacher behaviors |
| Polirstok and Greer (1977) | Teachers | Classroom | Assessed reciprocal teacher and child approval or disapproval responses |
| Rekers and others (1977) and Rekers, Amaro-Plotkin, and | Gender-disturbed boys | School and home | Recorded feminine behaviors |

| | | | |
|---|---|---|---|
| Low (1977) | | | |
| Rincover and Koegel (1977) | Autistic children | Experimental class | Monitored amount of unsupervised responding and academic progress |
| Rose (1978) | Hyperactive female child | Classroom | Out-of-seat, on-task, and aggressive behaviors |
| Russo and Koegel (1977) | Five-year-old autistic female | Kindergarten class | Described three-category coding system |
| Saudargas, Madsen, and Scott (1977) | Teachers and children | Classroom | Quantity of academic work completed, teacher behaviors (appropriate positive and negative responses and mistaken responses) |
| Schulman, Stevens, and Kupst (1977) | Hyperactive children | Classroom | Measured activity levels with biomotometer |
| Schulman and others (1978) | Hyperactive children | Classroom | Measured activity levels with biomotometer |
| Serbin, Tonick, and Sternglanz (1977) | Preschool children | Classroom | Employed an observational code with five categories for play behavior |
| Shafto and Sulzbacher (1977) | Hyperactive children (mentally retarded males) | School | Tracked frequency of activity changes under methylphenidate (Ritalin) treatment |

**Table 5. Recent Applications of Naturalistic Observation in School Settings (Continued)**

| Reference | Subjects | Setting | Behaviors Monitored |
|---|---|---|---|
| Sluckin and Smith (1977) | Preschool children | Preschool play group | Scanned groups for aggression, including initiator, those involved, incident, and outcome |
| Strain (1977) | Isolate preschool children | Experimental class | Employed coding system (Strain, Shores, and Kerr, 1976) to assess dyadic interactions; two behavioral classes, two classes of teacher behavior, and temporal sequence |
| Switzer, Deal, and Bailey (1977) | Children | Classroom | Provided a technique to assess and control theft in classrooms by introducing standard number of items to classroom and then counting missing items |
| Thomas and others (1978) | Children and teachers | Classroom | Monitored teacher approval rates on six categories of on-task behavior and three categories of off-task behavior of children |

| Trap and others (1978) | Children | Classroom | Assessed cursive letter formations using seven criteria of letter scoring with use of plastic scoring overlays |
|---|---|---|---|
| Van Houten and Van Houten (1977) | Children | Classroom | Number of words correctly or incorrectly read, number of lessons completed, and number of teacher praises and child comments |
| Wahler, House, and Stambaugh (1976) | Children | Home and school | Behavior code for home and school that allows record of interactions between target and peers or parents; five general behavior classes and six stimulus categories |
| Wellman and Lempers (1977) | Preschool children | Classroom | Employed an observation code for referential communications |
| Wing, Gould, and Yeates (1977) | Autistic and mentally retarded children | Home and school | Recorded three categories of symbolic play activities |

density on social behaviors. Similarly, Rekers and others (1977) and Rekers, Amaro-Plotkin, and Low (1977) employed observation in schools to record feminine behaviors of gender-disturbed boys. As with social behaviors, the typical format for these observations has included coding procedures implemented by external observers, although in the case of gender disturbance (Rekers and others, 1977) participant observers were utilized. Included among the functions of assessments just mentioned have been basic child research (Fagot, 1977a) and measurements of intervention outcomes (Fagot, 1977b; Rekers and others, 1977; Serbin, Tonick, and Sternglanz, 1977). Naturalistic observation has also been employed as a means of assessing the generalization of speech therapy training with mentally retarded subjects across classroom and home settings (Garcia, Bullet, and Rust, 1977) and to assess the spontaneous speech of disadvantaged children (Neville and Shemberg, 1978).

In the area of academic productivity, several investigators have employed measures of work completed (products of behavior) as a means of assessing the outcomes of treatment programs (Hay, Hay, and Nelson, 1977a; Humphrey, Karoly, and Kirschenbaum, 1978; Lahey and others, 1977b; Loos, Williams, and Bailey, 1977; Saudargas, Madsen, and Scott, 1977; Trap and others, 1978; Van Houten and Van Houten, 1977). These product-of-behavior measures would appear to have particular utility in the classroom since data such as written work are usually already available for assessment, as Lahey and others (1977b) have noted. In addition to product-of-behavior measures as a data source for assessing the effects of treatment, external observers have also been employed (Broden and others, 1978) for this purpose. Other investigators have employed both participant and external observers (Loos, Williams, and Bailey, 1977; Saudargas, Madsen, and Scott, 1977; Van Houten and Van Houten, 1977), reporting acceptable levels of agreement between these two data sources.

In classroom settings, a variety of problem behaviors have been targeted for assessment. For example, McGullough, Huntsinger, and Nay (1977) assessed verbally violent outbursts by a male adolescent. Out-of-seat behaviors (Bornstein, Hamilton, and Quevillon, 1977) and aggressive behaviors (Ginsburg, Pollman, and Wauson,

1977; Sluckin and Smith, 1977) have also been the subject of observation. In the evaluation of teachers as behavioral observers, Hay, Nelson, and Hay (1977) included observations of children's disruptive behaviors. Disruptive behaviors have also been the target of observation studies by a number of other investigators (Baer, Ascione, and Casto, 1977; Campbell, Endman, and Bernfeld, 1977; Deitz and others, 1978; Epstein and Goss, 1978; Foxx and Shapiro, 1978; Humphrey, Karoly, and Kirschenbaum, 1978; Jones, Fremouw, and Carples, 1977; Kent and others, 1977a; Kent and O'Leary, 1977; Lahey and others, 1977b; Marholin and Steinman, 1977; Marlowe and others, 1978; Plummer, Baer, and Leblanc, 1977; Rose, 1978). Noncompliant behaviors (Azrin, Azrin, and Armstrong, 1977; Wahler, House, and Stambaugh, 1976) and stealing (Switzer, Deal, and Bailey, 1977) have also been subjected to observation, as have autistic responses (Rincover and Koegel, 1977; Russo and Koegel, 1977; Wing, Gould, and Yeates, 1977). Several investigators have utilized observation procedures to assess children's hyperactive behaviors (Abikoff, Gittelman-Klein, and Klein, 1977; Schulman, Stevens, and Kupst, 1977; Schulman and others, 1978; Shafto and Sulzbacher, 1977). Kauffman, Hallahan, and Ianna (1977) assessed frequencies of tongue protrusions among retardates in a treatment program for reduction of that behavior.

While a majority of these assessments of problem behavior have served the function of evaluating treatment programs, some have been directed to the functional analysis of such behavior (Schulman, Stevens, and Kupst, 1977; Schulman and others, 1978; Wahler, House, and Stambaugh, 1976; Wing, Gould, and Yeates, 1977), and others have served a basic research function (Bornstein and others, 1977b; Ginsburg, Pollman, and Wauson, 1977; Hay, Hay, and Nelson, 1977a; Kent and others, 1977a; Rincover and Koegel, 1977; Rose, 1978; Sluckin and Smith, 1977). As with assessments of academic behaviors, several of these investigators have employed participant observers, primarily teachers (Bornstein, Hamilton, and Quevillon, 1977; Hay, Nelson, and Hay, 1977; Jones, Fremouw, and Carples, 1977; Kent and O'Leary, 1977; McGullough, Huntsinger, and Nay, 1977; Rincover and Koegel, 1977; Switzer, Deal, and Bailey, 1977), and several have reported acceptable agreement levels between participant observers (such as teachers and teacher aides) and external observers. For example, Rincover and Koegel (1977) reported agreement coefficients ranging from .96 to .99 between a teacher and external observers when monitoring task-oriented responses of autistic children. Likewise, adequate agreement between teachers and observers serving as teacher aides was reported by Switzer, Deal, and Bailey (1977) for recordings of theft in the classroom.

Observation procedures in classroom settings have also involved assessments of teacher behaviors. For example, teachers' verbal responses have been monitored to assess their input in altering the verbal responses of students (Broden and others, 1977), as have teachers' "approval" and "disapproval" statements as they influence aversive interactions with children (Polirstok and Greer, 1977) and children's behavior patterns (Thomas and others, 1978). Also, the initiations of activities by teachers have been assessed (Fagot, 1978), as have the effects of social attention on rates of teacher verbalizations (Moore and Stern, 1978). Kazdin (1977d) monitored both teacher and child behaviors to assess the vicarious effects of reinforcement to a target child upon unreinforced peers in a mental retardation class. And, in a unique design, Koegel, Clahn, and Nieminen (1978) assessed teacher's usage of behavior modification techniques with autistic children. These latter assessments have typically involved data collection by external observers and have been reported by several investigators (Kazdin, 1977d; Koegel, Russo, and Rincover, 1977; Switzer, Deal, and Bailey, 1977) to be sensitive to treatment effects.

In the application of naturalistic observation procedures in school settings, several recent publications are of note. Wahler, House, and Stambaugh (1976) reported on a general behavior code for children that may have utility for the school and home. This code encompasses nineteen response categories with five general classes of behavior (compliance or opposition, autistic, play, work, and social) and six stimulus categories that include both aversive and nonaversive occurrences of adult attention, adult instructions, and child attention. The scale may be used to record child-parent or child-peer interactions, and the authors have reported high interobserver agreement scores (80 percent). However, little information as to the validity correlates of the new coding system is yet available (Ciminero and Drabman, 1977). In an interesting application for the assessment of stealing behavior in the classroom, Switzer, Deal, and Bailey (1977) placed a uniform number of items (erasers, chewing gum, and pencils) commonly reported missing by teachers at specific locations in the classroom. Data collection (number of items present, absent, and returned) in fifteen-minute intervals by participant observers allowed assessment of stealing behaviors under two intervention strategies. Additionally, the authors assessed possible undesirable peer pressure to return items, activating a tape recorder during times when teachers were absent. Of note in this methodology is the attention paid to ethical principles. First, rather than introducing items that might have heightened the motivation to steal, the authors simply "controlled" items already common to the classroom. Second, peer reactions in the classroom were monitored to control for undue negative responses.

Koegel, Russo, and Rincover (1977) investigated teachers' use of behavior modification procedures with autistic children. These teacher assessments by external observers involved a code to record teachers' use of five aspects of behavior modification procedures, including instructions, prompts, shaping, consequences, and discrete trials. Among the response measures taken for children's performance were the categories of correct, incorrect, prompted, and approximations to the target behavior. Because there have been very few attempts to assess the adeptness of individuals in applying behavior modification techniques with autistic children, this assessment procedure addresses a particularly important topic.

Investigators have reported observation procedures in school settings to be sensitive to intervention-effected changes in such monitored behaviors as social responsiveness (Gottman, 1977a; Melahan and O'Donnell, 1978; Oden and Asher, 1977), sharing (Barton and Osborne, 1978), academic productivity (Hay, Hay, and Nelson, 1977a; Saudergas, Madsen, and Scott, 1977; Trap and others, 1978), attention in class (Kazdin, 1977c), various classroom problem behaviors (Bornstein, Hamilton, and Quevillon, 1977; Deitz and others, 1978; Epstein and Goss, 1978; Foxx and Shapiro, 1978; Humphrey and others, 1978; Kent and others, 1977a; Kent and O'Leary, 1977; Marholin and Steinman, 1977;

Marlowe and others, 1978; Rose, 1978; Russo and Koegel, 1977), and teacher behaviors (Van Houten and Van Houten 1977). A procedure for monitoring children's school attendance employed by Barber and Kagey (1977), however, had only limited sensitivity in reflecting changes in attendance patterns. Since the monthly percentage of attendance was a ratio of the total days all students were present during the month to the greatest possible number of days—on the assumption that all students had perfect attendance—only small percentage changes were reflected even when substantial changes in composite days occurred. For example, the authors reported that a change from 91 to 92 percent attendance represented an increase of as much as forty-five days in attendance for a typical month.

Campbell, Endman, and Bernfeld (1977) evaluated the utility of a behavior code in differentiating "true" hyperactives (high activity levels across situations) from situational hyperactives (moderately active children for whom heightened activity is situation specific), a distinction earlier drawn by Schleifer and others (1975). By employing fifteen hyperactives and sixteen controls, initial hyperactivity ratings were accomplished with the Werry-Weiss-Peters Activity Scale (Werry, 1968). Children were observed in regular classrooms with one thirty-minute observation period per child, with two alternating fifteen-minute blocks for both the target subject and classroom control. The observation code included six categories of child behavior (in-seat, out-of-seat, or off-task behavior, disruptive behavior toward teacher, disruptive behavior toward peers, attention soliciting, and disruption of class) and three categories of teacher behavior (positive feedback, negative feedback, directions). Following observation, teachers completed the Conners Teacher Rating Scale (Conners, 1969) on each target child. Data were analyzed for the total hyperactive group, with the control group split into "true" and "situational." The behavior code was sensitive both to the presence of hyperactives and to teacher style and reportedly allowed differentiation of the true and situational groups (discriminant validity). However, as is the case in many assessment procedures with hyperactive behavior, the behavioral code employed for child behaviors was weighted on the side of "problem" behaviors. As a result, the construct validity of this assessment instrument is open to question. As Haynes and Kerns (in press) have suggested in their critique of the coding system of Abikoff, Gittelman-Klein, and Klein (1977), failure to differentiate between classes of behavior (such as "hyperactivity" and "problem behavior") may confound interpretation of the construct validity of the assessment instrument.

Abikoff, Gittelman-Klein, and Klein (1977) recently reported on an attempt to validate a behavioral observation system for hyperactive children in the classroom—an attempt of particular interest owing to the lack of validation studies associated with observation systems. The authors adapted a coding system, previously employed by Tonick and others with "problem children," to include selected motor activities relevant to the assessment of hyperactivity. Elementary school children referred to an outpatient clinic for hyperactivity, identified as having behavior problems or as hyperactive by parents, and rated as hyperactive on Conners Teacher Rating Scale (Conners, 1969), along with a comparison group matched for sex and identified by teachers as "average" (no behavior problems), were observed in the classroom by trained observers; the observers viewed each hyperactive target child and an adjacent comparison child during alternating four-minute periods. Multiple correlated t-tests revealed that hyperactive children exhibited significantly higher behavior rates than did comparison children on twelve of the fourteen behavior categories. Additionally, particular-category dyads effectively differentiated a majority of hyperactive from nonhyperactive children. While the data for the discriminant validity of this instrument in identifying hyperactive children in the classroom are encouraging, interpretation of these results must be qualified by issues similar to those mentioned previously (Campbell, Endman, and Bernfeld, 1977). For example, the coding system utilized was originally designed to assess behavior problem children. Since some behavior codes may tap behavior problems in general, rather than behaviors idiosyncratic to hyperactivity (Haynes and Kerns, in press), a lack of differentiation among classes of problem behaviors leads to a confounding of the two constructs and leaves the construct validity of the assessment instrument open to question. Additionally, when classes of behavior are not sufficiently differentiated, the within-subject variability may be increased significantly; such variability within the hyperactive group was reported by Abikoff, Gittelman-Klein, and Klein (1977). Nevertheless, as one of the few attempts to validate a behavioral observation procedure for the assessment of hyperactivity in the classroom, this study is a welcome addition to the literature.

Evidence for the discriminant validity of naturalistic observation in evaluating teachers' use of behavior modification techniques with autistic children was reported by Koegel, Russo, and Rincover (1977) and described earlier in this section. In that study, teachers were to teach from one to four assigned target behaviors; each teacher worked with one child at a time. Independent observers scored the teachers as correct (fulfilled all aspects of the definition of the procedure for all trials within the thirty-second interval), incorrect (did not fulfill the definition in some way on one or more trials), or not applicable (procedure not observed during the thirty-second interval). The scoring categories included five classes of teacher instruction (discriminable, appropriate, consistent, uninterrupted, and given while child attending), the effectiveness of prompts, proper shaping procedures, and five classes of teacher consequences (immediate, contingent, unambiguous, consistent, and effective). In addition, children's performances were monitored on the task behaviors and scored as improved or deteriorated in comparison with the first ten trials of the session. Results indicated the assessment procedure to clearly differentiate between teachers with respect to the correct or incorrect use of defined behavior modification procedures. Additionally, scores of the teachers who used the behavior modification technique generally covaried with improvement or lack of improvement on child behavior measures, indirectly suggesting the construct validity of the teacher behavior measures. An exception was noted by the authors for one teacher during one baseline session, however; with a high level of correct teacher performance, there was no corresponding improvement in child performance, suggesting that other categories of teacher behavior may be important to measure.

In summary, naturalistic observation procedures have been applied extensively in schools and academically related settings to assess a variety of behaviors, including social interactions and skills, play activities, academic productivity and related behaviors, children's behavior problems, and teacher behaviors. These applications have served a basic child research function, as outcome measures of various treatment programs, and in the functional analysis of various problem behaviors. Despite the potential for preintervention assessment, however, there is little evidence of applications of such procedures to select target behaviors for intervention or to develop intervention strategies. A majority of the observation formats reviewed in this section have been found to reflect changes in targeted behaviors relatively quickly, supporting the sensitivity of the measures employed. The attempts of several of the investigations cited to evaluate the discriminant and criterion-related validity of observation instruments likewise represent an encouraging direction in the recent literature, although additional research is needed to further investigate issues of reliability and validity. Finally, while a limited number of recent studies reported adequate agreement levels between external observers and participant observers, further research will be necessary before definite conclusions may be drawn.

## Community Settings

In the recent literature, a number of investigators have reported interesting applications of naturalistic observation in a variety of community settings, including neighborhoods, restaurants, supermarkets, and apartment buildings. These studies have combined an evaluative research function with assessments of the effects of training and treatment programs. Table 6 summarizes the observational settings and the behaviors targeted for observation in these studies.

In the context of conservation programs, observations have been reported regarding participants' management of gasoline consumption (Foxx and Hake, 1977; Hake and Foxx, 1978) and electricity consumption (Hayes and Cone, 1977; Palmer, Lloyd, and Lloyd, 1977). In other applications, observation measures have involved evaluation of municipal policies, such as adherence to refuse-packaging guidelines (Stokes and Fawcett, 1977) and assessments of the effectiveness of saturation police patrols (Schnelle

**Table 6. Recent Applications of Naturalistic Observation in Community Settings**

| Reference | Subjects | Setting | Behaviors Monitored |
|---|---|---|---|
| Barnard, Christophersen, and Wolf (1977) | Male children | Supermarket | Assessed shopping behavior of boys relative to proximity to parent and product disturbance; also measured parent-consumer satisfaction |
| Bauman and Iwata (1977) | Adults | Home (kitchen/dining area, living/bath area) | Monitored household tasks including table setting and apartment cleaning |
| Clark and others (1977) | Children and parents | Supermarket | Monitored three categories of children's distracting behavior and five categories of parent-child conversations |
| Epstein and Martin (1977) | Overweight adults | Meal situations | Recorded food intake |
| Fawcett and Fletcher (1977) | Adults | Community neighborhood | Assessed manual designed to teach nonprofessionals to prepare instructional packages for administration by neighborhood residents |
| Foxx and Hake (1977) | College students | Automobile driving | Monitored gasoline conservation by taking odometer readings; field checks for car location |

| | | | |
|---|---|---|---|
| Hake and Foxx (1978) | College students | Automobile driving | Monitored gasoline conservation by taking odometer readings; field checks for car location |
| Hayes and Cone (1977) | Married students | Married student housing unit | Monitored power usage in kilowatt hours from meter boxes |
| Kleinknecht and Bernstein (1978) | Adults | Dental offices | Assessed dental fears through observation of overt behaviors (bodily movement), with respect to high- and low-anxiety subjects |
| Komaki and Barnett (1977) | Boys on football team | Practice field | Employed five-state checklist maintained by backfield coach to score execution of each running play |
| LeBow, Goldberg, and Collins (1976) | Adults | Restaurants | Methodology for observation of eating behavior through use of microphones and briefcase tape recorders |
| LeBow, Goldberg, and Collins (1977) | Adults | Quick service diner | Monitored chewing, hamburger bites, and eating french fries by means of a microphone-coding procedure |
| Marston and others (1977) | Obese and nonobese adults | Public cafeteria | Extraneous eating behaviors, bite frequencies, chews per bite, size of mouthful on five-point scale |

**Table 6. Recent Applications of Naturalistic Observation in Community Settings (Continued)**

| Reference | Subjects | Setting | Behaviors Monitored |
|---|---|---|---|
| Neef, Iwata, and Page (1978) | Retarded male student | Community bus routes | Monitored four categories (location, boarding, exiting, and signaling) to evaluate training in public transportation usage |
| Palmer, Lloyd, and Lloyd (1977) | Families | Home | Assessment of daily energy consumption measured in kilowatt hours of power consumed |
| Schnelle and others (1977) | Police patrols | Community patrol areas | Assessed effects of saturation police patrol with tachograph instrumentation providing data read-outs |
| Smith, Smoll, and Hunt (1977) | Football coaches | Practice field | Describes manual (Coaching Behavior Assessment System) to record ongoing coaching behaviors; twelve categories with applicability to all sports |
| Stokes and Fawcett (1977) | Adults | Neighborhoods | Refuse-packaging behavior assessed with six-category code for public policy assessment |

| Yeaton and Bailey (1978) | Children | Community intersections | Six categories of street-crossing skills (wait at curb, look, watch vehicle distance, walk, keep looking, use crosswalk) were tracked |

and others, 1977). Observation procedures have also been employed to evaluate the effects of manuals for training neighborhood residents to administer instructional skills packages to peers (Fawcett and Fletcher, 1977; Mathews and Fawcett, 1977), as well as to evaluate training programs for mentally retarded subjects in the use of public transportation (Neef, Iwata, and Page, 1978) and for children in pedestrian safety programs (Yeaton and Bailey, 1978). Parent-child interactions have been assessed to evaluate parent training procedures in controlling inappropriate behaviors of children in supermarkets (Barnard, Christophersen, and Wolf, 1977; Clark and others, 1977). Additionally, ingestive behaviors have been observed in restaurants (LeBow, Goldberg, and Collins, 1976), fast-food diners (LeBow, Goldberg, and Collins, 1977), cafeterias (Marston and others, 1977), and other public places (Epstein and Martin, 1977; Stunkard and Kaplan, 1977). Also, naturalistic observation has been employed to assess such sports activities as play execution in football (Komaki and Barnett, 1977) and coaching behaviors (Smith, Smoll, and Hunt, 1977). Finally, naturalistic observation has been employed in the assessment of dental fears among adults (Kleinknecht and Bernstein, 1978).

Observation procedures used in these community settings have also varied considerably. As is typical in naturalistic observation, behavior codes have been widely employed for direct observation of targeted behaviors by both external and participant observers. In some cases, direct observation has been supplemented with mechanical data collection procedures. For example, Foxx and Hake (1977) and Hake and Foxx (1978) utilized odometer readings in addition to observer sightings in assessing reductions in driving and gasoline consumption by college students. LeBow, Goldberg, and Collins (1977) integrated direct observation of eating behaviors with a mechanical data collection procedure by having observers make clicking and scratching sounds on a microphone to code response patterns for later analysis. In other studies, mechanical devices have served to collect naturalistic data for subsequent recording and analysis by observers. For example, electricity meters have provided observers with dependent measures in energy conservation programs (Hayes and Cone, 1977; Palmer, Lloyd, and Lloyd, 1977). In another study (Schnelle and others, 1977), the levels of saturation police patrols were recorded by observers using a commercial field chart analyzer from tachograph instrumentation in patrol cars—this instrumentation provides continuous, time-based, graphical read-outs of speed, distance, engine operation, and the use of emergency lights.

Several recent studies have employed innovative approaches to assessment in community settings. In programs designed to increase fuel conservation and to reduce driving among college students, Foxx and Hake (1977) and Hake and Foxx (1978) employed several special recording procedures to assure the accuracy of obtained data and to detect and reduce alteration of odometers. At each odometer check, the experimenters determined if each odometer was operational by driving .2 miles on a test track. Checks were also made of the make, model, year, and license number to ensure that the reading taken corresponded with the designated car. Means were also employed to determine that the subject was the actual driver of the car. This was accomplished by having drivers while in class indicate on a campus map the location of their cars; observers then went to those locations to determine that the specified cars were in the designated locations. An interesting methodology for observing and recording eating behaviors of obese and nonobese individuals in restaurants was reported by LeBow, Goldberg, and Collins (1977). Patrons were monitored by an observer (initially trained through videotapes) who was inconspicuously seated in one corner of the restaurant. Employing a tape recorder concealed in a briefcase, the observer made signals into the microphone to record foods eaten and eating behaviors. For example, taking a bite of hamburger was signaled by clicking a stopwatch, eating a french fry was signaled by scratching the surface of the microphone, and chewing was recorded by tapping the microphone.

Several other authors have provided data on the sensitivity of naturalistic observation in community settings. For example, Komaki and Barnett (1977) reported that scores on a five-stage checklist for football play execution were a sensitive measure of play performance, irrespective of game outcome. Barnard, Christophersen, and Wolf (1977) found observation of parent-child interactions in a supermarket to be sensitive to modification of parent-delivered consequences and to the quality and quantity of verbalized attention given to the child. Similarly, Clark and others (1977) found observation of distracting child behaviors and parent-child verbal interactions in supermarkets to be sensitive to parental consequation behaviors and also to the quality and quantity of verbalized attention. Additional evidence for the sensitivity of observations in community settings was reported by Neef, Iwata, and Page (1978) for assessments of public transportation training and by Yeaton and Bailey (1978) for assessments of pedestrian skill training. Likewise, Schnelle and others (1977), using the tachograph instrumentation previously mentioned to assess the effects of saturation police patrols, found this instrument to be sensitive in reflecting the degree to which patrol levels increased.

While we located no studies that directly assessed the content validity of observation procedures employed in community settings, several investigators have provided evidence of criterion-related validity. In the evaluation of refuse-packaging behavior, Stokes and Fawcett (1977) employed a six-category code of packaging violations. Prior to the arrival of sanitation crews, an observer was driven by car through the collection areas to code violations for residences, and sanitation crews were asked to rate the experimental areas on refuse-packaging behaviors. Results indicated that recorded levels of violations and percentages of residences in violation coincided with ratings by workers, suggesting the concurrent validity of this observation system. Evidence for the discriminant validity of observation procedures to differentiate eating patterns of obese and nonobese individuals in the natural environment was reported by Marston and others (1977). Employing four observation samples that included extraneous responses (such as looking at food and using a napkin), counts of chews per bite, frequency of bites, and typical size of mouthfuls on a five-point scale, observers found significant differences between eating patterns of obese and nonobese individuals. Similarly, LeBow, Goldberg, and Collins (1977) reported that the observation procedure described earlier reflected differential eating patterns between individuals classified as overweight or not overweight on the basis of such variables as arm fat and waist size. Evidence for the validity of naturalistic observation for assessing eating behavior, however, must be considered cautiously in light of the significant variations in eating patterns found among overweight individuals (LeBow, Goldberg, and Collins, 1977; Stunkard and Kaplan, 1977). Individual differences, as well as variation in methodologies and in the settings in which observations are made, make it difficult to evaluate the validity of assessments. Also of note with respect to the issue of discriminant validity of observations in the natural environment was the report by Kleinknecht and Bernstein (1978) of the failure of the observation procedures to discriminate between adults classified as high and low on a scale of dental fears.

In summary, naturalistic observation has been applied in a variety of community settings, including neighborhoods, restaurants, supermarkets, and apartment buildings. Similarly, a wide range of behaviors have been targeted for observation, including gasoline and electricity management, adherence to municipal policies, ingestive patterns, parent-child interactions, and athletic activities. In addition to the employment of behavior codes for direct observation of targeted behaviors by external and participant observers, these procedures in some cases have been supplemented with mechanical data collection procedures. In other investigations, mechanical devices have been utilized to collect naturalistic data for later transcription by observers. Consistent with observation applications described in previous sections of this chapter, the selection of assessment procedures often appears to be based on considerations of face validity and logical inference. Although a number of investigators have reported assessment approaches in community settings to be sensitive to changes in target behaviors, significantly fewer have reported support for the discriminant and criterion-related validity of observation procedures, although studies addressing these issues have reported encouraging findings. Along with the need for additional investigation of these issues, evidence for the content validity of observation instruments employed in community settings remains to be demonstrated.

## Issues in Naturalistic Observation

Considering the extensive application of observation in naturalistic settings as an assessment technique for the evaluation of treatment outcome and for the functional analysis of problem behavior, it is significant that it has seldom been the subject of validity evaluation. Few investigators have addressed the issues of the construct, content, or criterion-related validity of behavioral observation instruments. As Haynes and Kerns (in press) pointed out, a number of significant factors in the validity assessment of behavioral observation systems overlap with factors in the validity assessment of more traditional instruments. Along with the factors of content and criterion-related validity are factors such as observer accuracy, drift, and bias, reactive factors in measurement, variations in the complexity of instruments (for example, codes and the purposes for which they are utilized), and other variables, including the sampling procedures used (see Chapter Two), characteristics of the subjects themselves, and generalization factors associated with assessment procedures.

Of the studies reviewed in this chapter, a large number have provided indications of adequate agreement coefficients between observers, although few have evaluated observer accuracy (Kazdin, 1977a), an important aspect of criterion-related validity. For such accuracy assessments, comparisons of observer recordings with other criterion measures of the same behavior would be necessary. One might, for example, collect daily classwork papers (a product-of-behavior measure) as a criterion against which to compare observations of on- and off-task behavior in the classroom. Videotapes for comparison with observer scorings likewise can serve as a criterion against which to determine accuracy. Further, while observer training has been employed to enhance observer performance, only a limited amount of research has focused on this factor—a point also made by Wildman and Erickson (1977). Several additional issues are of significance with respect to the validity of observational measures and, although already described in greater detail in Chapter Two, they must be briefly reintroduced here.

Related to the performance of observers is the issue of observer *drift* (Johnson and Bolstad, 1973; O'Leary and Kent, 1973), that is, the deterioration of the accuracy of observers over time. Obviously, changes in recording performance will affect the validity of observational measures. Nevertheless, little in the way of evaluation of this issue has appeared in the recent literature. This has also been true regarding the issue of observer *bias* (Johnson and Christensen, 1975; Moore and Bailey, 1973; Schnelle, 1974), although it is to be expected that observer recordings, particularly those made by participant observers such as parents (Schnelle, 1974) or teachers in naturalistic environments may be subject to the influence of motivation or expectation; assessment of the naivete of observers may be desirable (Johnson and Christensen, 1975).

The *reactivity* of observation measures, likewise, poses a threat to validity. When a subject is aware of being observed, naturalness of behavior may be destroyed (Tunnell, 1977). Recently, for example, Forehand and Atkeson (1977) pointed out that parents may not adapt to the presence of observers. The utilization of participant observers in naturalistic environments (such as parents for family assessments or teachers for classroom observations) poses, in fact, an interesting dilemma. Use of participant observers might reduce reactive effects, since the observers would be less obtrusive, but might simultaneously introduce bias or other sources of error in the measures obtained. Conversely, while use of external observers might reduce some of the potential for bias (assuming naivete of observers), greater reactive effects might result.

Along with the potential threats to validity already discussed, several issues related to assessment instruments themselves deserve mention. Coding systems have ranged from very simple formats involving single-target behaviors to codes containing multiple behavioral categories. In the recent literature, a number of coding systems, particularly those aimed at treatment outcome, have been limited to single-target behaviors. It is also notable that few of these codes have been subjected to reliability or validity evaluations. For example, few have seen repeated application (at different time periods with the same groups) or application across different populations.

Although empirical data is generally lacking, several factors associated with assessment instruments themselves (see Chapter Two for a more detailed discussion) may influence the validity of measures obtained, particularly with respect to those obtained through the use of participant observers in the natural environment. For example, it could be expected that the specificity or generality of the behavioral definitions employed would differentially affect observer performance. Closely related to this issue is the issue of clarity of definitions. Increased clarity could influence the accuracy of observer recordings (and, in turn, their validity), as could the number of behaviors to be recorded, with the reliability and validity of obtained data expected to decrease as the number of behaviors targeted for observation increases (Haynes, 1978; Wildman and Erickson, 1977). However, while the reliability and validity of an instrument may be enhanced by limiting the number of behaviors simultaneously observed, this should not be interpreted as a recommendation to severely limit the number of behaviors sampled by an instrument. If a code does not adequately sample the targeted construct, the construct validity of the instrument will suffer; in this sense, multiple-assessment procedures would appear desirable (Forehand and Atkeson, 1977).

Associated with the determination of the number and types of behaviors sampled, of course, is the issue of the function for which the assessment instrument is to be employed. In developing general behavioral codes for the preintervention assessment of problem family interactions that involve complex antecedent and consequent events, it is critical that multiple behaviors be sampled. For the assessment of treatment outcomes, although the behaviors sampled may be fewer, it would likewise be important that recording formats include multiple behavioral measures since it is impossible to adequately assess intervention effects through reference solely to changes in main target behaviors (Haynes, 1978); multiple measures can allow assessment of intervention effects upon other than the main target behaviors (for example, effects on persons in the client's environment or on clients' behaviors across settings). Nevertheless, it seems desirable that the observation procedure employed not overburden the observers (Wildman and Erickson, 1977). In consideration of the issues just discussed, the question of the particular sampling technique employed becomes significant. Although the issue of sampling techniques was discussed more fully in Chapter Two, the potential influence on validity of the particular sampling strategies employed should be noted again. For example, quite different results may be obtained if observations are made during peak activity periods than if made during rest periods when assessing hyperactivity, and would likely be reflected in different levels of discriminant validity for the scale employed (Haynes and Kerns, in press).

Finally, as Tunnell (1977) has pointed out, the generalizability of obtained measures is not ensured by the use of naturalistic observation procedures. However, while the issue of generalization (external validity) is an important one, the varying aspects of generalizability, including setting generality (Bernal and others, 1976; Patterson, 1974) and the generality of treatment effects (Forehand and Atkeson, 1977), have received little attention in the recent research literature, although several authors have noted the necessity of generality assessment (Bernal and others, 1976; Cone, 1977; Forehand and Atkeson, 1977; Tunnell, 1977). In respect to temporal generality, Forehand and Atkeson (1977) have further commented on the need for more behavioral approaches, including more rigorous multiple-assessment procedures, such as those utilized by Patterson and others (1975). Regarding setting generality, data often are collected through parents' verbal reports (Forehand and Atkeson, 1977)—data for which the validity may be questioned on grounds of potential bias. A preferred approach, perhaps, would involve home observations over a variety of time periods. Likewise, assessment of behavioral generality frequently is confined to parental reports, although a few studies have recorded treated and nontreated behaviors (Forehand and Atkeson, 1977), a necessity in ascertaining behavioral generality. In this regard, the same authors also have suggested recording parental reactions to treated and nontreated behaviors.

In the recent literature on naturalistic observation, we located only a limited number of studies addressing the issue of generality. Among those, Peed, Roberts, and Forehand (1977) investigated setting generality through assessment of the effects of parental training in laboratory and home settings. Matson and Stephens (1978) found observation sensitive to generalization of treatment effects in psychiatric patients' living quarters. In another institutional setting, Rollings, Baumeister, and Baumeister (1977) evaluated generalization of the suppressive effects of overcorrection procedures (intervention with rocking and head-weaving behaviors of mentally retarded patients) from a treatment room to the general ward environment. Nutter and Reid (1978) found observation sensitive to generalization of training in clothing selection by mentally retarded females, and Neef, Iwata, and Page (1978) found observation sensitive to generalization with respect to training in public transportation usage for mentally retarded adults. Similarly, Strain (1977) reported generalization and maintenance of treatment effects among preschool social isolates from an experimental playroom to the classroom setting. Finally, Trap and others (1978) assessed the generalization of letter formations from those letters that were trained to untrained letters, and Parsonson and Baer (1978) investigated the effects of generalization training among preschool children.

To summarize, a number of issues influence the degree of confidence that can be placed in the validity of measures obtained through naturalistic assessment. These include factors associated with observer performance (the quality and internal consistency of observer data, along with observer training, bias, drift, and reactivity), subject factors such as reactivity, and characteristics of the instruments employed (definitional clarity within codes, number of behaviors coded, and specificity). There are also such considerations as the particular sampling techniques employed and the generalizability of measures obtained. Additional research, however, is needed to further delineate the relative influence of these factors upon the data generated.

### Product-of-Behavior Measures

Permanent products (product-of-behavior measures) have frequently been used as dependent measures in naturalistic settings. While these assessment measures cannot be characterized as observation procedures in the strictest sense, they may be employed as components of such assessment processes. Additionally, while these measures may be particularly suited for assessment in natural environments, they may also have utility for assessments in analogue settings such as those discussed in Chapter Four. In the recent literature, product-of-behavior measures have been employed in a variety of environmental settings, including schools, homes, hospitals, and institutions. One obvious advantage of product-of-behavior measures is, of course, their availability. For example, children's classwork in the form of workbook pages and completed assignment sheets represents a continuing source of data that might be employed by the behavior analyst to assess the effects of classroom interventions or as a means of preintervention assessment. Similarly, counts of soft-drink cans or bottles discarded may easily provide information as to soft-drink consumption in the home. An additional advantage of product-of-behavior measures is that they may be obtained in a relatively unobtrusive fashion. Accordingly, some of the reactive effects associated with more artificial dependent measures might be avoided.

Product-of-behavior measures potentially may be employed for preintervention assessment of target behaviors. For example, counts might be made of the number of cigarettes left in ashtrays in the home prior to intervention with smoking behaviors. Likewise, such measures can provide data for ongoing evaluations of treatment effects and to make decisions regarding treatment. As pointed out by Haynes (1978), adequate evaluation of intervention programs requires assessment of effects (both positive and negative) upon other than the main target behavior. For example, one might wish to determine that a classroom intervention procedure with a withdrawn child was not adversely affecting other aspects of the child's class performance. Thus, in addition to observations of the child's social interactions during treatment, the behavior analyst might also collect samples of the child's daily work to ensure that productivity levels did not decline as a result of intervention. In an extension of these applications, product-of-behavior measures can have utility as outcome measures of treatment; weighings can be employed with participants in weight reduction programs to evaluate the success of treatment. Finally, with respect to observation in the natural environment, product-of-behavior measures may be employed as a criterion against which to compare observational data for purposes of observer accuracy assessment.

In the school setting, Hay, Hay, and Nelson (1977a) employed students' workbook performances as product-of-behavior measures, along with behavioral observations to evaluate the effects of contingencies on on-task behaviors and on the rate and accuracy of academic performance; these behavior products were found to be sensitive measures of intervention effects. Additional product-of-behavior measures employed in conjunction with observational procedures in the classroom setting have included units of academic work completed under a classroom management pro-

gram (Jones, Fremouw, and Carples, 1977), the number of unit
assignments completed to an 80 percent criterion by students as
part of an evaluation of the effects of teacher aides in an open
classroom (Loos, Williams, and Bailey, 1977), and the number of
assignments completed under a program to evaluate the differential effects on academic production of two schedules of "home reports" (Saudargas, Madsen, and Scott, 1977). And, reporting on a
means of assessing and controlling theft in the classroom, Switzer,
Deal, and Bailey (1977) placed a standard number of common
classroom items in specific locations in the classroom. Subsequently,
the number of items present, absent, and returned were monitored
by independent observers (serving as teacher aides); measures were
found to be sensitive to the differential effects of lecture intervention versus group contingencies.

Product-of-behavior measures have also been employed in
the assessment of weight control programs. For example, Epstein
and Martin (1977) included weighing procedures both for purposes of preintervention assessment (percent overweight based on
midpoint of desirable weight range for appropriate height and
frame size according to the Metropolitan Life Insurance norms)
and as an outcome measure [weight reduction index according to
the formula: (weight loss/surplus weight) $\times$ (initial weight/target
weight)] of a self-control weight program. Similarly, Kingsley and
Wilson (1977) employed a subject's weight as a means of evaluating
the effects of a behavioral treatment for obesity. Herbert-Jackson
and Risley (1977) utilized a food-weighing procedure (described
earlier) along with observations of toddlers' eating behaviors, in an
attempt to identify foods eaten in sufficient quantity to produce
adequate nutrient intake. Also in an institutional setting, Magrab
and Papadopoulou (1977) employed weight, blood-urine-nitrogen
(BUN) levels, and potassium levels as product-of-behavior measures for four patients on a pediatric hemodialysis unit. Weight
gain between sessions was considered the primary measure of fluid
intake. (Interestingly, blood samples for these measures were obtained through dialysis lines and, thus, did not require additional
punctures.)

Assessments of enuretic children have also employed
product-of-behavior measures in home, hospital, and institutional

settings. For example, Doleys and others (1977a) employed parents as participant observers to monitor urine volume in evaluating the effects of dry-bed and retention control training with enuretic children. Similarly, Harris and Purohit (1977) employed a "water-load test" devised by Hallman (1950) to assess bladder capacity among enuretic and nonenuretic children. This technique involved administering from 500 to 1000 milliliters of water to children and instructing them to refrain from voiding for as long as possible. Each child's voidings in the subsequent period of four to six hours represented the dependent measures, with the largest single measure serving as an index of bladder capacity. Although this technique would appear susceptible to other sources of error, such as demand factors and immediate drinking history, or might reflect tendencies to withhold rather than actual bladder capacity, it was reported to be a sensitive measure with respect to the effects of bladder control training to increase bladder capacity among enuretic children. Finally, in a structured room in a mental retardation facility, Burleigh and Marholin (1977) recorded numbers of blocks properly stacked (on-task behavior) as one measure in the assessment of adverse side effects of verbal prompts in terminating a mentally retarded adult's aversive responding (placing hands over his eyes).

To summarize, because of their ready availability and relatively unobtrusive characteristics, product-of-behavior measures would seem especially suited for application in naturalistic environments. Functions of these instruments, as reflected in the recent literature, include preintervention assessment, ongoing evaluations of treatment, and measurement of outcomes of treatment. Additionally, product-of-behavior measures may have utility as criteria against which to compare observer data for observer accuracy assessments. Settings in which these measures have been employed have included schools, homes, and institutions, and the targets of assessments employing product-of-behavior measures have included work productivity in schools, classroom thefts, weight changes associated with weight control programs, children's eating behaviors, weight and blood-urine-nitrogen levels of hemodialysis patients under diet programs, measures of urine volume from enuretic children, and on-task behaviors of mentally retarded adults. While data are thus far limited with respect to the validity and reliability of these measures, several investigators have reported evidence for the sensitivity of the measures employed in reflecting behavioral changes as a function of treatment interventions. Owing to the potential utility of product-of-behavior measures for behavioral assessment, expansion of research investigations focusing on these measures is highly desirable.

## Summary

Naturalistic observation procedures have been utilized as an assessment strategy in a wide variety of settings and with extremely diverse populations and target behaviors. With few exceptions, the studies reviewed have reported that the observation instruments employed were sensitive to intervention effects in school, home, institutional, and community settings. Nevertheless, several parameters associated with the issue of sensitivity, such as the influence of the setting in which observations are made, the observation procedures themselves, and the characteristics of the behaviors observed, have not been sufficiently investigated. Naturalistic observation techniques have been reported by several investigators to significantly correlate with other criterion measures (concurrent validity) and to discriminate among groups of subjects classified on the basis of other criteria (discriminant validity). However, in contrast to reports of the sensitivity of instruments, the issues of criterion-related and content validity have much less frequently been examined. For naturalistic observation, methods typically are dictated by the settings in which observations are made. Conversely, analogue assessment settings, which are typically structured for purposes of observation, more easily support validation research through consistent use of similar settings and through the opportunity to vary those settings in a controlled fashion. Along these same lines, Tunnell (1977) has suggested that researchers may be attracted to naturalistic observation (field research) because of its apparently built-in external validity; researchers may thus give examination of external validity a lower priority than examination of internal validity. As already indicated, the very nature of observation in natural environments may, in part, dictate this phenomenon. Obviously, attempts to employ standardized settings risk disruption of the naturalness of behavior.

Product-of-behavior measures such as completed academic worksheets, food items remaining on plates, or measures of urine volume have received increased attention in recent literature. Although not constituting observation procedures in the strictest sense, these measures often are employed as components of such assessment procedures. Product-of-behavior measures would seem particularly suited for assessment in natural environments owing to their ready availability and relatively unobtrusive nature, although such measures may have utility for assessments in analogue settings as well. These instruments have served for preintervention assessment, for ongoing treatment evaluations, and as treatment outcome measures. Additionally, product-of-behavior measures may have utility as criteria against which to compare observational data for observer accuracy assessment. Although these instruments have frequently been reported as sensitive to treatment effects, only limited information is thus far available as to the criterion-related and content validity of product-of-behavior measures.

Another trend described in this chapter has involved the utilization of participant observers (such as parents, teachers, institutional staff members, and public employees) to monitor behaviors in naturalistic settings. Participant observers may have particular utility with respect to reduced time and cost constraints when compared with external observers. In family settings, a limited number of investigations have reported adequate agreement coefficients between external and participant observers, suggesting the utility of parents as observers of their children. Similarly, some limited evidence thus far exists with respect to the utility of teachers for observation of children's classroom behaviors. Investigations have also employed institutional staff members and public employees as participant observers. However, although staff members and public employees might have comparable utility as observers, such evaluations have less frequently been addressed. Finally, while the evidence thus far available with respect to the utility of participant observers for naturalistic observation is generally encouraging, the issues of validity and error sources have been insufficiently investigated.

Also of note have been the applications of several forms of instrumentation for data collection as components of observational procedures in naturalistic settings. Included among the instruments discussed was an electronic device (to be worn around the waist) that measures activity levels through displacement of mercury switches. In the assessment of environmental stimulation levels in hospital units for premature infants, light meters and sound pressure level meters have been employed along with observational procedures. For assessing staff members' accuracies in awarding contingency points to institutional residents, plastic overlays (templates) have been employed. Electricity meters and car odometers have provided data for evaluation of fuel and energy consumption programs, and tachograph instrumentation has been employed in patrol cars to assess the effects of saturation police patrols. Additionally, microphones and briefcase tape recorders have been employed to unobtrusively record observations of eating behaviors in restaurants. While reports of the sensitivity of these instruments in reflecting change in the behaviors monitored are encouraging, conclusions with respect to the criterion-related and content validity of these instruments must await further research.

Also discussed in this chapter were a number of issues related to, or potentially affecting, the reliability and validity of naturalistic observation. These included such factors as performance, drift, and bias of observers, reactive effects of measurement, various characteristics of the instruments employed (for example, the specificity and number of behaviors coded and the clarity of definitions), sampling procedures, and the generalizability of measures obtained. Although potentially significant in their impact on instrument validity and reliability, these issues have been infrequently addressed in the recent literature. Naturalistic observation has primarily served as a measure of treatment outcome or as a research tool in the evaluation of problem and social behaviors. The articles reviewed provide little evidence that naturalistic observation is being employed as a preintervention assessment instrument for the identification of target behaviors for intervention. As Ciminero and Drabman (1977) have suggested, however, such assessment data could be helpful not only in describing a behavior problem but also in selecting target behaviors and treatment strategies. Likewise, the use of such dependent measures would have implications for ongoing treatment decisions.

Finally, as Wildman and Erickson (1977) have pointed out, behavioral observation is the method of choice for many investigations. Naturalistic observation not only represents a desirable approach to assessment, owing to its greater apparent content validity, but it may also be the only viable approach for assessing the effect of intervention programs carried out in natural settings. However, additional evidence is needed with respect to the reliability and validity of such procedures. It is to be expected that this evidence will be provided as investigators more systematically and thoroughly report observational assessment procedures employed in naturalistic settings and as investigators become increasingly sensitive to issues associated with naturalistic observation.

# CHAPTER FOUR

# *Observation in Structured Environments*

As indicated in previous chapters, the behavioral construct system has had a major impact upon the philosophy and methodology of preintervention assessment; the desirability of observing behavior in the natural environment has been particularly emphasized. Although naturalistic observation is probably the assessment procedure most congruent with behavioral assumptions about the environmental determinants of behavior and with a preference for valid, generalizable, and noninferential assessment instruments, it is also costly and is not useful for the assessment of some target behaviors and populations. Naturalistic observation of parent-child interaction, marital interaction, food and alcohol intake, adult social interaction, and behavior in feared situations, for example, is desirable, but sometimes difficult and costly. One alternative to naturalistic observation is to observe target subjects within structured laboratory or analogue environments. An analogue assessment situation is one in which the target behavior is elicited in an environment that differs from the environment in which the behavior naturally occurs. Most often, analogue assessment occurs in clinic or laboratory rooms specially equipped for unobtrusive visual or auditory monitoring. The use of analogue assessment environments allows the behavior analyst to observe directly the subjects and behaviors of interest, with a more efficient use of time and financial expenditure than may often be the case for naturalistic observation.

Because of its *apparent* content validity and efficiency, analogue assessment has been utilized with a wide variety of target problems. For example, parent-child interaction is frequently observed in structured environments in outpatient clinics. Typically, a parent and child are instructed to play specific games or engage in specific tasks (such as cleaning up) in a playroom. Also, marital couples are sometimes observed in clinic observation rooms while they discuss areas of disagreement. Other examples of structured observation include the observation of speech-anxious subjects giving speeches, observation of the ingestive behaviors of overweight or alcoholic subjects, and observation of the behavior of subjects while approaching a feared stimulus. All of these examples are similar in that they involve direct observation or monitoring of targeted behavior in an analogue environment.

Structured observation procedures have also been utilized to assess a wide variety of behavior problems. Although many of the applications involve the assessment of social interactions, such as adult-child interaction, marital interaction, or adult social interaction, others involve the assessment of a single individual in a laboratory environment, such as eating or drinking behavior, child behavior, or behavior in feared situations.

There are several assumptions underlying the use of analogue assessment environments (Haynes, 1978). Most importantly, it is assumed that the behavior of target subjects in these situations is analogous to, will predict, or correlates with their behavior in the natural environment. This assumption is basic to the use of analogue assessment for diagnosis, screening, intervention planning, and outcome evaluation. However, this assumption has also been insufficiently tested, and factors affecting the degree to which data derived from analogue assessment can be generalized to the natural environment remain to be determined. Because of the untested assumptions that are central to the application of analogue assessment, a principal focus of this chapter is upon issues of the reliability, validity, and generalizability of analogue assessment. Because the procedures and issues in analogue assessment vary considerably as a function of the target behaviors, analogue assessment of each target behavior must be looked upon as a separate assessment instrument. Therefore, the chapter is divided into sections that reflect commonly selected target behaviors: parent-child interaction, child behavior, marital interaction, fear and anxiety, social skills, and ingestive behavior. The psychometric properties of each application will be discussed separately.

## Parent-Child Interaction

Several recently published studies have utilized analogue assessment environments to assess parent-child or adult-child interaction. These studies, summarized in Table 7, have typically involved parents and young children, although the social interactions of older children and between children and adults other than parents have also been assessed (Kent and others, 1977b). Analogue observation situations have been used for a variety of purposes in the assessment of adult-child interaction, including evaluation of the outcome of behavioral intervention programs (Forehand and King, 1977; Hobbs, Forehand, and Murray, 1978; Kent and others, 1977b; Koegel, Clahn, and Nieminen, 1978; Peed, Roberts, and Forehand, 1977), basic research on observation procedures (Reisinger and Ora, 1977; G. D. White, 1977; Zegiob and Forehand, 1978), and basic developmental research (Cantor and Gelfand, 1977; Eckerman and Whatley, 1977; Farran and Ramey, 1977; Field, 1977; Frisch, 1977; Lougee, Grueneich, and Hartup, 1977; Moskowitz, Schwarz, and Corsini, 1977; Mueller and others, 1977). The structured environments utilized have varied from basic clinic observation rooms with minimal modification to observation facilities that resemble the natural environment (Field, 1977; Snyder, 1977; G. D. White, 1977).

**Table 7. Recent Studies Involving Analogue Assessment of Adult-Child Interactions**

| Reference | Subjects | Assessment Situation | Comments |
|---|---|---|---|
| Cantor and Gelfand (1977) | Adults and children | Structured laboratory setting | Studied effects of children's behavior on adults |
| Eckerman and Whatley (1977) | Forty-four infant pairs with adults | Structured laboratory setting | Studied effect of presence or absence of toys on infant-infant and infant-adult interaction |
| Farran and Ramey (1977) | Infants in daycare center with parents, teachers, and stranger | Observation room; fourteen minutes with mother, teacher, and stranger | Investigated differences in interaction between infants and parents and infants and teachers |
| Field (1977) | Thirty-six infants with mothers | Structured laboratory furnished like living room in intensive care nursery | |
| Forehand and King (1977) | Parents and noncompliant children; eleven males, mean age 5.2 years | Structured laboratory setting | Behavioral intervention outcome study |
| Frisch (1977) | Twenty-four infants with adults | Laboratory playroom | Study of effect of sex-role labeling on adult-infant interaction |
| Hobbs, Forehand, and Murray (1978) | Twenty-eight mother-child pairs | Playroom equipped for observation; mother delivered commands on cue through bug-in-ear | Study of the effects of various time-out durations on noncompliance of children |

Table 7. Recent Studies Involving Analogue Assessment of Adult-Child Interactions (Continued)

| Reference | Subjects | Assessment Situation | Comments |
|---|---|---|---|
| Kent and others (1977b) | Parents and adolescents in behavioral intervention program | Parent-adolescent dyads discussed hypothetical and real conflicts | Behavioral intervention outcome study |
| Koegel, Clahn, and Nieminen (1978) | Parents and autistic children | Structured laboratory setting | Two studies on methods of teaching autistic children new behaviors |
| Lougee, Grueneich, and Hartup (1977) | Fifty-four nursery school children | Structured laboratory setting | Assessed verbal interaction among preschool children |
| Moskowitz, Schwarz, and Corsini (1977) | Twenty-four children, ages 2.9 to 3.4 years; with mother or stranger | Structured laboratory setting | Assessed social interaction of children at daycare center with mothers and strangers |
| Mueller and others (1977) | Three boys and parents | Laboratory playroom; thirty-minute observation sessions | Studied the development of verbal interaction among children |
| Peed, Roberts, and Forehand (1977) | Twelve mother-child pairs; participants in parent-training program | Laboratory setting | Behavioral intervention outcome study |
| Prinz and Kent (1978) | Thirty-eight distressed and forty nondistressed mother-adolescent dyads (adolescents between 10 and 15 years old) | Ten-minute conversation in which mother and adolescent discussed something adolescent wanted changed | Study of procedures for assessing the validity of parent-adolescent interactions in analogue setting |
| Reisinger and Ora (1977) | Ten behavior problem children and ten nonbehavior problem children with mothers | Playroom; free play with at least five commands from mother; twenty-minute session | Assessed convergent and divergent validity of structured observation |

| Study | Sample | Setting | Purpose/Findings |
| --- | --- | --- | --- |
| Snyder (1977) | 5-to-10-year-old boys with parents; ten problem and ten nonproblem families | Playroom/living room situation; forty-five minutes of undirected interaction | Assessed differences in interaction between problem and nonproblem families |
| G. D. White (1977) | Five families involving mother and two children | Resembled family living room | Demonstrated reactive effects of observers |
| Zegiob and Forehand (1978) | Twenty-eight mother-child pairs; lower- and middle-class families | Playroom equipped for observation; subjects were informed or uninformed of observation | Study of the reactive effects of observation and the effects of social class on mother-child interactions |

It would be expected that variance in structure (for example, toys present, size of observation room, or people present) of the observation environment or in assessment procedures would affect the resultant data and inferences. Physical structure and procedures are elements of the content validity of the assessment environment and have been discussed by Hughes and Haynes (1978). Several studies (Cantor and Gelfand, 1977; Eckerman and Whatley, 1977; Moskowitz, Schwarz, and Corsini, 1977; G. D. White, 1977; Zegiob and Forehand, 1978) have noted that modifications in the structure of the assessment environment or in the behavior of participants affect the behavior of the target subjects. Although these findings support the importance of structure as a factor affecting validity, they do not facilitate the identification of which structures or procedures might be associated with the greatest validity. Because the content validity of a particular analogue assessment situation depends upon its function, additional research is needed to determine which structures result in the most valid inferences for a particular function. Different structures, for example, will be required depending upon whether the analogue environment is utilized to assess the outcome of behavioral intervention, to diagnose dysfunctional families, or to assess parent-child interaction from a developmental perspective.

In reference to parent-child interaction, it is frequently important to identify the observation situation that results in the greatest degree of discriminant validity (the situation that best discriminates between families classed on the basis of another variable—such as clinic or non-clinic) or of criterion-related validity (the situation that best predicts, or is most highly correlated with, other measures of behavior emitted in the natural environment). It might be expected that structured environments resembling a living room, bedroom, or playroom, as opposed to "clinical observation" environments, would result in a greater degree of external validity (Hughes and Haynes, 1978), but the relationship between structure and validity has not been sufficiently investigated.

Recently published studies have noted changes in parent-child interactions in analogue environments as a result of behavioral intervention (Forehand and King, 1977; Hobbs, Forehand, and Murray, 1978; Kent and others, 1977b; Koegel, Clahn, and

Nieminen, 1978). Although changes in parent-child interaction in analogue observation situations suggest that this assessment instrument may be sensitive to intervention effects, it does not follow that similar behavior changes have occurred in the natural environment (Forehand and Atkeson, 1977), and caution should be exercised in evaluating intervention effects on the basis of analogue assessment. Additional criterion validity data are needed to assess generalization of these effects to the natural environment.

Several studies have addressed the issue of external and internal validity of analogue assessment procedures. Reisinger and Ora (1977) reported a well-conceptualized multimodal assessment study involving parent-child interaction and the effects of parent training for behavior problem children. Subjects were ten mother-child pairs with problem interactions and ten mother-child pairs that served as nonproblem controls. Parent-child interactions were observed for twenty minutes in a 3.5 by 4.5 meter observation room by two observers separated from each other by a wood partition. The observation situation was unstructured except that each mother was instructed to give at least five commands during the session. Mother and child behaviors were scored by both graduate students and parent volunteers, who used categories similar to those utilized by Wahler, House, and Stambaugh (1966). Parent-child interactions were also observed by two trained observers in the home for twenty minutes following clinic visits. During the home visits, parents were instructed to engage in routine activities, and mothers were equipped with radio transmitters. The transmitters, worn for two hours following the observation sessions, were automatically activated during the last thirty minutes of the two-hour period. Live observations and transmitted tapes were coded by the same system utilized for the analogue assessment.

Reisinger and Ora then utilized a multitrait-multimethod matrix model to evaluate the convergent and divergent validity of the two assessment procedures. Table 8, derived from a table presented by the authors, summarizes this application of standard measurement theory to behavioral observation data. Table 8 is a *model* correlation matrix representing a study in which three behaviors are observed by two different methods, such as self-monitoring and analogue observation, or in two different situations, such as the

**Table 8. Multitrait-Multimethod Matrix Model for Observation Data from Two Sources**

| | Observation Method 1 | | | Observation Method 2 | | |
| | Behavior 1 | Behavior 2 | Behavior 3 | Behavior 1 | Behavior 2 | Behavior 3 |
|---|---|---|---|---|---|---|
| **Observation Method 1** | | | | | | |
| Behavior 1 | a | d | d | b | c | c |
| Behavior 2 | d | a | d | c | b | c |
| Behavior 3 | d | d | a | c | c | b |
| **Observation Method 2** | | | | | | |
| Behavior 1 | b | c | c | a | d | d |
| Behavior 2 | c | b | c | d | a | d |
| Behavior 3 | c | c | b | d | d | a |

*Note:* $a$ = Monomethod-monobehavior (interobserver agreement), $b$ = Heterobehavior-monobehavior (validity), $c$ = Heterobehavior-heteromethod, and $d$ = Heterobehavior-monomethod.

*Source:* Reisinger and Ora (1977)

home and clinic. Inferences about the validity of the assessment methods or situations are derived by comparing correlation coefficients, $a$, $b$, $c$, and $d$. High criterion validity (and therefore construct validity) would be indicated by elevated correlation coefficients for $b$ (heteromethod-monobehavior) and low correlations for $c$ and $d$. This pattern of coefficients would suggest a high correlation between rates of the same behavior observed in the home and in the analogue situation. Assuming that other behaviors are not part of the same response class or that they do not covary, low correlation coefficients between different behaviors in the same situation and different behaviors in different situations would be expected. Monomethod-monobehavior coefficients ($a$) are derived from the agreement between two observers. Support for the construct validity of the naturalistic and analogue assessment procedures in the Reisinger and Ora study was suggested by correlation coefficients approximating .8 for two of the three $b$s and low correlations for the $c$s and $d$s. Although their study provides strong support for the validity of analogue assessment of parent-child interaction, its greatest contribution is that it serves as a general model for the criterion and construct validation of behavioral observation procedures.

A study by Snyder (1977) provided support for the discriminant validity of analogue assessment of parent-child interactions. Ten problem and ten nonproblem families, defined by Locke-Wallace marital adjustment scores, were observed for forty-five minutes in a structured environment resembling a playroom and living room. Interactions were videotaped and the behavior of each family member rated during six-second time samples. Snyder reported that parents in problem families emitted more aversive consequences and fewer positive consequences for prosocial behavior and more positive and fewer negative consequences for deviant behavior than those in nonproblem families.

Prinz and Kent (1978) reported one of the few studies in which analogue assessment was used with adolescent-parent dyads. Thirty-eight distressed and forty nondistressed mother-adolescent dyads were instructed to converse for ten minutes about an area of change desired by the adolescents (aged eleven to fifteen). Four raters, blind to experimental hypotheses and procedures, listened to the tape recordings of these discussions and afterward rated both mother and adolescent on the occurrence or nonoccurrence of thirty-one positive and negative behaviors. Ratings were summed across seven behavior categories and averaged across the four raters; all were found to discriminate between groups at the .01 level of confidence. The study therefore provided strong support for the discriminant validity of this analogue assessment procedure.

Support for the discriminant validity of analogue assessment of parent-child interaction is also evident in a study of Zegiob and Forehand (1978) in which twenty-eight mother-child pairs from middle and lower socioeconomic classes were observed for thirty-two minutes in a playroom equipped for observation. Eight mother and three child behaviors were coded, and the authors noted significant differences in behavior rates between the two groups of dyads. As part of the same study, the authors investigated the reactive effects associated with observation. In a counterbalanced design, each parent-child dyad underwent a sixteen-minute condition in which they were told they were being observed and a sixteen-minute condition in which they were told they were not being observed (they were told the equipment was broken). There were significant differences between the two conditions in all maternal behaviors except "negative verbal." Thus, the Zegiob and Forehand study provided support for the discriminant validity of analogue assessment of parent-child interaction and further documentation of the reactive effects associated with observation.

Two discussion articles with implications for analogue assessment of parent-child interactions have been published recently (Forehand and Atkeson, 1977; Hughes and Haynes, 1978). Forehand and Atkeson addressed the issues of generalization of treatment effects and stressed the importance of assessing temporal, setting, behavioral, and sibling generality. These authors reiterated the importance of assessing setting generality with respect to the effects of behavioral intervention programs in naturalistic settings as well as in analogue assessment environments. Hughes and Haynes (1978) reviewed studies involving the analogue assessment of parent-child interaction. To summarize, the authors noted: (1) a restricted age range of children served as target subjects—few adolescents had been assessed with analogue situations; (2) considerable variation among studies in the structure of assessment environments used; (3) considerable variation among studies in the behaviors targeted for observation and an underutilization of self-report measures; (4) satisfactory levels of interobserver agreement; (5) an acceptable degree of stability in behaviors across sessions in some studies but, generally, insufficient investigation of behavioral stability or reliability; (6) variance in the degree of stability as a function of the target behavior and structure of the assessment environment; (7) strong evidence supporting the sensitivity of analogue assessment to the effects of behavioral intervention; (8) varying degrees of content validity across studies; (9) support for the validity of analogue observation situations in discriminating problem and nonproblem families; and (10) insufficient research on the criterion-related validity (setting generality) of analogue assessment.

In view of the importance of analogue observation in behavioral assessment and the reactive effects possibly associated with this assessment instrument (Zegiob and Forehand, 1978), it is notable that we could locate only one recently published study (Reisinger and Ora, 1977) that directly assessed the criterion-related or external validity of analogue assessment of parent-child interaction. This deficiency is particularly significant in view of the frequency with which analogue assessment is used to evaluate the outcome of behavioral intervention. It is also notable that no recently published study used analogue observation as a preintervention assessment instrument to identify problem parent-child interactions. From recent publications, there is little indication that analogue assessment is being used to select target behaviors or to develop behavioral intervention strategies with families. The role of analogue observation in the assessment of parent-child interactions seems to be confined to basic research in developmental and child psychology and to one measure of behavioral intervention outcomes.

In summary, the assessment of adult-child interaction in analogue laboratory situations has played an important role in the evaluation of behavioral family intervention and in developmental and child psychology research. The importance of generalization from the laboratory to the natural environment, as well as the reliability and validity of this assessment procedure, has been emphasized by Forehand and Atkeson (1977) and Hughes and Haynes (1978). Only studies by Zegiob and Forehand (1978), Prinz and Kent (1978), Reisinger and Ora (1977), and Snyder (1977), however, have directly evaluated the validity of this assessment instrument. Additional validity studies, particularly those addressing external criterion validity, are needed, along with a further assessment of behavior stability across sessions, the content validity of various structured observation situations, and time-sampling and behavior-sampling parameters. The interdependence of structure, function, and application in analogue assessment should be stressed. The most valid structure for analogue assessment of parent-child interaction will vary as a function of whether the goal is to evaluate the outcome of behavioral intervention, select target behaviors for intervention, discriminate between subject groupings, or assess the effect of extraneous factors on parent-child interaction. Similarly, the importance and necessity of evaluating the external validity of the instrument will vary with its function. Therefore, an evaluation of the adequacy of an analogue observation situation must be sensitive to the idiosyncrasies of its application.

## Child Behavior

Table 9 presents an overview of recently published studies involving the analogue assessment of children, either alone or in interaction with peers. Inspection of this table reveals that a large proportion of recently published studies are concerned with developmental or child psychology rather than with behavior assessment or intervention. However, all involve analogue assessment and are included because of their implications for the sensitivity, reliability, and validity of this assessment instrument.

The children assessed within structured environments have included abused children (Reidy, 1977), a "pretranssexual" boy (Rekers and Varni, 1977), autistic children (Bittle and Hake, 1977; Foxx, 1977; Goren, Romanczyk, and Harris, 1977; Lovaas and others, 1977; Romanczyk, 1977; Solnick, Rincover, and Peterson,

**Table 9. Recent Studies Involving Analogue Assessment of Children**

| Reference | Subjects | Assessment Situation | Comments |
|---|---|---|---|
| Baer, Ascione, and Casto (1977) | Four behavior problem children (aged six to twelve years) in special education classroom | Structured observation room in school | Outcome study of behavioral token program |
| Barkley (1977b) | Thirty-six boys (aged five to twelve years); eighteen diagnosed as "hyperkinetic" | Variety of observation rooms: laboratory playroom, movie room, and so forth | Behavioral pharmacology study; assessed effects of methylphenidate (Ritalin) on activity level and attention |
| Berman, Monda, and Myerscough (1977) | Eighty children (aged thirty-two to sixty-three months) | Structured situation in day-care center | Studied reactions of young children to an infant |
| Bittle and Hake (1977) | Eight-year-old autistic boy with self-stimulatory behaviors | Several laboratory rooms | Studied generalization of behavioral intervention program across settings |
| Brody, Lahey, and Combs (1978) | Fifteen four-year-old children | Laboratory playroom | Assessed effects of intermittent modeling by adults |
| Bronson and Pankey (1977) | Forty male and female children | Laboratory playroom | Investigated children's reaction to strange environment |
| Foxx (1977) | Three autistic or retarded children (aged six to eight years) | Structured observation setting | Behavioral intervention outcome study using overcorrection avoidance to increase eye contact of subjects |

**Table 9. Recent Studies Involving Analogue Assessment of Children (Continued)**

| Reference | Subjects | Assessment Situation | Comments |
|---|---|---|---|
| Goren, Romancyzk, and Harris (1977) | Six autistic children with echolaliac speech | Observation setting in development disability center | Assessed effects of antecedent and consequent events on echolaliac speech |
| Hay (1977) | Sixteen normal infants | Suite of laboratory observation rooms | Assessed "following" and "exploration" behavior of infants |
| Jacklin and Maccoby (1978) | Thirty-three-month-old children | Structured observation setting with mothers present | Assessed social interaction between same-sex and opposite-sex pairs of children |
| Johnston and others (1977) | Eighteen nursery school children | Structured laboratory setting with toys | Found that laboratory measures of aggression were correlated with criteria measures |
| Lamb (1978) | Twenty-four infants and their preschool siblings | Structured observation setting; elements from typical home (couch, dishwasher, oven, slide, and toys) | Assessed interaction between infants and their preschool siblings and differences in behavior between the two groups |
| Lasky (1977) | Five infants | Structured observation setting | Assessed reaching, contact, and retrieval behavior of infants |
| Lieberman (1977) | Forty children (aged two to three years) | Structured observation setting; unstructured play | Assessed interaction with mother, stranger, or peers |
| Lovaas and others (1977) | Six autistic and normal children | Variety of structured observation environments | Assessed components of speech for autistic and normal children |

| Study | Sample | Setting | Description |
|---|---|---|---|
| Mueller and Brenner (1977) | Twelve male children | Television studio playroom | Investigated social skills and interaction among young children |
| Mueller and others (1977) | Three boys (aged twenty-one to thirty-three months) | Laboratory playroom; two thirty-minute sessions per week for eleven months | Investigated social interaction and verbal responsiveness |
| Pipp and Gaith (1977) | Infants | Structured observation setting | Assessed infant visual scanning as a function of stimulus characteristics |
| Reidy (1977) | Twenty abused, sixteen nonabused but neglected, and twenty-two normal children | Laboratory playroom; twenty-minute observation period | Focused on aggressive behavior; abused children emitted higher rates of aggressive behavior |
| Rekers (1975) | Normal and gender-disturbed boys | Laboratory playroom | Evaluated feminine mannerisms of normal and gender-disturbed boys |
| Rekers and Varni (1977) | Six-year-old "pre-transsexual" boy | Playroom situation with "masculine" and "feminine" toys | Behavioral intervention outcome study |
| Rekers and others (1977) and Rekers, Amaro-Plotkin, and Low (1977) | Forty-eight normal boys and girls | Structured observation setting | Established norms for sex-typed mannerisms of boys and girls |
| Rogers-Warren, Warren, and Baer (1977) | Eight four-year-olds | Daycare center playroom | Multiple-baseline study of sharing and effects of various interventions |

**Table 9. Recent Studies Involving Analogue Assessment of Children (Continued)**

| Reference | Subjects | Assessment Situation | Comments |
|---|---|---|---|
| Rollings, Baumeister, and Baumeister (1977) | Retarded children | Laboratory setting in mental retardation center | Behavior intervention outcome study that also investigated setting and response generalization |
| Romanczyk (1977) | Self-stimulating boy and girl | Structured observation setting | Behavioral intervention outcome study; assessed effects of varying contingency schedules on self-stimulation |
| Skarin (1977) | Thirty-two normal infants | Structured observation setting | Studied physiological and behavioral responses of infants to approach by stranger |
| Solnick, Rincover, and Peterson (1977) | Autistic children; six-year-old female, sixteen-year-old male | Structured observation setting | Behavioral analysis and intervention outcome study; studied tantrum behavior and effects of time-out |
| Spilton and Lee (1977) | Four-year-old normal children | Laboratory playroom | Assessed changes in speech of children as a function of the listener |
| Strain (1977) | Three behaviorally disordered preschool boys | Laboratory playroom | Investigated effects of peer initiation on social behavior of withdrawn boys |
| Strain, Shores, and Timm (1977) | Six behaviorally handicapped preschool boys | Laboratory playroom | Investigated dyadic interaction of withdrawn boys |

| | | | |
|---|---|---|---|
| Trause (1977) | Infants | Structured observation setting | Studied infants' response to strangers as a function of several factors |
| Wells, Forehand, and Hickey (1977) | Two brothers, ten years old; emotionally disturbed and mentally retarded | Laboratory playroom | Behavioral intervention outcome study; assessed effects, side effects, and generalization of overcorrection procedures |
| Wells and others (1977) | Two brothers, ten years old; emotionally disturbed and mentally retarded | Laboratory playroom | Behavioral intervention outcome study that investigated response generalization |
| Young-Browne, Rosenfeld, and Horowitz (1977) | Twenty-four infants | Structured observation setting | Assessed infants' visual discrimination of facial expressions |

1977), children variously characterized as "behavior problems," "retarded," "developmentally disabled," "emotionally disturbed," or "emotionally handicapped" (Baer, Ascione, and Casto, 1977; Foxx, 1977; Newsom and Simon, 1977; Rollings, Baumeister, and Baumeister, 1977; Strain, 1977; Strain, Shores, and Timm, 1977; Wells, Forehand, and Hickey, 1977; Wells and others, 1977), hyperkinetic children (Barkley, 1977b), and "normal" children and infants (Berman, Monda, and Myerscough, 1977; Brody, Lahey, and Combs, 1978; Bronson and Pankey, 1977; Hay, 1977; Jacklin and Maccoby, 1978; Johnston and others, 1977; Lamb, 1978; Lasky, 1977; Lieberman, 1977; Pipp and Gaith, 1977; Rogers-Warren, Warren, and Baer, 1977; Trause, 1977; Young-Browne, Rosenfeld, and Horowitz, 1977). Table 9 confirms the point made in the previous section of this chapter that structured assessment settings are seldom utilized in the assessment of adolescents.

In the assessment of child behaviors, the structure of the analogue environment has varied widely. As indicated in Table 9, some investigations used a minimally modified laboratory or clinic setting equipped with observation and recording facilities. Others utilized assessment settings that were designed to approximate the natural environment—for example, a living room or playroom. Some studies (Baer, Ascione, and Casto, 1977; Barkley, 1977b; Berman, Monda, and Myerscough, 1977; Goren, Romanczyk, and Harris, 1977; Rogers-Warren, Warren, and Baer, 1977; Rollings, Baumeister, and Baumeister, 1977) involved the isolation or modification of a part of the natural environment to serve as an analogue assessment environment. The functions of the analogue assessment with children have also varied widely. In addition to its use for basic developmental and child psychology research, analogue assessment has been used to assess the effects of behavioral intervention programs with children (Baer, Ascione, and Casto, 1977; Bittle and Hake, 1977; Foxx, 1977; Rekers and Varni, 1977; Romanczyk, 1977; Wells and others, 1977), for systematic behavioral analysis of problem child behaviors (Goren, Romanczyk, and Harris, 1977; Lovaas and others, 1977; Rekers, 1975; Romanczyk, 1977; Strain, Shores, and Timm, 1977), and to establish normative data for sex-role behaviors of children (Rekers and others, 1977; Rekers, Amaro-Plotkin, and Low, 1977). As in the assessment of parent-child interaction, there is little indication that analogue assessment is being used as a preintervention assessment instrument for the identification of problem behaviors or program planning. When structured assessment situations are utilized in conjunction with behavioral intervention programs, the programs are designed independently of data derived from the assessment.

Several recently published studies have indicated that analogue assessment can be sensitive to the effects of behavioral intervention and result in data with discriminant and criterion validity. All previously cited behavioral intervention studies using analogue assessment reported significant changes in the behavior of target children as a function of behavioral intervention. In addition, several studies (Barkley, 1977b; Bronson and Pankey, 1977; Goren, Romanczyk, and Harris, 1977; Hay, 1977; Jacklin and Maccoby, 1978; Pipp and Gaith, 1977; Skarin, 1977; Spilton and Lee, 1977; Strain, 1977; Trause, 1977) have noted that the behavior of subjects within analogue settings varies according to the stimuli within the assessment environment (such as the behavior of others or modification of physical stimuli). The sensitivity of analogue assessment is further exemplified by the finding of several researchers (Mueller and Brenner, 1977; Spilton and Lee, 1977; Strain, 1977) that the behavior of target subjects is influenced by the behavior of other participants in the environment. The implication of this finding is that, because of the sensitivity of analogue assessment to transient environmental factors, researchers and clinicians using this procedure with children need to exert special care in structuring the analogue environment.

Several innovative applications of analogue assessment with children should be noted. Rekers (Rekers and Varni, 1977; Rekers and others, 1977; Rekers, Amaro-Plotkin, and Low, 1977) used structured observation settings to investigate gender identity problems under the assumption that boys who emit a high frequency of "feminine" behaviors are likely to encounter adverse social reactions in later life. Rekers set up an analogue laboratory situation involving "boy" and "girl" toys and activities. The dependent variable was the proportion of time spent in gender-specific activities. This analogue situation was used as a method of assessing the outcome of behavioral intervention programs. Although the studies may be questioned on the basis of social mores (boys with gender identity problems are rated as "improved" if they play with toys such as rubber knives and toy guns), this assessment procedure has been shown to discriminate among normal boys, normal girls, and boys with gender identity problems and to be sensitive to the effects of intervention.

Barkley (1977b) used analogue assessment situations to evaluate the effects of methylphenidate (Ritalin) on the activity level and attention of eighteen hyperkinetic and eighteen normal boys. In a cross-over design involving drug and placebo ingestion, Barkley employed a number of assessment instruments (such as a stabilimetric chair and a reaction-time test) and a grid-marked playroom to investigate placebo and drug effects on activity level and attention span. All measures except seat movement were consistent with the hypothesis that methylphenidate was more effective than the placebo in decreasing activity levels of hyperkinetic children. Attention span, indicated by the number of toy changes and mean time spent with each toy in the structured environment, was also noted to increase with methylphenidate ingestion. Unfortunately, the authors did not evaluate the generalization of these changes to the natural environment.

Several studies have evaluated the criterion validity of analogue assessment of child behaviors by utilizing other dependent measures of the target behaviors. Skarin (1977) monitored heart rate, selected behaviors, and facial expression of thirty-two infants (aged five to seven months and ten to twelve months) in the home and in a structured laboratory situation. The behavior of each infant in these two situations was assessed with its mother present, with its mother absent, and when approached by a stranger. Increases in heart rate were associated with behavioral indicators of distress (crying and other negative responses). Significant differences in responses were found between the home and the laboratory settings and between older and younger infants. Although these results were interpreted within a developmental context, they also suggest that the behavior of infants when approached by a stranger in a laboratory setting is not indicative of their responses to a stranger at home.

Although deviating from a behavioral construct system,

Lieberman (1977) utilized a multimethod assessment approach in evaluating the "social competence" of forty children (aged two to three). Assessment procedures included home observations of mother-child and stranger-child interactions, interviews with mothers about anxiety, dependency, and social behaviors of the child, and questionnaires. The social interaction of the children was also observed while they were in an unstructured analogue situation. Ratings of social adequacy with peers in the analogue observation setting (peer competence, responsiveness, and reciprocal interaction) were significantly associated with reports of low anxiety at home and inversely related to "maladaptive maternal attitudes toward the expression of aggression" and "restrictive maternal attitudes" (1977, p. 1277). In sum, the social behavior of the target children in an analogue assessment situation was found to be significantly related to a number of parental self-report and questionnaire measures. In another nonbehavioral study, Johnston and others (1977) observed aggressive behaviors of preschool children in a laboratory playroom. Eighteen nursery school children were independently observed for ten minutes in a playroom containing toys. Four indices of aggression were recorded: kicking or hitting a doll, throwing toys, pounding toys in ground, and hitting a puppet or stuffed bear. The authors reported that observation measures of aggression correlated significantly with peer ratings of aggressiveness (.76) and with teacher ratings of aggressiveness (.57) but did not significantly correlate with self-ratings of aggressiveness.

A study examining setting generality was reported by Bittle and Hake (1977), who utilized four different assessment-intervention settings in treating a nine-year-old autistic boy for self-stimulatory behavior. Two rooms served for treatment and two additional rooms served to assess generalization of treatment effects. Although inferences about the generality of assessment data were confounded with the generality of treatment effects, the authors implemented a multicomponent intervention program and reported that decreases in self-stimulation rates in the treatment rooms were accompanied by corresponding decreases in the rate of those behaviors in assessment rooms in which treatment had not occurred. Romanczyk (1977) also reported a study in which the self-stimulatory behavior of both a young girl and a young boy was suppressed with variable- and fixed-ratio punishment. (Reduction in self-stimulation accompanying punishment was also associated with reductions in self-stimulatory behavior in rooms in which contingencies were not applied.) In addition, Romanczyk reported that significant positive side effects, such as increased play, social behavior, and academic performance, accompanied the reduction in self-stimulatory behavior.

Rollings, Baumeister, and Baumeister (1977) assessed the setting generality of overcorrection treatment of stereotypic behaviors of retarded individuals. Intervention and assessment in two single-subject (A-B-A-B) studies occurred in a structured laboratory setting in a mental retardation center, and the authors assessed generalization to the natural environment (a ward of the retardation center). The authors demonstrated that, although intervention effects were under the control of specific discriminative stimuli (distance between experimenter and subject), they were able to generalize from laboratory treatment setting to the natural environment. As noted, caution must be exercised in interpreting the studies cited above because they are primarily tests of the setting generality of *intervention* rather than of assessment. Nevertheless, these studies are consistent in suggesting that the behavior of children in analogue observation settings is significantly correlated with their behavior in naturalistic settings.

In summary, some, but not all, recently published studies have suggested that the rates of certain child behaviors in analogue observation settings are significantly related to other measures of the same or collateral behaviors. Although these studies tend to support the validity and generalizability of analogue assessment of child behavior, several limitations should be noted. First, not all criterion-related measures are convergent with behavior rates derived from analogue assessment (as in Johnston and others, 1977). Second, although the correlation coefficients between measures are statistically significant, in most cases the proportion of variance ($R^2$) in behavior rates in one assessment situation accounted for by knowledge of data from another situation is unimpressive. For example, in the study by Johnston and others, only 36 percent of the variance in rate of aggressive behavior in the analogue assessment situation was accounted for by measures of teacher ratings of aggression. This suggests that, although the aggressive behavior of children in a structured observation setting may be significantly correlated with their behavior in the natural environment or with the teacher's perception of their behavior, naturalistic behavior or others' perception of it is more complexly determined. Because of situation specificity and variance in behavior determinants, it is illogical to expect that one assessment procedure will account for nearly all the variance on another measure.

Several recently published articles have also presented evidence relating to the discriminant validity of analogue assessment of child behaviors. *Discriminant validity* is most clearly indicated by the degree to which data from analogue assessment can be used to correctly identify subjects who are classed on the basis of naturally occurring events, such as hospitalized versus nonhospitalized. Rekers (1975), Rekers, Amaro-Plotkin, and Low (1977), and Rekers and others (1977) provided evidence that analogue assessment can discriminate among normal boys, normal girls, and "pretranssexual" boys on measures of sex-role play and mannerisms, noting that the rate of "feminine" mannerisms and the characteristics of toy play (amount of play with "masculine" and "feminine" toys) validly discriminated among these groups of subjects. Reidy (1977) assessed the rates of aggressive behavior of twenty abused children, sixteen nonabused but neglected children, and twenty-two normal children in an analogue observation setting. Two trained observers rated the frequency of aggressive behaviors during a twenty-minute session in a laboratory/playroom situation. Abused children emitted higher rates of aggressive behavior than did nonabused; this finding was corroborated by teacher ratings of aggressiveness. Lamb (1978) observed eighteen-month-old infants and their preschool siblings in an analogue setting and noted significant differences in a number of behaviors (such as responses to commands and frequency of imitative behavior) between the two age groups. Jacklin and Maccoby (1978) observed same-sex pairs and opposite-sex pairs of thirty-three-month-old children in an analogue setting and noted significant differences in the behavior of the children as a function of the sex of their partner.

Analogue assessment has thus been used with a variety of child behaviors and behavior problems. The evidence from re-

cently published studies is rather consistent in suggesting that
analogue assessment can be sensitive to the effects of behavioral
intervention with children, that behavior emitted in structured settings can be significantly related to other measures of the same
behavior and to measures of the same behavior in other situations,
and that analogue assessment can discriminate among groups of
children classified on a number of dimensions. Despite the strong
evidence for the sensitivity and validity of this assessment procedure with children, there has been insufficient investigation of a
number of components affecting its utility, including: (1) content
validity of various physical environments and instructions, (2) reliability and temporal factors of the situation, and (3) appropriateness of analogue assessment for different child behaviors.

## Marital Interaction

We could locate only a few recently published studies involving analogue assessment of marital interaction. Brady (1977) briefly
summarized a study, originally published in *Acta Psychiatrica Scan-
dinavia,* in which behavioral intervention procedures were used in
group treatment of dysfunctional marital couples. Structured observation situations (incompletely described) were utilized to assess
communication before and after treatment and were sensitive to
the effects of behavioral intervention. Jacobson (1977) reported a
study in which ten dissatisfied marital couples received either "minimal treatment" or behavioral intervention involving positive interaction training and problem solving. Before and after the interventions, couples were videotaped while trying to resolve an area of
conflict. Trained observers utilizing the Marital Interaction Coding
System (MICS) assessed each couple's skill in problem solving and
determined the rate of reward and punishment behaviors. Significant improvement was noted for the behavioral group but not for
the "minimal treatment" control group. Margolin and Weiss (1978)
presented a single case study illustrating the use of analogue assessment. At each assessment period couples engaged in two videotaped negotiation sessions in which they attempted to resolve a
current problem in their relationship. Each session lasted ten min-

utes, and couples were measured on the degree of "helpfulness" of each spouse's comments and on indices of mutual agreement. The specific behaviors identified as helpful were selected on the basis of interviews with the couple as to which behaviors they found most facilitative (an example of social validation). The results of these studies are consistent with previous findings (reviewed by Haynes, 1978) that analogue assessment of marital communication can provide a sensitive and valid index of communication problems. It has been shown to be sensitive to the effects of behavioral intervention and to discriminate between functional and dysfunctional married couples.

O'Leary and Turkewitz (1978) pointed out some methodological difficulties in using structured communication exercises in the assessment of marital and family functioning. They noted that the content of the conflicts discussed is very seldom controlled but that it can have a critical influence on the data obtained. They also suggested the operation of an age factor (or duration-of-marriage factor) in that, with older couples, a higher degree of induced conflict is usually necessary before the assessment situation can discriminate between functional and dysfunctional couples. They suggested having couples discuss topics related to, but not identical with, marital problems.

Inferences that analogue assessment can function as a valid measure of marital dissatisfaction are constrained by two other considerations. First, the utility of this assessment procedure may be confined to verbal components of the marital relationship. Structured assessment situations have been used primarily to assess verbal interactions and communication skills of married couples and may not be as sensitive to such other marital difficulties as a low rate of reciprocal reinforcement or sexual dysfunction. Although it is likely that verbal interaction covaries with other characteristics of the marital relationship, the specific applicability of analogue assessment of nonverbal components of marital interaction remains to be investigated. Second, analogue structures such as communication exercises, decision making, or game playing are likely to be differentially sensitive to various types of marital dissatisfaction, and researchers should be cognizant of these limitations and attend to the issue of content validity.

## Fear and Anxiety

Analogue observation settings and behavioral avoidance tests (BATs) have frequently been used to assess overt behavioral, physiological, and subjective components of fear and anxiety. In the typical assessment situation, a subject is requested to approach a feared object or stimulus or engage in a feared behavior. Dependent measures may include subjective reports of discomfort during the approach to the feared stimulus, distance of the closest approach to the feared stimulus, physiological indices of arousal during the approach, and behavioral indices of anxiety (such as hands shaking and tremors). Table 10 summarizes recently published studies involving analogue assessment of fear behavior.

Analogue observation settings have been used in the assessment of a variety of fears, although target stimuli have involved relatively specific fears—for example, fears of small animals, tests, speeches, and heights. Specific fears are, undoubtedly, more amenable than general fears, such as fear of rejection or failure, to assessment in analogue situations. The content and structure of the assessment situation have been similar across studies; in most cases, subjects have been requested to physically approach the feared stimulus or perform a feared behavior in an environment dissimilar to the natural environment. Except for a study by Jeger and Goldfried (1976), all recently published studies involving the analogue assessment of fear have been used only to assess the outcome of behavioral intervention.

The sensitivity of analogue fear assessment to intervention effects is indicated by the finding that in all cited studies at least one dependent measure taken during the analogue assessment changed to a significant degree as a function of treatment or that the analogue situation discriminated between subjects undergoing different interventions. Thus, within the constraints of the population and structures utilized, analogue assessment appears to be a sensitive measure of treatment effects on fear behavior. However, it should also be noted that several authors reported that some dependent variables monitored during the analogue fear assessments were insensitive to treatment effects (Fremouw and Zitter, 1978; Gallagher and Arkowitz, 1978; Peck, 1977; Wroblewski, Jacob, and

**Table 10. Recent Studies Involving Analogue Assessment of Fear**

| Reference | Subjects | Assessment Situation | Comments |
|---|---|---|---|
| Barrera and Rosen (1977) | Snake-fearful subjects | Standard behavioral avoidance test (BAT) with snakes | Assessed components of self-administered desensitization |
| Cohen (1977) | Height-fearful subjects | Approaching window, stairwell, and railing on fourteenth-fifteenth floor of building | Criterion validity study with multiple dependent measures of fear of heights |
| Efran and others (1977) | Subjects with miscellaneous fears (spiders, rats, snakes, and beetles) | Standard BAT situation | BAT was sensitive to treatment instructions |
| Fremouw and Zitter (1978) | Speech-anxious undergraduate students | Four-minute speech | Controlled study of effects of skills training and cognitive restructuring on speech anxiety |
| Gallagher and Arkowitz (1978) | Subjects with test anxiety | Timed anagrams test | Controlled study of effects of covert modeling on test anxiety |
| Gatchel and others (1977) | Speech-fearful subjects | Three-minute speech with observers present | Behavioral intervention outcome study comparing heart-rate control and relaxation |
| Gautheir and Marshall (1977) | Rat-fearful subjects | Standard BAT with rats | Evaluated effects of various exposure durations in flooding intervention |

**Table 10. Recent Studies Involving Analogue Assessment of Fear (Continued)**

| Reference | Subjects | Assessment Situation | Comments |
|---|---|---|---|
| Goldfried and Goldfried (1977) | Speech-fearful subjects | Four-minute speech preceded by five-minute preparation; videotaped | Behavioral intervention outcome study comparing hierarchy and relaxation components of self-desensitization |
| Goldfried, Lineham, and Smith (1978) | Test-anxious undergraduate students | Tested in small groups on tests derived from Wechsler Adult Intelligence Scale (WAIS) and Wonderlic personnel test; informed that IQ was being assessed | Controlled study of effects of cognitive restructuring on test anxiety |
| Hamilton and Bornstein (1977a) | Speech-fearful subjects | Speech given in front of two other individuals; behavior covertly recorded | Assessed component of self-monitoring and instructions program for speech skills |
| Hekmat (1977) | Snake-fearful subjects | Standard BAT with snakes | Assessed outcome of semantic behavior therapy |
| Jeger and Goldfried (1976) | Speech-fearful subjects | Speech situation in which subjects were informed that they would be observed | Criterion validity assessment of speech in structured observation situation |
| Kirsch and Henry (1977) | Speech-fearful subjects | Four-minute speech | Behavioral intervention outcome study assessing desensitization and control procedures |

| Author (Year) | Subjects | Situation/Measure | Description |
|---|---|---|---|
| Lineham and others (1977) | Multiple fears (spiders, height, and speech) | Height—subjects attempted to climb fire escape; spider—standard BAT; speech—three-minute speech on fixed topic while the experimenter watched | Behavioral intervention outcome study with modeling |
| Marchetti, McGlynn, and Patterson (1977) | Test-anxious subjects | Structured test-taking situations with physiological measures | Behavioral intervention outcome study on relaxation procedures |
| Marshall, Stoian, and Andrews (1977) | Speech-fearful subjects | Speech situation | Behavioral intervention outcome study involving desensitization and skills training |
| Peck (1977) | Mildly retarded height- or rat-fearful subjects | Standard BAT (approaching metal escape grate for fear of heights) | Behavioral intervention outcome study with desensitization; BAT was not sensitive |
| Rosen, Glasgow, and Barrera (1977) | Snake-fearful subjects | Standard BAT with snakes | Assessed predictive validity of several measures of treatment success |
| Rosenthal, Hung, and Kelley (1977) | Snake-fearful subjects | Standard BAT with snakes | Assessed effects of social influence on performance during BAT |
| Slutsky and Allen (1978) | Speech-anxious undergraduate students | Two and one-half minute speech on assigned topic | Controlled study of effects of desensitization and contextual cues in treatment of speech anxiety |

**Table 10. Recent Studies Involving Analogue Assessment of Fear (Continued)**

| Reference | Subjects | Assessment Situation | Comments |
|---|---|---|---|
| Sullivan and Denny (1977) | Snake-fearful subjects | Standard BAT with snakes | Assessed effects of expectancy and fear level on desensitization outcome |
| Thomas and Rapp (1977) | Man with eyepatch phobia | BAT with eye patch | Behavioral intervention outcome study of flooding |
| Weissberg (1977) | Speech-fearful subjects | Speech situation | Behavioral intervention outcome study involving desensitization and skills training |
| Wroblewski, Jacob, and Rehm (1977) | Subjects with dental fears | BAT involving dental office situation | Behavioral intervention outcome study involving relaxation and symbolic modeling; BAT nonsensitive |

Rehm, 1977). This finding supports the contention that validity is a function not only of the structure of a particular analogue assessment situation but also of the dependent measures selected. For example, it is a logical but unsupported assumption that a behavioral avoidance test (BAT) may be a more valid indicator of behavioral than of cognitive components of fear behavior.

Several types of dependent measures have been used in BATs. Because almost all BATs involve approaching a feared stimulus in a graded series of steps, the most common dependent measure is the number of graded steps completed (or final distance between subject and stimulus). This provides one measure of degree of behavioral avoidance. Thus, subjects have been scored on their approach to and contact with snakes, rats, and spiders or on their approach to acrophobic stimuli (looking out windows). As indicated by Cohen (1977), however, such data are not on an interval scale but are often treated with statistics that are based on interval scale requirements. Self-reports of subjective discomfort or anxiety during analogue fear assessment have also been monitored in recently published studies. Typically, subjects are asked to indicate verbally their level of discomfort on a predetermined scale at various stages of approach to the feared stimulus. Although not done in recently published studies, a comparison of subjective and behavioral fear measures might help identify classes of fear behavior (anxious-nonavoidance, nonanxious-avoidance) and might be helpful in selecting the most appropriate intervention.

Psychophysiological measures have also been used in several analogue fear assessment studies (Gatchel and others, 1977; Gautheir and Marshall, 1977; Goldfried and Goldfried, 1977; Marchetti, McGlynn, and Patterson, 1977; Peck, 1977; Slutsky and Allen, 1978; Thomas and Rapp, 1977). The use of psychophysiological measures provides another means of establishing the internal criterion validity of the assessment instrument and provides data on an important component of fear (see discussion on response fractionation in Chapter Eight). Direct behavioral observation by external observers of subjects during behavioral avoidance tests has also been used as a dependent measure (Fremouw and Zitter, 1978; Gatchel and others, 1977; Gautheir and Marshall, 1977; Goldfried and Goldfried, 1977; Hamilton and Bornstein, 1977a; Jeger and

Goldfried, 1976; Lineham and others, 1977; Marshall and others, 1977; Marshall, Presse, and Andrews, 1977; Marshall, Stoian, and Andrews, 1977; Slutsky and Allen, 1978). Behavioral indices of anxiety (such as hand tremors and verbal dysfluencies) were observed either directly by external observers or through scoring of videotapes. In most cases of direct observation of subjects during analogue fear assessment, however, unvalidated observation and rating systems have been applied (see Chapter Two). Several researchers (Gatchel and others, 1977; Goldfried and Goldfried, 1977; Marshall and others, 1977; Marshall, Presse, and Andrews, 1977; Marshall, Stoian, and Andrews, 1977; Peck, 1977; Slutsky and Allen, 1978) commendably utilized multiple measures during analogue fear assessment. The use of psychophysiological, subjective, and behavioral measures facilitates comprehensive evaluation of the internal validity of the assessment instrument, is highly congruent with the multiple factors in the construct of "fear," and provides a comprehensive evaluation of the outcome of intervention programs.

As noted throughout this chapter, analogue assessment is insufficient to evaluate intervention effects when behavior change in the natural environment is the primary goal. Several recently published studies have provided data on the criterion-related validity (setting generality) of analogue fear assessment. Marchetti, McGlynn, and Patterson (1977), for example, took several measures of test anxiety (physiological measures made during an analogue test-taking situation, the S-R Inventory of Anxiousness, and the Test Anxiety Scale) and found nonsignificant relationships between physiological indices during the structured test-taking situation on the one hand and self-report measures on the other. Hamilton and Bornstein (1977a) utilized self-monitoring and instructions to treat twenty-eight undergraduate students with speech anxiety. To evaluate the outcome of the intervention program, subjects gave a speech in front of two other individuals, and their behavior was recorded for later coding. The authors reported an "impressive" correspondence between self-monitoring data and data from the analogue speech situation.

Research on the criterion-related validity of analogue assessment of speech anxiety was also reported in several recent articles. Jeger and Goldfried (1976) found that a structured observation setting in which subjects were informed that they would be observed when making a speech resulted in a level of anxiety comparable to that elicited in naturalistic speech situations. Goldfried and Goldfried (1977), however, reported nonsignificant correlations between measures of speech anxiety and behavior during an analogue speech situation and the results of several questionnaires (Personal Report of Confidence as a Speaker—Paul, 1966; S-R Inventory of Anxiousness—Endler, Hunt, and Rosenstein, 1962; Fear of Negative Evaluation—Watson and Friend, 1969). Slutsky and Allen (1978) evaluated individual differences in response to desensitization and placebo interventions with speech anxiety and noted congruence in questionnaire and analogue measures in indicating the superiority of desensitization. Marshall, Stoian, and Andrews (1977) utilized several questionnaire measures in addition to analogue assessment for speech anxiety as outcome measures of a self-administered desensitization program. Although a correlation matrix was not provided, the authors reported that all measures demonstrated significant changes as a function of the intervention.

Other studies have noted a correspondence between intervention-effected changes in analogue fear assessment and changes on other measures of the same construct (Goldfried, Lineham, and Smith, 1978; Weissberg, 1977). Peck (1977) used various forms of desensitization to reduce acrophobic behavior in adult retardates. Dependent measures included climbing to the fifth floor of a metal grate fire escape and leaning over and looking at the ground for thirty seconds, Fear Thermometer (subjects were asked how afraid they were), pulse rate, and Fear Survey Schedule. Peck presented a matrix of correlation coefficients among these dependent measures. The subjects' performance on the BAT (approach to the fire escape) correlated .43 with their Fear Survey Schedule (the author did not mention which fear questionnaire was used) and .47 with a behavior checklist involving anxiety signs during the BAT. Peck also noted that the behavior checklist, Fear Thermometer, Fear Survey Schedule, and pulse rate did not demonstrate significant changes as a function of intervention.

A lack of covariance among measures taken during analogue fear assessment and criterion measures has been reported by other authors. Wroblewski, Jacob, and Rehm (1977) compared the effects of symbolic modeling and relaxation on subjects with dental fears. The BAT consisted of successive approximations to full dental treatment beginning with observation of a confederate dentist manipulating dental tools. The final step was allowing a dentist to perform an examination. Scores on several dependent measures (BAT; the Fear Survey Schedule—Rubin and others, 1969; and the Dental Anxiety Scale) were not sensitive to treatment effects, but a measure of the number of subjects performing the terminal response (completing dental treatment) did reflect significant changes following intervention.

Cohen (1977) reported an excellent example of criterion-related validity assessment utilizing multiple dependent measures of acrophobic behavior. Acrophobic subjects were exposed to three behavioral avoidance tests: (1) taking eight graded approach steps to a fourteenth-floor hallway that ended in front of a plate glass window, (2) approaching a fourteenth-floor railing and looking down, and (3) approaching a concrete-walled railing on the fifteenth floor and leaning over the railing. Subjects were also administered the Fear Survey Schedule III, the Willoughby Personality Inventory, and a specially designed Acrophobia Questionnaire (see Chapter Six). Correlation coefficients among the three BATs were .68, .74 and .56, suggesting a moderate level of concordance. On preintervention administration, the correlation coefficient between the BAT and the Acrophobia Questionnaire (avoidance factor) was −.32. The BAT was not significantly related to the Fear Survey Schedule or the Willoughby. Cohen addressed the issue of low correlations between the BAT and other measures but did not find this outcome surprising in view of the fact that the BAT does not involve a naturalistic situation, resultant data are not on an interval scale, and reactive effects attributable to the presence of an observer during the BAT are possible.

Goldfried, Lineham, and Smith (1978) employed multiple measures in the assessment of two cognitive interventions with test anxiety. The analogue assessment occurred in small groups in which the Wonderlic Personnel Test and Digit Span tests from the Wechsler Adult Intelligence Scale (WAIS) were administered after subjects were told that they were going to be administered elements from an IQ test. Subjects were also given a state-trait Anxiety Scale, an anxiety differential, the Worry Scale, and the Taylor Anxiety Scale. Although significant changes were found for all measures after intervention, only one questionnaire measure (the Worry Scale) differentiated between the two experimental cognitive anxiety-reduction procedures. Lick and Unger (1977) also addressed the issue of the external validity of analogue fear assessment. These authors noted that the level of association between measures is probably a function of such factors as the reactivity due to the artificial laboratory situation and the demand characteristics of the assessment situation. They suggested that higher correlation coefficients could be expected if the content of the self-report measures were similar to the stimuli encountered in the analogue situation.

The articles cited above suggest that analogue assessment of fear behavior can have a moderate to high degree of external validity but that the degree of association with criteria measures is a function of several variables, particularly the degree of similarity between stimuli on the BAT and stimuli on the criterion measure. Another factor affecting the validity of analogue fear assessment is the reactivity inherent in the assessment instrument. Performance in the analogue situation is therefore probably indicative of performance in the natural environment only when the conditions in the natural environment approximate those of the analogue situation.

The degree of concordance between measures of behavior in analogue and naturalistic environments reflects on the content validity of the analogue assessment situation. Those analogue situations that resemble the natural environment would be expected to provide a more generalizable measure of the targeted behavior. This issue was addressed by Thomas and Rapp (1977), who noted that inconsistent findings about the effects of implosive therapy may be as easily attributable to inappropriateness of the analogue assessments employed as to ineffectiveness of the procedure. They stressed the importance of multimodal measures in analogue evaluation of fear and intervention outcome because the mode of expected effect varies between therapies. Implosive therapy, for example, may be expected to produce maximum effects in psychophysiological response systems while covert rehearsal procedures may produce maximum effects in overt approach behaviors.

As noted previously, several researchers (Goldfried and Goldfried, 1977; Hamilton and Bornstein, 1977a; Jeger and Goldfried, 1976) found that the presence of an observer during an analogue speech by a speech-anxious subject or informing the subject that the speech would be observed from behind a one-way mirror increased the sensitivity and validity of the analogue assessment. These findings serve to underscore the assumption that inferences about the validity of a specific analogue situation for assessing fear are limited to the specific assessment procedures and stimuli used. It cannot be assumed that high validity coefficients for one analogue assessment situation are generalizable to other analogue situations or to the assessment of other target behaviors in the same analogue situation.

Recently published studies also have implications for the utility of analogue fear assessments in *predicting* the outcome of interventions designed to reduce fear. Rosen, Glasgow, and Barrera (1977) analyzed data from a previous study involving the treatment of snake-fearful subjects. Subjects had participated in preintervention and postintervention analogue assessments, and at a two-year follow-up the authors ascertained the degree to which the subjects were able to engage in previously avoided activities in the natural environment. The authors reported a modest correlation coefficient (.25) between performance on the postintervention BAT and improvement noted at follow-up. Correlations between follow-up reports on the one hand and Fear Survey Schedule and general ratings of fear level on the other, however, were stronger (−.46 and −.64, respectively). This study, therefore, provided only weak support for the predictive validity of analogue fear assessment but stronger support for the validity of self-report measures in predicting behavior change in the natural environment at a two-year follow-up. Sullivan and Denny (1977) assessed the relationship between performance on a preintervention analogue fear assessment and the outcome of an intervention program aimed at decreasing snake anxiety. They reported no significant relationship between the BAT and therapy outcome.

In summary, analogue assessment has recently been applied with a variety of fears, including speech and test anxiety, fear of small animals and heights, and dental fears. The majority of studies have employed analogue assessment as one of several measures of treatment outcome and have indicated that, in most cases, it appears to be a sensitive indicator of treatment effects. Several types of dependent measures have been taken during the analogue assessments, including approximation to a feared stimulus, self-report of discomfort, psychophysiological measures, and direct observation of "anxiety" behaviors. Evidence is generally consistent in supporting the internal and external criterion-related validity of this assessment procedure, but the degree of generalizability varies and is probably a function of the dependent variables selected and the structure and content validity of the analogue assessment situations. Several authors have noted a lack of covariance between analogue and criterion measures, and findings concerning the validity of analogue measures in predicting treatment effects have been mixed. Issues of reactivity, constraints on inferences of validity, and sources of error were noted.

## Social Skills

Several recently published studies have involved analogue assessment of social skills. Targeted populations have included psychiatric inpatients (Bellack, Hersen, and Turner, 1978; Finch and Wallace, 1977; Marziller and Winter, 1978; Matson and Stephens, 1978), heterosexuals and homosexuals (Russell and Winkler, 1977), drug abusers (Zeichner, Pihl, and Wright, 1977), children (Bornstein, Bellack, and Hersen, 1977), alcoholics (Kelly and others, 1978), and the elderly (Edinberg, Karoly, and Gleser, 1977). These studies, as well as studies dealing with college student populations, have been summarized in Table 11.

Two studies will be presented to illustrate the typical format of analogue assessment of social skills. D.P. Greenwald (1977) assessed differences on a number of measures between high-frequency and low-frequency female daters. Greenwald suggested that, because the roles and behavior patterns of males and females differ in dating situations, different skills are required for each and inferences derived from research on one sex probably cannot be generalized to the other. In Greenwald's study, high- and low-

**Table 11. Recent Studies Involving Analogue Assessment of Social Skills**

| Reference | Subjects | Assessment Situation | Comments |
|---|---|---|---|
| Bellack, Hersen, and Turner (1978) | Psychiatric inpatients | Behavioral assertiveness test—response to social cues presented by model | Two studies evaluating the reliability, validity, and generalizability of role-playing tests of social skills |
| Bornstein, Bellack, and Hersen (1977a) | Unassertive children | Nine role-playing situations in studio; same-and opposite-sex role models | Multiple-baseline behavioral intervention outcome study of assertive training program with children |
| Edinberg, Karoly, and Gleser (1977) | Elderly subjects | Role-playing situations in which an assertive response was appropriate (such as being told that one was ineligible for Social Security) | A multimodal program for the assessment of assertive skill in the elderly |
| Finch and Wallace (1977) | Socially unskilled male schizophrenics | Role-playing and spontaneous situations requiring assertive response (such as refusing unreasonable request, initiating conversation, and expressing opinion) | A behavioral intervention outcome study |
| Fischetti, Curran, and Wessberg (1977) | Socially skilled and unskilled males | Behavior analogue situation in which subjects pressed switches to facilitate | A study designed to isolate components of social skill deficits |

| Study | Subjects | Procedure | Purpose |
|---|---|---|---|
| D. P. Greenwald (1977) | Low-frequency and high-frequency college female daters | interaction by a female speaker; Covert observation of interaction with male confederate; role-playing interaction with males—asked to get acquainted | Assessed criterion validity and sensitivity of various measures of social skill in college females |
| Kelly and others (1978) | One male alcoholic | Role-playing scenes drawn from situations reported by the subject to be problematic | Case study of commendatory assertiveness training |
| Little, Curran, and Gilbert (1977) | Heterosexually anxious college students | Role-playing situation in which subjects pretended to be in a pizza parlor with opposite-sex confederate and wanted to ask for a date | A study investigating the effects of different methods of subject recruitment; behavioral intervention outcome study |
| Marziller and Winter (1978) | Four psychiatric patients | Five-minute conversation with an untrained stooge | Presentation of social skills training program and analysis of individual differences in response of patients |
| Matson and Stephens (1978) | Four chronic female psychiatric patients | Ten role-playing scenes | Description and evaluation of social skills training program for decreasing arguing and fighting of inpatients |

**Table 11. Recent Studies Involving Analogue Assessment of Social Skills (Continued)**

| Reference | Subjects | Assessment Situation | Comments |
|---|---|---|---|
| Royce and Arkowitz (1978) | Male and female socially isolated college students | Ten-minute conversation with another subject | Controlled outcome study of effects of practice interactions on social skill and social anxiety |
| Russell and Winkler (1977) | Homosexuals | Cafeteria situation in which subjects approached others and initiated conversations; phone calls to police station | Behavioral intervention outcome study in which homosexuals were taught to feel less anxiety and to be more expressive about their sexual preference |
| Trower and others (1978) | Socially unskilled and socially phobic patients | Role-playing situation; not described in detail | Controlled study comparing anxiety-reduction and skills acquisition programs for treating social problems |
| Turner and Adams (1977) | Unassertive college students | Role-played scenes described by experimenters; interpersonal encounters with female confederates | Behavior intervention outcome study; assessed several components of assertive training program |
| Warren and Gilner (1978) | Forty-one dating or married couples | Role-playing test for positive assertive behavior | Developed and evaluated role-playing test for positive assertive behavior (test of tenderness expression) |

| Wolfe and Fodor (1977) | Unassertive behavior of college females | Subjects responded to eleven assertion situations presented on a tape recorder | Study of assertive responses of college females |
| Zeichner, Pihl, and Wright (1977) | Drug abusers and nonabusers | Simulated social interactions similar to those used by Rehm and Marston | Assessment of social skills of drug abusers |

frequency female daters, selected on the basis of self-report questionnaires, were exposed to several analogue observation situations involving social interaction. First, female subjects were placed in a waiting room with attractive males who were posing as subjects in the same experiment. The male confederates had been trained to maintain moderate eye contact and a friendly attitude and had specific guidelines for initiating and responding to conversation. Interactions were recorded on videotape, and the females were later rated by two female high-frequency daters on overall social skill, social anxiety, physical attractiveness, and estimated dating frequency. Trained observers also recorded time spent talking, talk-time percentage, percentage of initiations, number of verbal recognitions, head nods, action latency, and lack of eye contact. Although no significant differences in behavior between the two groups were noted, low-frequency daters, in comparison to high-frequency daters, were rated as significantly less attractive and less socially skilled and were judged to have a lower estimated dating frequency.

Subjects were then exposed to three one-minute role-playing situations in which they listened to several audiotaped scenarios that involved verbal interaction with a male acquaintance before class, meeting a male at a McDonald's Restaurant, and being introduced to an unknown male at a party. Then subjects acted out each of these situations by responding to a male confederate who, in turn, responded in a moderately positive way to the female's initiations. Effects similar to those found in the first assessment situation were noted except that only marginal differences were found between high- and low-frequency daters in overall social skill. There were no significant differences between low-frequency and high-frequency daters on measures of behavior in the role-playing situation. On self-report measures, however, high-frequency daters rated themselves as making a better impression and as better able to carry on a conversation, and they judged themselves able to do better in real life than was reflected in the role-playing situations. The study by Greenwald did not provide support for the discriminant validity of behavioral measures during analogue assessment of high- and low-frequency daters. Because overall peer ratings of the two groups of females were different, it must be assumed that raters were responding to variables that were not tapped by the behavioral codes used and that elements of the content (instructions, males used, and situations used) of the analogue assessment situation and codes were not appropriate for the targets under study. A less likely, although possibly valid, inference is that there were no actual behavioral differences between the two groups.

Russell and Winkler (1977) presented another interesting application of analogue assessment of social behavior, although their procedures could as easily be classified as naturalistic assessment. Interested in assisting homosexuals to become more accepting and assertive about their sexual orientation, these authors exposed homosexuals to behavioral and nonbehavioral group interventions to facilitate this process. As part of preintervention and postintervention assessment, homosexuals were asked to engage in a series of structured tasks requiring assertive responses. Subjects were instructed to (1) walk through a university cafeteria carrying a folder on which were stickers declaring support of homosexual rights while observers in the cafeteria rated them on the manner in which the folder was carried; (2) approach three different tables in the university cafeteria and pass out leaflets about homosexual law reform and make a brief statement about the issue while observers again scored their performance; (3) ask students at the cafeteria to sign a homosexual rights petition; and (4) call a police station and question police about homosexual rights. A tape recorder and FM transmitter were used to record responses of the subjects for later scoring. The analogue assessments were not sensitive to treatment effects: most subjects refused to engage in any of the assigned tasks, five subjects participated in only one of the assessment tasks, and six successfully completed all of the assessment tasks and therefore could not have improved on follow-up measures. In effect, the assessment concept exemplified in this study is original and noteworthy, but the content and structure of the assessment procedures did not exhibit satisfactory discriminant or content validity. The lack of content validity is especially perplexing in view of the fact that the tasks were designed after consulting with homosexual rights groups on campus.

With social skills, analogue assessments have been utilized in most cases to assess the effects of behavioral intervention programs. In some studies (Edinberg, Karoly, and Gleser, 1977; D. P. Greenwald, 1977; Kelly and others, 1978; Little, Curran, and Gilbert, 1977; Marziller and Winter, 1978; Zeichner, Pihl, and Wright, 1977), however, this assessment instrument has been used to identify components of social behavior or to study subject recruitment procedures. Analogue assessment was used to help select target behaviors for the social skills training programs described in two recent articles. Marziller and Winter (1978) reported on a social skills training program for four psychiatric inpatients. Individual social deficits were identified with the help of an analogue assessment situation in which subjects interacted for five minutes with an untrained stooge. Matson and Stephens (1978) also used preintervention analogue assessment to identify social deficits of four chronic psychiatric inpatients. Each subject was exposed to a series of role-playing situations in which a narrator described a situation and the subject then interacted with a role-playing accomplice. Situations commonly experienced on an inpatient ward were used. In both of the studies cited above, analogue assessment was used to tailor the social skills training programs to the needs of individual patients. However, the degree of benefit derived from such individualized programs remains to be evaluated.

Warren and Gilner (1978) reported on the development of an instrument for the analogue assessment of positive assertive behaviors (Behavioral Test of Tenderness Expression). This assessment instrument is designed to evaluate positive expressive behaviors normally found in intimate relationships. Forty-one heterosexual couples who were married or had been dating for at least nine months participated in the role-playing test. Fifty role-playing items (such as appreciation, saying thanks, expressing interest in the other person, tolerance, and sincere apologies) were compiled, and each couple responded to fifteen items presented on tape. Their responses were recorded and rated on a four-point scale by independent raters; each subject also rated the responses of his or her partner to provide a measure of criterion validity. The results indicated: (1) high interrater reliability, (2) high indices of homogeneity (split-half reliability), (3) high indices of concurrent validity—agreement between partners and independent raters, (4) no sex differences, and (5) generally significant correlations of the analogue test with four questionnaire measures of positive assertiveness. The study by Warren and Gilner is notable because it represents one of the first attempts to develop and empirically evaluate an analogue assessment instrument for positive assertive behavior.

Dependent measures of social skill derived from analogue assessment procedures have included verbal latency (D. P. Greenwald, 1977; Royce and Arkowitz, 1978), verbal fluency and content (Finch and Wallace, 1977; Matson and Stephens, 1978), other paralinguistic factors such as voice firmness and affect (Bellack, Hersen, and Turner, 1978; Wolfe and Fodor, 1977), self-report measures of anxiety (Fischetti, Curran, and Wessberg, 1977), nonverbal behaviors such as posture (Trower and others, 1978), and response timing skill and anxiety ratings (Little, Curran, and Gilbert, 1977). Most of the dependent measures have been derived from direct observation of the behavior of subjects during analogue assessment, although nonobservational measures such as self-report have also been used. We could locate no recently published article that utilized physiological measures during analogue assessment of social skills.

As noted by Curran (1977) in his review of heterosexual social skills training, multiple dependent measures are highly desirable in assessing social skills because of the complexity of the construct. Although he was suggesting the use of a variety of measurement instruments (such as questionnaires or direct observation), the same principle applies to dependent measures within analogue assessments. As noted in Chapter One, and more recently by Turner and Adams (1977), the constructs of social anxiety and social skill encompass a diversity of components, including behavioral skill, physiological reactions to social stimuli, and subjective perceptions and cognitive interpretations of social events. Recent studies have tended to utilize a rather narrow range of measures *within* an analogue assessment, although most studies also incorporated nonanalogue measures. The most frequent use of analogue assessment of social skill is in the evaluation of behavioral intervention outcome. Except for a study by Russell and Winkler (1977), all other studies involving analogue assessment of social skill have found significant changes in dependent measures as a function of intervention. It should be reiterated, however, that sensitivity to intervention effects is a function of the dependent measures utilized as well as of the overall structure of the assessment situation. Most studies also reported differences among measures in the degree or occurrence of change; some behavioral measures did, but others did not, demonstrate significant changes as a function of intervention.

The issue of content validity in the analogue assessment of social skill is particularly important in view of the situation specificity of the construct (Curran, 1977; Turner and Adams, 1977). Situation specificity was illustrated in a study by Edinberg, Karoly, and Gleser (1977) in which assertive behaviors of the elderly were evaluated. A series of questionnaires, interviews, and role-playing measures of assertive behaviors of elderly subjects were utilized to ascertain the importance of situational versus personality variables (traits). The results suggested that the greatest proportion of variance in responses was accounted for by an interaction between subjects and situations. The implication is that assertive behaviors of the elderly are highly situation specific; assertive behavior of a subject in one situation cannot be predicted validly from knowledge of the assertive behavior of the subject in other situations. The type of situation utilized to assess assertive behaviors, therefore, will have significant impact upon the sensitivity and validity of the assessment procedure. This assumption was supported by Kelly and others (1978), who found that changes in commendatory assertive skills did not generalize to refusal skills in a training program with a male alcoholic.

In most cases, the content of the assessment situations for the analogue assessment of social skills was apparently derived from logical inference or from a review of previous applications. Kelly and others (1978), however, structured the analogue assessment situations after interviewing the target subject about the situations that caused the most difficulty. In developing analogue assessment situations to use with psychiatric inpatients, Matson and Stephens (1978) consulted ward staff about situations that typically precipitated problematic social behaviors by the subjects. In the study by Russell and Winkler (1977) assertive situations with homosexuals were constructed after consultation with a homosexual students' organization at a university. Although the assessment situations proved to be insensitive to intervention effects, their study exemplified a potentially valid method of selecting assessment stimuli. These studies suggest that consultation with unassertive or unskilled individuals or with other individuals familiar with the target subjects about problematic interactions may prove a useful method of constructing analogue situations.

As indicated by Finch and Wallace (1977), several types of situations in the analogue assessment of social skills can enhance the content validity, criterion validity, and generalizability of the assessment procedure. Finch and Wallace used both spontaneous and role-playing situations to assess assertive behaviors of schizophrenics, and Edinberg, Karoly, and Gleser (1977) used several situations to assess the generalization of treatment effects. Multiple situations were also used by Kelly and others (1978), Matson and Stephens (1978), and Warren and Gilner (1978). Restricting analogue assessment to one setting may seriously impede the generalizability of inferences, is inconsistent with the assumption of situation specificity of behavior, and may not provide sufficiently comprehensive assessment of the complex factors involved in most target behaviors. Several studies have reported data that are relevant to an evaluation of the criterion validity of analogue assessment of social interaction. Most of the studies that used analogue assessment as a measure of behavioral intervention outcome also concurrently administered other measurement instruments. Although levels of covariance or correlation coefficients among measures were usually not reported, the majority of studies noted similar changes among measures. Additional support for the criterion validity of analogue assessment of social skills has been noted by D. P. Greenwald (1977) and Turner and Adams (1977).

Bellack, Hersen, and Turner (1978) reported two studies evaluating the reliability and criterion validity of analogue assessment of social assertive skills. The first experiment examined the relationship between performance on the Behavioral Assertiveness Test and evaluation by mental health experts of the target subjects' social skills. Five female psychiatric patients participated in role-playing situations in a structured laboratory setting. A narrator from another room described social situations requiring positive and negative assertive behavior, and the subject responded to a role model who was sitting next to her. The behavior of each subject was rated by two sets of raters on a number of specific behavioral dimensions and by ten mental health experts on effectiveness and quality of the response. Correlation coefficients between observation data on the one hand and ratings of effectiveness and quality on the other were moderate; most failed to reach significance. The authors also constructed stepwise regression equations to identify variables that were the best predictors of quality and effectiveness ratings. Although they suggested that the predictor variables accounted for 90 to 96 percent of the variance, cautious interpretation of their inferences is suggested because predictors generated from use of stepwise regression in this manner seldom replicate. Also based on their stepwise regression equations, the authors suggested that (1) the specific components contributing to the quality and effectiveness of a response will vary as a function of the type of response (negative versus positive), (2) the contribution of components within a response class will vary according to the specific definition of response adequacy of social skill (effectiveness versus quality), and (3) response components predict response adequacy much better in combination than they do individually.

In their second experiment, Bellack, Hersen, and Turner (1978) utilized a similar analogue assessment procedure with ten male and ten female psychiatric inpatients. As criterion measures, each subject also participated in a standardized interview situation and was observed during a group setting. There were no significant correlation coefficients between the analogue assessment measures and the criterion measures. The authors also assessed the between-scene stability of behavior during the role-playing situation and noted that, in most cases, the Pearson correlations were above .80. These studies, taken together, are difficult to interpret but provide evidence for individual differences in response styles and for the presence of multiple components in assertive behaviors. They give only mixed support, however, for the situation specificity and criterion validity of assertive social behavior. Because analogue assessment and its criterion measures are usually situation specific, the degree of covariation between measures would probably be a function of the degree of similarity among stimuli in the assessment instruments. As noted by Heimberg and others (1977) and Wolfe (1978), more extensive criterion validity studies of analogue assessment of social skills are needed as prerequisites to confident application of this assessment instrument.

Several recently published studies have assessed the discriminant validity of analogue assessment of social behavior. As noted previously, D. P. Greenwald (1977) found no significant differences between low- and high-frequency daters in the rates of specific behaviors emitted in analogue assessment situations, although global ratings by observers did validly discriminate between groups (a finding consistent with that of Arkowitz and others, 1975; and Borkovec and others, 1974). Zeichner, Pihl, and Wright (1977) assessed social skills of drug users and nonusers and found no significant differences between the two groups. As in other cases of negative findings, however, lack of discriminant validity may be attributable to a lack of real between-group differences as well as to invalidity of the measurement instrument. Findings supporting the discriminant validity of analogue assessment of social skills were reported by Little, Curran, and Gilbert (1977) for two groups of subjects solicited through different recruitment procedures and by Fischetti, Curran, and Wessberg (1977) for males with high and low heterosexual anxiety.

The articles reviewed in this section on social skills have all involved environmental analogues in which inferences of generalization have to be made across environments (between the analogue and naturalistic environment). Fischetti, Curran, and Wessberg (1977) assessed social skills using behavioral analogues as well as environmental analogues. As part of a larger study assessing the social skills of males with high and low heterosexual anxiety, subjects were placed in a simulated dating interaction situation. The subject's task was to press two switches (the switches indicated gestural or vocal responses) at appropriate times to make it easy for a female speaker to talk to him. Data consisted of the frequency and timing of these analogue behaviors. Criterion levels for the frequency and timing of responses were first established with a group of socially competent males, and the response patterns of subsequent groups of anxious and nonanxious males were con-

trasted to those of the original criterion group. Significant
between-group differences were found for the timing but not for
the frequency of responses.

In summary, analogue observation assessment of social skills
has involved a variety of target populations, target behaviors, and
assessment situations. Typically, subjects are requested to participate in role-playing or spontaneous social situations while subjective and behavioral measures are taken. This assessment instrument has been shown to be sensitive to the effects of behavioral
intervention in most studies, but there has been insufficient examination of criterion-related and discriminant validity. Issues of
content validity and reliability have also been insufficiently
investigated.

## Ingestive Behavior

Ingestive behavior, particularly consumption of food and
alcohol, has been the target of analogue assessment for a number
of years. Analogue observation has provided data on the characteristics and determinants of ingestive behavior and has
supplemented information derived from interviews and questionnaires. Targeted populations have most frequently been overweight individuals or alcoholics. Several recent articles have also
assessed ingestive behaviors in analogue observation settings and
are outlined in Table 12. In one study (Conners, Maisto, and Sobell,
1978) the validity of a taste test for evaluating alcohol preferences
was examined. Thirty-two male undergraduates—considered
moderate or heavy drinkers—were presented with two beakers
containing orange juice and were instructed to rate the drinks on
more than two dozen dimensions. One beaker was labeled "alcohol" and had four milliliters of grain alcohol floating on top with
the rim of the glass swabbed in alcohol. The beakers were rated as
significantly different on 52 percent of the dimensions. The authors noted that this was the first study in which an own-subject
control has been used, and the analogue assessment situation appeared to be sensitive to some dimensions of alcohol preference.

Because of the small number of recently published studies
using analogue assessment and the diversity of assessment proce-

dures, settings, target populations, and target behaviors associated with these studies, it is difficult to draw valid inferences concerning the reliability or validity of analogue assessment of ingestive behavior. However, it should be noted that these studies, along with studies previously published (Haynes, 1978), have suggested that analogue assessment measures of ingestive activity significantly correlate with measures of that behavior in the natural environment. As with other populations and behaviors, the factors affecting criterion validity, content validity, and reliability of the structured assessment settings require additional attention.

Table 13 presents a brief overview of several additional applications of analogue assessment situations that were not amenable to classification within the previous sections of this chapter. Although the idiosyncratic nature of these applications makes it difficult to discuss issues of reliability or validity, they do support the applicability of analogue assessment to a broad range of behaviors.

## Summary

Analogue assessment has been used with a wide variety of target populations and behaviors. The applicability of this assessment instrument would seem to be constrained only by the amenability of the target problem to being elicited in controlled environments, and this is primarily a function of the specificity and public nature of the response, the probability of its occurrence, and the degree of reactivity associated with it. For these reasons, some behavior patterns, including phobic or self-deprecatory thoughts, fears of rejection, or enuresis, may be less amenable to analogue assessment.

The issue of reactivity is of particular importance in analogue assessment because reactivity influences the probability that the behavior will occur and the validity of inferences that can be drawn. Therefore, it is important to evaluate the degree to which behavior rates and relationships observed in analogue assessment correspond to the same behaviors emitted in the natural environment. A model for this evaluation, derived from Reisinger and Ora (1977), was presented. The degree of correspondence between behavior rates or topography in analogue and natural

**Table 12. Recent Studies Involving Analogue Assessment of Ingestive Behavior**

| Reference | Subjects | Assessment Situation | Comments |
|---|---|---|---|
| Adams and others (1978) | Sixty-one obese, normal, and thin women | Observation room of psychiatric clinic in which a free-choice lunch was provided | Study assessed the validity of this analogue situation for evaluating the eating behavior of obese and nonobese women |
| Conners, Maisto, and Sobell (1978) | Moderate or heavy drinking college students | Taste test involving orange juice disguised as alcoholic drink | Assessed validity of the taste test analogue as a measure of alcohol preference |
| Davidson and Bremser (1977) | Two male alcoholics | Laboratory chamber in which subjects pressed lever on various schedules of reinforcement | Assessed DRL (Differential Reinforcement of Low-Rate Behavior) schedules of reinforcement in facilitating controlled drinking |
| Dericco, Brigham, and Garlington (1977) | Twenty-four smokers | Laboratory settings primarily used for suppression of smoking (using shock) | Behavioral intervention outcome study; laboratory data were not primary source of outcome data (used self-monitoring and interviews) |
| Doleys and others (1977b) | Three adult male alcoholics | Experimental laboratory chamber; measured alcoholic intake through glass motions | Assessed effects of aversive conditioning procedure on alcohol intake in the laboratory |

| Garlington and Dericco (1977) | Drinking behavior of three male college students | Simulated tavern; used twelve-ounce calibrated beer glass; observers served as bartenders | Behavioral intervention (modeling) outcome study was sensitive to treatment effects |
|---|---|---|---|
| Herbert-Jackson and Risley (1977) | Preschool children | Daycare center | Food intake |

**Table 13. Additional Recent Applications of Analogue Assessment**

| Reference | Subjects and Target Behaviors | Assessment Situation | Comments |
|---|---|---|---|
| Brodzinsky (1977) | Fourth-grade children; humor responses | Experimenter presented children with jokes and recorded responses of children | Developmental psychology study of factors affecting humor response in children |
| Burleigh and Marholin (1977) | Adult retardates; aversive and on-task behavior | Structured setting in institution; block manipulation activity | Assessed effects of verbal prompts and reinforcement on aversive and on-task behaviors of adult retardates |
| Hall, Baker, and Hutchinson (1977) | Schizophrenics; verbal behavior | Conversation test derived from Baker; twenty simple questions requiring a variety of responses | Evaluation of institutional treatment of chronic schizophrenic patients |
| Mathews and Fawcett (1977) | Community proctors | Role-playing situation in which proctor trainees were observed for the occurrence or nonoccurrence of proctor behaviors | A behavioral intervention outcome study on the feasibility of training community residents as instructional proctors |
| Resick and others (1978) | Six stutterers | Recorded stuttering in several situations involving talking to a stranger on telephone and conversation with a stranger | Behavioral intervention outcome study on the effects of systematic slowed speech on stuttering |
| Turner, Hersen, and Bellack (1977) | Adult female psychotic; self-report of auditory hallucinations | Structured laboratory setting used for treatment and assessment of auditory hallucinations | Evaluated effect of several intervention procedures on self-reports of auditory hallucinations |

environments will be a function of numerous factors and should be the subject of intensive study. It would be illogical, in view of the situation specificity of behavior, to expect a high degree of correspondence between behaviors emitted in two such dissimilar situations. Dissimilarity between naturalistic and analogue situations in the rates of targeted behaviors does not, however, imply lack of covariation or validity.

Many, but not all, of the studies have reported that analogue assessment is sensitive to the effects of intervention, is significantly correlated with other criterion measures, and can discriminate among groups of subjects classified on the basis of other criteria. Nevertheless, a considerable amount of research will be required before factors affecting its validity can be identified. Specifically, the effects on validity of variation in instructions to subjects, subject expectancies, the physical or sequential structure of the assessment situation, behavior monitoring procedures, the types of behaviors coded, and time sampling or other temporal factors of the situation remain to be evaluated.

Several recently published studies have evaluated the degree of generalization between analogue assessment situations or between analogue and naturalistic settings, and most noted generally high correlations. Edinberg, Karoly, and Gleser (1977), however, noted a lack of predictive validity among analogue assessment situations with the elderly. It was noted that the degree of generalization will probably vary with the similarity among assessment instruments and that the relationship between content similarity and derived correlation coefficients deserves further study. As noted by Hughes and Haynes (1978), the use of analogue assessment is based, in part, on the assumption that it is more efficient than naturalistic observation for deriving information about target populations and behaviors. Of course, the issue of efficiency is relevant only when issues of validity have been satisfactorily addressed, but the relative efficiency of structured observation settings has not been systematically investigated. Additional research on structured observation situations should be directed toward a comparative evaluation of the amount of information gained per unit of professional time, client time, and financial expenditure.

The issue of consistency or reliability of behavior across time or assessment administration has been previously addressed. Indices of reliability and consistency affect the degree of confidence that can be placed in data derived from one administration of an assessment instrument and affect decisions about the number or duration of assessment sessions necessary for reliable estimates of behavior rates. In most cases, analogue assessment has been administered only once prior to, and once following, intervention (or only a single time in nonintervention studies). As a consequence, recent studies have not contributed to an understanding of the reliability or determinants of analogue assessment.

The reliability and validity of analogue assessment are intimately tied to the structure and content of the assessment situation and the time and behavior sampling parameters used. As noted in several studies (such as Wroblewski, Jacob, and Rehm, 1977), the validity of structured observation assessment depends upon which dependent measures (physiological, specific behavior codes, or self-report) are taken, the criteria measures against which they are compared, the structure of the assessment environment, and time-sampling parameters (duration of intervals and number of sampling intervals). Because the content validity of analogue assessment affects criterion validity and sensitivity, analogue situations and stimuli should be constructed only after careful observation of, or interviews with, target subjects, consultation with mediators in the natural environment, or recourse to empirical literature.

Structured assessment situations have apparently been used primarily as a research rather than a clinical tool. Although this conclusion is based upon a survey of journal articles and may simply reflect the inherent emphasis upon research applications in these articles, we are familiar with only a few recent studies that have based intervention strategies upon the results of analogue assessment. One impediment to the clinical utility of analogue assessment is the dearth of normative data. For structured assessment settings to be optimally useful in clinical behavior therapy, there must be a set of norms against which the behavior of a target subject or client can be compared. Normative data concerning typical rates of social, assertive, ingestive, or other behaviors would assist the behavior analyst in pinpointing behavioral deficits and excesses and in controlling stimuli. In the absence of normative data, the behavior analyst must rely upon subjective inferences and subjective norms in interpreting the outcome of this assessment procedure. The most frequent application of analogue assessment is in the evaluation of the outcome of behavioral intervention. Although there are strong indications that analogue assessment situations are sensitive to the effects of intervention, their application as outcome measures implies that they are valid measures of the construct under study. For example, the assessment of intervention outcome with withdrawn subjects is based upon the assumption that analogue assessment instruments can discriminate between withdrawn and nonwithdrawn children. However, in most analogue assessment of intervention outcomes, there has been insufficient prerequisite research on the criterion or discriminant validity of the instrument for the targeted construct.

# CHAPTER FIVE

# *Self-Monitoring*

In recent years, the systematic application and evaluation of self-monitoring procedures have enjoyed increased attention, attributable perhaps to two primary factors. First, for certain target behaviors, such as obsessive ruminations or headaches, data collection by independent observers or through other external means may be impossible. Self-monitoring techniques, however, may also be applied to such overt behaviors as drinking, smoking, or hair pulling for which observation by external observers is time consuming, costly, or inefficient. Second, demonstration of reactive effects associated with self-monitoring has generated interest in its potential as an intervention procedure. Thus, as has been indicated elsewhere (Haynes, 1978; Nelson, 1977), self-monitoring, that is, the observation and systematic recording of one's own behavior, may serve both assessment and intervention functions.

In the realm of assessment, self-monitoring may provide a means of gaining information about targeted behaviors prior to intervention—for example, the frequency, duration, antecedents, and consequences of targeted behavior—and, when applied throughout an intervention program, may provide measures of the effectiveness of treatment. From a therapeutic standpoint, self-monitoring may serve an educational function by increasing clients' discriminability of their behavior, as well as by increasing clients' awareness of the effects their behavior has on others and, conversely, the effects of the environment upon their own behavior. Furthermore, self-recording may have reactive effects on the targeted behavior, producing changes in the frequency of behaviors monitored. These changes may be of therapeutic significance in that they often occur in desirable directions (Nelson, 1977); self-monitoring may increase those behaviors judged as positive by clients and may decrease those judged as negative. In examining the recently published studies relevant to self-monitoring, subsequent sections of this chapter will focus on the application and utility of this procedure, on methods of self-recording and associated reactive effects, and on information regarding the validity of data so obtained.

## Applicability

As an assessment and intervention instrument, self-monitoring has recently been applied in diverse settings and with a variety of behaviors, both overt and covert, including ingestive and addictive behaviors, psychophysiological responses, sexual behaviors, conservation and work behaviors, emotional responsibility, and academic behaviors. These applications have also involved a variety of populations, such as children, adolescents, college students, teachers, adult outpatients, families, and institutionalized individuals. Table 14 summarizes recent applications of self-monitoring, along with recording procedures and behaviors targeted for monitoring.

Smoking behavior has been a frequent target of self-monitoring. Conway (1977) requested undergraduate males to tally the number of cigarettes smoked from assigned packs during baseline, treatment, and posttreatment periods. Subjects began each day with a predetermined number of cigarettes that was checked by witnesses. As a part of an aversive conditioning treat-

**Table 14. Recent Applications of Self-Monitoring**

| Reference | Application | Recording Method | Behaviors Monitored |
|---|---|---|---|
| *Ingestive Behavior* | | | |
| Conway (1977) | Smoking behavior | Tally sheets | Number of cigarettes smoked from assigned pack |
| Dawley and Sardenga (1977) | Smoking behavior | Not reported | Not reported |
| Dericco, Brigham, and Garlington (1977) | Smoking behavior | Data sheets | Number of cigarettes smoked daily, including time and physical setting |
| Dericco and Garlington (1977) | Alcohol consumption | Data sheets | Amount consumed daily |
| Epstein and Martin (1977) | Food intake | Not reported | Amount of food consumed daily |
| L. Green (1978) | Ingestive and discriminative stimuli | Daily weighings plotted on graphs | Food items and liquids consumed; discriminative cues for eating; moods |
| Hay, Hay, and Nelson (1977b) | Alcohol consumption | Self-report postcards | Quantity and type of alcohol consumed daily/weekly/monthly |
| Kilmann, Wagner, and Sotile (1977) | Smoking behavior | Recording on charts | Number of cigarettes smoked daily |
| Lando (1977) | Smoking behavior | Pocket-sized booklets | Number of cigarettes smoked |
| Miller (1978) | Alcohol consumption | Daily record cards | Number of drinks during each week of treatment |
| Rozensky (1974) | Smoking behavior | Recording before or after smoking | Number of cigarettes smoked |

| Reference | Topic | Method | Measure |
|---|---|---|---|
| Thompson and Conrad (1977) | Drug urges | Logbook | Frequency of drug urges and anxiety reactions |
| *Physical and Psychophysiological Behavior* | | | |
| Beiman, Graham, and Ciminero (1978) | Hypertension | Sphygmomanometer | Daily recording of blood pressure in the home |
| Epstein and Abel (1977) | Headache | Six-point scale | Headache pain and disruptive effects |
| Feuerstein and Adams (1977) | Headache | Daily headache form | Frequency, duration, and intensity of migraine and muscle-contraction headaches |
| Horne (1977) | Trichotillomania | Diary | Hair-pulling behavior and successful resistance to hair-pulling urges |
| Kleinman and others (1977) | Hypertension | Sphygmomanometer | Daily recording of blood pressure |
| Lick and Heffler (1977) | Insomnia | Not reported | Not reported |
| Lubar and Shouse (1977) | Seizures | Not reported | Alpha patterns and seizure frequency |
| McLaughlin and Nay (1977) | Trichotillomania | Not reported | Eyelash pulling and hair pulling |
| Mitchell and White (1977a) | Headache | Weekly monitoring form | Migraine frequency, symptoms, time of day, and antecedents |
| Ribordy and Denny (1977) | Review of behavioral treatment of insomniacs | Subjective reports | Feelings of being rested; reports of sleep latency |

**Table 14. Recent Applications of Self-Monitoring (Continued)**

| Reference | Application | Recording Method | Behaviors Monitored |
|---|---|---|---|
| Schulman, Stevens, and Kupst (1977) | Physical activity | Biomotometer | Activity level (bodily) |
| *Sexual Behavior* | | | |
| Bronwell, Hayes, and Barlow (1977) | Heterosexual versus deviant behavior | Not reported | Sexual urges and fantasies |
| Maletzky (1977) | Sexual activity | Not reported | Sexual activity |
| Rekers and Varni (1977) | "Pretranssexual" behavior | Wrist counter | Frequency of play with "masculine" toys |
| Rekers and others (1977) and Rekers, Amaro-Plotkin, and Low (1977) | Cross-gender behavior | Videotaped behavior | Feminine voice and cross-gender behavior frequencies |
| *Conservation and Work Behavior* | | | |
| Bauman and Iwata (1977) | Household behaviors | Charts | Table setting and general household tasks |
| Foxx and Hake (1977) | Fuel conservation | Personal fuel consumption worksheets | Miles driven per day |
| Palmer, Lloyd, and Lloyd (1977) | Fuel conservation | Electricity meters and feedback sheets | Number of kilowatt hours of electricity used and conservation attempts |
| Paulsen and others (1977) | Impulsive spending | Not reported | Money spent in categories of personal care, transportation, and entertainment |

*Thoughts*

| Study | Target | Measurement | Description |
| --- | --- | --- | --- |
| Emmelkamp and Kraanen (1977) | Compulsive rituals | Precoded observation forms | Three relevant categories of each subject's compulsive ritual by frequency and duration |
| Emmelkamp and Kwee (1977) | Obsessive ruminations | Counting device and eight-point distress scale | Number of obsessions and total number of ruminations each day; ratings of distress |
| Hamilton and Bornstein (1977a) | Speech anxiety | Not reported | Objective indicators of anxiety, speech dysfluencies |
| Hamilton and Bornstein (1977b) | Anxiety | Recording sheets | Date, anxiety-eliciting situation, and subjective units of disturbance |
| Hay, Hay, and Angle (1977) | Drug urges | Not reported | Drug taking and drug-related thoughts |
| Mathews and Shaw (1977) | Generalized anxiety | Detailed diary and ten-point rating | Ratings of "anxious mood"; estimated number of minutes spent thinking target thoughts |
| Novaco (1977) | Anger | Diary; seven-point scale of anger and anger management | Degree of anger arousal and degree of anger management |
| Turner, Hersen, and Bellack (1977) | Hallucinations | Physical signal | Frequency of occurrence and duration of hallucinations |

**Table 14. Recent Applications of Self-Monitoring (Continued)**

| Reference | Application | Recording Method | Behaviors Monitored |
|---|---|---|---|
| *Academic and School-Related Behavior* | | | |
| Bornstein, Hamilton, and Quevillon (1977) | Out-of-seat behavior | Not reported | Frequencies of out-of-seat behavior |
| Dahlkoetter and Foster (1978) | Participation in track team workouts | Daily record cards | Daily attendance; number of minutes spent exercising |
| Hundert and Batstone (1978) | Arithmetic assignments | Report slips | Number of arithmetic questions answered correctly |
| Hundert and Bucher (1978) | Arithmetic assignments | Self-reports on folded paper | Number of correct answers |
| Jones, Trap, and Cooper (1977) | Written work | Self-recording sheets | Manuscript letter stroke errors |
| Kirschenbaum and Karoly (1977) | Mathematics calculations | Not reported | Accurate and inaccurate solutions |
| Meyers, Nathan, and Kopel (1977) | Library usage and journal reshelving | Counting instructions and tallies | Number of books shelved and unshelved |
| Nelson and others (1977) | Teacher verbalization | Not reported | Positive versus negative verbalization frequencies |
| Nelson, Lipinski, and Boykin (1978) | Classroom verbalizations | Hand-held versus belt-worn counters | Frequencies of appropriate verbalizations |
| Piersel, Brody, and Kratochwill (1977) | Test performance | Recording of points earned | Correct and incorrect responses on WISC-R |
| Plummer, Baer, and Leblanc (1977) | Rate of teacher instructions | Recording sheets | Elapsed time and number of instructions delivered |
| G. J. Schwartz (1977) | Remedial reading program | Not reported | Time spent reading under summer program contract |

ment procedure, Dericco, Brigham, and Garlington (1977) asked subjects to monitor daily frequencies of cigarettes smoked, along with corresponding information as to environmental setting and the time of occurrence (smoking of any portion of a cigarette was tallied as one cigarette smoked). Subjects were required to deliver the data to the experimenters on a daily basis. Follow-up measures were accomplished through telephone requests for self-monitoring; family members were reliability observers. While self-monitoring was apparently sensitive to treatment effects, actual data were not reported. In a design employing both male and female undergraduates, Kilmann, Wagner, and Sotile (1977) requested participants to chart the number of cigarettes smoked each day with recordings made following each cigarette smoked. In contrast, Rozensky (1974) had subjects monitor their smoking behavior by recordings made prior to each cigarette smoked. Lando (1977) utilized pocket-sized booklets to monitor smoking behavior of male and female adults who had responded to a newspaper advertisement for a smoking treatment program. These booklets were mailed to the participants, along with self-addressed return envelopes to facilitate data collection.

Self-monitoring has also been utilized in the assessment of alcohol consumption. In one of these investigations (Hay, Hay, and Nelson, 1977b), self-report postcards were employed to obtain information regarding the quantity and type of alcohol consumed. Similarly, Dericco and Garlington (1977) used prepared data sheets that required alcoholic patients to record the quantity of alcoholic beverage consumption on a daily basis, while Miller (1978) employed daily record cards for self-monitoring of alcohol consumption among problem drinkers. In a weight control program, Epstein and Martin (1977) had subjects monitor food intake and at the same time employed frequencies of social interaction and blood pressure levels as outcome measures. L. Green (1978) required obese subjects to plot daily weights on graphs in an investigation of the relationship of temporal and stimulus factors to weight loss.

Self-monitoring procedures have also been utilized in the assessment of physical and psychophysiological response patterns. Schulman, Stevens, and Kupst (1977) described the biomotometer, an electronic package worn around the waist that measures bodily activity levels by angular displacement of mercury switches. Such instrumentation would appear to have potential for the self-monitoring of activity levels in that the apparatus provides tabulation of total activity, measures of overactivity by tabulation of the number of times the subject exceeds designated criterion levels of activity during a preset interval, and auditory feedback through a crystal earphone each time a subject's activity level exceeds the criterion. In a biofeedback treatment procedure, Lubar and Shouse (1977) requested adolescent patients to self-record seizure activity. Applying self-recording in a biofeedback training program for tension headaches, Epstein and Abel (1977) had subjects record headache pain and tension disruption produced by headaches for a one-week period on a six-point self-monitoring scale. Similarly, Feuerstein and Adams (1977) found self-monitoring sensitive to treatment effects in a biofeedback intervention program for subjects with muscle-contraction and migraine headaches. Each patient monitored headaches on a daily headache form that included frequency, duration, and intensity across baseline, treatment, and posttreatment phases. In a further application of self-monitoring with migraine subjects, Mitchell and White (1977a) had participants record migraine frequency, time of day, and symptoms before and after on weekly self-monitoring forms. In addition to the self-monitoring of blood pressure by hypertensives (Kleinman and others, 1977; Beiman, Graham, and Ciminero, 1978), self-recording has also been applied with trichotillomania (abnormal desire to pull one's own hair) and dermatological disorders. In a baseline phase prior to treatment, McLaughlin and Nay (1977) had a seventeen-year-old female self-monitor frequencies of eyelash and hair pulling. Similarly, Horne (1977) found self-monitoring to be a sensitive measure of hair-pulling behavior and resistance to hair-pulling urges for both a male and a female in behavior therapy treatment programs. Finally, self-monitoring procedures have been utilized in treatment programs for insomnia (Lick and Heffler, 1977; Mitchell and White, 1977b; Ribordy and Denny, 1977). In those investigations reviewed by Ribordy and Denny (1977), most monitoring procedures involved subjective reports of feeling rested and reports of sleep latency—measures unfortunately subject to considerable bias.

Several investigators have applied self-monitoring techniques in the assessment of sexual behavior. In an aversion therapy program dealing with homosexual and exhibitionistic patients, Maletzky (1977) employed self-monitoring of sexual activity, along with corresponding reports from participant observers. Bronwell, Hayes, and Barlow (1977) requested subjects to keep notebooks in which they recorded occurrences and types of sexual urges and fantasies. Rekers and Varni (1977) reported a case in which a six-year-old "pretranssexual" boy self-monitored play with "masculine" toys; recording in this case was accomplished by means of a wrist counter. With an eight-year-old male in treatment for a gender-role disturbance Rekers and others (1977) and Rekers, Amaro-Plotkins, and Low (1977) employed videotape as a format for self-observation to aid in discriminating the occurrence of feminine voice inflections and mannerisms.

Applications of self-monitoring for conservation and work behaviors have also appeared in recent publications. In a program to initiate and maintain tasks such as table setting and apartment cleaning, Bauman and Iwata (1977) utilized self-monitoring as an assessment and intervention procedure. University students who labeled themselves impulsive overspenders were instructed by Paulsen and others (1977) to self-monitor money spent in such specified categories as personal care, transportation, and entertainment. As part of a gasoline conservation program, college students were asked to maintain daily personal fuel conservation worksheets by Foxx and Hake (1977). In the assessment of energy conservation procedures, Palmer, Lloyd, and Lloyd (1977) required an adult family member to see that family members read and initialed daily feedback messages regarding daily energy consumption. Subjects were also asked to save the messages in a file provided and to note any conservation measures they attempted.

Self-monitoring has also been employed with such covert behaviors as hallucinatory and obsessive thoughts, anxiety, and drug-related thoughts and urges, as well as with overt compulsive rituals and anger reactions. Although not requiring that the patient record events, Turner, Hersen, and Bellack (1977) requested a female psychotic patient to self-observe the occurrence and duration of auditory hallucinations by raising a finger and keeping it raised throughout each hallucinatory event. Emmelkamp and Kraanen (1977) employed self-monitoring with obsessive-compulsive patients, requiring each subject to observe three components of his or her compulsive rituals and to record the frequency and duration of these actions on precoded observation forms. Similarly, Emmelkamp and Kwee (1977) utilized self-monitoring to assess obsessional ruminations; subjects kept track of obsessions with a counting machine and, at a certain hour each day, made a note of the total number of obsessions. Hamilton and Bornstein (1977b) required an adult male experiencing pervasive anxiety to self-record the anxiety-eliciting situation and its date, as well as subjective units of disturbance. These same authors (1977a) required undergraduate participants in a speech anxiety treatment program to evaluate their progress by self-monitoring objective indicators of anxiety-related cognitions. Mathews and Shaw (1977) requested patients to keep detailed diaries in which they were to record every three hours (from 9:00 A.M. to 9:00 P.M.) their "anxiety mood" on a ten-point scale, along with an estimate of the number of minutes spent thinking the specified target thought in the preceding three hours. Also employing a diary format, Novaco (1977) required a depressive patient to self-monitor anger experiences (the degree of anger aroused and the degree of anger management) on a seven-point scale. In a study involving behavioral treatment of drug dependence, Thompson and Conrad (1977) employed self-monitoring as a means of assessing drug treatment and antecedent overt and covert stimuli to drug usage. Self-observation in this case involved a log in which drug urges and three categories of anxiety (interpersonal anxiety, feeling upset, and restlessness) were recorded. Similarly, a twenty-one-year-old college student self-recorded drug taking and drug-related thoughts (Hay, Hay, and Angle, 1977) as part of a behavioral assessment program over a three-week period.

A number of investigators have utilized self-monitoring procedures with academic and school-related behaviors. An interesting application of self-monitoring with implications for environmental design (Meyers, Nathan, and Kopel, 1977) involved library staff members who self-recorded the number of journals that they reshelved daily. The staff members were provided with specific counting instructions, and one dependent measure was the number of bound journals not reshelved each day. With minority group children, self-recording of points earned on WISC-R short forms has also been employed (Piersel, Brody, and Kratochwill, 1977). In another application (G. J. Schwartz, 1977), students were asked to self-monitor reading behavior as a component of a summer remedial reading contract subsequent to a reading treatment program. Also, in a design with significant implications for the reactivity of self-monitoring, Kirschenbaum and Karoly (1977) employed both positive and negative self-monitoring with college students on mathematics tasks similar to those on graduate admissions tests. During the initial phase of a treatment program to modify out-of-seat behavior in a classroom setting, Bornstein, Hamilton, and Quevillon (1977) requested a target child to monitor his own out-of-seat behavior. Also in a classroom setting, Jones, Trap, and Cooper (1977) had first-grade children self-monitor the production of manuscript letter strokes using self-recording sheets and overlays (as outlined in Helwig and others, 1976). In the classroom, Nelson and others (1977) applied self-monitoring procedures to such teacher behaviors as positive and negative verbalizations. As a part of a classroom behavioral intervention program by Plummer, Baer, and Leblanc (1977), teachers self-monitored the number of instructions given and time elapsed as a means of determining whether to increase, decrease, or maintain the rate of instructions given during a treatment program. Nelson, Lipinski, and Boykin (1978) required mentally retarded adolescents to self-record appropriate verbalizations, using either belt-worn or hand-held counters. Hundert and Batstone (1978) and Hundert and Bucher (1978) required students to self-monitor the number of arithmetic problems answered correctly; these studies investigated the accuracy of self-reporting. And Dahlkoetter and Foster (1978), in assessing reactive effects, requested participants on a university women's track team to self-monitor daily attendance and behavior during workouts.

In summary, recently published studies reflect the application of self-monitoring procedures with a wide variety of target populations and with both overt and covert behaviors. However, while any response that can be defined, observed, and monitored by a client may be amenable to assessment through self-monitoring, it cannot be assumed that the resultant data represent valid indicators of the characteristics or rates of the monitored behaviors. The utility and applicability of self-monitoring cannot be assessed without regard for the validity of the measures obtained, but some inferences may be drawn. For example, application of self-monitoring with covert behaviors such as those already cited might provide more valid assessments than would such procedures as interviews or independent observers. Advantages become apparent in terms of monitoring low-frequency behaviors as well; infrequent seizure activity might more efficiently be assessed through self-monitoring than through the use of external observers. Additionally, self-monitoring may represent the assessment instrument of choice when its validity is contrasted with that of alternative procedures. For example, utilization of external observers to monitor target behaviors in a social setting may produce reactive effects not only upon the behavior of the client under observation but conceivably upon the behavior of others in the social setting, thus influencing the validity of measures of the target behavior and of antecedent and consequent social interactions.

## Methods and Derived Measures
## of Self-Monitoring

As selection of an appropriate recording procedure depends in large part upon the nature of the target behavior, a variety of recording formats have appeared in the recent literature, including ratings, narrative accounts, frequency and duration measures, and product-of-behavior measures. A number of authors have utilized self-administered rating scales to record covert behaviors. Epstein and Abel (1977) employed a six-point rating scale for headache pain and its disruptive effects on behavior. Ratings of feeling rested are frequently used in insomnia research (Haynes, Follingstad, and McGowan, 1977) and were reviewed by Ribordy and Denny (1977). Likewise, Emmelkamp and Kwee (1977) utilized an eight-point distress scale for rating distress associated with obsessive ruminations. Hamilton and Bornstein (1977b) had anxious patients rate subjective units of disturbance, while Novaco (1977) reported the use of a seven-point scale for rating degree of anger arousal and anger management. Similarly, Mathews and Shaw (1977) employed a ten-point rating scale for rating clients' "anxious mood." Clients have also generated written narrative reports as a means of recording self-report information. Diaries have been employed to monitor hair-pulling behavior (Horne, 1977), sleep latency of insomniacs (Ribordy and Denny, 1977), and anger (Novaco, 1977). Mathews and Shaw (1977) required subjects to maintain a detailed diary in which they recorded ratings of "anxious mood," along with estimates of the number of minutes spent thinking specified target thoughts. In a somewhat similar fashion, Palmer, Lloyd, and Lloyd (1977) required subjects participating in an energy conservation program to record attempts at conservation.

A number of investigators have employed frequency counts as a means of gathering self-monitored data for discrete behaviors. In assessing smoking behaviors, for example, Conway (1977) employed tally sheets for the number of cigarettes smoked daily from assigned packs. Recording charts for the number of cigarettes smoked have also been utilized by Kilmann, Wagner, and Sotile (1977) and by Rozensky (1974). Dericco, Brigham, and Garlington (1977) required subjects to record frequency, time, and situational factors for daily smoking patterns. Similarly, Lando (1977) provided subjects with pocket-sized booklets for recording numbers of cigarettes smoked, as well as self-addressed mailing envelopes for return of the data. Frequency recording has also been utilized to monitor the frequency of drug urges (Hay, Hay, and Angle, 1977; Thompson and Conrad, 1977) and the frequency of drug taking (Hay, Hay, and Angle, 1977). Assessment of physiological responses such as migraine and muscle-contraction headaches (Feuerstein and Adams, 1977; Mitchell and White, 1977a) and seizure activity (Lubar and Shouse, 1977) has also been accomplished through frequency counts. Frequency recording has been applied in assessing compulsive rituals (Emmelkamp and Kraanen, 1977), obsessive ruminations (Emmelkamp and Kwee, 1977), anxiety responses (Hamilton and Bornstein, 1977a), and hallucinatory thoughts (Turner, Hersen, and Bellack, 1977). In academic settings and with related academic behaviors, frequency recording has also been utilized to assess out-of-seat behavior (Bornstein, Hamilton, and Quevillon, 1977), book shelving (Meyers, Nathan, and Kopel, 1977), instructions delivered by teachers (Plummer, Baer, and Leblanc, 1977), children's classwork (Hundert and Batstone, 1978; Hundert and Bucher, 1978), children's test performances (Piersel, Brody, and Kratochwill, 1977), appropriate classroom verbalizations by mentally retarded adolescents (Nelson, Lipinski, and Boykin, 1978), and compliance with exercise schedules (Dahlkoetter and Foster, 1978). Finally, application of frequency recording has involved charts to monitor general household work, such as table setting and apartment cleaning (Bauman and Iwata, 1977).

As indicated previously, the selection of a format for recording self-monitored behavior depends largely upon the characteristics of the targeted behavior. While frequency counts are applicable with discrete target behaviors and provide information regarding event occurrence, the durations of occurrence of such behaviors are often also of interest. As an assessment format, duration measures are sensitive to varying time intervals (Nelson, 1977); that is, duration measures reflect amounts of time consumed by the occurrence of a target behavior and are thus often employed, either alone or in combination with other measures such as frequency counts, to monitor the total duration of target behaviors. A combination of frequency and duration measures of self-monitored behaviors has been utilized by Feuerstein and Adams (1977) with muscle-contraction and migraine headaches, by Emmelkamp and Kraanen (1977) with compulsive rituals, by Turner, Hersen, and Bellack (1977) with hallucinatory experiences of a psychotic patient, and by G. J. Schwartz (1977) with reading time. Additional measurement procedures utilized in self-monitoring have included data sheets for recording the amount of alcohol consumed daily (Dericco and Garlington, 1977; Miller, 1978) and self-report postcards, such as those employed by Hay, Hay, and Nelson (1977b) for alcohol consumption (recording in that investigation was first required on a daily basis and was later reduced to weekly and then monthly recordings). Similarly, Palmer, Lloyd, and Lloyd (1977) had subjects monitor kilowatt hours of electricity used, and Paulsen and others (1977) required participants to record amounts of money spent in specified categories of personal care, transportation, and entertainment.

## Reactivity of Measures

As indicated earlier, self-recording may produce reactive effects on targeted behaviors, producing changes in the topography or rates of the behavior monitored. Because of this, self-monitoring has significance as an intervention as well as an assessment procedure. In the recent literature, reactive effects have been reported for self-monitoring of ingestive behaviors. Kilmann, Wagner, and Sotile (1977) reported that, with a sample of eighty-nine male and female undergraduate students, self-monitoring following each cigarette smoked produced significant changes in rate of cigarette consumption for some but not all subjects. In assessing the temporal effects of self-monitoring, Rozensky (1974) found that self-recording prior to the occurrence of smoking behavior was more effective in reducing cigarette smoking than was self-monitoring following the smoking response. Interestingly, L. Green (1978) reported that, with obese individuals, temporal order (premonitoring versus postmonitoring) did not independently affect weight reduction, although temporal factors did interact with stimulus factors; that is, premonitoring produced greater effects when monitoring ingestive stimuli (caloric intake), while postmonitoring produced greater effects when monitoring discriminative stimuli (cues associated with eating, such as preceding events, urges, and situations).

Reactive effects have also been reported in the behavioral treatment of trichotillomania (Horne, 1977). Frequencies of hair pulling during a self-monitoring phase were reported to decrease by one third, although no information was provided as to the longevity of the reported change. Rekers and Varni (1977) reported reactive effects of self-monitoring for a boy who crossdressed; the child was allowed to press a wrist counter only when playing with "masculine" toys. Although this was reported to produce 100 percent play with "masculine" toys, these results must be interpreted with caution; because the child probably had no values favoring "masculine" play, it is possible that the behavior change may have been a function of other reinforcers introduced by the experimenters. In data reported by Foxx and Hake (1977), self-monitoring was associated with a reduction in gasoline consumption by college students, although evidence for a reactive effect was confounded by monetary contingencies for fuel conservation. Clearer evidence for reactive effects of self-monitoring has been reported by Hay, Hay, and Angle (1977) in a single-subject design involving a twenty-one-year-old college student who self-recorded drug taking and drug-related thoughts. Following three weeks of monitoring drug-taking behavior, the frequency of dexedrine tablet ingestion was markedly reduced and remained so for the duration of the self-recording period, with similar results reported for drug-related thoughts.

Reactive effects have been demonstrated in investigation of academic and school-related behaviors as well. Kirschenbaum and Karoly (1977) assigned college students to several experimental conditions, including positive self-monitoring (monitoring of accurate solutions) and negative self-monitoring (monitoring of inaccurate solutions). The authors reported that negative self-monitoring on mathematics tasks led to decreased accuracy in performance, less favorable self-evaluations, and fewer problems attempted. In a study by Nelson and others (1977), teachers who self-monitored positive verbalizations were found to increase their rates of positive statements, while teachers who self-recorded negative statements decreased their rates of negative verbalizations. Along these same lines, Nelson, Lipinski, and Boykin (1978) reported increases in appropriate classroom verbalizations among adolescent mentally retarded subjects as a function of self-monitoring.

Of those studies addressing reactive effects in the current review, a large majority have reported behavior change properties for self-monitoring, consistent with findings reviewed elsewhere (Haynes, 1978; Nelson, 1977). But the skewed nature of the reports in favor of reactive effects reviewed here, although suggestive, may be somewhat misleading since an equally large number of recent investigations employing self-monitoring either have not addressed this issue or have not reported outcome data. Clear interpretation has in other cases been precluded through the confounding of possible reactive effects with other treatment manipulations. For example, Hundert and Batstone (1978) and Hundert and Bucher (1978) reported increases in numbers of arithmetic questions solved, as well as increased accuracy, for subjects self-reporting their work to a teacher for reinforcement (and with the threat of punishment for inaccuracies). These changes, however, cannot be interpreted independently of the reinforcement contingencies employed. Similarly, Dahlkoetter and Foster (1978) reported increased reactivity as a result of public posting of data relating to adherence to training schedules by university athletes. Since coaches were, however, not blind to treatment group memberships and thus may have differentially responded to members of the treatment group, these data likewise must be interpreted cautiously; other reinforcers might have operated.

In contrast to those studies providing evidence for reactive effects, other studies have reported minimal or no reactive effects from self-monitoring (Haynes, 1978). A number of variables seem to have significance for the reactive effects of self-monitoring.

## Variables Influencing Reactivity

The occurrence, extent, and duration of reactive effects from self-monitoring may be viewed as dependent variables under the control of other variables. Factors potentially contributing to the reactive effects of self-monitoring include valences attached to behaviors monitored, contingencies associated with self-monitoring, the relative obtrusiveness of the recording devices employed, temporal aspects of recording procedures, contiguity of the behavior and its recording, monitoring of behavior or behavior products, schedules of self-monitoring, the number of target behaviors monitored, experimenter instructions, training in self-monitoring, the nature of the target behavior, and motivational factors.

Several investigators (Haynes, 1978; Kazdin, 1974; Nelson, 1977) have postulated that the *valence* associated with the behavior being monitored (the value placed on the behavior by the target subject) can influence the occurrence or direction of reactive effects; that is, self-monitoring of a positive behavior such as classroom tasks completed or assertive responses might be associated with increases in the frequencies of that behavior, while self-monitoring of negative behaviors such as hair pulling or smoking might lead to decreases in the frequencies of those behaviors. Consistent with these predictions, increases in such positively valued behaviors as appropriate classroom verbalizations (Nelson, Lipinski, and Boykin, 1978) and positive teacher verbalizations (Nelson and others, 1977) have been reported to be associated with positive self-monitoring. Similarly, other investigators have reported reductions in such negatively valued behaviors as negative teacher verbalizations (Nelson and others, 1977), hair pulling (Horne, 1977), drug ingestion and drug-related thoughts (Hay, Hay, and Angle, 1977), and fuel consumption (Foxx and Hake, 1977).

In an investigation of weight reduction among obese females, L. Green (1978) suggested that the greater reactive effects produced by self-monitoring caloric intake than by self-monitoring discriminative stimuli associated with eating might be related to performance standards implicit in the self-monitoring of calories and to the culturally accepted negative valence associated with caloric intake. With respect to the lack of effects demonstrated for the monitoring of discriminative stimuli, Green further suggested the possibility that there may be few, if any, negative cultural values (valences) regarding the range of discriminative stimuli for eating (such as occasions, times, feelings, and activities) that subjects monitored; only if associations were established between such stimuli and eating in inappropriate situations would reactive effects as a function of negative valences thus be expected.

Additional information on the role of behavior valence in reactive effects has been provided by Kirschenbaum and Karoly (1977). In that study, college students solving either simple or difficult mathematics problems were assigned to conditions of negative self-monitoring (monitoring inaccuracies), positive self-monitoring (monitoring accuracies), no self-monitoring but immediate performance feedback, and no self-monitoring with no feedback. Findings indicated that negative self-monitoring led to lower self-evaluations, to decreased favorableness of self-consequations (reinforcement or punishment), and to a somewhat increased association of anxiety with performance, a suggestion also offered by Cavior and Marabotto (1976). Negative self-monitoring also led to decreased accuracy in performance, although as compared with positive self-monitoring it facilitated sustained self-recording when tasks were simple. All groups decreased self-monitoring when tasks were difficult. Accordingly, outcomes from this investigation generally confirmed a "closed-loop hypothesis"; relative to positive self-monitoring, negative self-monitoring produces less favorable self-evaluations, self-consequations, and increased negative affect, a finding consistent with that of Piersel, Brody, and Kratochwill (1977) in children's self-monitoring of positive and negative responses on standardized intelligence tests.

These findings are likewise consistent with Kanfer's (1970) suggestion that, when individuals monitor positively or negatively valenced behaviors, they are more likely to self-impose contingencies that may affect the probabilities of that behavior's future occurrence (Mahoney, 1974). The Kirschenbaum and Karoly (1977) data also are generally supportive of an activation arousal hypothesis; that is, negative self-monitoring will be detrimental to sustained self-monitoring performance of a complex task but will facilitate self-monitoring of a simple task. When confronted with difficult tasks, subjects attempted fewer problems and were less accurate; when tasks were simple, negative self-monitoring as compared with positive self-monitoring facilitated sustained self-monitoring. Clearly, then, while the degree of reactivity seems partially a function of the degree to which monitored behavior is valued or devalued, this valence factor does not account for all the variance in reactive effects.

Along with the influence of behavior valence and overt and covert self-delivered contingencies, *social contingencies and other external reinforcers* may likewise play a role in affecting the occurrence, direction, or degree of reactivity. According to Haynes (1972), unpredictable social contingencies frequently accompany self-recording. For example, although some individuals in the subject's natural environment may encourage an overweight individual who is attempting to control his weight through self-recording of bites of food taken, others may provide unwanted and possibly negative sorts of attention that correspondingly may influence not only the degree of reactivity but also the probability that monitoring will continue. In this regard, there is some evidence that public recording of the occurrence of behaviors may have an effect on the social environment different from that of private monitoring. Thus, Dahlkoetter and Foster (1978) reported significantly greater reactive effects for self-monitoring of exercise activities by athletes when this data was publicly displayed, raising the possibility that subtle environmental contingencies may have operated to encourage enhanced performance under this condition. As noted earlier, however, these data must be interpreted cautiously since coaches were not blind to experimental group membership. Certainly, additional research to evaluate the influence of social contingencies is desirable.

*Obtrusiveness* of the recording method may also affect reactivity. Obviously, recording procedures that produce chastisement from the social environment should be avoided unless one is monitoring a negative behavior with the hope of decreasing its frequency. Unobtrusive recording procedures may minimize such adverse social consequences and enhance the probability of continued self-monitoring. At the same time, several authors (Maletzky, 1974; Nelson, 1977; Nelson, Lipinsky, and Boykin, 1978) have suggested that the self-recording device may serve a discriminative stimulus function in producing increased frequencies of self-monitored responses. In this sense, a more obtrusive device might produce greater behavior change than a less obtrusive one (Nelson, Lipinski, and Boykin, 1978). In evaluating the obtrusiveness of recording devices, Nelson, Lipinski, and Boykin (1978) had mentally retarded adolescents self-monitor the frequency of appropriate classroom verbalizations with either a hand-held counter (more obtrusive) or a belt-worn counter (less obtrusive). Although differences were not statistically significant, the hand-held counter was associated with higher frequencies of appropriate verbalizations and more accurate recordings. The authors suggested that a more obtrusive recording procedure may thus be associated with greater reactivity than a less obtrusive one.

The *temporal relationship* between self-monitoring and the target behavior may also affect reactivity. In contrasting the effects of monitoring before or after eating behavior, Bellack, Rozensky, and Schwartz (1974) found greater weight loss for individuals who monitored themselves prior to bites taken, and they suggested that prebehavior monitoring may have the effect of disrupting a response chain, a suggestion likewise proposed by Kanfer (1970). In contrast, L. Green (1978) more recently reported that temporal order of self-recording did not independently affect weight reduction. At follow-up, however, temporal order interacted significantly with stimulus patterns; that is, premonitoring was more effective when calories were being monitored, and postmonitoring was more effective when discriminative cues for eating were being monitored. For smoking behaviors, Rozensky (1974) reported greater reductions when responses were recorded before rather than after smoking. Although the data are thus far limited, evidence reported would tentatively suggest that, at least for adults, monitoring that follows (as compared with monitoring prior to) behavioral events *may* be less reactive, suggesting also that, for purposes of preintervention assessment, postbehavioral self-monitoring may have the greater relative utility. However, further investigation to delineate these relationships is indicated.

Also potentially affecting reactivity is the *contiguity* between targeted behaviors and their recording. Although no research has appeared that directly assesses this relationship, it could be expected not only that immediacy of recording would increase accuracy by reducing the probability of omissions or errors associated with delayed recording but also that immediacy of recording would generate greater reactivity if, in fact, assumptions regarding overt and covert self-administered contingencies are valid. Another factor affecting the degree of reactivity involves whether monitoring is directed at the targeted behavior or at the product of the targeted behavior; that is, whether *behavior* or *product-of-behavior* measures are obtained. For example, self-monitoring of daily caloric intake and weight (Romanczyk, 1974) has been reported to produce greater weight loss in subjects than does self-monitoring of weight alone, suggesting that direct monitoring of behavior is more reactive than monitoring of behavior products. As Haynes (1978) has pointed out, products of behavior may be the dependent variable of choice if the aim of self-monitoring is to provide a nonreactive baseline against which later intervention effects may be assessed.

while direct monitoring of behavior may be the preferred approach if self-monitoring is to serve an intervention function.

   *Schedules* of self-monitoring have also been reported to affect
reactivity. For example, Mahoney and others (1974) reported that
continuous recording of correct responses on an academic task
resulted in increased study time as compared with intermittent
recording. Frederiksen, Epstein, and Kosevsky (1975) and
Mahoney and others (1974) have proposed that continuous self-
monitoring may maximize the operation of self-reward factors, and
Frederikson, Epstein, and Kosevsky (1975) have noted that the optimal schedule for self-monitoring may be a function of the rate
and variability of the behavior. In other words, high-frequency
behaviors may require continuous and immediate recording, while
easily discriminable, low-frequency behaviors may be validly monitored over relatively longer intervals, although reactivity may be
somewhat reduced (Haynes, 1978). An additional consideration is
the *number* of behaviors monitored (Haynes, 1978; Nelson, 1977).
Not only may increases in the number of behaviors monitored
correspondingly decrease reactivity, but in terms of the demands
made upon subjects the monitoring of multiple behaviors may also
produce aversive effects that could result in cessation of self-
monitoring. For example, Haynes and Follingstad (in press) found
that a high percentage of marital couples failed to produce self-
monitored data, despite numerous prompts, when asked to record
three behaviors. This finding was consistent with earlier reports
from undergraduates about the aversive nature of monitoring
multiple behaviors (Haynes, 1972).

   While little evidence appears in the recent literature, *experimenter instructions* to clients for self-monitoring during baseline or
treatment phases may be an important determinant of the frequency of reported behaviors. For example, it is possible that during baseline phases experimenters might give instructions not to
change behavior rates or during intervention phases might give
instructions to engage in the behavior as many times as possible.
While these represent attempts to enhance the accuracy of baseline
measurement or to demonstrate the effectiveness of treatment,
such instructions may confound interpretation, particularly if assessment of self-monitoring effects is the primary aim. Although

few studies have thus far focused on this issue, some evidence exists that valence induction by experimenters produces differential behavioral change through self-monitoring (Nelson, 1977).

Closely related to the potential effects of experimenter instructions is the question of the effects of *training* for accuracy in self-monitoring. Attempts at increasing the accuracy (one aspect of validity) of self-recorded data might result in increased reactivity by focusing greater attention upon the behavior, by making the behavior more discriminable, or through the possible introduction of contingencies. From an assessment standpoint, this would represent an undesirable outcome. Although evidence related to this question is limited, two recent investigations have addressed it. As part of an investigation that evaluated self-monitoring training as a means of increasing accuracy of self-recording of speech behaviors among adult volunteers, Bornstein and others (1978) reported that, while training increased accuracy, this was not differentially associated with greater reactivity; control subjects who self-monitored their behavior without training were as reactive as trained individuals, although they were less accurate. Along these same lines, Nelson, Lipinski, and Boykin (1978) found training to increase the accuracy but not the reactivity of self-monitoring among adolescent retarded subjects in an investigation involving training in self-monitoring of appropriate verbalizations. While additional investigation of this relationship should be pursued, the available data tentatively suggest that heightened reactivity may not necessarily be the price for increased accuracy. As with experimenter instructions to clients for self-monitoring, little evidence exists about the relationship between the *nature* or *characteristics* of the targeted behavior and reactivity. While further research is needed, it may be expected that behaviors that are easily discriminable (for example, smoking or eating) would produce greater reactive effects than behaviors less easily discriminable, such as sequences of cognitive events that might be recorded by some as discrete events and by others as a single occurrence.

Additionally, reactive effects of self-monitoring potentially may be affected by subject *motivation*. Although little is reported in the literature regarding motivational effects, reactivity likely would be enhanced for individuals motivated for behavior change. For example, self-monitoring by motivated individuals might also be associated with greater numbers of self-administered contingencies, expectancies, or demands. Similarly, unmotivated subjects engaged in self-monitoring would be expected to self-administer fewer contingencies or to have fewer expectancies for change than motivated subjects, resulting in lesser degrees of reactivity. In this regard, one recent study by Komaki and Dore-Boyce addressed the issue of motivation in self-monitoring. College students, categorized as to high or low motivation for behavioral change according to questionnaire responses, were requested to self-monitor their talking during discussion group periods. Although it was reported that subjects high in motivation for change significantly increased the amount of time spent talking (over baseline levels) and subjects judged low in motivation for change did not, clear interpretation of these results is precluded by problems in the reporting of measures obtained (event recording was apparently utilized, but data were reported as the percentage of time spent talking—a duration measure) and in the analysis of the obtained data (comparisons of means across the two groups of subjects could not take into account the slopes and variability in data for individual subjects apparent from visual inspection). Thus, conclusions regarding the relationship between reactive effects of self-monitoring and motivational levels of subjects must await further research.

Other factors also may potentially affect the reactivity of self-monitoring. For example, reactivity may be differentially affected by whether a subject monitors occurrences or nonoccurrences of the target behavior. Variations in settings (such as schools, clinics, or the home) may likewise influence reactivity differentially. Similarly, little is known regarding the differential influences of variations in sampling formats (duration versus frequency recording) upon reactivity. Demographic variables such as age, sex, or intellectual level may also influence the reactivity of self-monitoring. And, finally, little is known of the generalization of reactive effects across behaviors or settings.

In summary, reactive effects are reported in some studies, but not in others. Evidence has appeared in the recent literature to suggest that a number of factors influence the reactivity of self-monitoring. These include: (1) valences of the target behavior; (2) social contingencies associated with self-monitoring, including the effects of public recording; (3) the relationship of the obtrusiveness of the recording device to reactivity; (4) the temporal order of recording; and (5) the number of behaviors monitored. While the influence of training in self-monitoring was addressed, evidence thus far suggests that reactivity is not significantly influenced by such attempts to increase accuracy of recording. Although one study reviewed did address the factor of motivation and its influence upon reactivity, additional research will be necessary before tentative conclusions can be drawn. Finally, a number of additional factors, although not addressed in the recent literature, may affect the reactivity of self-monitoring. These include: (1) contiguity between the behavioral event and its recording; (2) whether behavior or behavior products are targeted for monitoring; (3) the particular schedule of self-monitoring that is employed; (4) the influence of experimenter instructions (demand characteristics); (5) the nature of the behaviors targeted for self-monitoring; and (6) factors such as the settings and demographic characteristics of populations in which self-monitoring procedures are undertaken.

## Validity of Self-Monitoring

The validity of self-monitoring is a major determinant of its utility as a preintervention assessment procedure. Validity estimates of self-monitoring typically are based upon comparisons between data obtained through self-recording and data obtained through concurrent assessment of the same target behavior by other means or through correlations with assessment instruments administered at other times. Before confidence in self-monitoring as an assessment instrument is possible, correspondence between data so obtained and other measures of the targeted behavior must be assessed. For example, self-recorded frequencies of cigarette smoking should accurately reflect the actual number of cigarettes smoked. The validity of the procedure for assessment purposes would otherwise be negated. However, it should additionally be noted that, owing to the potential dual function of self-monitoring, evidence suggesting invalidity of self-monitoring for assessment purposes would not necessarily preclude its validity as a behavior change procedure. The reactive effects associated with self-monitoring make the issue of validity of particular importance. Because self-monitoring may function to modify the rates of targeted behaviors, resultant data may be of little utility for assessment. Also, data obtained through self-recording may accurately reflect a *current* behavior rate, while not accurately reflecting behavior rates prior to self-monitoring or behavior rates when self-monitoring is not occurring.

In the recent literature, the major focus for validity assessment has been on evaluation of the accuracy of self-monitoring through comparison of behavior rates obtained from self-recording with rates for the same behavior obtained concurrently from other assessment instruments. As indicated by Nelson (1977), comparison data for assessment of accuracy in self-monitoring may be obtained by comparing concurrent recordings by self-observers and independent observers, by comparing concurrent recordings from self-observers and from mechanical devices, or by comparing self-recordings with some product-of-behavior measure assumed to be related to the self-monitored target behavior. By far, the most frequently used of these accuracy assessment procedures has been that of comparisons between self-monitored recordings and simultaneous recordings made by independent observers. Important to the interpretation of such comparisons, however, is the distinction emphasized by several investigators (Johnson and Bolstad, 1973; Lipinski and Nelson, 1974; Nelson, 1977) between accuracy and agreement evaluations. In other words, when comparisons are made between self-recorded data and data simultaneously recorded by independent observers, a measure of observer *agreement* is derived; when self-monitored data are compared with criterion measures, measures of *accuracy* are derived. Although two observers may be in agreement, neither of their recordings may truly reflect actual target behavior occurrences (Lipinski and Nelson, 1974; Nelson, 1977). While the following discussion employs the term *accuracy* in referring to both of these comparison formats, the reader should bear this distinction in mind.

As previously indicated, a number of investigators have assessed the accuracy of self-monitoring through comparison of behavior rates derived through self-monitoring with concurrent external observation of these same behaviors, either by employing participant observers such as family members (Dericco, Brigham, and Garlington, 1977; Dericco and Garlington, 1977; Hay, Hay, and Nelson, 1977b), roommates (Dericco, Brigham, and Garlington, 1977), friends (Epstein and Martin, 1977; Lando, 1977), teacher aides (Bornstein, Hamilton, and Quevillon, 1977), and employers and coworkers (Dericco, Brigham, and Garlington, 1977; Meyers, Nathan, and Kopel, 1977) or through utilization of trained observers, including undergraduate students (Hamilton and Bornstein, 1977a; Nelson and others, 1977) and adults (Jones, Trap, and Cooper, 1977; Nelson and others, 1977).

Several investigators have employed external observers to assess accuracy of self-recording of ingestive behaviors. For example, in a smoking treatment program for undergraduates, Conway (1977) had witnesses check tallies of the number of cigarettes smoked daily by participants, with each subject starting the day with a predetermined number of cigarettes. Agreement between the witnesses and subjects in this case could have been compared against the available standard (number of cigarettes remaining) for a measure of criterion-related validity; unfortunately, however, no validity data were reported. Similarly, while Lando (1977) and Dericco, Brigham, and Garlington (1977) employed outside observers to simultaneously record the smoking behavior of participants who were self-recording smoking frequencies, they did not report agreement data. Hay, Hay, and Nelson (1977b), however, reported accuracy for self-monitoring of drug usage by corroborating self-observations of an adult male alcoholic (quantity and type of alcohol consumed) through telephone calls to a family member. Dericco and Garlington (1977) reported an agreement coefficient of .927 (a range of .88 to 1.00) between external observers and an alcoholic patient monitoring daily alcohol consumption. For self-monitoring of other ingestive behaviors such as food intake, however, reported accuracy assessments have been less encouraging. Epstein and Martin (1977) had participant observers assess the accuracy of self-monitored food intake of subjects in a weight reduction group. Comparisons between external observers and self-observers indicated coefficient ranges of .66 to 1.00 for one group and .41 to .90 for a second group, reflecting considerable variability in agreement between the two measures.

Comparisons between external observers and self-observers have also been reported in the assessment of academic and school-related behaviors. Assessing positive and negative teacher verbalizations, Nelson and others (1977) found only moderate correlations between teachers' self-monitored data and data from external observers, although a coefficient of .95 was found for agreement between external observers. Again, however, it should be noted that in cases of observer agreement the assumption that observations by external observers are the valid criterion against which to make comparisons is problematic; it cannot simply be assumed that self-monitoring is invalid since it is always possible that error might be a function of the external observers. Nevertheless, in assessing accuracy of self-reporting among schoolchildren, Hundert and Batstone (1978) and Hundert and Bucher (1978) found exaggerations in students' reports to teachers of performance on mathematics assignments when reinforced for self-reporting, although accuracy was increased and maintained when a surveillance condition (comparisons with teacher recordings) was instituted.

High accuracy coefficients were reported for comparisons of appropriate classroom verbalizations by Nelson, Lipinski, and Boykin (1978); for subjects untrained in self-monitoring, a correlation coefficient of .78 was obtained, and for subjects trained in self-monitoring a coefficient of .91 was reported. Bornstein, Hamilton, and Quevillon (1977) obtained satisfactory agreement between a schoolchild's self-monitored data for out-of-seat behavior and data from external observers (a teacher and teacher's aide); 92 percent of the child's ratings were within one of that recorded by the first observer. Further, 83 percent of the child's recordings perfectly matched those of the first observer and 78 percent perfectly matched those of the second observer. Comparisons between the two external observers yielded an average agreement coefficient (calculated by dividing the smaller frequency by the larger) of .88, with a range from .79 to .95. In a design employing three groups of first-grade children trained to self-record correct manuscript letter strokes through the use of plastic overlays, Jones, Trap, and Cooper (1977) reported coefficients for averages of agreement with external observers (also trained in the use of overlay scoring) of .79, .82, and .84. And, in a study that assessed journal reshelving in a university library, Meyers, Nathan, and Kopel (1977) employed an outside rater and library personnel to count the number of unshelved volumes each day. A correlation coefficient of .87 for interobserver agreement was obtained for the experimental phases; during follow-up, perfect agreement was obtained.

In applications of self-monitoring with household behaviors, Bauman and Iwata (1977) reported high agreement between self-observations and external observers. For monitoring of dinner and kitchen areas, agreement coefficients were .88 and .75; for living and bath areas, they were .80 and .78. These coefficients, however, were based on averages across days, a somewhat less sensitive and powerful method of comparison than those based on day-by-day assessments. Of interest to the question of comparability of recordings between self-observations and observations by others, Richards, Anderson, and Baker (1978) compared self-monitoring with external monitoring, with and without feedback. Self-observers (college students) and external observers monitored the use of first-person pronouns (I or we) during a sentence-completion task. One half of the subjects saw a digital tally of usage of the target pronoun. Findings indicated that self-monitoring with feedback resulted in data that were significantly different from data from external monitoring without feedback. This suggests that only when information feedback is held constant can it be concluded that data from self-observers and external observers are similar.

As evidenced by the studies cited above, recently published research has focused on one aspect of validity—accuracy, or, more specifically, agreement between data derived from self-observers and from external observers. Clearly lacking in the literature is evidence for the degree to which self-monitoring measures correlate with instruments administered at a different time or for the degree to which such measures discriminate between groups of subjects classified on the basis of independent criteria. Thus, one might have groups varying across one dimension (obese versus nonobese or anxious versus nonanxious, for example) self-monitor as a means of assessing discriminant validity. In such a design, investigators likewise could manipulate other variables such as contiguity of recording or could record behavior versus behavior products to assess differential effects of these parameters on validity. Considering the limited proportion of recently published studies that have assessed the validity of data derived from self-monitoring, and in view of the indications that self-monitoring can be associated with significant degrees of reactivity, inferences that self-monitoring can be used as an assessment instrument to validly predict behavior must be drawn cautiously.

## Variables Affecting
## Validity

A number of variables may affect the validity of measures derived through self-monitoring. Included among the threats to validity are those variables that increase reactivity. As indicated previously, data derived from self-monitoring may accurately reflect current behavior rates but may not accurately reflect rates prior to self-monitoring or when self-monitoring is not occurring. Accordingly, any factors that increase the behavior change qualities of self-monitoring (such as valences of targeted behaviors, social contingencies, or experimenter instructions) may also adversely affect the criterion-related validity of self-monitoring. Where self-recording produces significant behavioral change, one cannot assume that the resultant data are predictive of that same behavior under natural conditions or that such data would covary with data derived from assessment procedures other than concurrent observation (Haynes, 1978). Thus, factors that influence reactivity may affect criterion-related validity, and such threats to validity may or may not be reflected in a measure of accuracy based on agreement comparisons between observers.

Inspection of the recently published literature reveals several attempts to enhance accuracy of self-monitoring (Bornstein and others, 1977a; Bornstein and others, 1977b; Bornstein and others, 1978). For example, Bornstein and others (1977b) assessed the effects of "enhancers" upon the fidelity (accuracy) of self-recorded measures through three procedural manipulations: (1) foot-in-the-door techniques, (2) induced self-esteem techniques, and (3) guilt-induction techniques. The dependent variable employed was "unreliability," operationally defined as the number of subject-recorded pass/fail deviations from prerecorded tapes with possible scores ranging from zero (perfect correspondence) to twenty-four (no correspondence). Results indicated that self-monitoring accuracy (fidelity) was greater for "enhancement" subjects than for controls. This finding was likewise supported in a similar enhancement procedure (Bornstein and others, 1977a); enhancement manipulations in that design included cueing statements, classification of consequences, cognitive consistency, and public commitment. In an additional investigation (Hamilton and Bornstein, 1977a), both accuracy instructions and an enhancement procedure (false feedback regarding subjects' honesty) were found to improve accuracy of self-monitoring of verbal responses among speech-anxious subjects. The enhancement procedure was found to be superior to the accuracy instructions only when the target behavior was easily discriminable. The relative degree of attained accuracy, however, is unclear since change scores (error rates) rather than accuracy data were reported. Similar improvements in accuracy of self-monitoring through an enhancement procedure were likewise reported by Hamilton and Bornstein (1977b) in the case of an adult male client experiencing pervasive anxiety.

While providing evidence for the utility of enhancement procedures to increase accuracy of self-monitoring, Hamilton and Bornstein's (1977a) research also suggested that training in self-monitoring can influence the validity of self-monitoring. In their study, subjects who received training in self-monitoring demonstrated greater accuracy in recording than did subjects not exposed to training. This finding has several implications, as does the related finding that only when the target behavior was clearly discriminable were enhancement procedures (subjects were told on the basis of personality assessment that they were honest in evaluating their own performance and that this characteristic was important for accuracy in self-monitoring) superior to accuracy instructions (subjects were told that their self-monitoring data were the only data obtainable from the study and were thus important). Not only may training significantly affect accuracy of recording, but, additionally, such training may increase a subject's ability to clearly discriminate those target behaviors under observation. Additional evidence for the influence of training in increasing the accuracy of self-recordings was provided by Jones, Trap, and Cooper (1977). These authors provided both the self-observers (first-grade children) and the external observers with varying amounts of discrimination training in scoring errors for manuscript letter strokes and found improved agreement coefficients between self-recorders and external observers with increased training. Assessing the effects of training in self-monitoring upon accuracy among adolescent retarded subjects, Nelson, Lipinski, and Boykin (1978) similarly found accuracy to be significantly greater for trained than for untrained subjects. As previously discussed, however, studies reporting simultaneous evaluation of potential reactive effects accompanying such training have provided evidence that enhancement of accuracy through training may not affect reactivity (Bornstein and others, 1978; Nelson, Lipinski, and Boykin, 1978).

As already indicated, increased accuracy in self-monitoring as a function of training may, in part, represent a facilitation of subjects' capacities to discriminate the target behavior. Subjects' awareness and recognition of the occurrence of the behavior thus influence accuracy. For example, Rekers and others (1977) described an eight-year-old boy who reported that, until trained to self-record cross-gender mannerisms on videotape, he had been unaware of engaging in behaviors that produced ostracism. Covert behaviors such as obsessive ruminations or hallucinatory experiences are also difficult to discriminate, suggesting the influence upon accuracy of characteristics of the target behavior itself. For example, interpretation and comparison of patients' self-recorded frequency data for obsessive ruminations, such as those reported by Emmelkamp and Kwee (1977), is problematic since some patients might make clear distinctions between obsessive thoughts, even though these might occur in sequence, while others might score such a sequence as a single obsession. Discrimination and, in turn, accuracy may thus be influenced by characteristics of the individual target behavior.

As stated earlier, any procedure that increases the behavior change qualities of self-monitoring may also affect the criterion-related validity of data so obtained. Just as contingencies for self-monitoring have consistently been shown to affect accuracy (Nelson, 1977), so those variables previously discussed as influencing reactivity may be expected to correspondingly affect criterion-related validity. In employing self-monitoring as an instrument for assessment, the behavior analyst should likewise be aware of the potential for bias in reporting. For example, in an effort to demonstrate adherence to treatment programs, teachers or parents may overreport frequencies of reinforcement directed toward a child. Similarly, obese individuals may underreport urges for food or frequencies of eating between meals. As already discussed, the findings reported by Hundert and Batstone (1978) for children's exaggerations in self-reporting of math problems solved under conditions of reinforcement for self-reporting point up the need for such cautions.

Studies reviewed in the recent literature have generally supported the accuracy of self-monitoring. Additionally, evidence has appeared demonstrating that accuracy may be increased through such means as enhancement procedures and training in self-monitoring. Numerous other factors (variables affecting reactivity, bias in reporting, and so forth) may function to adversely affect the validity of self-recorded data. Additionally, it should be noted that accuracy is but one aspect of validity. While accuracy has been typically assessed through observer agreement coefficients, little evidence for the criterion-related validity of self-monitoring has appeared.

## Summary

In recent years, the systematic application and evaluation of self-monitoring as an instrument of behavioral assessment and behavior change have enjoyed increased attention. Self-monitoring has utility as a means of assessing covert and low-frequency behaviors not easily assessed through other means. Self-monitoring has been applied with a wide variety of overt and covert behaviors, such as ingestive and addictive behaviors, psychophysiological re-

sponses, sexual behaviors, conservation and work behaviors, emotional responsivity, and behaviors in academic settings, as well as
with a wide range of populations (children, adolescents, college
students, teachers, adult outpatients, families, and institutionalized
individuals). Methods of recording have included ratings, narrative
accounts, frequency and duration measures, and product-of-
behavior measures.

Significant reactive effects (behavior change properties)
have also been demonstrated as a function of self-monitoring—
effects that may reduce its effectiveness as an assessment instrument. Variables that influence the degree of reactivity include the
valence of the monitored behavior, social contingencies associated
with self-monitoring, the obtrusiveness of the recording device, the
temporal order of recording, the number of behaviors monitored,
subject motivation for change, and training in self-monitoring. A
second group includes the contiguity between the behavioral event
and its recording, whether behavior or behavior products are monitored, the schedule of self-monitoring employed, the influence of
experimenter instructions, the nature of behaviors targeted for
monitoring, and various situational and demographic variables.
While evidence for the reactivity of the former variables has appeared in the recent literature, evidence for the relationship of the
latter variables to reactive effects in self-monitoring has not appeared. Several studies have suggested that self-monitoring is an
accurate assessment method, but while accuracy may be enhanced
through training or reinforcement, it may also be negatively influenced by those same variables associated with reactivity. Finally,
while the validity of self-monitoring as an assessment instrument
has usually been evaluated through concurrent observation of the
targeted behavior, significantly lacking in the literature is evidence
for the criterion-related validity of data so obtained.

# CHAPTER SIX

# *Behavioral Questionnaires*

$W$hile a behavioral construct system emphasizes direct observation of behavior, numerous questionnaires with potential utility for the behavior analyst have been published in recent years. Questionnaires have been utilized in the assessment of a variety of behaviors, including assertive behaviors, social and marital interactions, ingestive behaviors (alcohol and food ingestion), fears, sexual behaviors and orientations, problem behaviors and traits, and other miscellaneous behaviors. The various functions of behavioral questionnaires have included identification and description of target behaviors and relevant antecedent and consequent events, derivation of historical information, identification of potential reinforcers, assessment of covert processes (such as feelings, cognitions, physiological events), assessment of mediation potential, and derivation of quantitative measures. Questionnaires have accordingly been employed as preintervention assessment instruments, as a means of evaluating outcomes of intervention programs, and as research instruments for the analysis of behavior disorders.

Presented in Table 15 are a number of questionnaires with demonstrated or potential utility for behavioral assessment. As the number of questionnaires available to behavior analysts runs into the hundreds (Bellack and Hersen, 1977; Haynes, 1978; Walls and others, 1977), this table is meant to provide the reader with an overview of questionnaires available while extending that previously published by Haynes (1978). While some questionnaires such as the Fear Survey Schedule or the Behavior Problem Checklist focus on the identification of specific behaviors, behavior problems, or anxiety-producing situations and are useful across a variety of subjects, others such as the Marital Precounseling Inventory are designed for application with specific populations and typically provide an index of the level of dysfunction. To the extent that a questionnaire may generate valid information, its efficiency may make it the instrument of choice, particularly when other, more direct methods of assessment are not feasible. Questionnaires may be administered with minimal time and financial expense and have been found to be useful assessment instruments with those subjects who are not part of an observable social system (Haynes, 1978). When it may not be feasible to send observers into clients' work or social environments, instruments such as questionnaires or self-monitoring procedures often may be the primary source of behavioral data. Interest in questionnaires as data collection procedures has also been enhanced by the recent increased interest in cognitive therapy with its underlying assumption that beliefs and values influence, and can account for, a substantial percentage of behavior variance (Mahoney, 1977).

The most appropriate response format for a behavioral questionnaire will depend upon its particular function; that is, if the questionnaire is designed simply to indicate areas of difficulty or the presence or absence of certain symptoms or feelings, a checklist format may suffice. As Walls and others (1977) pointed out, checklists typically are not employed for reporting accurate frequencies or durations of behavior but instead usually involve recordings of the capacity of a subject to emit given behaviors. At

**Table 15. Questionnaires with Demonstrated or Potential Utility for Behavioral Assessment**

| Questionnaire | Comments | Representative References |
|---|---|---|
| *Questionnaires Measuring Assertiveness* | | |
| Action Situation Inventory | Measure of degree of assertiveness in a range of situations | Friedman (1971) |
| Adult Self-Expression Scale | Forty-eight-item self-report measure of assertiveness for adults | Gay, Hollandsworth, and Galassi (1975) and Hollandsworth, Galassi, and Gay (1977) |
| Assertion Inventory | Respondents indicate degree of discomfort to a range of situations calling for an assertive response, the probability of engaging in specific assertive behaviors, and those situations they would like to handle more assertively | Gambrill and Richey (1975) |
| Assertiveness Scale | Measures ability of college students to turn down unreasonable requests; gives options for each of thirty-five items; measures typical response and degree of discomfort to request | McFall and Lillesand (1971) |
| College Self-Expression Scale | Assertiveness in college students across a wide range of situations; taps positive and negative assertiveness, self-affirmation, and self-denial | Galassi and Galassi (1974, 1975), Galassi and others 1974, 1976) |

Table 15. Questionnaires with Demonstrated or Potential Utility for Behavioral Assessment (Continued)

| Questionnaire | Comments | Representative References |
|---|---|---|
| Constriction Scale | Respondents indicate their assertive social behaviors to forty-three items; forced-choice format | Bates and Zimmerman (1971) |
| Generalized Expectations of Others Questionnaire | Designed to assess differences between individuals high and low in assertiveness with respect to expectations of others in everyday situations; estimates of how often five specified reactions are expected from others | Eisler and others (1978) |
| Rathus Assertiveness Schedule | Measure of assertion developed and validated on college populations; respondents indicate how characteristic or uncharacteristic of them are a number of specific assertive behaviors | Rathus (1973) and Vaal (1975) |
| Wolpe-Lazarus Assertion Scale | Subjects indicate in a true/false format answers to a number of items describing assertive social interactions | Wolpe and Lazarus (1966) |
| *Questionnaires Measuring Social Interactions* | | |
| Dating Frequency Questionnaire | Thirty-five questions regarding dating behavior frequencies; information as | Klaus, Hersen, and Bellack (1977) |

| Instrument | Description | References |
|---|---|---|
| Dating History Questionnaire | to problems encountered on dates, factors limiting dating, and degree of difficulty with various aspects of dating<br>Elicits demographic information and previous dating history | Curran and Gilbert (1975), Curran, Gilbert, and Little (in press), and Little, Curran, and Gilbert (1977) |
| Fear of Negative Evaluation | Items measuring fear of negative social evaluation | Watson and Friend (1969) |
| Peer Contact Form | Parental questionnaire as to the frequency and duration of infants' contact with other children up to age six for prior weeks | Becker (1977) |
| Preschool Behavior Questionnaire | Thirty-item questionnaire on which preschool teachers rate child in context of the peer group; ratings on a three-point scale | Behar (1977) |
| Social Activities Questionnaire | Survey of dating behaviors; comfort levels, skill, and satisfaction with current dating behaviors | Arkowitz and others (1975), Glasgow and Arkowitz (1975) |
| Social Anxiety Inventory | One hundred sixty-six items measuring social anxiety; good assessment of factors | Richardson and Tasto (1969) |
| Social Avoidance and Distress Scale | Measure of distress, fear, and anxiety in social situations | Glasgow and Arkowitz (1975), Watson and Friend (1969), and Weissberg (1977) |

**Table 15. Questionnaires with Demonstrated or Potential Utility for Behavioral Assessment (Continued)**

| Questionnaire | Comments | Representative References |
|---|---|---|
| Social Behavior Scale | Children's behavioral choice card; distinguishes among four social behavioral categories as prosocial or competitive | Knight and Kagan (1977) |
| Social Competence | Items relating to dating history and confidence in heterosexual situations | Lanyon (1967) |
| Social Competence Scale | Assesses overt classroom behavior with respect to interpersonal relationships; range from healthy to disturbed in preschool setting | Kohn (1977) |
| Social Performance Survey Schedule | Rating of frequencies of fifty positive and fifty negative behaviors; scoring adjusted for specific groups | Lowe and Cautela (1978) |
| Survey of Heterosexual Interactions | Items concerning past dating history and assertiveness with females in specific social situations | Twentyman and McFall (1975) |
| Survey of Heterosexual Interactions for Females | Contains four questions on dating frequencies and twenty questions on heterosexual situations in which respondent rates on five-point scale her ability to initiate or carry on conversation | Williams and Ciminero (1978) |

*Questionnaires Measuring Marital Interaction and Satisfaction*

| | | |
|---|---|---|
| Areas of Change Questionnaire | Assesses the degree of behavior change that partners indicate for selves and spouses in thirty-four typical problem areas | Birchler and Webb (1977) and Weiss, Hops, and Patterson (1973) |
| Dyadic Adjustment Scale | Appropriate for either married or unmarried couples; measures several factors, including adjustment, cohesion, consensus, and affectional expression | Spanier (1976) |
| Knox Marital Adjustment Scale | Assesses overall marital happiness, happiness in specific areas, and areas of conflicts and goals | Knox (1971) |
| Locke-Wallace Marital Adjustment Scale | Measures overall level of marital adjustment and adjustment in specific areas | Kimmel and Van der Veen (1974) and Locke and Wallace (1959) |
| Marital Activities Inventory | Assesses eighty-five leisure-time activities, including sex, in which the individual engaged with spouse, alone, and with others during previous month | Birchler and Webb (1977) |
| Marital Conflict Form | Questionnaire designed to aid identification of problem areas; list of twenty-six potential problem areas | Weiss and Margolin (1977) |
| Marital Happiness Scale | Respondents indicate degree of current marital satisfaction in ten areas, including sex and finances | Azrin, Naster, and Jones (1973) |

**Table 15. Questionnaires with Demonstrated or Potential Utility for Behavioral Assessment (Continued)**

| Questionnaire | Comments | Representative References |
|---|---|---|
| Marital Precounseling Inventory | Highly detailed, behaviorally oriented inventory that elicits information regarding satisfaction in specific areas, pleasant interactions, goals, and perception of partner's happiness | Stuart and Stuart (1972) |
| Sexual Compatibility Test | Paper-and-pencil scale assessing sexual interaction; eleven sexual scales in MMPI-type profile sheet; twelve sexual content subtests, six dysfunctional scores, and overall sexual satisfaction score | Foster (1977) |
| *Questionnaires Measuring Ingestive Behaviors* | | |
| Alcohol Consumption Inventory | Elicits information regarding alcoholic beverage consumption patterns | Cahalan, Cisin, and Crossley (1969) |
| Behavioral Alcohol Interview Questionnaire | Functional analysis of antecedents, response parameters, and consequences of alcoholics' drinking patterns | and Higgins and Marlatt (1975) Hay, Hay, and Nelson (1977b) |
| Dash-Brown Survey of Fact and Fiction in Weight Reduction | Three parts: Pt. I relates to common beliefs about weight reduction, obesity, and overweight dieters' fantasies; Pt. II requires recognition of foods to eat | Dash and Brown (1977) |

| | | |
|---|---|---|
| Drinking Profile | or avoid for weight loss; and Pt. III requires recognition of caloric value of foods and ratings of liking | Marlatt (in press) |
| | Elicits information regarding demographic characteristics, initial drinking pattern development, current consumption patterns, behaviors, and symptoms associated with drinking, beverage preference, and motivation for drinking | |
| Eating Patterns Questionnaire | Questionnaire measuring patterns of eating | Wollersheim (1970) |
| Institutionalized Chronic Alcoholic Scale | Derived alcoholism scale from MMPI long form; used to differentiate alcoholics from neurotics | Atsaides, Neuringer, and Davis (1977) |
| Scale of Internal Versus External Control of Weight | Five-item scale that asks whether weight is hereditary, due to childhood problems, or due to the need for tangible reinforcement | Tobias and MacDonald (1977) |
| Session Evaluation Scale | Seven-point ratings of degree to which weight control booster sessions help, along with rating of therapist helpfulness | Ashby and Wilson (1977) |
| *Questionnaires for the Identification and Measurement of Fears* | | |
| Achievement Anxiety Test | Questionnaire measuring anxiety in academic achievement situations | Alpert and Haber (1960), Johnson and Sechrest (1968), and Ryan, Krall, and Hodges (1976) |

**Table 15. Questionnaires with Demonstrated or Potential Utility for Behavioral Assessment (Continued)**

| Questionnaire | Comments | Representative References |
|---|---|---|
| Acrophobia | Fifteen items to assess fear of heights | Bootzin and Kazdin (1972) |
| Acrophobia Questionnaire | Forty-item self-report scale for fears of height; zero-to-six-point anxiety scale; two-point scale for degree of avoidance; yields separate anxiety and avoidance scores | Cohen (1977) |
| Behavioral Fear Questionnaire | Self-report concerning fears of nonpoisonous snakes, spiders, rats, beetles, and roaches | Efran and others (1977) |
| Fears of Heights | Twenty scaled items measuring fear of heights | Baker, Cohen, and Saunders (1973) |
| Fear of Snakes | Thirty-item questionnaire measuring fear of snakes | Lang, Melamed, and Hart (1970) |
| Fear of Spiders | Thirty-item questionnaire measuring fear of spiders | Lang, Melamed, and Hart (1970) |
| Fear Rating | Rating of degree of fear on a ten-point scale at closest point in an approach sequence | Rosenthal, Hung, and Kelley (1977) |
| Fear Survey Schedule I | A list of fifty common fears; rated on a seven-point scale | Lang and Lazovik (1963) |
| Fear Survey Schedule II | Five-item fear scale; good analysis of internal consistency, criterion validity, and sex differences; most empirically constructed of the three Fear Survey Schedules | Bernstein and Allen (1969), Geer (1965), and Rubin and others (1968) |

| Fear Survey Schedule III | Seventy-five-item fear scale; five-point scale | Curran and Gilbert (1975), Hersen (1971), Wein, Nelson, and Odom (1975), and Wolpe and Lang (1964) |
| Fear Thermometer | Self-report of feelings of fear during behavior avoidance test (snake) | Gautheir and Marshall (1977), Moss and Arend (1977), and Walk (1956) |
| Fear Thermometer | Estimate of the degree of anxiety upon completion of speeches; 100-point scale | Marshall, Presse, and Andrews (1977) and Marshall, Stoian, and Andrews (1977) |
| Israeli Fear Survey Schedule | Ninety-seven items; seven items are specific to Israeli situation; relevant to everyday life | Goldberg and Yinon (1977) and Goldberg, Yinon, and Cohen (in press) |
| Mathematics Anxiety Scale | Questionnaire measuring anxiety about mathematics | Richardson and Suinn (1973) |
| Personal Report of Confidence as a Speaker | Behavioral checklist of anxiety during speeches | Paul (1966) |
| Snake Anxiety Questionnaire | Questionnaire measuring fear of snakes | Klorman and others (1974) and Rosen, Glasgow, and Barrera (1976) |
| Snake Fear Questionnaire | Eight-item questionnaire; fear rated on seven-point scale | Suedfeld and Hare (1977) |
| Spider Anxiety | Sixty items describing various situations involving spiders; five-point anxiety scale | Denny and Sullivan (1976) |
| Suinn Test Anxiety Behavior Scale (STABS) | Fifty-item questionnaire measuring test-taking anxiety | Suinn (1969) and Zemore (1975) |
| Subjective Units of Disturbance Scale (SUDS) | Presents fourteen hypothetical situations involving public speaking; subjects rate each item on 100-point scale; SUDS score is sum of ratings | Marshall, Stoian, and Andrews (1977) |

**Table 15. Questionnaires with Demonstrated or Potential Utility for Behavioral Assessment (Continued)**

| Questionnaire | Comments | Representative References |
|---|---|---|
| Temple Fear Survey Inventory | One-hundred-item fear scale; based on previously published Fear Survey Schedules | Braun and Reynolds (1969) |
| Test Anxiety Scale | Assesses anxiety associated with test taking | Richardson and others (1977) and Sarason (1972) |
| *Questionnaires Measuring Sexual Attitudes and Behaviors* | | |
| Bem Sex-Role Inventory | Includes masculinity, femininity, and social desirability scales | Bem (1974) and Winkler (1977) |
| Body-Type Preference | Questionnaire for assessing preference for specific body types | Wiggins, Wiggins, and Conger (1968) |
| Femininity Study | Two-hundred-item questionnaire assesses female self-concepts and states that represent typically feminine behaviors | Pishkin and Thorne (1977), Thorne (1977), and Thorne and Pishkin (1977) |
| Negative Attitudes Toward Masturbation Inventory | Thirty-item scale measuring masturbation guilt | Abramson and Mosher (1975) |
| Sex Guilt | Forced-choice questionnaire measuring sex guilt | Mosher (1966, 1968) |
| Sex Inventory | Two-hundred-item questionnaire dealing with sexual behavior and deviant sexual behavior; designed to | Thorne (1966) |

| Instrument | Description | References |
| --- | --- | --- |
| Sexual Activities Checklist | screen potential sex offenders; utility for behavioral assessment remains to be demonstrated | |
| | A behavior checklist in which respondents indicate types of heterosexual behaviors engaged in | Bentler (1968) |
| Sexual Attitudes | Patients rate twenty sexual and nonsexual concepts on thirteen bipolar scales | Marks and Sartorius (1968) |
| Sexual Interaction Inventory | Measures current and desired satisfaction with frequency of several sexual interactions and current and desired pleasure from sex; for self and spouse, seventeen heterosexual behaviors; results in eleven scales of pleasure, satisfaction | LoPiccolo and Steger (1974) |
| Sexual Interaction Rating Scale | Self-report of arousal to eight types of persons (young, preadolescent, and adolescent girls and boys, and men and women); seven-point rating scale | Levin and others (1977) |
| Sexual Orientation Questionnaire | Respondents indicate their responses to 120 male and female items on a six-point adjective scale; used to assess heterosexual versus homosexual interest | Feldman and others (1966), Feldman and MacCulloch (1971), MacDonough (1972), Philips (1968), and Turner, James, and Orwin (1974) |

**Table 15. Questionnaires with Demonstrated or Potential Utility for Behavioral Assessment (Continued)**

| Questionnaire | Comments | Representative References |
|---|---|---|
| *Questionnaires Measuring Problem Behaviors and Traits* | | |
| Affect Adjective Checklist | List of twenty-one affectively toned adjectives used to describe one's current emotional states | Zuckerman (1977) |
| Aggression Rating | Peer raters assess child on four scales (starting fights, target of other's aggression, verbal aggression, unpopularity); card-sort procedure | Oliveus (1977) |
| Anger Inventory | Eighty situational descriptions; respondent rates anger on a five-point scale | Novaco (1975, 1977) |
| Antidepressive Behavior Questionnaire | Composed of 100 items assessing behaviors that individuals emit to combat depression | Rippere (1976) |
| Anxiety Differential | Subjective reports of tension | Husek and Alexander (1963), Israel and Beiman (1977), and Kirsch and Henry (1977) |
| Beck Depression Inventory | Items assess depressed mood, feelings, affect, and behavior; good validity and reliability although primarily nonbehavioral in orientation | Beck (1967), Forrest and Hokanson (1975), Klein and Seligman (1976), and Lester and Beck (1977) |

| Instrument | Description | Reference |
|---|---|---|
| Behavior Problem Checklist | Fifty-five behavioral descriptions clustered into four domains (conduct problems, personality problems, inadequacy-immaturity, and socialized delinquency) for rating problem behaviors and traits occurring in childhood and adolescence | Peterson and Quay (1967), Quay (1972, 1977), and Quay and Peterson (1975) |
| Brief Outpatient Psychopathology Scale | Used to evaluate therapeutic effect of antidepressant drugs in outpatient settings | Free and Overall (1977) |
| Checklist for Communication at Home | Five-point self-report rating scale of quality and frequency of problem-solving behaviors, communication skills, and specific conflicts | Kent and others (1977b) |
| Child Behavior Profile | Parent report and checklist; 118 behavior problem items plus three social competence domains | Achenbach (1978) |
| Children's Behavioral Classification Project | Scale to establish behaviorally based nosology for children's and adolescents' emotional disorders; 274 behavioral items (twenty-six factors) endorsed as true/false by parent; requires parental reading level of fourth grade; also three demographic items | Dreger (1977) and Baker and Dreger (1977) |

Table 15. Questionnaires with Demonstrated or Potential Utility for Behavioral Assessment (Continued)

| Questionnaire | Comments | Representative References |
|---|---|---|
| Conners Abbreviated Teacher Rating Scale | A modification of the Conners Teacher Rating Scale | Pelham (1977), Sleator and von Neumann (1974) |
| Conners Teacher Rating Scale | Ten-item scale for assessing hyperactive children (restlessness, inattention, impulsive behavior, and so forth) | Conners (1969), and Werry, Sprague, and Cohen (1975) |
| Daily Menstrual Symptom Scale | Similar to that of Chesney and Tasto, but additionally requires recording of amount of menstrual medication used and invalid hours | Cox (1977) |
| Depression Adjective Checklist | Questionnaire measuring depression; seven forms; can be rapidly administered; primarily nonbehavioral in orientation | Levitt and Lubin (1975) and Lubin (1967) |
| Depression Experiences | Assesses a wide range of experiences that are frequently associated with depression; sixty-six items | Blatt, D'Afflitti, and Quinlan (1976) |
| Drug-Use Questionnaire | For each targeted drug, four questions asked: Have you used? Regular user? Frequency? If used but no longer—how long since stopped? | Ferguson (1974) and Huntwork and Ferguson (1977) |

| Instrument | Description | References |
|---|---|---|
| Eysenck Personality Inventory | Inventory used to infer "neuroticism" and "introversion" | Best (1975), Eysenck and Eysenck (1968), and Farley and Mealiea (1971) |
| Hyperactivity Rating Scale | Eleven categories of behavior with three items per category (restlessness, impulsiveness, and others) | Spring, Greenberg, and Yellin (1977) |
| Irrational Beliefs Test | One hundred statements believed to reflect irrational or illogical thinking | Jones (1968) and Rimm and others (1977) |
| Leyton Obsessional Inventory—Modified | Paper-and-pencil modification of Leyton Obsessional Inventory to facilitate group administration | Cooper (1970) and Kazarian, Evans, and Lefave (1977) |
| Life History Questionnaire | An instrument useful in a questionnaire or interview format that assesses developmental events and behavior problems | Wolpe (1969) |
| Louisville Behavior Checklist | Behavior checklist containing eight scales within three broad-based factors (aggression, inhibition, and learning disability) | Kent and O'Leary (1977), Miller (1967), and Miller and others (1971) |
| Menstrual Symptom Questionnaire | Employed to psychometrically identify two types of primary dysmenorrhea (spasmodic and congestive); defines types of menstrual symptoms, not severity | Chesney and Tasto (1975) |
| Modified Behavior Problem Checklist | Modification of the Behavior Problem Checklist to reflect the respondent's feeling about the disturbing nature of items | Algozzine (1977) |

**Table 15. Questionnaires with Demonstrated or Potential Utility for Behavioral Assessment (Continued)**

| Questionnaire | Comments | Representative References |
|---|---|---|
| New Physicians' Rating List | Rating scale to follow patient interviews by health professionals; nineteen symptom and behavior rating constructs; four major components of outpatient discomfort (anxiety, psychomotor activation, depression, and somatization) | Free (1974) |
| Nurse's Observation Scale of Inpatient Evaluation | Rating scale to assess change in long-stay schizophrenic patients; thirty items grouped in six scales relating to patients' ward behavior | Dolan and Norton (1977), Honigfeld Gillis, and Klett (1966), and Philip (1977) |
| Obsessive-Compulsive Questionnaire | Thirty-item questionnaire involving factors of checking, cleaning, slowness, and doubting | Hodgson and Rachman (1977) |
| Parent Attitude Test | Set of four measures (school attitudes, home attitudes, behavior rating scale, and adjective checklist) | Cowen and others (1970) |
| Pittsburgh Adjustment Survey Scale | Contains items to identify problem and prosocial behaviors of boys aged six to twelve years | Ross, Lacey, and Parton (1965) |
| Preschool Personality Questionnaire | Parallel instrument to the Children's Behavioral Classification Project; obtains child's point of view | Baker and Dreger (1977) |

| Name | Description | Reference |
|---|---|---|
| Problem-Oriented Record | Questionnaire for identification of specific problems and treatment for psychiatric patients; also used for ongoing evaluation of therapy | Grant and Maletsky (1972), Weed (1970), and Wolff and Epstein (1977) |
| Psychotic Inpatient Profile | Inventory to quantify currently observable ward behavior and self-reports of psychiatric inpatients; separate norms for drugged and nondrugged patients | Knight and Blaney (1977) and Lorr and Vestre (1968, 1969) |
| Reaction Inventory-Interference | Rating scale to identify obsessive thoughts and compulsive acts that interfere with daily activities; forty items; five descriptions of extent to which client would like to get rid of problem | Evans and Kazarian (1977) |
| Rutter Teacher Questionnaire | Consists of twenty-six specific behaviors; teacher notes whether each behavior doesn't apply, applies somewhat, applies very much | Rutter (1967) |
| School Behavior Checklist | Ninety-six items of deviant and prosocial behavior; seven scales | Camp and others (1977) and L. C. Miller (1972) |
| Self-Rating Checklist | A seventy-three-item checklist useful for identifying goals of clients in early stages of assessment | Cautela and Upper (1975) |
| Self-Report Questionnaire | To differentiate obsessive-compulsive personality traits from obsessive-compulsive symptoms; | Kazarian, Evans, and Lefave (1977) |

**Table 15. Questionnaires with Demonstrated or Potential Utility for Behavioral Assessment (Continued)**

| Questionnaire | Comments | Representative References |
|---|---|---|
| | rating scale for each of thirty-nine "resistance" items consisting of five descriptions of extent to which the respondent experiences difficulty in stopping behavior; degree of resistance is the sum of the thirty-nine values | |
| Situation Specific State-Trait Test | Consists of twenty situations to which respondent describes responses on sixteen scales for each; factors include fear arousal, positive affect, attentive coping, and sadness | Zuckerman (1977) |
| Social Desirability Scale | Questionnaire assessing probability that subjects' responses will be biased because of concern with social values | Crowne and Marlowe (1964), Farley and Mealiea (1971), and Watson and Friend (1969) |
| S-R Inventory of Anxiousness | Measures autonomic arousal experienced by individual when anxious; helps identify specific autonomic responses to stress | Conger, Conger, and Brehm (1976), Endler, Hunt, and Rosenstein (1962), Schroeder and Rich (1976), and Wein, Nelson, and Odom (1975) |
| Staff Attitude Questionnaire | Completed by residential ward coordinators at end of each shift; nine items yield overall level of difficulty experienced with children | Cawson and Perry (1977) and D. N. Martin (1977) |

| Instrument | Description | Reference |
|---|---|---|
| State-Trait Anxiety Inventory | Questionnaire measuring state and trait anxiety; measure of situational or basal levels of anxiety | Curran and Gilbert (1975), Kendall and others (1976), Ryan, Krall, and Hodges (1976), and Spielberger, Gorsuch, and Lushene (1970) |
| Student Problem Listing | Student selects from list of twenty potential problems (getting enough attention, sufficient extracurricular activities, and others) | Azrin, Azrin, and Armstrong (1977) |
| Suicidal Intent Scale | Administered in form of structured interview (self-report); objective fifteen-item scale; quantifies relevant facets of attempter's verbal and nonverbal behavior prior to and during suicidal act; items one to eight involve objective circumstances surrounding attempt (this portion can also be completed for suicides actually carried out); items nine to fifteen cover attempter's perception of method's lethality and fantasies regarding possibility of rescue or intervention | Kovacs and Beck (1977) |
| Survey of Problem Behavior | General behavior rating scale; thirty-eight behavioral descriptions to be rated on four-point scale | Upper, Lochman, and Aveni (1977) |
| Teacher Problem Listing | Teacher indicates common problems from list of fifty-eight items; forty-two are conduct related, others represent classroom problems | Azrin, Azrin, and Armstrong (1977) |

**Table 15. Questionnaires with Demonstrated or Potential Utility for Behavioral Assessment (Continued)**

| Questionnaire | Comments | Representative References |
|---|---|---|
| Werry-Weiss-Peters Activity Rating Scale | Scale to assess effects of drug treatment; parents report frequencies of specific activities | Werry and others (1966) |
| Willoughby Personality Schedule | Questionnaire assessing general levels of "neurosis" with particular relevance to anxiety and discomfort in social situations | Wolpe (1969) |
| *Questionnaires Measuring Miscellaneous Other Behaviors* | | |
| Attitude Toward Behavior Modification Scale | Likert-type scale for assessing attitudes toward behavior modification in business organizations | Dubno and others (1978) |
| Autonomic Perception Questionnaire | Twenty-eight items; twenty-one deal with perceptions of bodily sensations during anxiety states; seven are related to pleasure states | D. Carroll (1977), Mandler, Mandler, and Uviller (1958), Mandler and Kremen (1958), and Whitehead and others (1977) |
| Behavioral Self-Concept Scale | Presents thirty-six pairs of items verbally and pictorially to students; items are related to classroom activities; children specify at which of each pair they are better | Williams and Workman (1978) |

| Instrument | Description | Reference |
|---|---|---|
| Child's Report of Parental Behavior Inventory | Fifty-six item questionnaire to assess children's perceptions of parent's child-rearing behaviors (accepting or rejecting, psychological autonomy or control, firm or lax control) | Margolies and Weintraub (1977) |
| Counselor Effectiveness Scale | Likert-type rating scale; representativeness of thirty behaviors judged for therapeutic camp counselors on six-point scale; overall effectiveness index | Deysach, Ross, and Hiers (1977) |
| Daily Teacher Questionnaire | Report-card format; teacher responds to ten class rules questions, one teacher satisfaction question, one classwork section to score daily points, and one grade section | Schumaker, Hovell, and Sherman (1977b) |
| Foster Home Reinforcement Survey Schedule | Twenty-four items rated on a four-point scale to determine reinforcers to be used in contracts for contingency programs | Upper, Lochman, and Aveni (1977) |
| Lead Exposure Questionnaire | Thirty items cover specific kinds of pica activity, as well as possibilities of exposure to airborne lead | David and others (1977) |
| Leisure Questionnaire | Open-ended question format regarding hobbies and recreation center usage (mental retardation center); elicits estimates of frequency of participation in twenty-nine activities on a five-point scale | Johnson and Bailey (1977) |

**Table 15. Questionnaires with Demonstrated or Potential Utility for Behavioral Assessment (Continued)**

| Questionnaire | Comments | Representative References |
|---|---|---|
| Rating Scale of Teacher Characteristics and Practices | Twenty-seven Likert-type items; five choices ranging from "strongly agree" to "strongly disagree"; assesses dimensions of warmth and support, use of harsh disciplinary practices, and amount of structure | Huston-Stein, Friedrick-Cofer, and Susman (1977) |
| Reinforcement Menu | A questionnaire designed to identify current or potential reinforcers | Homme and others (1969) |
| Reinforcement Survey Schedule | Questionnaire designed to identify potential and current reinforcers for use in behavior therapy | Cautela (1972), Cautela and Kastenbaum (1967), Kleinknecht, McCormick, and Thorndike (1973), Thorndike and Kleinknecht (1974) |
| Reinforcer Item Questionnaire | Ten-item questionnaire to determine reinforcers in a county prison | Bassett, Blanchard, and Koshland (1977) |
| Rotter I-E Locus of Control Scale | Measures client's perceived control over reinforcers; may indicate whether client perceives reinforcement as occurring as a function of external agents or as a function of client's own behavior | Rotter (1966) and Wener and Rehm (1975) |
| Therapy Sessions Assessment Questionnaire and Progress Assessment Questionnaire | Questionnaires that elicit information regarding perceptions of clarity of imagery and emotional arousal during sessions and frequency of practice between sessions | Diament and Wilson (1975) |

Toy-Use Questionnaire

Questionnaire to assess toy safety, durability, and appeal in play situations; identifies problems associated with toy management, safety, and durability

Quilitch, Christophersen, and Risley (1977)

the same time, if the intent of the questionnaire is to generate a sensitive index of a construct such as fear or depression, scaling procedures may be appropriate. Questionnaires appearing in the literature typically have been designed to provide either self-report measures from clients or ratings of clients by others (see Table 15). As checklist and scale formats are not, for the most part, treated separately in subsequent sections, considerations of sensitivity, reliability, and validity for questionnaires must take into account the response format employed as well as the respective data sources.

Within a behavioral construct system, it is important that questionnaires provide quantitative data on *specific behaviors* in *specific situations*. In this regard, behavioral questionnaires may provide indices of the rate of specific behaviors that are elements of the construct under investigation. When scales generate only an index of adjustment in specific areas, the utility and content validity of such scales within a behavioral construct system are limited since they do not provide quantitative data on behavior rates and maintaining contingencies or sufficient specification of target behaviors. Not only must behavioral questionnaires generate an overall index with adequate reliability and validity, but they must provide a great range and specificity of data to function adequately as preintervention behavioral assessment instruments.

Subsequent sections of this chapter review questionnaire applications according to the categories of behavior targeted for assessment. Since a principal aim of the chapter is to evaluate issues of reliability and validity, studies having implications for these topics will be emphasized. But it may be helpful to briefly reintroduce the principles of reliability and validity (see Chapter One) as they pertain to the psychometric evaluation of questionnaires. The procedures involved in assessing reliability of questionnaires essentially involve correlating scores derived from separate administrations of the questionnaire (stability) or from separate components of the questionnaire (internal consistency). In those cases where questionnaires involve ratings by external observers, calculations of interobserver agreement have also been employed. In respect to the reliability of questionnaires, it should be remembered that some behaviors may be expected to vary across time (for example, depressive feelings or patterns of marital interaction).

The stability of a questionnaire measure may thus be confounded with the stability of the client's behavior (Walls and others, 1977). For repeated measures, therefore, lack of stability may make the data uninterpretable.

Validity assessment of a questionnaire involves correlating scores with the outcome of other instruments or with subjects grouped by naturally occurring events (for example, depressed versus nondepressed clients). To review, validity components of interest may include:

1. Discriminant validity—the degree to which a questionnaire generates differential scores for subjects classed by naturally occurring events
2. Concurrent validity—the degree to which a questionnaire correlates with other, previously validated questionnaires or other assessment procedures administered at similar points in time
3. Predictive validity—the degree to which scores on target questionnaires correlate with data on target subjects derived from other instruments administered at a later point in time
4. Construct and content validity—construct validity is assessed through a series of criterion-related validity assessments and through evaluation of hypotheses derived from the construct system upon which the test is based; content validity refers to the degree to which items in the questionnaire adequately sample the dimensions being measured

### Assertiveness

In the recent literature, questionnaires have been utilized to assess assertive behaviors among adults (Hollandsworth, Galassi, and Gay, 1977; Wolfe and Fodor, 1977), including drug abusers (Zeichner, Pihl, and Wright, 1977) and psychiatric patients (Eisler and others, 1978; Finch and Wallace, 1977; Rathus and Nevid, 1977), as well as to assess assertive behaviors among college students (Hull and Hull, 1978; Nevid and Rathus, 1978; Nietzel, Martorano, and Melnick, 1977; Quillin, Besing, and Dinning, 1977; Turner and Adams, 1977). Typically, the scales employed have been of the self-report variety and have focused on such behaviors as interpersonal skills (Finch and Wallace, 1977), social skills (Zeichner, Pihl, and Wright, 1977), social expectations (Eisler and others, 1978), verbal responses (Wolfe and Fodor, 1977), and responsiveness to assertion skill training (Nietzel, Martorano, and Melnick, 1977; Turner and Adams, 1977). In several studies, questionnaires have been employed as treatment outcome measures (through pretreatment and posttreatment administrations) for assertiveness training (Finch and Wallace, 1977; Nietzel, Martorano, and Melnick, 1977; Wolfe and Fodor, 1977). Turner and Adams (1977) employed the Rathus Assertiveness Schedule for preintervention assessment and subject selection. In other studies (Hollandsworth, Galassi, and Gay, 1977; Quillin, Besing, and Dinning, 1977; Rathus and Nevid, 1977; Zeichner, Pihl, and Wright, 1977), questionnaire measures of assertiveness have served a research purpose in the functional analysis of behavior. Several of the questionnaire instruments employed in the assessment of assertiveness are presented in Table 15.

For the most part, recent investigations have reported the assertiveness questionnaires employed to be sensitive measures in reflecting changes in behavior as a function of intervention, although Wolfe and Fodor (1977) reported that an assertiveness questionnaire employed with female adults for the assessment of verbal assertive responses was insensitive. Similarly, Zeichner, Pihl, and Wright (1977) reported that a questionnaire measuring social skills did not discriminate between drug abusers and drug nonabusers. Although most of the evidence for the validity of questionnaires in the assessment of assertiveness appearing in the recent literature has been limited to reports of instrument sensitivity (one aspect of validity), a few investigators have additionally addressed other issues of validity. For example, Hollandsworth, Galassi, and Gay (1977) reported a validation study of the Adult Self-Expression Scale (ASES)—an assertiveness scale for adults that was reported earlier by Gay, Hollandsworth, and Galassi (1975). This forty-eight-item self-report measure of assertion was reported to correlate well with adjective checklist scales and to show moderate to high construct and concurrent validity, as well as high test-retest reliability (Gay, Hollandsworth, and Galassi, 1975).

In the most recent investigation of the Adult Self-Expression Scale (Hollandsworth, Galassi, and Gay, 1977), the convergent and discriminant validity of the scale was assessed in two studies. In the first, the ASES was administered, along with the abasement, dominance, and aggression scales of an adjective checklist (Gough and Heilbrun, 1965) and a Behavior Questionnaire consisting of ten items from the ASES rewritten in the form of observer ratings for peer evaluations of assertion, to a sample of normal adults, college students, and psychiatric inpatients. In the second study, the ASES was administered, along with the Rathus Assertiveness Schedule (Rathus, 1973) and three subscales of the Buss-Durker Inventory (Buss, 1961), to a population of assaultive and nonassaultive criminal offenders. Two independent judges (blind to the research aim) put subjects' behaviors into five categories ranging from "not aggressive" to "aggressive to an extreme," based on prior criminal records. Findings in the first study indicated a significant correlation between the ASES and the Rathus Assertiveness Schedule, supporting the convergent validity of the ASES when self-report was used as a measure of assertion. A significantly negative correlation with abasement scales on the adjective checklist also was obtained, likewise providing support for the convergent validity of the ASES. The discriminant validity of the ASES—reflected by stronger correlations between self-reports of assertion on the ASES and peer-rated assertion on the Behavior Questionnaire than between self-reported assertion and peer-rated aggression—was supported only for the group of normal adults. However, results in the second study yielded further support for the discrimination validity of the ASES in that the relationship between self-reports on the ASES and Rathus Assertiveness Schedule was greater than that between self-reports on the ASES and Buss-Durker Inventory of aggression. Taken together, these findings are generally supportive of the discriminant validity of the ASES, as well as of moderate to strong convergent validity across a variety of populations. While this evidence, along with the strong relationship found with respect to other self-report instruments, suggests the potential utility of the ASES as a measure of assertive behavior for use with adults in general, evidence thus far is limited and must be interpreted cautiously. For example, a recent investigation by DeGiovanni and

Epstein (1978) found a significant correlation between the ASES and the aggression dimension of a behavior checklist, suggesting a possible confounding between assertion and aggression on such scales.

Also appearing in the recent literature have been two reports (Nietzel, Martorano, and Melnick, 1977; Rathus and Nevid, 1977) relating to the validity of the Rathus Assertiveness Schedule (Rathus, 1973). With respect to the concurrent validity of the scale in applications with psychiatric populations, Rathus and Nevid (1977) administered the questionnaire to 191 psychiatric patients (neurotics, schizophrenics, and individuals with personality disorders). Findings supportive of the concurrent validity of the scale were reported in that Rathus Assertiveness Schedule measures correlated highly (.80 for all diagnostic categories) with therapists' ratings of assertiveness on a semantic differential scale (see Rathus and Nevid, 1977). Split-half reliability coefficients for internal consistency were reported as .84 for neurotics, .73 for schizophrenics, and .91 for individuals with personality disorders—coefficients generally supportive of the internal consistency of the questionnaire. However, these coefficients should be interpreted cautiously since split-half reliability coefficients are sensitive to the particular method employed in deriving the two halves and thus represent a less powerful method of assessing internal consistency. With respect to discriminant validity, Nietzel, Martorano, and Melnick (1977) recently reported that the Rathus Assertiveness Schedule differentiated between groups of assertive and nonassertive male and female students. While Hull and Hull (1978) reported a finding of no sex differences with respect to total score on the Rathus Assertiveness Schedule among undergraduates, a significant sex-by-question interaction was reported. A factor analysis yielded twelve main factors for males, eleven main factors for females, and eleven main factors for males and females combined. Because of the large number of approximately equally weighted factors, Hull and Hull suggested that assertion may be situation specific rather than representative of a generalized trait.

In summary, questionnaires have been employed with a variety of adult populations in the assessment of assertiveness. These questionnaires have been employed as outcome measures of assertiveness training, as a means of preintervention assessment and subject selection, and for purposes of research in scale evaluation and functional behavior analysis. A majority of investigators have reported the scales employed to be sensitive measures with respect to changes in behavior. Nevertheless, except for reports of instrument sensitivity, investigators have infrequently addressed issues of scale validity, although tentative evidence for the convergent and discriminant validity of the Adult Self-Expression Scale was recently reported, as was additional data supportive of the concurrent and discriminant validity of the Rathus Assertiveness Schedule. Typically, scales employed in the assessment of assertiveness have been nonspecific (trait oriented), although adequate function as a preintervention assessment instrument requires specificity of data. Two additional issues addressed in this section that are deserving of additional investigation are those of situational specificity in the assessment of assertiveness and the potential confounding of the dimensions of assertion and aggression within the scales employed.

## Social Interactions

In the assessment of social interactions, the populations with which questionnaires have been utilized are varied and have included infants (Becker, 1977), preschoolers (Behar, 1977), and school-aged children (Knight and Kagan, 1977; Lambert, Essen, and Gead, 1977; Oden and Asher, 1977), as well as adults (Eisler and others, 1978; Farrell, Wallander, and Mariotto, 1978; Fischetti, Curran, and Wessberg, 1977; D. P. Greenwald, 1977; Klaus, Hersen, and Bellack, 1977; Little, Curran, and Gilbert, 1977; Lowe and Cautela, 1978; Trower and others, 1978). Several of the questionnaire instruments employed in the assessment of social interactions are presented in Table 15. The formats of the questionnaires employed typically have included teacher ratings (Behar, 1977; Lambert, Essen, and Gead, 1977) and caretaker ratings (Becker, 1977), as well as self-report measures by adults (Eisler and others, 1978; Farrell, Wallander, and Mariotto, 1978; Fischetti, Curran, and Wessberg, 1977; D. P. Greenwald, 1977; Greenwald, 1978; Klaus, Hersen, and Bellack, 1977; Little, Curran, and Gilbert, 1977;

Lowe and Cautela, 1978; Trower and others, 1978; Williams and Ciminero, 1978) and children (Knight and Kagan, 1977). Included among those child behaviors targeted for assessment by questionnaire instruments have been social interactions (Behar, 1977; Knight and Kagan, 1977), social isolation (Oden and Asher, 1977), peer contacts of infants (Becker, 1977), and social inappropriateness (Lambert, Essen, and Gead, 1977). For adults, behaviors targeted for questionnaire assessment have included dating activity (D. P. Greenwald, 1977; Greenwald, 1978), dating frequency, patterns, and problems (Klaus, Hersen, and Bellack, 1977), heterosexual interactions (Williams and Ciminero, 1978), and heterosexual social anxiety (Farrell, Wallander, and Mariotto, 1978; Fischetti, Curran, and Wessberg, 1977; Little, Curran, and Gilbert, 1977). While a majority of the questionnaires applied to social interactions have been for the purpose of research, including subject screening (Farrell, Wallander, and Mariotto, 1978) and subject selection (Williams and Ciminero, 1978), Oden and Asher (1977) did report the use of a rating questionnaire with social isolates as an outcome measure of intervention through administration of the questionnaire before and after treatment.

Reports of the sensitivity of questionnaire measures to social interactions have been somewhat inconsistent. While several investigators have not addressed this issue, others have reported evidence for the sensitivity of questionnaire measures in reflecting changes in social interactions among children (Behar, 1977; Knight and Kagan, 1977; Lambert, Essen, and Gead, 1977) and among adults (Eisler and others, 1978; Klaus, Hersen, and Bellack, 1977; Little, Curran, and Gilbert, 1977). With regard to a rating scale assessment of socially isolated children, however, Oden and Asher (1977) found the scale to be insensitive as an outcome measure of treatment effects. As in the case of questionnaire assessment of assertiveness mentioned previously, reports of the validity of social interaction questionnaires, when addressed at all, have been based largely on instrument sensitivity.

Recently, Behar (1977) reported on the development of the Preschool Behavior Questionnaire (a modification of the Children's Behavior Questionnaire developed by Rutter (1967), a thirty-item scale to rate children in the context of the peer group by preschool teachers. Standardization involved administration of the scale to children ages three to six. The standardization sample was comprised of 496 "normal" children and 102 children professionally diagnosed as emotionally and behaviorally disturbed. A root-number, root-plot factor analysis yielded a three-factor solution; dimensions included: (1) hostile-aggressive, (2) anxious-fearful, and (3) hyperactive-distractible. Discriminative power of the scale was reduced by less than .5 percent when items that did not discriminate were dropped. Interrater agreement coefficients between two groups of raters (teachers and aides) yielded an overall agreement coefficient of .84, with coefficients of .81, .71, and .67 for factors one, two, and three, respectively (reliability decreased as factor size decreased).

With respect to dating behaviors, Klaus, Hersen, and Bellack (1977) employed a self-report questionnaire consisting of thirty-five questions regarding the frequency of dating behaviors, specific problems encountered on dates, and desirable dating patterns. Subjects were also asked to specify those factors that limited their dating behaviors, the degree of difficulty they had with various aspects of dating (rated on a five-point scale), and the stage of the dating relationship during which they were likely to engage in various behaviors. Subjects rated the degree of difficulty encountered relative to each activity on a five-point scale ("no difficulty" to "extreme difficulty"). Pearson product-moment correlations among the variables associated with dating frequency, dates desired, and difficulties encountered yielded acceptable levels of significance, except for items dealing with difficulties reported in avoiding or curtailing sex and the number of dates desired monthly. The authors also reported the scale to be sensitive to differences between high- and low-frequency daters (discriminant validity). Also related to social interactions, the Dating History Questionnaire (Curran, Gilbert, and Little, in press) has recently been employed in the investigation of heterosexual social anxiety (Curran, 1977; Little, Curran, and Gilbert, 1977). Utilizing two different subject recruitment procedures (advertisement of a therapy analogue study and selection of subjects from undergraduate classes), Little, Curran, and Gilbert (1977) reported evidence for the discriminant validity of the scale; scale measures corresponded to behavioral measures of anxiety and behavioral ratings of skill, which in turn differentiated between the two groups.

Recently, Williams and Ciminero (1978) reported the development of the Survey of Heterosexual Interactions for Females, a self-report measure containing four questions on dating frequency and presenting twenty heterosexual situations in which the subject rates (on a five-point scale) her ability to initiate or carry on a conversation in that situation. Initial data obtained with a population of female undergraduates yielded an alpha coefficient (for internal consistency) of .89 and a test-retest correlation of .62. Additionally, a correlation of .558 was reported between this scale and the Rathus Assertiveness Schedule and a correlation of −.404 with the Trait portion of the State-Trait Anxiety Inventory. While this scale appears to have potential utility for subject selection, additional information will be necessary to evaluate its utility as an outcome measure.

Also reported in the recent literature was the development of the Social Performance Survey Schedule (Lowe and Cautela, 1978). The scale involves self-ratings of the frequency of social behaviors on a five-point Likert scale. Part A consists of 50 positive social behavior items and Part B consists of 50 negative social behavior items. An initial pool of social traits was generated by undergraduates; next, these items were behaviorally defined to generate comprehensive behavioral descriptions of the most common and important descriptors of social behavior (100 items). The scale requires subjects to rate frequencies with which they engage in the 100 behaviors on a five-point scale (zero to four) ranging from "not at all" to "very much." Interestingly, the scale may be scored by two different methods. Through the first method it is assumed a priori that better social performance is reflected if greater frequencies of positive than negative social behaviors occur. Part A (positive behavioral items) is thus scored with four points for responses of "very much," and Part B (negative behavioral items) is reverse-scored with four points for "not at all"; scores for Part A and Part B are then summed. The alternative scoring procedure allows for scoring according to judgments of various populations. Thus, judges rate ideal frequencies for each of the 100 behaviors. The average for judges' ratings, accordingly, represents the "ideal" frequency for each item. The absolute difference between the mean rating for the item and the item score for the particular subject is then taken for each item and subtracted from the score of four; the sum of the 100 resulting scores constitutes the adjusted total, and higher adjusted A and B scores reflect more ideal frequencies. Reliability estimates employing Pearson test-retest correlations were: (1) total test = .87 for unadjusted and .86 for adjusted scores; (2) Part A = .76 for unadjusted and .88 for adjusted scores; and (3) Part B = .87 for unadjusted and .85 for adjusted scores. Alpha coefficients for internal consistency were .88 and .94 for unadjusted and adjusted scores, respectively. Also reported was a moderate and inverse correlation with the Social Avoidance and Distress Scale (Watson and Friend, 1969), a predicted relationship between social performance and social anxiety.

In summary, questionnaires have recently been employed in the assessment of social interactions of infants, preschool and school-aged children, and adults. With regard to format, questionnaires typically have involved teacher and caretaker ratings for child behaviors and self-report measures for adults. Child behaviors assessed with questionnaires have included social interactions, isolation, and nonconformity. Adult behaviors assessed have included dating patterns and heterosexual social anxiety. Although most often serving the purpose of research in the functional analysis of social interaction, questionnaires have also been employed as intervention outcome measures through comparisons of pretreatment and posttreatment responses. Finally, to the extent that investigators have addressed the issue of validity, attention has largely been confined to reports of questionnaire sensitivity in reflecting changes in observed behaviors. Although little has appeared in the recent literature with respect to construct or criterion-related validity, some recent evidence was reported with respect to the discriminant validity of a scale for the measurement of dating behaviors and a scale designed to assess heterosexual social anxiety. Also discussed was the development of a social performance scale that may have utility for preintervention assessment of social skills, as was a newly developed scale that may have utility for subject selection for analogue research in heterosexual social skills. Additionally, reports on a scale designed to assess children in the context of the peer group have been initially promising. Finally, while many of the questionnaires employed generate a general index of behavior, only a few provide information regarding behavioral frequencies, even though it is desirable within a behavioral construct system that questionnaires provide quantitative data on specific behaviors in specific situations.

## Marital Interaction and Satisfaction

Several investigators have recently employed self-report questionnaires in the assessment of marital interaction and satisfaction. While a majority of these assessments have focused on marital discord (Jacobson, 1977; Newmark, Woody, and Ziff, 1977; Oltmans, Broderick, and O'Leary, 1977; Snyder, 1977) and marital stress (Margolin and Weiss, 1978), questionnaires have also been utilized in the assessment of sexual activities (Birchler and Webb, 1977; Foster, 1977) and other interactions, including leisure-time behaviors (Birchler and Webb, 1977) among problem and nonproblem couples. In contrast to the somewhat infrequent reports of the application of questionnaires as preintervention instruments with other categories of behavior, a majority of those studies reviewed in this section have utilized questionnaires for preintervention assessment (Jacobson, 1977; Margolin and Weiss, 1978; Newmark, Woody, and Ziff, 1977; Oltmans, Broderick, and O'Leary, 1977; Snyder, 1977). With marital interaction, questionnaires have also served a research function (Birchler and Webb, 1977; Newmark, Woody, and Ziff, 1977) and as outcome measures of treatment effects (Birchler and Webb, 1977) through pretreatment and posttreatment administrations. Furthermore, investigators have consistently reported the questionnaires employed to be sensitive indicators of changes in the behaviors targeted for assessment. Several of the questionnaire instruments employed in the assessment of marital interaction and satisfaction are presented in Table 15.

Recently, Foster (1977) reported on the development of a paper-and-pencil self-report questionnaire, the Sexual Compatibility Test, that assesses the sexual interaction of married couples. Employing a sample of 200 men and women (matching the characteristics of the U.S. married population for age, income, education, and race), the 101-item scale was administered to assess the full range of their sexual activities with their respective partners. From these test responses, eleven sexual scales were constructed and arranged in an MMPI-type profile sheet; normative data for twelve sexual content subtests, for six dysfunctional scores, and for overall sexual satisfaction were obtained. In support of the internal consistency of the scales, Foster reported alpha coefficients ranging from .90 to .96. Test-retest Pearson product-moment correlations for the seven scales ranged from .79 to .97. Also with respect to marital interaction, some evidence was recently reported by Birchler and Webb (1977) for the discriminant validity of the Marital Activities Inventory, which assesses eighty-five leisure-time activities, including sex, in which individuals have participated with their spouses (alone or with others) over the previous month, and for the discriminant validity of the Areas of Change Questionnaire, which assesses the degree of behavior change that partners indicate for self and spouse in thirty-four typical problem areas. These questionnaires were administered to fifty happy couples (staff volunteers) and fifty unhappy couples (persons seeking treatment) at the University of Oregon Marital Studies Center; the scales were found to differentiate between the two groups in that problem couples differed in rates of intercourse, proportion of free-time activities engaged in together, and the number of unresolved problems reported.

Finally, in the questionnaire assessment of problem family interactions, Snyder (1977) has reported further evidence for the criterion-related validity of the Locke-Wallace Marital Adjustment Scale and the Quay-Peterson Behavior Problem Checklist. In a structured observation setting, family interactions (mother-father-child) were observed through use of the Patterson coding and sampling system. Problem families were defined as those achieving low scores (marital dissatisfaction), that is, scores below 95 on the Locke-Wallace or scores of 11 or less on the Problem Behavior Checklist. Ten problem and ten nonproblem families (as distinguished by the questionnaire criteria) were thus observed; subsequent observation revealed the problem families to provide more aversive and fewer positive consequences for prosocial behavior, as well as more positive and fewer negative consequences for deviant behaviors, than did nonproblem families, reflecting evidence for the discriminant validity of the questionnaires and for the observation system employed.

In summary, questionnaires employed in the assessment of marital interaction and satisfaction have been of the self-report format. Most frequently, these assessments have involved marital discord, although some investigators have utilized questionnaires to assess sexual activities and other behaviors. Typically the function of these questionnaires has been for preintervention assessment (identification of problem behaviors), although some have been employed as outcome measures of treatment and for the functional analysis of behavior. Again, however, the degree of behavioral and situational specificity associated with questionnaire measures in the assessment of marital interaction and satisfaction is somewhat limited. While the sensitivity of questionnaires in reflecting changes in behavior has consistently been reported, only limited information has appeared with respect to other investigations of questionnaire validity. Some evidence, however, has appeared with respect to the discriminant validity of the Quay-Peterson and Locke-Wallace scales in differentiating problem from nonproblem families in regard to interactions. Likewise, some evidence has appeared suggesting the discriminant validity of the Marital Activities Inventory and the Areas of Change Questionnaire in differentiating problem from nonproblem married couples. Also reported in the recent literature was the development of a new questionnaire (the Sexual Compatibility Test) for the assessment of the sexual interactions of married couples.

## Ingestive Behaviors

In the recent literature, the application of questionnaires for the assessment of ingestive behaviors has included populations of obese and overweight adults (Ashby and Wilson, 1977; Dash and Brown, 1977; L. Green, 1978; Kingsley and Wilson, 1977; Quereshi, 1977; Steffen and Myszak, 1978; Tobias and MacDonald, 1977) and alcoholic adults (Atsaides, Neuringer, and Davis, 1977; Davidson and Bremser, 1977; Hay, Hay, and Nelson, 1977b; Miller, 1978; Sobell and Sobell, 1978), as well as adult smokers (Blittner,

Goldberg, and Merbaum, 1978; Emmelkamp and Walta, 1978). These questionnaires have typically been of the self-report format. With respect to eating behaviors, Tobias and MacDonald (1977) collected self-report information regarding demographic and eating characteristics. Similarly, Quereshi (1977) employed a questionnaire to investigate behaviors and life-style characteristics of obese persons. Kingsley and Wilson (1977) employed a dieting history questionnaire with obese persons, while Dash and Brown (1977) explored cognitive and behavioral variables related to dietary issues through the use of a questionnaire. Finally, Ashby and Wilson (1977) utilized a questionnaire to assess treatment session and therapist helpfulness among overweight adults. In regard to drinking behaviors, questionnaires have been utilized to assess antecedent response parameters and consequences of drinking patterns (Hay, Hay, and Nelson, 1977b) and to evaluate MMPI responses on a derived alcoholic scale (Atsaides, Neuringer, and Davis, 1977). Table 15 presents questionnaire instruments employed in the assessment of ingestive behaviors.

The functions of questionnaires in the assessment of ingestive behaviors have included pretreatment and posttreatment measures for evaluations of intervention outcomes of obesity programs (Ashby and Wilson, 1977; Dash and Brown, 1977; Tobias and MacDonald, 1977) and smoking programs (Blittner, Goldberg, and Merbaum, 1978). Questionnaires have also been used to assess expectancies for success in obesity treatment programs (Steffen and Myszak, 1978) and as outcome measures of treatment for alcoholism (Davidson and Bremser, 1977). Additionally, questionnaires have served as preintervention assessment devices with obese subjects (Dash and Brown, 1977; Kingsley and Wilson, 1977; Quereshi, 1977) and alcoholic subjects (Hay, Hay, and Nelson, 1977b; Miller, 1978), as diagnostic instruments with adult alcoholics (Atsaides, Neuringer, and Davis, 1977), and for subject assignments to obesity research groups (L. Green, 1978) and subject selection for smoking treatment programs (Emmelkamp and Walta, 1978).

As with the application of questionnaires in the assessment of other categories of behavior, scales employed in the assessment of ingestive behaviors have generally been reported to be sensitive (quick to reflect changes in the behaviors under investigation). Tobias and MacDonald (1977) published the Scale of Internal Versus External Control of Weight, a five-item questionnaire that includes subject reports of whether weight is hereditary, whether there is a need for tangible motivation to lose weight, and whether weight is due to early problems in childhood. In a comparison of several treatment approaches to weight loss, the scale was reported to demonstrate significant decreases across time; test-retest reliability was .52 on a control sample. Also bearing on the issue of weight control, Dash and Brown (1977) recently reported on an attempt to develop a self-rating instrument that would have predictive value with regard to subjects' abilities to lose weight. This new scale, the Dash-Brown Survey of Fact and Fiction in Weight Reduction, contains three major parts. Part I consists of thirty-five statements (twenty items are related to common beliefs regarding weight reduction and obesity and fifteen items involve commonly held fantasies of overweight dieters) that are rated on a seven-point scale as to accuracy. In Part II, the subject is presented with a list of ten food items and asked which to eat and which to avoid in order to lose weight. Part III presents a list of twenty food items and requires the subject (1) to circle the correct number of calories for each from five choices and (2) to rate how much the food item is liked on a seven-point scale, with one equaling "great dislike" and seven equaling "very much liked." Preliminary evidence for construct and content validity was reported, along with test-reliability coefficients (obtained from samples of high school seniors and college nutrition students) ranging from .635 to .892, with a total coefficient of .948.

In an investigation of the psychosocial correlates of obesity control, Quereshi (1977) employed the Rating of Self-Status, a self-rating questionnaire primarily consisting of multiple-choice items dealing with behaviors and life-styles of obese individuals. Of the sixty-nine items, fifty deal with behavior patterns and nineteen involve biographical and biosocial items. From a weight loss organization, female members of chapters showing the highest average weight loss (for one year) and of chapters showing the lowest average weight loss were asked to complete the questionnaire. Subsequently, a multivariate analysis of variance (MANOVA) and a factor analysis employing Pearson product-moment correlations were performed on the data; data analysis resulted in twenty-four factors. Although MANOVA comparisons of high-weight-loss and low-weight-loss chapters on the twenty-four dependent variables did not reflect significant differences, a subsequent MANOVA that contrasted remedially and nonremedially obese individuals (regardless of chapter membership) was reported by the authors to yield highly significant overall results on ten of the twenty-four factors; of these, eight were in the predicted direction. While these data suggest that certain behavioral and biosocial characteristics may reliably and validly distinguish between remedially and non-remedially obese subjects (discriminant validity), these results must be interpreted with caution since the criterion of significance employed ranged from a confidence level of .10 to .001.

Finally, Atsaides, Neuringer, and Davis (1977) recently reported on the development of a questionnaire to differentiate alcoholics from neurotic subjects. For 70 male alcoholic and 70 male neurotic subjects, MMPI long-form responses were obtained. Item frequencies of the first set of 35 patients from each group were compared by a chi-square or Fisher's exact test; using a .05 confidence level, a set of items was generated. This procedure was repeated with the second set of patients. Using items that were significant for both sets of subjects, the MMPIs of all 140 subjects were then scored on the derived alcoholism scale, followed by an evaluation to establish a maximum efficiency cutoff score that would correctly diagnose most patients while minimizing false negatives and false positives. The evaluation yielded an eight-item scale. Data indicated the scale to correctly identify approximately 85 percent for each group (discriminant validity). It should be noted further, however, that the utility of the scale may be limited to diagnosis of male inpatients.

To summarize, the recent applications of questionnaires for the assessment of ingestive behaviors have primarily been directed toward populations of obese and alcoholic adults and typically have been of the self-report variety. Targets of questionnaire assessments have included demographic characteristics and dieting histories of obese individuals, helpfulness of therapists in treatment programs for obesity, antecedent and response parameters of drinking behaviors and, in a few cases, smoking behaviors. With regard to ingestive behaviors, questionnaires have functioned as outcome measures of treatment for obesity and alcoholism, as preintervention assessment instruments with obese and alcoholic patients as well as smokers, and as diagnostic instruments with alcoholic adults, although the scales so employed typically have not provided quantitative data on situational aspects or frequencies of the targeted behaviors. While a majority of investigators have reported the scales employed to be sensitive to behavioral changes, only limited evidence has appeared relative to other aspects of scale validities.

### Fears

One of the most frequent applications of behavioral questionnaires appearing in the recent literature has been in the assessment of fear responses, as Table 15 illustrates. Typically, these assessments have been directed at male and female adult populations, including one investigation involving adult retardates (Peck, 1977). The great majority of questionnaires employed in the assessment of fear responses have utilized a self-report structure, although Peck (1977) employed a checklist format as part of the assessment of acrophobia among adult retardates. Similarly, Gautheir and Marshall (1977) employed a checklist along with self-report measures in the assessment of snake phobias among female undergraduates.

Among the behaviors targeted for questionnaire assessment have been spider phobias (Efran and others, 1977; Lineham and others, 1977), rat phobias (Efran and others, 1977; Lick, Sushinsky, and Malow, 1977; Peck, 1977; Smith and Coleman, 1977), and snake phobias (Denny and Sullivan, 1976; Efran and others, 1977; Gautheir and Marshall, 1977; Lick, Sushinsky, and Malow, 1977; Moss and Arend, 1977; Rosenthal, Hung, and Kelley, 1977; Suedfeld and Hare, 1977; Sullivan and Denny, 1977). Fears of height have also been the target of questionnaire assessment (Bootzin and Kazdin, 1972; Cohen, 1977; Lineham and others, 1977; Peck, 1977), as have dental fears (Mathews and Rezin, 1977; Wroblewski, Jacob, and Rehm, 1977), fears of public transportation (Hayes and Barlow, 1977), and fears of tissue damage and bodily injury (Beiman and others, 1978). Investigators have also employed questionnaires in the assessment of an eyepatch phobia (Thomas and Rapp, 1977) and to assess social and heterosexual phobias (James, 1978). Additionally, questionnaires have been utilized with public speaking and speech anxieties (Gatchel and others, 1977; Fremouw and Zitter, 1978; Giesen and McGlynn, 1977; Goldfried and Goldfried, 1977; Kirsch and Henry, 1977; Lineham and others, 1977; Marshall, Presse, and Andrews, 1977; Marshall, Stoian, and Andrews, 1977; Weissberg, 1977), in the evaluation of achievement anxiety (Snyder and Deffenbacher, 1977) and test anxiety (Holroyd, 1978), to assess generalized anxiety (Horne and Matson, 1977; Ollendick and Nettle, 1977), and in the investigation of general and specific traits in the assessment of anxiety (Mellstrom, Zuckerman, and Cicala, 1978).

While the primary function of questionnaires for fear assessment in the recent literature has been as an outcome measure of intervention procedures (through pretreatment and posttreatment administrations), several investigators have employed questionnaires as a means of preintervention assessment for such behaviors as fears of snakes and rats (Efran and others, 1977), fears of spiders (Efran and others, 1977; Lineham and others, 1977), fears associated with speech behaviors including public speaking anxiety (Giesen and McGlynn, 1977; Lineham and others, 1977) and generalized anxiety (Horne and Matson, 1977). Recently, Gatchel and others (1977) employed a questionnaire as a diagnostic measure of speech-anxious subjects. In other investigations, Beiman and others (1978), Fremouw and Zitter (1978), and Lineham and others (1977) utilized questionnaires as a means of subject selection. Finally, in one recent investigation (Gautheir and Marshall, 1977) a questionnaire was employed not only as an outcome measure of an intervention with females with snake phobias but also in decisions for treatment termination. Although the majority of studies just discussed have reported that the questionnaires employed were sensitive, in that they quickly reflected changes in the behaviors under investigation, several have reported the opposite. For example, Wroblewski, Jacob, and Rehm (1977) reported a self-report questionnaire to be insensitive as an outcome measure with subjects manifesting dental fears. As an outcome measure of public speaking anxiety, Weissberg (1977) likewise reported on the insensitivity of a self-report questionnaire employed to assess treatment outcome. As an outcome measure of an intervention with fears of heights among adult retardates, Peck (1977) found the questionnaire employed to be insensitive in reflecting treatment effects.

In addition to reports of questionnaire sensitivity in the assessment of various fear responses, several investigators have reported evidence for the criterion-related validity of questionnaires in fear assessment. With respect to fears of snakes, for example, Moss and Arend (1977) reported a correlation of .79 between a behavior avoidance test and the Fear Survey Schedule III (Wolpe and Lazarus, 1966), suggesting the concurrent validity of that scale in the assessment of snake fears among college students. In addition, Moss and Arend (1977) employed a variation of Walk's (1956) Fear Thermometer to assess subjects' self-report feelings during a behavior avoidance test; this instrument was found to be sensitive to treatment effects and to correlate .42 with the Fear Survey Schedule III. Finally, the Rotter (1966) Locus of Control I-E Scale was found to correlate .43 with change in the behavior avoidance test, providing further evidence of the criterion-related validity of Rotter's scale.

A Snake Fear Questionnaire employed by Suedfeld and Hare (1977) likewise was reported to be highly correlated with the Fear Survey Schedule, as well as with heart-rate data. Criterion-related validity was also reported by Rosenthal, Hung, and Kelley (1977) for a Fear Rating (similar to a Fear Thermometer); at the closest point to the fear stimulus, clients were asked to rate the degree of fear "right now" on a ten-point scale. Correlations between ratings and a behavior avoidance test were significant. Finally, Schroeder and Craine (1971) found a correlation of .41 between a snake-touching behavior avoidance test and scores on the Lang Fear of Snakes Questionnaire, providing additional evidence for the criterion-related validity of that questionnaire. With respect to the assessment of public speaking anxiety, two investigations have generated evidence for the criterion-related validity of the questionnaires employed. Giesen and McGlynn (1977), in an investigation of public speaking anxiety involving sixty fearful and sixty nonfearful college students, asked subjects to complete Paul's

(1966) Personal Report of Confidence as a Speaker Scale (PRCS), a thirty-item self-report scale yielding scores for public speaking anxiety, along with Geer's (1965) Fear Survey Schedule II (an inventory questionnaire of fifty objects and situations involving fear levels on a one (no fear) to seven (terror) scale; a criterion of score levels of one to two defined nonfearful subjects). Although comparisons with physiological data (heart rate and skin conductance) suggested that relatively responsive speech-fearful subjects can be obtained through these self-report measures (discriminant validity), analysis of variance calculations indicated a lack of correlation between psychophysiological responsiveness and self-reported fears of public speaking.

In an investigation with students with cockroach phobias, Fazio (1969) reported actual behaviors (picking up a cockroach) to correlate .37 with a specially inserted cockroach item on the Fear Survey Schedule and .41 with a composite of six insect items. Smith and Coleman (1977), utilizing the Temple Fear Survey Inventory (Braun and Reynolds, 1969) to assess fears of rats among females, reported that the scale effectively discriminated among subjects, although a behavior avoidance test did not. Cohen (1977) recently reported the development of an Acrophobia Questionnaire (AQ). This self-report instrument consists of forty items, twenty of which involve common height-related situations. A zero-to-six-point scale for anxiety and a two-point scale for degree of avoidance are included to yield separate anxiety and avoidance scores. In an initial investigation, acrophobics were observed under three structured observation situations and were administered the Acrophobia Questionnaire, the Fear Survey Schedule III, the Willoughby Personality Schedule, and the Marlowe-Crowne Social Desirability Scale as pretest and posttest measures. Subsequent data analysis (which included a principal components analysis) yielded significant correlations between pretest behavioral measures and Acrophobia Questionnaire anxiety scores (−.32) and avoidance scores (−.46); behavioral measures were not significantly related to other questionnaire measures on pretest. On posttest, behavioral measures were significantly related to Acrophobia Qusetionnaire anxiety change (.42) and avoidance change (.40), as well as to the Fear Survey Schedule III change (.53). In emphasizing the low correlation between behavioral and nonbehavioral measures, Cohen suggested that this may have resulted from difficulties with the behavioral test; that is, (1) the test did not approximate real-life situations, and (2) the behavioral tests were not on an interval scale. However, these findings may also be a function of the fact that the different tests measure different aspects of anxiety. Additionally, it should be noted that, to obtain an index of concurrent validity between a questionnaire and behavioral measures, it would be desirable to administer the questionnaire *during* the behavioral test.

Finally, an analysis of the Test Anxiety Scale (Sarason, 1972) with respect to the components of test anxiety was recently reported by Richardson and others (1977). The scale was administered to 1200 undergraduates (839 females and 361 males); a matrix of intercorrelations of subjects' scores was factored using a principal axes method. Two factors accounting for 84.95 percent of the variance were then rotated by the varimax method. Components of Factor I were cognitive concern and worry about oneself and one's performance on tests, as well as apparent consequences of this worry such as interference and physiological indices of anxiety. Factor II involved reaction to emotional stress or aversion to the stress; this did not involve cognitive worry or autonomic arousal. Items correlating .35 or higher with either factor were then used to construct a sixteen-item Factor I and a fourteen-item Factor II subscale. Along with a significant correlation (−.24) reported between the two subscales, a high internal consistency coefficient (.90) was reported for the sixteen-item scale.

In summary, a frequent application of behavioral questionnaires in the recent literature has been in the assessment of fear responses. Typically, such questionnaire assessments have been directed toward adult populations and have been primarily of the self-report variety, although a limited number of checklists have also been employed. As with many other questionnaire instruments, those employed in the assessment of fear responses generally provide data in the form of indices rather than in terms of behavioral frequencies. Fears targeted for questionnaire assessments have included spider, rat, and snake phobias, acrophobia, dental and public transportation phobias, public speaking and speech anxieties, and achievement and generalized anxieties. While the major function of questionnaires in fear assessment has been as an outcome measure of intervention, several investigators have employed questionnaires for preintervention assessment, for subject selection, and in decisions regarding treatment termination. A majority of studies cited reported the questionnaires employed to be sensitive to changes in behavior, although a self-report scale of dental fears was insensitive to treatment outcomes. Likewise, a self-report questionnaire for measuring public speaking anxiety was reported insensitive, as was a questionnaire employed with adult retardates to assess fears of heights. Encouraging evidence for the criterion-related validity of several questionnaires for the assessment of snake, rat, and cockroach fears, as well as for public speaking anxiety, was also noted. Also appearing in the recent literature was the development of an acrophobia questionnaire that may have utility in the assessment of fears of height. Evidence for the factor structure and internal consistency of the Test Anxiety Scale has also appeared.

## Sexual Attitudes and Behavior

Questionnaires have been employed for the assessment of sexual attitudes and behaviors by several investigators. Presented in Table 15 are several of the instruments available for these assessments. Populations to which these assessments have been directed have included both children (Smith and Daglish, 1977) and adults (Auerbach and Kilmann, 1977; Heilbrun and Landauer, 1977; Kantorowitz, 1978; Levin and others, 1977; Maletzky, 1977; Pishkin and Thorne, 1977; Russell and Winkler, 1977; Thorne, 1977; Thorne and Pishkin, 1977; Zeiss, Rosen, and Zeiss, 1977). Included within adult female populations have been alcoholic and schizophrenic subjects (Pishkin and Thorne, 1977; Thorne and Pishkin, 1977), married women (Zeiss, Rosen, and Zeiss, 1977), and female undergraduates (Pishkin and Thorne, 1977; Thorne and Pishkin, 1977). Male adult populations have included subjects experiencing orgasmic problems (Kantorowitz, 1978), pedophiliac subjects (Levin and others, 1977), homosexual subjects (Maletzky, 1977; Russell and Winkler, 1977), and exhibitionistic subjects (Maletzky, 1977). The questionnaire formats employed with these subjects have been exclusively of the self-report type. Behaviors targeted for questionnaire assessment have included masculine and feminine patterns among children (Smith and Daglish, 1977), feminine role "inadaptability" (Pishkin and Thorne, 1977), and feminine self-concept (Thorne, 1977), as well as other feminine behaviors (Thorne and Pishkin, 1977). Additionally, questionnaires have been employed to assess sexual performance and satisfaction among adults (Auerbach and Kilmann, 1977), orgasmic responses (Kantorowitz, 1978; Zeiss, Rosen, and Zeiss, 1977), homosexual behaviors (Russell and Winkler, 1977), and reinforcing imagery and feared stimuli (Levin and others, 1977).

With respect to the assessment of sexual attitudes and behavior, questionnaires have primarily served as outcome measures (determined from pretreatment and posttreatment questionnaire responses) of intervention programs (Auerbach and Kilmann, 1977; Maletzky, 1977; Russell and Winkler, 1977; Zeiss, Rosen, and Zeiss, 1977). We located only two recent studies involving the utilization of questionnaires for the purpose of preintervention assessment (Levin and others, 1977; Russell and Winkler, 1977). One additional investigation employed questionnaires for purposes of subject selection (Kantorowitz, 1978). With regard to the sensitivity of questionnaires, investigators who have addressed this issue have reported the scales employed to quickly reflect changes in the behaviors targeted for assessment.

Recently, several investigators (Posavac and others, 1977; Pishkin and Thorne, 1977; Thorne, 1977; Thorne and Pishkin, 1977) have reported on the Femininity Study (Thorne, 1965), a 200-item questionnaire designed to assess female states and self-concepts representing feminine behaviors. Thorne (1977) reported that this unipolar instrument was designed to reflect differences across time among females with different demographic characteristics. Normative rates were established empirically by actual base rates of different clinical groups; item retention was a function of base rates' differentiation power among different groups. Each of eleven areas of adjustment was empirically sampled by twenty items, and this sampling yielded ten factors. Pishkin and Thorne (1977), in administering the scale to a sample of 31 alcoholics, 146 college students, and 152 schizophrenic females, identified five factors through factor analysis: (1) heterosexual social role instability,

(2) parental role inadaptability, (3) homemaker role inadaptability, (4) general affective (neurotic) instability, and (5) maternal role inadaptability. Base rates for these populations were reported to form a continuum from (presumably) normal female college students through alcoholic to institutionalized schizophrenic groups. Thorne and Pishkin (1977), employing a cluster analysis with data derived from student, alcoholic, and schizophrenic females, found item responses to be generally consistent across subgroups. Likewise, Posavac and others (1977) reported some evidence for the ability of the scale to discriminate among groups. Interpretation of these findings as supportive of the discriminant validity of the scale must be tempered, however, by the additional finding (Thorne and Pishkin, 1977) that the different populations showed wide differences in factorial composition of femininity at different points in time.

In summary, populations with which questionnaires have been employed in the assessment of sexual attitudes and behaviors have included both children and adults; behaviors targeted for investigation have included masculine and feminine patterns, sexual performance and orgasmic responses, and homosexual behavior. These questionnaires have been exclusively of the self-report format and have functioned primarily as outcome measures of intervention programs. The use of questionnaires for purposes of preintervention assessment and diagnosis has been quite limited, perhaps as a result of the limited behavioral and situational specificity of many of these scales. While several investigators have reported questionnaires to be sensitive to changes in behavior, not all have addressed this issue. Except for these reports of scale sensitivity and the initial investigations of the Femininity Study, little has appeared in the recent literature about other aspects of questionnaire validity in the assessment of sexual attitudes and behaviors.

## Problem Behaviors
## and Traits

Perhaps the most frequent application of behavioral questionnaires appearing in the recent literature has been in the assessment of problem behavior and traits. These assessments have focused on a variety of populations, including children (Abikoff, Gittelman-Klein, and Klein, 1977; Achenbach, 1978; Barkley, 1977b; Bolstad and Johnson, 1977; Bugental, Whalen, and Henker, 1977; Camp and others, 1977; Coleman, Walkind, and Ashley, 1977; Dreger, 1977; Forehand and King, 1977; Harris, Drummond, and Schultz, 1977; Johnston and others, 1977; Karoly and Rosenthal, 1977; Kent and O'Leary, 1977; Kohn, 1977; Minde, 1977; Oliveus, 1977; Quay, 1977; Reidy, 1977; Yepes and others, 1977), children and their parents (Dreger, 1977; Oltmans, Broderick, and O'Leary, 1977; Peed, Roberts, and Forehand, 1977), adolescents (Hodges and Deich, 1978; Huntwork and Ferguson, 1977; Murphy and Zahm, 1978; Wolff and Epstein, 1977), and adolescents and their parents (Kent and others, 1977b). Additional populations have included schizophrenics (Herr, Eaves, and Algozzine, 1977; Philip, 1977), neurotics (Free and Overall, 1977; Kenny, Mowbray, and Lalani, 1978), and other adults (Bumberry, Oliver, and McClure, 1978; Cautela, 1977; Cox, 1977; Dolan and Norton, 1977; Evans and Kazarian, 1977; Hodgson and Rachman, 1977; Hoffman and Overall, 1978; Hollandsworth and Cooley, 1978; Kazarian, Evans, and Lefave, 1977; Kovacs and Beck, 1977; Lanyon, 1977; Lester and Beck, 1977; Lubin, Marone, and Nathan, 1978; Novaco, 1977; O'Leary and others, 1977; Rimm and others, 1977; Rozensky and Rehm, 1977; Schrader, Craighead, and Schrader, 1978). Also the subjects of questionnaire assessment of problem behaviors and traits have been teachers and students (Azrin, Azrin, and Armstrong, 1977) and treatment staff members (D. N. Martin, 1977). Table 15 illustrates a number of questionnaire instruments available for the assessment of problem behaviors and traits.

The formats of questionnaires employed likewise have varied and have included ratings by others (Abikoff, Gittelman-Klein, and Klein, 1977; Achenbach, 1978; Barkley, 1977b; Bolstad and Johnson, 1977; Bugental, Whalen, and Henker, 1977; Dolan and Norton, 1977; Dreger, 1977; Evans and Kazarian, 1977; Forehand and King, 1977; Free and Overall, 1977; Hodges and Deich, 1978; Johnston and others, 1977; Kohn, 1977; Lubin, Marone, and Nathan, 1978; D. N. Martin, 1977; Minde, 1977; Murphy and Zahm, 1978; Oliveus, 1977; Peed, Roberts, and Forehand, 1977; Philip, 1977; Spring, Greenberg, and Yellin, 1977; Yepes and others, 1977) and self-reports and ratings (Bumberry, Oliver, and McClure, 1978; Cox, 1977; Harris, Drummond, and Schultz, 1977; Hodgson and Rachman, 1977; Hollandsworth and Cooley, 1978; Huntwork and Ferguson, 1977; Kazarian, Evans, and Lefave, 1977; Kenny, Mowbray, and Lalani, 1978; Kovacs and Beck, 1977; Lester and Beck, 1977; Novaco, 1977; O'Leary and others, 1977; Oltmans, Broderick, and O'Leary, 1977; Rozensky and Rehm, 1977; Schrader, Craighead, and Schrader, 1978). Additionally, a number of investigators have employed checklist formats for completion by mediators (Achenbach, 1978; Azrin, Azrin, and Armstrong, 1977; Camp and others, 1977; Herr, Eaves, and Algozzine, 1977; Hoffman and Overall, 1978; Karoly and Rosenthal, 1977; Kent and O'Leary, 1977; Lubin, Marone, and Nathan, 1978; Minde, 1977; Peed, Roberts, and Forehand, 1977; Quay, 1977).

With respect to children, behaviors targeted for assessment have included conduct problems in the school setting (Bolstad and Johnson, 1977; Kent and O'Leary, 1977), aggressive behaviors (Camp and others, 1977; Johnston and others, 1977; Oliveus, 1977; Reidy, 1977), noncompliant behaviors (Forehand and King, 1977; Peed, Roberts, and Forehand, 1977), hyperactivity (Abikoff, Gittelman-Klein, and Klein, 1977; Barkley, 1977b; Bugental, Whalen, and Henker, 1977; Spring, Greenberg, and Yellin, 1977; Yepes and others, 1977), and emotional and other behavioral disturbances (Achenbach, 1978; Azrin, Azrin, and Armstrong, 1977; Coleman, Walkind, and Ashley, 1977; Dreger, 1977; Harris, Drummond, and Schultz, 1977; Karoly and Rosenthal, 1977; Kohn, 1977; D. N. Martin, 1977; Oltmans, Broderick, and O'Leary, 1977; Quay, 1977). Among adolescent populations, behaviors targeted for questionnaire assessment have included drug usage (Huntwork and Ferguson, 1977) and disturbed behaviors within families (Kent and others, 1977b).

Behaviors targeted for questionnaire assessment within adult populations have included suicidal intent (Kovacs and Beck, 1977), suicidal wishes (Lester and Beck, 1977), other depressive behaviors (Bumberry, Oliver, and McClure, 1978; Lubin, Marone, and Nathan, 1978; O'Leary and others, 1977; Rozensky and Rehm, 1977; Schrader, Craighead, and Schrader, 1978), psychopathological symptom complaints (Hoffman and Overall, 1978), neurotic outpatient behaviors (Free and Overall, 1977), illogical thoughts of those with phobias (Rimm and others, 1977), and obsessive-compulsive complaints (Evans and Kazarian, 1977; Hodgson and Rachman, 1977; Kazarian, Evans, and Lefave, 1977; Kenny, Mowbray, and Lalani, 1978). Questionnaires have also been employed to assess changes in the ward behavior of schizophrenic patients (Dolan and Norton, 1977; Philip, 1977), adjustment problems of schizophrenic patients (Herr, Eaves, and Algozzine, 1977), and other psychiatric problems (Minde, 1977; Wolff and Epstein, 1977), as well as behavioral problems and deficits among retardates (Hodges and Deich, 1978; Murphy and Zahm, 1978). Also included among questionnaire assessments have been problem behaviors such as anger (Hollandsworth and Cooley, 1978; Novaco, 1977), stuttering (Lanyon, 1977), menstrual symptoms (Cox, 1977), and pain (Cautela, 1977).

   In regard to problem behaviors and traits, one of the most frequent purposes of questionnaires has been for the development and evaluation (of the utility and validity) of the questionnaires themselves. Additional functions of questionnaire applications have included preintervention assessments (Achenbach, 1978; Azrin, Azrin, and Armstrong, 1977; Kent and others, 1977b; Lanyon, 1977; Wolff and Epstein, 1977; Yepes and others, 1977), outcome evaluations of treatment programs through comparisons of pretreatment and posttreatment measures (Achenbach, 1978; Barkley, 1977b; Camp and others, 1977; Dolan and Norton, 1977; Forehand and King, 1977; Free and Overall, 1977; Hodges and Deich, 1978; Hollandsworth and Cooley, 1978; Karoly and Rosenthal, 1977; Kenny, Mowbray, and Lalani, 1978; Kent and O'Leary, 1977; Murphy and Zahm, 1978; Oltmans, Broderick, and O'Leary, 1977; Peed, Roberts, and Forehand, 1977; Yepes and others, 1977), diagnosis (Herr, Eaves, and Algozzine, 1977), the ongoing evaluation of therapy (Wolff and Epstein, 1977), and subject selection (Achenbach, 1978; Schrader, Craighead, and Schrader, 1978). A majority of these investigations have reported the questionnaires employed to be sensitive in reflecting changes in behavior as a function of intervention, although not all authors have addressed this issue. In contrast, Herr, Eaves, and Algozzine (1977) indicated questionable sensitivity for a checklist employed for the purpose of diagnosis of schizophrenic and adjustment reactions. Likewise, Kent and O'Leary (1977) found a teacher checklist of children's conduct problems in school to be insensitive as a measure of intervention outcome.

With respect to the validity of questionnaire assessments of depression, several recent studies (Bumberry, Oliver, and McClure, 1978; Lester and Beck, 1977; Lubin, Marone, and Nathan, 1978; Rozensky and Rehm, 1977) are of note. Rozensky and Rehm (1977) classified subjects referred to the psychology service of a Veterans Administration hospital on the basis of the Beck Depression Inventory. Individuals classified as to high or moderate depression were compared with a control group with respect to amounts of self-delivered reinforcement on a memory task; as expected, "highs" self-delivered fewer rewards, providing evidence for the construct validity of that scale. Additional evidence for the concurrent validity of the Beck Depression Inventory was recently reported by Bumberry, Oliver, and McClure (1978). Drawing on a college student population and employing psychiatric ratings of depth of depression as a criterion, a Pearson correlation of .77 between the ratings and the Beck Depression Inventory was reported. Accordingly, the authors suggested this evidence to be supportive of the concurrent validity of the instrument for assessments of depression in university populations when psychiatric estimates of the depth of depression are employed as the standard.

Also employing the Beck Depression Inventory, Lester and Beck (1977) administered the scale to 188 hospitalized depressive patients who manifested some degree of suicidal ideation; factorial structures of responses on the depression inventory were similar for groups of both suicidal ideators and suicide attempters. Kovacs and Beck (1977) reported on the Suicidal Intent Scale, a questionnaire administered in the form of a structured interview, to assess the seriousness of suicidal intent. This objective, fifteen-item scale quantifies relevant facets of the attempter's verbal and nonverbal behavior prior to and during suicidal acts. Each item includes three choices (0, 1, 2; the higher the score, the greater the seriousness of the attempt). Part I (items one to eight) assesses objective circumstances surrounding the attempt (including preparation, setting, prior subject cues to facilitate or hamper discovery). Part II (items nine to fifteen) covers the perception of the attempter of the lethality of the method, fantasies regarding the possibility of rescue or intervention, the extent of premeditation, and the reported subjective purpose of the attempt. High internal consistency and interrater reliability for the Suicidal Intent Scale were reported earlier by Beck, Schuyler, and Herman (1974), as was evidence for its concurrent and construct validity (Beck, Morris, and Lester, 1974; Minkoff and others, 1973).

With respect to the assessment of depression through checklist formats, Lubin, Marone, and Nathan (1978) recently reported an investigation involving a comparison of obtained scores on a Depression Adjective Checklist (Lubin, 1967) under two administration formats: (1) examiner-administered and (2) self-administered. Within a population of psychiatric inpatients, no significant differences between scores under the two administration formats were found, suggesting the acceptability of examiner administration with clients such as functional illiterates. Also appearing recently (Hoffman and Overall, 1978) was an investigation of the factor structure of the Symptom Checklist-90, a ninety-item checklist of psychopathological symptoms and complaints. Employing the scale with unselected psychiatric patients (a 75 percent female population), a principal components analysis that included a varimax rotation yielded five factors (depression, somatization, phobic anxiety, functional impairment, and hostile suspiciousness). Internal consistency for items within factors was found to be high (.94–.83), and the total score was found to be highly correlated with each factor (.92–.74). A Spearman-Brown split-half reliability coefficient between odd and even items was .976, and an alpha coefficient obtained for the total test was .975. The authors reported the depression, somatization, and phobic anxiety factors to be most clearly defined, with somatization possibly a more independent dimension. The authors further suggested (because of high factor intercorrelations) that the instrument may generate a dimension of general complaints and discomfort rather than distinct dimensions of pathology; the instrument, however, may have utility as a global index of psychopathology.

The Behavior Problem Checklist (Peterson and Quay, 1967; Quay, 1972; Quay and Peterson, 1975), most recently reviewed by

Quay (1977), involves a three-point scale for rating problem behaviors and traits occurring in childhood and adolescence. The scale consists of three primary subscales: (1) conduct problems, (2) personality problems, and (3) inadequacy-immaturity. These subscales were derived from a factor analysis of ratings on both deviant and nondeviant students. A fourth scale (socialized delinquency) represents items derived from a factor analysis of case history records. The first three scales were developed from ratings by teachers for 831 kindergarten through sixth-grade children. With respect to content validity, the scale items were originally selected by noting referral problems from case folders of 400 child guidance clinic referees. For the assessment of behavioral problems among children, several investigators (Harris, Drummond, and Schultz, 1977; Oltmans, Broderick, and O'Leary, 1977; Quay, 1977; Reidy, 1977) have recently reported support for the validity of the Behavior Problem Checklist (BPC). For example, Oltmans, Broderick, and O'Leary (1977) recently reported the scale to differentiate effectively between problem and nonproblem families when it was administered to the parents of 62 children referred to a behaviorally oriented psychology clinic, as compared with a sample obtained for 31 nonreferred children of the same age and socioeconomic status. Reidy (1977) reported the scale to discriminate among abused children, nonabused but neglected children, and normal children; abused children reflected higher aggression scores than did the other two groups.

Also related to the Behavior Problem Checklist, Harris, Drummond, and Schultz (1977) reported an investigation of the relationship between teacher ratings of behavior and children's self-ratings. The checklist was completed by 13 teachers for a sample of 254 students, grades one through eight. Students aged six to eight completed the Early School Personality Questionnaire (Coan and Cattell, 1972); students aged eight to twelve completed the Children's Personality Questionnaire (Porter and Cattell, 1972); and students aged eleven to eighteen completed the Junior-Senior High School Personality Questionnaire (Cattell and Cattell, 1969). Findings indicated the strongest correlation between the Behavior Problem Checklist and inventories with respect to teachers' accurate ratings of deviant behavior in grades four to six; less support was indicated for grades one to three and seven to eight. While these data suggest some support for the construct validity of the Behavior Problem Checklist, the authors noted incongruence at grades one to three and seven to eight, suggesting the need for additional investigation. Finally, Herr, Eaves, and Algozzine (1977) recently reported an investigation of the validity of the Behavior Problem Checklist in discriminating between schizophrenic and adjustment reactions among adolescents. Special education teachers in four hospitals completed the scale for fifty-six students. Schizophrenics were rated on flag items ("face-valid" items intended to serve for identification of possible psychoticism; see Quay and Peterson, 1967) and on the inadequacy-immaturity dimension. Significant errors were reported to result when either of these criteria was used independently; use of the flag items resulted in misdiagnosis of 35 percent of the schizophrenic adolescents and 25 percent of the adjustment reaction patients. Use of the inadequacy-immaturity dimension criteria was estimated to misdiagnose over 21 percent of subjects. Certainly these estimated error rates may make the scale unacceptable for clinical purposes.

In an investigation of the relationship between staff attitudes and "behavioral incidents" in a residential center, D. N. Martin (1977) recently employed a behavioral questionnaire containing nine items that yields an overall level of difficulty experienced with children during work shifts and that generates an index of "incident proneness" (the number of incidents on the shift is divided by the number of shifts worked). Additionally, staff attitudes were assessed with a questionnaire developed by Cawson and Perry (1977) to aid in the description of school regimens; the fifty-one items on that scale are organized into six subscales: (1) traditional control, (2) work, (3) passivity, (4) distance, (5) suppression of problems, and (6) staff status. Incident proneness scores were found to positively correlate with the scales of the attitude questionnaire, and attitudes expressed correlated with the behavior of the children during shifts. Further, expressed attitudes were related to staff behaviors, suggesting that the Cawson-Perry Questionnaire is a valid measure of significant variables of the school regimen.

With respect to the questionnaire assessment of hyperactivity, Spring, Greenberg, and Yellin (1977) recently reported on a comparison of the Hyperactivity Rating Scale, which contains eleven categories of behavior with three items per category. In that study, eight scales (restlessness, impulsiveness, distractability, work fluctuations, excitability, rapid tempo, poor coordination, and low perseverance) that had been shown in a previous validation study (Spring and others, in press) to separate hyperactive from normal children were employed. Mothers and teachers rated forty-five children at the end of a two-week period during which methylphenidate treatment was temporarily terminated; psychological tests were also administered at that time. Findings indicated that six of thirty-two comparisons between teacher ratings and psychological tests were significantly and negatively correlated (these involved tests requiring sustained attention), while for mothers four of thirty-two comparisons were significantly and positively correlated. These contrasting findings suggest that, while teachers were oriented to attentional tasks, mothers were oriented to some other aspect of children's behavior. The authors suggested that home tasks possibly require less sustained attention. Also bearing on the use of questionnaires to assess hyperactive behavior, evidence for the discriminant validity of the Conners Teacher Rating Scale (Conners, 1969) was recently reported by Abikoff, Gittelman-Klein, and Klein (1977). In that study, sixty children referred to outpatient clinics for hyperactivity and sixty same-sex normal children were observed by independent observers in a classroom setting. The children were also rated by teachers on the Conners Teacher Rating Scale. Results indicated significantly greater elevations of scores for the hyperactive than for the normal children, corresponding also to the observational data obtained for the groups. Finally, Yepes and others (1977) reported on the use of the Conners Teacher Rating Scale (Conners, 1969, 1973) and the Werry-Weiss-Peters Activity Rating Scale in the assessment of the relative effectiveness of two psychotropic drugs on hyperactivity. Significant correlations between the two scales were reported when parents served as raters. Additionally, high correlations between parent ratings of behavior change on the two scales reflected consistency in parental evaluations and concurrent validity for the two scales.

In the recent literature, Evans and Kazarian (1977) reported the development of the Reaction Inventory-Interference, a rating scale to identify obsessional thoughts and compulsive acts that interfere with persons' daily activities. Internal consistency for the forty-item scale was reported to be .95; a correlation obtained between this scale and the Leyton Obsessional Inventory (a card-sort inventory for yes/no responses to sixty-nine questions, forty-six of which differentiate between selected obsessive-compulsive patients and normal persons) was reported to be .66, supporting the concurrent validity of the Leyton Obsessional Inventory. Additionally, Kazarian, Evans, and Lefave (1977) reported on the modification of the Leyton Obsessional Inventory (Cooper, 1970) to a paper-and-pencil form to facilitate group administration. A factor analysis on the modified version from replies of 173 college students, however, only replicated two of the original three factors extracted by Cooper and Kelleher (1973).

Also with respect to the assessment of obsessive-compulsive complaints, Hodgson and Rachman (1977) reported the development of a questionnaire; apparently item selection was based upon literature surveys, "hunches about etiology," and interviews with 30 obsessional patients (it was unclear as to how or by whom these patients were diagnosed). From this, sixty-five items were assembled (items that failed to discriminate between a group of obsessional and a group of neurotic patients were discarded). This number was ultimately reduced to thirty items that differentiated between groups on both parametric and nonparametric (t-test, chi-square) analyses. A principal components analysis with oblique rotation on the responses of 100 adult obsessionals (50 from the original group and 50 more from other hospitals who were selected on the criteria of observable obsessive-compulsive behaviors, chronic treatment, and not psychotic) resulted in a four-component solution that accounted for 43 percent of the variance; factors were checking, cleaning, slowness, and doubting. Alpha coefficients (which average the intercorrelation among all items in a particular subscale to indicate the extent of cohesiveness of the items as a measure of a single dimension) for the four subscales were .7, .8, .7, and .7, respectively. Scale validation involved comparisons of scaled scores with the authors' ratings on 42 individuals in the sample that they had treated. (It should be noted that this may not represent an independent data sample; in questionnaire validation, it is important to validate a questionnaire on a sample that differs from the one initially used to develop the questionnaire.)

Recently, Free and Overall (1977) reported on the development of the Brief Outpatient Psychopathology Scale, a rating scale to be employed in the context of structured interview formats to characterize presenting pathology and to measure degrees of change for neurotic clients in outpatient settings. The scale was designed to evaluate the therapeutic effects of antianxiety drugs in outpatient settings and represents a modest revision of the New Physicians' Rating List (Free, 1974). Through a principal components analysis, four major components of outpatient discomfort were separated: (1) anxiety, (2) psychomotor activation, (3) depression, and (4) somatization. A factor analysis was reported by Free and Overall (1977) to suggest that the Brief Outpatient Psychopathology Scale adequately distinguishes treatment effects on the four dimensions. With respect to the construct validity of the Eysenck Personality Inventory, Martin and Moltmann (1977) administered that scale to residents of a state hospital where a combination token economy and step system were in effect; the steps were hypothesized to be inversely related to the degree of stimulation provided, with the highest step involving the lowest stimulation. Results supported this hypothesis; extraversion correlated significantly with ward behavior ratings, and decreasing extraversion scores (14.2, 12.2, 8.9) were found for each step, suggesting that extraverts need more stimulation at lower steps than do other groups. Neuroticism did not correlate significantly with steps.

Evidence recently reported by Knight and Blaney (1977) and by Huntwork and Ferguson (1977) is of note with respect to the validity of questionnaire measures. Knight and Blaney (1977) assessed the interrater reliability of the Psychotic Inpatient Profile (Lorr and Vestre, 1968, 1969), an inventory designed to quantify currently observable ward behavior and self-reports of psychiatric inpatients (separate norms are employed for drugged and nondrugged patients). Interrater reliabilities for all scales were calculated on the basis of nurse and psychiatric aide ratings; quite low reliability levels were found (levels well below those reported in the scale manual), suggesting the utility of the instrument to be questionable. As the authors pointed out, until higher levels of reliability are established, the validity of the instrument will remain in doubt. With respect to a four-question drug-use questionnaire (Have you ever used the drug? Are you a regular user? How often do you use the drug? If you have stopped—how long ago?) developed by Ferguson (1974), Huntwork and Ferguson (1977) recently reported consensual validation support; however, as the drug-use score has been validated only in the consensual sense, it is unclear how this score reflects drug-use behavior.

Cox (1977) recently reported on an evaluation of the Menstrual Symptom Questionnaire, originally developed by Chesney and Tasto (1975) to psychometrically identify two types of primary dysmenorrhea: (1) spasmodic, which refers to distress during the flow period associated with excessive muscle tension; and (2) congestive, which refers to premenstrual tension related to water retention. Initial reports on the scale (Chesney and Tasto, 1975) indicated test-retest reliability of .87; discrimination between spasmodic and congestive women also was reported to be highly significant, with twenty-nine of forty-eight women tested identified as spasmodic (questionnaire scores between 82 and 102), while nineteen scored in the congestive range (46 to 48). No women were reported to score in the midrange of 69 to 81, suggesting that two unique types of primary dysmenorrhea are identifiable by the scale. More recently, however, data reported by Cox (1977) did not support these earlier findings. Employing the scale with fourteen distressed and fourteen nondistressed college women, Cox found an equal proportion of respondents in each third of the distribution, suggesting that the congestive-spasmodic dimension is a continuous rather than a dichotomous dimension as reported earlier. Additionally, patients completed a daily symptom scale that included reports of the amount of menstrual medication used and the number of invalid hours; while differences between distressed and nondistressed groups would suggest concurrent scale validity, no differences were found between the two supposed groups (congestive and spasmodic).

Preliminary information on an attempt to establish a behaviorally based nosology for children's and adolescents' emotional disorders was recently reported by Dreger (1977). The Children's

Behavioral Classification Project contains a duplicated list of 274 behavioral and 3 demographic items (age, sex, and clinic or nonclinic status). Behavioral items are endorsed as either true or false by the parent (usually the mother) or parent-surrogate. The scale requires a fourth-grade reading level on the part of the respondent; scoring is accomplished by totaling factor structure weights for items endorsed true for each factor, and the authors reported that internal consistency for the scale was associated with the number of items contained in a factor. For individual factors, estimates for the internal consistency reliability yielded mean and median correlations of .64 for both. With respect to reliability, however, Dreger additionally reported apparent fatigue associated with responding to the rather long scale; respondents tended to utilize more of the items in the first half than in the second half of the scale.

Finally, Achenbach (1978) recently reported on the development (and standardization for boys aged six to eleven) of the Child Behavior Profile, a parent report/checklist questionnaire that may have utility as a descriptive classification system to group children for clinical and research purposes, as an assessment instrument to delineate problem and adaptive behaviors, and as a means of quantitatively assessing behavior change. The scale contains 118 problem behavior items, along with additional items that comprise three social competence domains: (1) activities scale, (2) social scale, and (3) school scale. A factor analysis of the protocols of 450 disturbed boys yielded these behavior problem scales: Somatic Complaints, Social Withdrawal, Hyperactive, Aggressive, Delinquent, Schizoid, Depressed, Uncommunicative, Obsessive-Compulsive. Comparisons of disturbed and normal boys were reported by the author to show significant differences on all behavior problem and social competence scales, suggesting some evidence for the discriminant validity of the scale. Test-retest correlations were reported to average .89, while interparent correlations for the standardization sample were reported to average .74.

In summary, the questionnaire assessments of problem behaviors and traits have involved a variety of populations, including children and their parents, adolescents, schizophrenic and neurotic adults, teachers, and treatment staff members. Behaviors targeted

for these assessments likewise have been varied and have included
children's conduct problems, noncompliance, hyperactivity, and
other behavioral disturbances. Among adolescent populations, behaviors targeted have included drug usage and disturbed behaviors
within families. Adult behaviors targeted for questionnaire assessments have included suicidal intent, depression, neurotic outpatient behaviors, illogical thoughts, obsessive-compulsive complaints, ward behaviors of psychotic subjects, anger, stuttering,
menstrual symptoms, and pain. Questionnaire formats for the assessment of problem behaviors and traits have included ratings by
others, self-reports and self-ratings, and various checklist formats.
The functions served by these various questionnaires have included the development and evaluation of the scales themselves,
preintervention assessment, outcome evaluations of intervention
measures (both pretreatment and posttreatment measures), diagnosis, and the ongoing evaluation of therapy. However, the scales
employed in the assessment of problem behaviors and traits typically result in indices of dysfunction, not in frequencies of occurrence of target behaviors. Likewise, these scales often have not
provided sufficient information as to the situational specificity of
targeted behaviors. As regards the validity of questionnaires thus
employed, a majority of investigators have reported evidence for
the sensitivity of these measures, although not all authors have
addressed this issue. In contrast, a lack of sensitivity was reported
for a diagnostic checklist of schizophrenic and adjustment reactions
and for a teacher checklist of children's conduct problems as an
outcome measure of intervention.

    In the assessment of depression, additional evidence for the
construct and concurrent validity of the Beck Depression Inventory was recently reported, as was internal consistency, along with
concurrent and construct validity, for the Suicidal Intent Scale.
With regard to behavior problems among children, additional evidence for the discriminant validity of the Behavior Problem
Checklist in delineating problem from nonproblem families was
also reported, as was its discriminative power in differentiating
abused from both nonabused but neglected children and normal
children with respect to aggression scores. Limited evidence for the
construct validity of the Behavior Problem Checklist was also re-

cently reported, although grade-level inconsistencies in obtained scores suggest the need for additional investigation. Finally, an application of that scale to discriminate between schizophrenic and adjustment reactions in adolescents yielded generally unacceptable error rates, suggesting that the utility and validity of the scale for such diagnostic purposes are questionable.

Evidence for the concurrent validity of a recently developed questionnaire to assess or describe school regimens has also appeared in the recent literature, as has some support for the discriminant validity of the Hyperactivity Rating Scale. But inconsistencies between mothers' and teachers' ratings were also reported, suggesting that, while teachers were oriented to attentional tasks, mothers were oriented to some other aspect of children's behavior (possibly tasks that do not require sustained attention). Also with respect to hyperactivity, evidence for the discriminant validity of the Conners Teacher Rating Scale was recently reported, along with evidence for the concurrent validity of both the Conners Teacher Rating Scale and the Werry-Weiss-Peters Activity Rating Scale for the assessment of the effects of drug treatments. Support for the concurrent validity of the Leyton Obsessional Inventory for the assessment of obsessive-compulsive behaviors has also recently been reported, along with reports of adequate concurrent validity and internal consistency for the Reaction Inventory-Interference, a rating scale to identify obsessive thoughts and compulsive acts that interfere with daily activities. Also of interest in the recent literature was the report on development of the Brief Outpatient Psychopathology Scale, a scale that may have utility in evaluating the therapeutic effects of antianxiety drugs in outpatient settings.

Evidence in support of the construct validity of the Eysenck Personality Inventory has also appeared with respect to the extraversion dimension, as compared with ward behavior ratings and associated degrees of stimulation provided under a combination token economy and step system. Also related to assessments of psychotic inpatients, an investigation was recently reported involving the Psychotic Inpatient Profile; low interrater reliability coefficients between nurses and aides as raters, however, suggest that the utility of the scale needs further investigation. Likewise, while a recently reported drug-use questionnaire was validated in a consensual sense, it is unclear how well its drug-use scores reflect actual drug-taking behavior, and further investigation is needed. And, while earlier reports on the Menstrual Symptom Questionnaire suggested the discriminant validity of the scale in identifying a dichotomous congestive-spasmodic dimension, a more recent investigation did not support the earlier findings; patients' responses tended to reflect a continuous dimension. Additionally, patients' responses to a daily symptom scale that included reports of the amounts of menstrual medication used did not result in group differences, drawing into question the concurrent validity of the scale. Finally, a preliminary report on the attempt to establish a behaviorally based nosology for children's and adolescents' emotional disorders was noted. The Children's Behavioral Classification Project includes 274 behavioral items that are endorsed as either true or false by the parent or parent-surrogate. However, as data are thus far limited, decisions as to the utility of this scale must await further investigation. Likewise, while initial reports of the Child Behavior Profile suggest potential utility for the scale as a classification and assessment instrument, further research will be necessary before conclusions can be drawn.

## Miscellaneous Questionnaire Applications

In addition to the applications previously discussed, questionnaires have been employed with a variety of other behaviors (see Table 15), including heartbeat perceptions of adults (D. Carroll, 1977; Whitehead and others, 1977), pain experiences of adults (Craig, Best, and Best, 1978), developmental behaviors among children (Colligan, 1977), toy use by children (Quilitch, Christophersen, and Risley, 1977), teacher satisfaction with child behaviors (Schumaker, Hovell, and Sherman, 1977b) and with academic remediation programs (Foxx and Jones, 1978), children's self-concepts associated with classroom activities (Williams and Workman, 1978), and parents' childrearing behaviors (Margolies and Weintraub, 1977). Additionally, questionnaires have been employed to assess leisure behaviors of mentally retarded females (Johnson and Bailey, 1977), counselor effectiveness (Deysach, Ross, and Hiers, 1977), sources of reinforcement (Bassett, Blanchard, and Koshland, 1977; Upper, Lochman, and Aveni, 1977), and perceptions of reinforcers (Serralde de Scholz and McDougall, 1978). Questionnaires have also been employed in assessing the acceptability of treatment procedures (Foxx and Shapiro, 1978), attitudes toward behavior modification in business settings (Dubno and others, 1978), room- and cabin-cleaning behaviors among adolescents (Peacock, Lyman, and Rickard, 1978; Wood and Flynn, 1978), driving habits of college students (Hake and Foxx, 1978), and the range of motion and ambulation as a measure of client gains in physical therapy programs (Greene and others, 1978).

Formats of the questionnaires employed have included self-reports (Bassett, Blanchard, and Koshland, 1977; D. Carroll, 1977; Craig, Best, and Best, 1978; Dubno and others, 1978; Hake and Foxx, 1978; Johnson and Bailey, 1977; Quilitch, Christophersen, and Risley, 1977; Serralde de Scholz and McDougall, 1978; Whitehead and others, 1977), ratings (Colligan, 1977; David and others, 1977; Deysach, Ross, and Hiers, 1977; Foxx and Jones, 1978; Foxx and Shapiro, 1978; Greene and others, 1978; Huston-Stein, Friedrick-Cofer, and Susman, 1977; Margolies and Weintraub, 1977; Upper, Lochman, and Aveni, 1977; Williams and Workman, 1978), and checklists (Peacock, Lyman, and Rickard, 1978; Schumaker, Hovell, and Sherman, 1977b; Wood and Flynn, 1978). In addition to basic research functions involving scale evaluations (Colligan, 1977; Deysach, Ross, and Hiers, 1977; Dubno and others, 1978; Huston-Stein, Friedrick-Coffer, and Susman, 1977; Margolies and Weintraub, 1977; Peacock, Lyman, and Rickard, 1978; Quilitch, Christophersen, and Risley, 1977; Williams and Workman, 1978), the functions of questionnaires cited above have also included preintervention assessments (Bassett, Blanchard, and Koshland, 1977; D. Carroll, 1977; Foxx and Shapiro, 1978; Johnson and Bailey, 1977; Upper, Lochman, and Aveni, 1977; Whitehead and others, 1977) and treatment outcome assessments (Foxx and Jones, 1978; Greene and others, 1978; Schumaker, Hovell, and Sherman, 1977b; Wood and Flynn, 1978), as well as subject selection and functional behavior analysis (Hake and Foxx, 1978). While several investigators have reported questionnaires to be sensitive in reflecting changes in the behaviors under investigation (Colligan, 1977; Quilitch, Christophersen, and Risley, 1977;

Schumaker, Hovell, and Sherman, 1977), others have reported the insensitivity of questionnaires in the assessment of heartbeat perception (Whitehead and others, 1977) and of hyperactive behavior associated with lead exposure (David and others, 1977).

Recent reports on the criterion-related validity of the Autonomic Perception Questionnaire (Mandler, Mandler, and Uviller, 1958), a twenty-eight-item self-report scale of perceptions of bodily sensation during the states of anxiety and pleasure, have been somewhat equivocal. In contrast to earlier reported findings of modest correlations with autonomic activity reported by Mandler and Kremen (1958) and Mandler, Mandler, and Uviller (1958), findings recently reported by Whitehead and others (1977) failed to demonstrate significant correlations between the Autonomic Perception Questionnaire and either initial voluntary control of heart rate or learning of heart-rate control. These findings are similar to those of several investigations reviewed recently by D. Carroll (1977), and they suggest caution in accepting the predictive validity of the questionnaire as a preintervention instrument.

For the assessment of children's perceptions of their parent's childrearing behaviors, Margolies and Weintraub (1977) recently reported on the reliability and factor structure of the Child's Report of Parental Behavior Inventory, a 56-item revision of an earlier 260-item questionnaire (Schaefer, 1965). Along with the report of high test-retest reliability at one- and five-week intervals, factor analysis revealed three orthogonal factors describing dimensions of childrearing behavior: (1) acceptance or rejection, (2) psychological autonomy or psychological control, and (3) firm control or lax control. These same three factors were found consistently across a wide range of populations, including American elementary, high school, and college students, and Canadian high school and college students. In the evaluation of toy safety, durability, and appeal, Quilitch, Christophersen, and Risley (1977) have reported evidence for the criterion-related validity of a Toy-Use Questionnaire. At the end of each day, an observer who had monitored children's play activities in a structured playroom completed the Toy-Use Questionnaire that identified problems associated with toy management, durability, and frequencies of use; questionnaire data were reported to correlate well with such separate observational measures as durations of play with specific toys and frequencies of choice (concurrent validity). Additionally, the questionnaire was found to be a reliable predictor of the appeal of a toy across subjects and settings (external validity).

David and others (1977) employed the Lead Exposure Questionnaire, a thirty-item parent-report questionnaire involving specific kinds of pica activity (such as eating dirt or plaster) and possible exposure to airborne lead, as a dependent measure (along with measures of blood-lead levels) in the investigation of hyperactivity. Correlations between the questionnaire data and blood-lead levels were, unfortunately, low (.36). Additionally, while the physiological measures differentiated between groups with reference to lead accumulation, the questionnaire did not, suggesting either the scale's lack of discriminant validity or the possibility that differences in lead levels may not be a function of differential exposure but may rather reflect an inability to excrete lead once it is ingested. With respect to self-concept in children, Williams and Workman (1978) reported on the development of a Behavioral Self-Concept Scale related to children's classroom activities. This self-rating scale presents thirty-six pairs of classroom activities verbally and pictorially; subjects specify at which activity within each pair they are better. A subject's self-concept relative to a given activity is defined as the number of times the subject ranks that activity over other activities. Test-retest coefficients of .85 for males, .82 for females, and .90 for males and females combined were reported. Finally, Dubno and others (1978) recently reported on a questionnaire to assess attitudes toward behavior modification in business organizations. While no validity data are thus far available, the authors reported a test-retest coefficient of .70. Additionally, a split-half reliability coefficient of .88 and a coefficient of .92 between odd and even items were reported. While this questionnaire has potential utility for investigations of the relationship between attitudes toward behavior modification programs and their effectiveness, further scale evaluation will be required before conclusions can be drawn.

In summary, questionnaire applications discussed in this last section have involved a variety of behaviors, including adults' perceptions of autonomic activity, children's toy use, teacher charac-

teristics and responses to children's behaviors, parents' childrearing behaviors, leisure behaviors of retarded subjects, and counselor
effectiveness. Questionnaire formats have included self-reports,
ratings, and checklists, and the functions served by the various
questionnaires have involved preintervention and treatment outcome assessments, as well as subject selection and scale evaluations.
While the majority of studies reviewed in this section did not address the issues of reliability and validity, evidence for the sensitivity of questionnaires to teacher satisfaction and child behaviors, as
well as to children's toy use, were reported. With respect to toy use,
evidence for criterion-related validity was also reported. In contrast, data were reported suggesting the apparent lack of validity of
a questionnaire developed for the assessment of autonomic perceptions and of a questionnaire to assess lead exposure among
hyperactive children. As with many other questionnaires, those discussed in this section often do not generate the degree of behavioral and situational specificity desirable within a behavioral construct system.

## Variables Influencing the
## Validity of Questionnaires

As indicated elsewhere (Haynes, 1978), questionnaire validity can be considered a dependent variable influenced by numerous other variables. Among the variables potentially affecting the
validity of questionnaires (aside from method of item selection,
item comprehensiveness, method of scale construction, and question format) are response bias, social desirability, demand factors,
expectancies, population characteristics, observer reactivity, situation and behavioral specificity, and scale length.

*Response bias* refers to the serial dependency of responses to
questionnaire items. In other words, since questionnaires may require a series of responses, the response to one item may not be
independent of previous item responses. Response bias means that
different item arrangements and scale constructions may generate
different responses to items, thus affecting the validity of obtained
scores. Fidler and Kleinknecht (1977) recently described a randomized response procedure (see Chapter One for a more detailed

description) for reducing error and response bias in self-reports—a procedure that could have utility for questionnaire procedures. A related issue is that of *social desirability*. On questionnaire items, responses may be influenced by the social values associated with the particular items. For example, it may be expected that individuals might underreport behaviors of perceived negative value (such as child abuse or anxieties) while overreporting behaviors of perceived positive valence (such as the number of reinforcers delivered to a child). Likewise, *demand factors* may affect the validity of questionnaire data. For example, Lick (1977) reported higher fear scores for subjects who were informed that their scores would determine whether or not they would receive therapy; similarly, higher fear scores were found when subjects were informed that research credits would be available for those selected to participate. Lick, Sushinsky, and Malow (1977) suggested that correlations between self-report and avoidance measures of fear may increase under low-demand (for approval) conditions, a point earlier proposed by Bernstein (1973) and by Hodgson and Rachman (1974).

Individual responses on questionnaire items may also be influenced by client *expectancies*. For example, a teacher's knowledge of the previous success of a treatment procedure in producing behavioral change might influence his or her reports of hyperactivity during an intervention procedure. Similarly, self-reported reductions in fear level might accompany a client's expectation of the success of therapy. Bornstein, Hamilton, and Quevillon (1977) employed an "expectancy control manipulation" as part of a classroom treatment program for out-of-seat behavior. For the measure of behavioral expectation, the teacher was asked to complete a ten-point Likert-type scale prior to a positive practice condition, a differential reinforcement of other behaviors (DRO) reversal condition (in which the teacher was led to expect further decrements in the target behavior), and a second positive practice condition. In all three instances, the teacher circled a score of eight, indicating a consistent, firm expectation for decrements in the target behavior across the first-intervention phase, the reversal phase, and the second-intervention phase. Additionally, Sullivan and Denny (1977) reported expectancy manipulations in a desensitization procedure with subjects with snake phobias. Measures of how subjects expected their fear levels to change were accomplished through questionnaires purportedly required by a human subject experimentation committee. Subjects were also administered a Snake Anxiety Questionnaire and the Snake Fear Inventory (Denny and Sullivan, 1976). The authors reported that all measures were sensitive and that expectancy manipulations were effective, although no correlations among the measures were reported. Given the evidence for expectancy effects on questionnaire responses, caution is indicated when employing these instruments to assess ongoing effects of treatment or as outcome measures of treatment.

Because inferences of validity are limited to the populations studied (Haynes, 1978), care should be taken in the validation of instruments to adequately sample those populations with which a questionnaire is likely to be employed. Also with respect to *population characteristics*, caution should be employed in the application and interpretation of a questionnaire that has not undergone adequate validation with that population from which the client is drawn. For example, assumptions as to the validity of scores obtained from noncollege populations on assertiveness questionnaires developed on college student populations should be undertaken cautiously.

Another potential threat to the validity of questionnaire data is that of *observer reactivity*. While considerable evidence for the reactive effects of self-monitoring has appeared in the literature (see Chapter Five), little has appeared for the reactive effects associated with self-report (questionnaire) data. Nevertheless, self-report instruments and self-monitoring procedures are similar in that both require some degree of self-observation for reporting, and it may thus be expected that the administration of self-report questionnaires will affect the targeted behavior. Reflecting an awareness of these potential effects, the Sullivan and Denny (1977) study mentioned earlier included a "nonreactive" measure of the expectancy manipulations, although no empirical test was made of the degree of reactivity associated with the questionnaire. Temporal factors shown to be associated with reactive effects in self-monitoring (such as the fact that recordings made prior to or during the occurrence of targeted behaviors may produce greater reactive effects than recordings made subsequent to those behaviors—see Chapter Five) likewise may have implications for questionnaire assessments. Although not directly addressed in the literature, it might thus be expected that, while retrospective self-reports (such as those employed by Gautheir and Marshall (1977) at the completion of a behavioral avoidance test) may not be as sensitive or valid as ongoing self-reports obtained during behavioral avoidance tests, ongoing self-reports may be more reactive. Likewise, for obtaining data having external validity, questionnaire assessments subsequent to behavior require the subject to accurately *recall* the behavior in question (Bellack and Hersen, 1977). In this sense, it is possible that the requirements for a behaviorally oriented questionnaire (emphasizing specificity and quantitative information) cannot completely be met. For example, in a depression questionnaire it is necessary to know how many social contacts occurred during the previous week. A depressive individual, however, may not be able to accurately report that information. Similarly, an alcoholic may not know (or recall) how many drinks were taken during the previous week. Thus, obtained data may not be valid.

Also potentially affecting the validity of questionnaire instruments is the *situational and behavioral specificity* of the particular instrument. Bellack and Hersen (1977) recently noted that the less specific and concrete the wording of items, the greater the probability of item misinterpretation, and hence of lowered validity with respect to measures obtained. Lick, Sushinsky, and Malow (1977) also addressed the question of descriptive detail in questionnaire items. In two studies, the authors investigated whether increases in the descriptive detail of a Fear Survey Schedule item would increase the correlation of the item with a subsequent avoidance measure. In the first study, a correlational analysis reflected progressively stronger relationships between self-report and avoidance measures as self-report items more closely described the avoidance test. Similarly, a correlational analysis in the second study indicated that self-report and avoidance measures became more and more correlated as the descriptive detail of the fear schedule item increased. Finally, it can be expected that greater item specificity will result in greater utility (Bellack and Hersen, 1977); in that sense, since checklists do not usually generate specific behavior counts, their utility as compared with other scales may be somewhat lessened. The validity of questionnaire instruments additionally may be influenced by the *length* of the particular scale employed (Haynes, 1978). For example, when employing scales rather than checklists, the behavior analyst may be faced with an interesting dilemma; a two-point scale ("always" or "never") may produce greater reliability but less sensitivity and criterion-related validity than a ten-point scale (such as "always," "very frequently," "frequently," and so forth). Similarly, while greater variance in test-retest responses could be expected with a longer scale that demands more difficult discriminations between points, a shorter scale with few units of choice might not be as sensitive or valid a measure of the construct under investigation.

Finally, two additional issues are of note with respect to validity evaluations of questionnaire instruments. First is the concept of *attitudinal lag* (Hersen, 1973), a term describing the occurrence of improved motor function prior to proportional changes in cognitive functioning within the same behavioral intervention program. As Bellack and Hersen (1977) have suggested, low correlations between self-report and behavioral (motoric) indices, such as those reported by Wicker (1969) with respect to behavioral measures of fear, need not be taken as a general indictment of self-report measures. Since many behavioral intervention procedures focus on behavioral (motoric) changes, differential changes in cognitive and behavioral functioning perhaps are to be expected unless each response system is treated independently to minimize these effects (Bellack and Hersen, 1977; Lang, 1971). The second additional issue involves the use of questionnaire responses for an *idiographic function* rather than a nomothetic one. As Bellack and Hersen (1977) have pointed out, it is quite possible that responses to individual items may be valid even though grouped data (summative scores) may not significantly correlate with external criteria. Similarly, Haynes (1978) has emphasized that behavioral questionnaires should stress the "derivation of quantitative data on *specific* behaviors and in *specific* situations" (p. 314). To the extent, then, that questionnaires are limited to an overall index of adjustment, rather than providing information on specific behavior rates, their utility and content validity within a behavioral construct system may be limited.

## Summary

Questionnaires described in this chapter have been utilized in the assessment of assertive behaviors, social and marital interactions, ingestive behaviors, fears, sexual behaviors and orientations, problem behaviors and traits, and other miscellaneous behaviors. In the assessment of assertiveness, the investigations involved a variety of adult populations, with questionnaires employed as outcome measures of assertiveness training, as a means of preintervention assessment and subject selection, and for purposes of research in scale evaluation and functional behavior analysis. A majority of investigators reported the scales employed to be sensitive to changes in behaviors targeted for investigation—an important consideration, since without demonstration of an instrument's ability to reflect changes in the behavior under observation, it might be assumed that behavior change did not occur when, in fact, it did. However, except for such reports of instrument sensitivity, investigators have only infrequently focused on other issues of questionnaire validity, although evidence for the discriminant and convergent validity of the Adult Self-Expression Scale has recently appeared, as has additional evidence supporting the concurrent and discriminant validity of the Rathus Assertiveness Schedule.

The social interactions of infants, children, and adults have also been the focus of questionnaire assessments. Typically, the questionnaire formats of these assessments have involved ratings of children by teachers and caretakers and self-report measures with adults. Included among the behaviors assessed have been social interactions, inappropriate behaviors, and behavioral deficits among children, as well as dating patterns and heterosexual social anxiety among adults. While most often serving a research purpose in the functional analysis of social interaction, questionnaires have also been employed as intervention outcome measures for social interaction assessments. As with assessments of assertiveness, validity investigations in the recent literature have largely been confined to reports of questionnaire sensitivity. While little has appeared with respect to criterion-related and construct validity, some recent evidence was described relating to the discriminant validity of a dating behavior scale and of a heterosexual social anxiety scale. Also promising were initial reports on a scale for the assessment of children in the peer-group context.

Questionnaires employed to assess marital interaction and satisfaction typically have been of the self-report format and most frequently have involved marital discord and, to a lesser extent, sexual activities and problem behaviors. In most cases, the function of these questionnaires has been for preintervention assessment; they have been employed less frequently to assess the effects of treatment programs and for functional behavior analysis. The sensitivity of questionnaires in reflecting changes in behavior has been consistently cited. And, although only limited evidence for other types of validity has been reported, additional evidence for the discriminant validity of the Quay-Peterson and Locke-Wallace scales in differentiating problem from nonproblem families on the basis of interactions has been recently reported, as has evidence suggesting the discriminant validity of the Marital Activities Inventory and the Areas of Change Questionnaire in differentiating problem from nonproblem marital couples. Also reported in the recent literature was the development of a new questionnaire, the Sexual Compatibility Test, that may have utility for the assessment of the sexual interaction of married couples.

In the assessment of ingestive behaviors, the targets of self-report measures have included demographic and dieting histories of obese individuals, therapist helpfulness in obesity programs, and antecedent and response parameters of drinking behaviors. For questionnaires used as outcome measures of treatment, as diagnostic instruments with alcoholic adults, and as preintervention assessment instruments with alcoholic and obese patients, a majority of investigators have reported evidence for their sensitivity. But only limited evidence has appeared in recent literature as to other aspects of scale validities. One of the more frequent applications of behavioral questionnaires has been in the assessment of fear responses. Typically involving self-report formats with adult populations, questionnaires have been employed in the assessment of phobias (rats, spiders, snakes, and heights), as well as in the assessment of public speaking, speech, and achievement anxieties. Most often these questionnaires have served as outcome measures of intervention, but some have been employed for preintervention assessment, for subject selection, and for decisions regarding treatment termination. While a self-report scale of dental fears as an outcome measure, a self-report questionnaire of public speaking anxiety, and a self-report questionnaire employed with adult retardates to assess fears of heights were noted to be insensitive, the remaining investigations that addressed this issue have reported positive findings. Also encouraging was evidence for the criterion-related validity of several questionnaires for the assessment of phobic and anxiety responses. Additionally reported in the recent literature was evidence for the factor structure and internal consistency of the Test Anxiety Scale and the development of an Acrophobia Questionnaire having potential utility for assessment of fears of height.

Questionnaires applied to sexual attitudes and behavior have focused on masculine and feminine behavior patterns of children and on sexual performance, orgasmic responses, and homosexual behaviors among adults. Exclusively of the self-report format, these questionnaire assessments have primarily served as treatment outcome measures; applications for preintervention assessment and diagnosis have been quite limited. Except for reports by several investigators of scale sensitivity (not all investigators addressed this issue) and recent investigations of the Femininity Study, which assesses female states and self-concepts, little has appeared recently with regard to other aspects of validity for these scales.

The questionnaire assessment of problem behavior and traits represents perhaps the most frequent application of questionnaires in the recent literature. Targeted for assessment have been children's noncompliance, conduct problems, and hyperactivity, drug usage and behavioral disturbances among adolescents, and adult behaviors such as depression, suicidal intent, neurotic outpatient behaviors, obsessive-compulsive complaints, psychotics' ward behaviors, anger, stuttering, menstrual symptoms, and pain. Questionnaire formats have included self-reports, ratings, and checklists, with functions including scale development, preintervention assessment, outcome evaluations, diagnosis, and ongoing therapy evaluations. A majority of investigators have reported findings for the sensitivity of the scales employed, although a lack of sensitivity for a diagnostic checklist of schizophrenic and adjustment reactions and for a teacher checklist of children's conduct problems was also reported. In the assessment of depression, evidence supportive of the construct validity of the Beck Depression Inventory has recently appeared, as has evidence for the concurrent and construct validity of the Suicidal Intent Scale. Likewise, evidence for the discriminant validity of the Behavior Problem Checklist for assessing behavior problems among children was recently reported, as was limited evidence for its construct validity. With respect to hyperactivity, additional evidence for the discriminant validity of the Conners Teacher Rating Scale was reported, along with evidence for the concurrent validity of both that scale and the Werry-Weiss-Peters Activity Rating Scale in assessing the effects of drug treatment. Along with evidence for the concurrent validity of the Leyton Obsessional Inventory and reports of adequate concurrent validity and internal consistency for the Reaction Inventory-Interference (a rating scale to identify obsessive-compulsive acts disruptive to daily activity), the development of the Brief Outpatient Psychopathology Scale, which may have utility for the evaluation of the effect of antianxiety drugs in outpatient settings, was also reported. Also appearing in the recent literature was a preliminary report on the Children's Behavioral Classification Project—an attempt to establish a behaviorally based nosology for children's and adolescents' emotional disorders. Initial reports on the Child Behavior Profile, a scale having potential utility as a classification and assessment instrument, also appeared in the recent literature.

Other questionnaire applications have included assessments of such behaviors as heartbeat perceptions, developmental and toy-use behaviors of children, teacher satisfaction, parents' child-rearing behaviors, leisure behaviors, teacher behaviors, and counselor effectiveness. While several investigators have reported scale sensitivity for these assessments, a questionnaire assessing heartbeat perception and another assessing hyperactive behavior associated with lead exposure were found to be insensitive to changes in behavior. In contrast to earlier reports, equivocal findings were reported for the criterion-related validity of the Autonomic Perception Questionnaire. An investigation of the reliability and factor structure of the Child's Report of Parental Behavior Inventory was also recently reported, as was evidence for the criterion-related (concurrent and predictive) validity of a Toy-Use Questionnaire that used adult observers as respondents. As already indicated, a Lead Exposure Questionnaire for the assessment of hyperactive behavior was found to be insensitive.

Also described in this chapter were a number of variables potentially affecting the validity of questionnaire measures. These included response bias, social desirability, demand factors, expectancies, population characteristics, observer reactivity, situational and behavioral specificity, and scale length. While the factors of demand, expectancy, and situational and behavioral specificity have received some empirical attention in the literature, these other factors, while addressed, have not been the subject of empirical investigation. Given the potential influence of these factors upon the validity of questionnaire data, however, further systematic evaluation is essential. As indicated in various sections of this chapter, demonstrations of questionnaire sensitivity have frequently appeared in the recent literature. This is an important consideration since a questionnaire that is not relatively quick to reflect changes in the behavior under observation might lead to assumptions that behavior had not changed when, in fact, it had. Much less frequent have been investigations of other aspects of questionnaire validity. The suggestion that needless measurement duplication exists in the assessment of fear and social skills (Hersen and Bellack, 1976a; Hersen, 1973) would appear in like manner to apply to the areas of questionnaire application described in preceding sections. As those authors suggested, one significant reason for such duplication seems to be that investigators often independently develop their own assessment devices for behavioral intervention assessments rather than cross-validating scales already available and for which some degree of reliability or validity has already been demonstrated. As a result, researchers continue to design and apply their own instruments, often without evaluating them, and this procedure often results in the utilization of unvalidated questionnaires to assess intervention outcomes.

Several other considerations also are deserving of attention with respect to questionnaire instruments. Along with the need for additional systematic investigation of the external and internal validity of those questionnaires currently being employed, it is also apparent that, while the more recent behavioral questionnaires, such as those for assertiveness, reflect an increased empirical sophistication (Haynes, 1978), the questionnaires currently available still do not generate information with the degree of specificity demanded by the behavior analyst. For example, in the assessment of depression, no questionnaires currently available provide quantitative information with regard to likely antecedent events, responses of others, or sources of reinforcement. Like most other scales, depression questionnaires result in scores useful primarily for classification purposes (Haynes, 1978). As indicated previously, to the extent that questionnaires provide reliable, valid measures of behaviors targeted for assessment, they may be the assessment instrument of choice, particularly with respect to cost and time factors and for those situations where direct observation is not easily accomplished. The degree to which various questionnaire instruments can accurately predict or covary with behaviors measured by other instruments and in other settings largely remains to be determined through extended empirical and systematic investigation.

# CHAPTER SEVEN

# *Behavioral Interviews*

---

The interview is perhaps the most frequently used, least systematically applied, and least frequently evaluated behavioral assessment instrument. Intervention with any family, couple, school, institution, individual client, or social system necessitates personal communication or interviews among the client, change agent, and behavior analyst. The function of this contact varies and may include gathering information about client concerns and goals, identifying factors that maintain or elicit problem behaviors, eliciting historical information, identifying environmental reinforcers, assessing mediation potential, educating the client, obtaining informed consent, and communicating explicitly about the procedures and goals of the assessment and intervention programs.

An interview is here defined as any structured interaction between target subjects or mediators and the behavior analyst for the purposes delineated above. In view of the importance of the interview in the intervention process, it is surprising that the significance of this social interaction has been consistently underestimated in published behavioral research. The structure, content, and process of the interview will affect the quality of the intervention program and the attitudes and behavior of the participants. Thus, the preintervention interview is likely to have a significant impact on the success of a behavioral intervention program. This chapter will examine recently published articles with implications for the reliability, validity, or utility of behavioral interviews. The application of behavioral interviews, along with current issues in behavioral interviewing, will be considered in separate sections. Sources of error and bias associated with the various applications of the behavioral interview will also be considered. Table 16 summarizes recently published behavior therapy articles that used the interview as an assessment instrument. Subsequent sections of this chapter will consider more closely many of these articles, as well as nontherapy articles that also used behavioral interviews.

**Table 16. Recently Published Behavior Therapy Articles Utilizing the Interview**

| Reference | Targets | Application |
|---|---|---|
| Ashby and Wilson (1977) | Obesity | Screening |
| Beiman and others (1978) | Specific fears | Screening and criterion validity of interview reports |
| Bloom and Cantrell (1978) | Essential hypertension | Screening and client information |
| Bollard and Woodroffe (1977) | Enuresis | Treatment planning |
| Borkovec and Hennings (1978) | Sleep disturbance | Client information; expectancy manipulation |
| Cautela (1977) | Pain | Diagnosis; discussion article |
| Eisler and others (1978) | Social skills deficits in psychotic and nonpsychotic subjects | Diagnosis and screening |

**Table 16. Recently Published Behavior Therapy Articles**
**Utilizing the Interview (Continued)**

| Reference | Targets | Application |
|-----------|---------|------------|
| Emmelkamp, Kuipers, and Eggeraat (1978) | Agoraphobia | Screening and client information |
| Epstein and Abel (1977) | Muscle-contraction headache | Diagnosis and screening |
| Fawcett and Fletcher (1977) | Individual in community | Program development |
| Foa and others (1977) | Rat phobia | Outcome evaluation |
| Goldfried and Goldfried (1977) | Speech anxiety | Client education and information |
| Hall, Baker, and Hutchinson (1977) | Chronic schizophrenia | Predictor variables; treatment outcome |
| Haynes, Sides, and Lockwood (1977) | Insomnia | Diagnosis and screening |
| Horne (1977) | Trichotillomania | Treatment planning |
| James (1978) | | Client information |
| Jeffrey, Wing, and Stunkard (1978) | Obesity | Screening |
| Jehu and others (1977) | Enuresis | Outcome evaluation |
| Kantorowitz (1978) | | Client information and screening |
| Kenny, Mowbray, and Lalani (1978) | Hypertensives | Identification of factors causing stress |
| Knight and Kagan (1977) | Children | Identification of reinforcers |
| Lanyon (1977) | Stuttering | Screening |
| Leiblum and Kopel (1977) | Sexual dysfunctions | Historical factors to assess mediation potential |
| McGullough, Huntsinger, and Nay (1977) | Violent outbursts | Treatment planning |
| B. Martin (1977) | Disturbed families | Screening, treatment planning, and client education and information |
| Marziller and Winter (1978) | Social skills | Treatment planning |
| Mathews and Shaw (1977) | Anxiety | Diagnosis and screening, treatment planning, and outcome evaluation |

**Table 16. Recently Published Behavior Therapy Articles
Utilizing the Interview (Continued)**

| Reference | Targets | Application |
|---|---|---|
| Obler (1973) | Sexual dysfunction | Outcome evaluation |
| Palmer, Lloyd, and Lloyd (1977) | Electricity conservation | Program evaluation |
| Perri, Richards, and Schultheis (1977) | Smoking | Treatment planning |
| Rekers and Varni (1977) | Sexual dysfunction | Outcome evaluation |
| Rosen and Kopel (1977) | Transvestite-exhibitionist | Client education and information |
| Steffen and Myszak (1978) | Obesity | Client information; expectancy manipulation |
| Suarez, Crowe, and Adams (1978) | Depression | Diagnosis and screening |
| Teasdale and Rezin (1978) | Depressive thoughts | Client information and training |
| Trower and others (1978) | Social problems | Screening |
| Vogler, Weissbach, and Compton (1977) and Vogler and others (1977) | Alcoholism | Treatment planning |
| Wincze, Hoon, and Hoon (1978) | Female sexual arousal | Screening, diagnosis, and outcome evaluation |

## Applications of the
## Behavioral Interview

The behavioral interview has been used for a variety of functions in recently published articles, including the diagnosis and screening of potential clients for participation in behavioral intervention programs, the identification of cognitive events for intervention purposes, and as part of behavioral research, preintervention assessment to help devise intervention programs, and the measurement of intervention outcomes. These applications will be considered in subsequent sections.

*Diagnosis and Screening.* As indicated in Table 16, the behavioral interview perhaps has been most frequently used to screen clients for participation in intervention programs and to put clients into diagnostic categories for clinical and research purposes. Interviews have been used frequently as diagnostic instruments with psychophysiological disorders (such as headaches or insomnia) and sexual dysfunctions (Bancroft, 1974; Kantorowitz, 1978; Kinsey, Pomeroy, and Martin, 1948; Obler, 1973; Rosen and Kopel, 1977) in which self-report is the primary means of problem identification and diagnosis. Preintervention interviews are frequently used to select subjects with a sufficient degree of psychophysiological disturbance (such as minimal headache frequency or sleep-onset latency for insomnia) to be included in an intervention program or with symptoms congruent with diagnostic criteria. In studies by Haynes and others (1975) and Epstein and Abel (1977) that involved behavioral intervention with headaches, a preintervention diagnostic interview was utilized to assist in the differential diagnosis of headache types. Criteria for the diagnosis of headache as either muscle-contraction or migraine are based upon self-reports of its location, duration, and intensity, sensory disturbances accompanying it, effects of medication on it, auras, the client's family history of headache, and sensitivity to environmental stimuli, neurological findings, and the presence or absence of nausea and vomiting. Although these factors could be ascertained through questionnaires, interviews have also functioned as assessment instruments for headaches.

Interviews have also been used by Haynes, Sides, and Lockwood (1977) to select insomniac subjects for inclusion in behavioral intervention and etiology research studies. Insomniacs diagnosed as primarily of the sleep-onset variety were those reporting a minimal sleep-onset latency of sixty minutes, difficulties with sleep onset at least four times per week, a minimal history of two years of sleep disturbances, and the absence of clinically significant psychological or organic disturbance. Cautela (1977) described a Pain Survey Schedule that evidently can be utilized in either a questionnaire or interview format to assess various types of pain. Kleinman and others (1977) interviewed hypertensive patients about currently experienced stress involving work, sickness, or family. Hypertensives were classified as experiencing high or low stress in order to evaluate the covariation of stress with blood pressure.

The interview has also been used as a diagnostic tool with depression. Shaw (1977) compared the effectiveness of behavioral and cognitive therapy for depressives and utilized a preintervention, structured interview that focused on the depressed subject's recent behaviors. The responses to open-ended interview questions were used to select depressed patients for inclusion in the study. Subjects selected were those who were diagnosed as "depressed" but not sufficiently depressed to warrant hospitalization. Suarez, Crowe, and Adams (1978) utilized the interview to help diagnose depressed women. Subjects who were diagnosed as "depressive reaction" were included in the study, but criteria for the diagnosis were not presented. In a study with implications for the validity of interviews in the diagnosis of depression, Natale (1977) induced mood changes (elation, depression, and neutral) midway during a simulated initial interview and found that significant behavior changes were associated with the depressed and elated states. Although Natale's study suggests that discrete and identifiable behavior changes may be associated with mood states such as depression, the study utilized base rates obtained prior to mood change for comparison. Unfortunately, the interviewer dealing with clients in a clinical situation seldom has predepression samples of behavior to facilitate comparison of moods. The study by Natale, however, was consistent with earlier findings by Pope and others (1970), who found significant differences in verbal behavior of hospitalized patients depending on their level of depression.

Interviews have been used as screening and diagnostic instruments with several other behavior disorders. B. Martin (1977) utilized a preintervention interview to select families with sufficient degrees of behavioral disturbance for inclusion in a treatment program and to identify problem interactions of those families. A preintervention screening interview also was utilized by Mathews and Shaw (1977) to select subjects with frequent and intense anxiety. Lanyon (1977) employed an informal initial interview with stutterers and selected for inclusion in a biofeedback program those who stuttered on at least 35 percent of the words of a passage read during a preintervention interview. Hall, Baker, and Hutchinson (1977) interviewed chronic schizophrenic patients to identify variables that might predict the effectiveness of a token economy. The authors utilized a 179-item checklist on which the presence or absence of symptoms and other behaviors was noted by two independent raters. Ashby and Wilson (1977) used an initial interview to screen subjects for inclusion in a behavioral weight control program. Volunteers who were not at least fifteen pounds or 10 percent overweight, as well as those who had other physical difficulties, were excluded from the study. Subjects were screened in an initial interview in an orgasmic conditioning study by Kantorowitz (1978). Subjects who evidenced anxiety regarding their sexual functioning or those with abnormal sexual histories were omitted from the treatment program. Eisler and others (1978) utilized a screening interview as part of a social skills training program with psychotic and nonpsychotic hospitalized patients. Each participant was interviewed by both a psychologist and a psychiatrist to ascertain psychiatric diagnosis and suitability for the study. Patients who were diagnosed as schizophrenic or nonpsychotic by both interviewers were selected for inclusion in the intervention program. Wincze, Hoon, and Hoon (1978) utilized a screening interview to select five women for inclusion in a behavioral intervention program for low sexual arousal. Criteria for acceptance into the program included: (1) report of a satisfactory marital relationship, (2) report that the sexual dysfunction consisted of low levels of sexual arousal and pleasure, and (3) an absence of psychotic and neurotic disorders. The use of interviews to assist in screening overweight subjects for behavioral intervention and research was also reported by Jeffrey, Wing, and Stunkard (1978).

Herjanic and Campbell (1977) utilized a structured interview with matched groups of mothers and children from psychiatric and pediatric clinics. The interview was in the form of a symptom checklist on relationship problems, behavior at school, school learning problems, "neurotic" symptoms, symptoms of "psychosis," and antisocial behavior. Although the study has some methodological difficulties (there were no data on "normalcy" of the pediatric group, and the authors did not account for the age factor in symptoms), the authors reported that, except for "psychosis," the number of symptoms reported reliably discriminated disturbed from nondisturbed children.

As evidenced by the previously cited studies, the preintervention interview has frequently been used as a diagnostic and screening instrument in recently published research. Inferences that the interview can be validly applied for this purpose, however, are indirect and derive primarily from the observation that subjects classified into divergent groups on the basis of the interview are significantly different on some other measures, such as questionnaire scores or overt behavior. Assessment of the validity of the interview as a diagnostic instrument is hampered by several factors: (1) specific components or questions used in the interview are infrequently reported, (2) criterion levels for the various diagnostic categories are infrequently reported, and (3) the reliability (internal and external) of the diagnostic process is infrequently assessed. Evaluation of the construct and criterion validity of the interview for diagnosis necessitates reporting of the interview procedures, stimuli, reliability, and diagnostic criteria. Inadequate description of interview procedures means that the validity of the construct being identified cannot be assumed. It is unclear, for example, whether the headaches being treated in the studies cited earlier are actually muscle-contraction headaches. This failure to adequately describe the diagnostic procedures of interviews suggests that caution should be exercised in interpreting results. It should also be reiterated that the validity of an instrument is situation specific, and evidence that the interview can be utilized validly in the diagnosis of specific psychophysiological disorders does not mean that the interview will be a valid diagnostic instrument with other disorders.

The behavioral interview has been utilized as an instrument for placing subjects into diagnostic categories without sufficient assessment of its validity as a method for making such decisions. Inferences of its validity as a diagnostic instrument are usually based upon "face validity," that is, the apparent relevance of client responses to the constructs being considered. Thus, behavior analysts assume that a subject's report of depression, sexual anxiety, or social inhibition is a valid indicator of those constructs and that it can be used to place subjects in different categories. Obviously, the validity of the interview for classifying subjects will depend on many factors, including the structure of the interview, characteristics of the interviewer, and the target responses.

*Identification of Cognitive Events.* Another prevalent use of preintervention interviews in clinical behavior therapy is in the identification of cognitive components of behavior disorders. Such cognitive elements as self-concept, attribution of causality, self-statements, expectancies, and misinformation are assumed to be important etiological components of many behavior disorders. Cognitive factors are frequently assessed in interviews in clinical behavior therapy, but the applicability of the interview for this purpose has not been subjected to substantial investigation. One attempt to identify cognitions was reported by Mathews and Shaw (1977). In an uncontrolled pilot study, the authors utilized interviews to evaluate the cognitive behaviors of ten individuals with generalized anxiety. The authors reported that anxious patients frequently reported repetitive anxiety-associated thoughts. These thoughts were often about aversive or threatening events. The etiological role of cognitive factors in depression has been emphasized frequently. Researchers such as Beck, Mahoney, Meichenbaum, and Seligman have noted the etiological significance of cognitive events and have, in the past, reported research findings supporting this assumption. Beck, Laude, and Bohnert (1974), for example, noted that during interviews depressed individuals emitted a high rate of specific thoughts relating to possible aversive events such as illness, death, or social rejection. However, the interview as an instrument for the assessment of cognitive factors in depression has not been systematically evaluated.

In summary, it is in the area of cognitive assessment that the divergence between clinical application and research involving the interview is most evident. In behavioral intervention, cognitive target events and etiological factors are probably most frequently identified during personal communication between client and behavior analyst, but research on cognitive elements in behavior disorders has relied almost exclusively on questionnaires. The utility of behavioral interviews in the assessment of cognitions will be a function of the ability of subjects to accurately and reliably report cognitive events, the type of cognitive event targeted, and the content validity of the interview situation. Obviously, a great deal of research is needed on interview assessment of cognitive factors. This research should be particularly concerned with the applicability, reliability, and criterion-related validity of the interview as an instrument for assessing cognitive events.

*Design of Intervention Strategies.* Several studies have utilized interviews to derive information to help plan intervention programs, as indicated in Table 16. Because a behavioral construct system assumes multiple causality and individual differences in the etiological and maintaining factors of behavior, preintervention assessment is necessary for implementation of an optimally effective intervention program. In clinical behavior therapy, identification of target variables for intervention, the selection of contingencies, and general intervention planning frequently occur during preintervention interviews (Kanfer and Grimm, 1977). As with other applications of the behavioral interview, however, clinical application has not been accompanied by a commensurate amount of empirical research. Marziller and Winter (1978) made extensive use of preintervention interviews to formulate intervention strategies and to select target behaviors in a social skills training program. All clients were interviewed by one or both authors, who also made commendable attempts to interview relatives, acquaintances, or "significant others." Numerous authors (see Table 16) have reported using the interview for program planning, but systematic investigation of the validity of derived information or parameters affecting validity has not been undertaken.

The interview has been used in recently published research to develop a variety of interventions and has been applied to a variety of target behaviors and clients. Bollard and Woodroffe (1977) utilized an initial interview with parents to plan dry-bed training with enuretic children. As previously mentioned, Cautela (1977) published a Pain Survey Schedule that allows the behavior analyst to identify the etiological factors and characteristics of a pain response that may be helpful in planning interventions. Horne (1977) interviewed two patients manifesting trichotillomania and used the information to help design a behavior therapy program. B. Martin (1977) employed a preintervention interview to pinpoint parent-child interaction difficulties prior to initiating family therapy. In a study with ten anxious patients, Mathews and Shaw (1977) identified anxiety-associated cognitions and then instituted a behavioral treatment program to reduce those cognitions. Kenny, Mowbray, and Lalani (1978) interviewed obsessive-compulsive patients to help plan intervention programs. In a program designed to treat the violent behavior of a sixteen-year-old male, McGullough, Huntsinger, and Nay (1977) utilized a preintervention interview to pinpoint the sequence of events preceding a violent outburst. Based on this information, the adolescent was taught to monitor the chain of events (subvocal cursing, feeling of noncooperation, and so forth) and institute self-control procedures to break the chain. In another self-control study, Perri, Richards, and Schultheis (1977) interviewed smokers to pinpoint factors causing or associated with smoking. This information was incorporated in an intervention program to assist the clients in developing self-control skills to reduce cigarette consumption. Vogler and others (1977) and Vogler, Weissbach, and Compton (1977) discussed the importance of assessing drinking patterns prior to designing intervention programs for alcoholics. They suggested that moderate drinking may be an appropriate intervention goal with some alcoholics and that the success of such programs varies with a number of factors, such as degree of preintervention alcohol intake, age, secondary symptoms of alcoholism, history of hospitalization, and work history. For other alcoholics, however, abstinence training may be the most effective treatment strategy.

The evidence supporting the utility and validity of the interview in planning intervention programs is indirect: behavioral intervention programs based on information derived from the interview have been effective. However, this type of information provides only weak support for the validity of data derived from the interview. In addition to basic research on the reliability and validity of the preintervention interview, research is needed in several other areas to more fully evaluate the interview as a source of data for program planning: (1) determining the most appropriate interview structure and content for providing the greatest amount of information, as well as the most valid information, for program development; (2) evaluating the covariance between changes in interview-derived information and the type of behavioral intervention implemented; and (3) comparing the efficacy of interview and noninterview sources of data for planning interventions.

*Measurement of Intervention Outcome.* As shown by Table 16, the interview has been used as a measure of intervention outcome in a number of studies (Epstein and Abel, 1977; Wincze, Hoon, and Hoon, 1978; Foa and others, 1977; Hall, Baker, and Hutchinson, 1977; Jehu and others, 1977; Mathews and Shaw, 1977; Obler, 1973; Rekers and Varni, 1977; Vogler, Weissbach, and Compton, 1977; Vogler and others, 1977). In none of the studies cited, however, was the interview described in sufficient detail for evaluation of its criterion or content validity, potential biasing components, or other sources of error. Typically, clients or mediators (such as parents or teachers) are interviewed following treatment about their perception of treatment effects and side effects. Although the interview is used as only one of several dependent measures, it is obvious that researchers are drawing inferences about intervention effects from the data derived from interviews. As in other applications of the interview, however, the interview as outcome measure is not being treated with the empirical care devoted to other outcome assessment instruments. Little effort is typically made to report the identity of the interviewers, the content of the interview, the interview situation, or the reliability and criterion validity of the information derived. As a result, it is impossible to have confidence in inferences drawn from most of the cases in which interviews are used as outcome measures.

Other recent applications of the preintervention interview include the identification of historical data about sexual and marital histories prior to intervention (Leiblum and Koepel, 1977; Wincze, Hoon, and Hoon, 1978), the assessment of mediation potential or prognosis (Ciminero and Drabman, 1977; Leiblum and Kopel, 1977), and informing or educating clients about the therapy contract or the causes of behavior (Bollard and Woodroffe, 1977; Goldfried and Goldfried, 1977; B. Martin, 1977; Rosen and Kopel, 1977; Teasdale and Rezin, 1978). One further application of interviewing should be noted—computer interviewing. This phrase has been applied to various procedures that use multiple-choice or true/false questions on an interactive computer system. The use of computers to gather self-report information is certainly a significant development in behavioral assessment but to classify this as an "interview" technique is arbitrary. It could as easily be classified as a "computer-questionnaire" technique. Because computer assessment procedures cannot be classed directly as either interviewing or questionnaire modes of assessment, they were discussed in Chapter One.

The interview is thus frequently employed in diagnosis and screening, but its validity for this purpose has not been frequently evaluated. Information from preintervention interviews has contributed to the development of intervention programs, but its efficiency, relative to information from other sources, also remains to be evaluated. The interview is seldom utilized as the primary outcome measure but is frequently used to draw inferences about outcome. It is evident from this review of recent applications of the interview in behavioral assessment that in most cases it is being used informally and unsystematically. The format of its current application as an outcome measure is analogous to utilizing questionnaires by informally jotting down a few questions, administering them to clients in an unstructured way, and not reporting the content of the questions or the assessment situation. The interview probably has a significant impact in most therapy programs and the content, style, format, and structure of the interview can influence the data derived from it. Interpretation of interview-derived information, as well as a more sophisticated understanding of the interview as an assessment instrument, may be facilitated by more carefully constructing interview situations and stimuli, controlling for potential biasing factors, and reporting interview procedures in research presentations in a more comprehensive way. The utilization of the behavioral interview in diagnosis and screening, in the assessment of cognitive events, to derive information for designing intervention programs, and to evaluate the outcome of those programs underscores the importance of assessing the validity of the interview. Significant decisions and inferences are made on the basis of information derived from the interview, and their validity is de-

pendent upon the validity of the interview procedures and content.
The following section will consider the issues of the reliability and
validity of the behavioral interview more closely.

## Reliability and
## Validity of the
## Behavioral Interview

As noted in the preceding discussion, the validity of behavioral interviews has been insufficiently investigated. Ciminero and
Drabman (1977) noted a dearth of studies on the validity of interviews with children and particularly with parents and teachers. The
lack of research on the behavioral interview is particularly disturbing in view of its important functions in behavioral assessment and
intervention. However, there have been several recently published
studies with implications for the reliability or validity of behavioral
interviews. The validity of a behavioral interview can be evaluated
in several ways. In *criterion-related evaluation,* the data from interviews are compared with data from other assessment instruments.
The *discriminant validity* of interviews can be ascertained by noting
the degree to which data derived from the interview can discriminate between groups classed on the basis of other criteria—
preferably naturally occurring criteria (such as married versus divorced couples). Validity can also be assessed through *manipulation,*
in which some parameters in the interview, such as instructions to
clients, are manipulated and changes in the behaviors of the interviewed clients between conditions are noted. The *content validity*
and *interrater reliability* of the interview can also be evaluated.

In studies assessing the criterion-related validity of interviews, criteria have either been alternative measures of the information targeted in the interview or variables different from, but
presumed to correlate with, the targeted information. Vogler,
Weissbach, and Compton (1977), for example, found that drinking
history and demographic variables may be particularly strong predictors of treatment outcome for alcoholics. Because the criterion
(response to treatment) is not another measure of the target variables (drinking patterns and history), findings such as these pro-

vide only indirect support for the validity of the interview. In another study providing indirect support for the validity of interviews, Kleinman and others (1977) interviewed hypertensives about stress and found a significant correlation between the amount of stress reportedly experienced by the subjects and their blood pressure level. In a more direct assessment of criterion-related validity, Herjanic and Campbell (1977) compared childrens' verbal reports on a wide range of questions to those of their parents. The authors found an average agreement of approximately 80 percent and noted that the agreement rates varied according to the type of information solicited. Girls' responses were slightly more reliable than those of boys. Bronson and Pankey (1977) interviewed parents in their homes about their children's reactions in the presence of unfamiliar adults. Simultaneously, an observer rated the child in the presence of the visitors; the correlation coefficient between the two sets of data was calculated to be .74.

Beiman and others (1978) utilized a behavioral interview as one dependent measure of fear behavior. The experimenters employed a semistructured interview to determine whether subjects reacted with discomfort to slide presentation and/or avoided naturally occurring fear-related stimuli. While results concerning subjective discomfort were not analyzed, information about naturally occurring avoidance behavior was coded according to a binary system. Fifteen subjects classified by other methods as being high in fear reported avoiding stimuli like hospitals, injections, and gory movies. Only a single low-fear subject indicated similar avoidance behavior; chi-square analysis suggested a confidence level for this finding of .001. The correlation coefficients between self-reported avoidance behavior and other dependent measures revealed mixed results. Reported avoidance was significantly correlated with State-Trait Anxiety Inventory scores but not with Anxiety Differential scores or skin conductance levels. Thus, the results of the Beiman study provide only moderate support for the criterion-related validity of self-reported fear behavior. Support for the criterion-related validity of self-reported sexual dysfunctions in women was found in a study by Wincze, Hoon, and Hoon (1978). The authors noted that women's reports of low sexual arousal and low anxiety in sexual situations were substantiated by responses on the Sexual Arousability Inventory (Hoon, Wincze, and Hoon, 1976).

Several researchers have observed significant changes in the behavior of clients when the interview conditions were manipulated. As previously noted, Natale (1977) induced elated, depressed, or neutral mood states in subjects during a simulated telephone interview, and significant changes were noted by observers in response latencies, speech rate, articulation rate, and frequency of silent pauses. Similar differences in verbal behavior were noted by Pope and others (1970) and Waxer (1976) with psychosomatic patients interviewed during depressed and nondepressed days. Rosenthal, Hung, and Kelley (1977) interviewed snake-fearful subjects prior to a behavior avoidance test (BAT). In the first of two studies, subjects underwent a structured twenty-minute interview in which the interviewer was either empathic and warm or unempathic and critical. Subjects undergoing the stern interview evidenced greater approach responses to the snake and reported less fear than those in the other group. In the second study, subjects were either actively encouraged to approach the snake or merely instructed to engage in the BAT. The high-demand condition resulted in greater approach responses than the other condition when the two groups were tested immediately after the interview, but no significant between-group differences were found at follow-up.

In a study with implications for the utility and validity of preintervention interviews, Schiederer (1977) exposed potential clients at a mental health center to one of four conditions prior to an intake interview: (1) modeling, (2) detailed instructions, (3) detailed instructions plus modeling, and (4) no manipulation. All the preinterview manipulations were designed to increase the number and rate of self-disclosing statements and problem descriptions and decrease impersonal descriptions and discussions during the intake interview. The author reported that detailed instructions about how to behave in the interview were sufficient to significantly increase the rate of problem description and self-disclosure; the addition of modeling to the instructions did not significantly enhance the interview process. In addition, therapists rated subjects in the manipulation groups as more helpful than those in the control

groups, and subjects in the manipulation groups rated their interviewers as more concerned. But these findings are inconsistent with
recommendations by others; Pope and others (1972), for example,
suggested minimizing the degree of structure of the intake interview. The studies that demonstrated changes in client behavior as a
function of manipulation in the interview instructions or conditions
are particularly significant because they indicate that the type,
amount, rate, and validity of information derived from an interview can be affected by factors within the interview situation. The
implications for research in this area are clear: More investigation
is needed on variables that influence the validity, efficiency, and
utility of the interview process.

Several investigators have noted that the behavior of clients
during interviews varies according to the classification of clients
along various dimensions (discriminant validity). Thus, the previously described study by Natale (1977) reported that client behavior
during the interview varied according to the mood state induced in
the client. Although not operating within a behavioral construct
system, Waxer (1977) also noted differences in the behavior of
subjects during an interview as a function of level of anxiety. Waxer
videotaped twenty one-minute segments of interviews with
psychiatric patients who varied in level of anxiety; the tapes were
then scored by forty-six raters. Nonverbal cues such as finger
twitching and shifting eyes were significantly related to anxiety
ratings. These findings are consistent with previous work by Waxer
(1974, 1976) in which nonverbal behaviors were also found to significantly discriminate between subjects with respect to the occurrence and degree of depression. Perri, Richards, and Schultheis
(1977) reported that retrospective data derived from a structured
interview could discriminate between clients who did and who did
not successfully apply self-control techniques to stop smoking. The
authors used a yes/no format, five-point Likert scales, and open-
ended questions focusing on a variety of smoking history and
treatment factors (such as the subject's smoking problem and how
the program was implemented). The previously cited research by
Kleinman and others (1977) indicated that data on stress derived
from a structured interview were significantly related to level of
blood pressure.

The content validity of behavioral interviews is an important consideration but has also been the subject of little research. Content validity here refers to the degree to which the elements in the interview situation are appropriate to the constructs and population being investigated. Content validity may be reflected in the specific behaviors emitted by the interviewer (such as questions asked or nonverbal cues) or in the context or situation within which the interview occurs. Thus, factors such as who is present during the interview, the stressfulness of the interview, the degree of structure (Pope and others, 1970, 1972), the focus of the interview, and the format of stimuli (for example, open-ended or yes/no questions—Perri, Richards, and Schultheis, 1977) affect the sensitivity and validity of derived data. Levy (1976), for example, noted that schizophrenic symptoms are more likely to occur in some types of interpersonal situations than in others. Whether or not an interview elicited behaviors that discriminated among paranoid schizophrenics, nonparanoid schizophrenics, and nonschizophrenics was found to vary with manipulations in the degree of interpersonal reciprocity in the interview. As noted previously, one of the most powerful methods of investigating the parameters of the interview situation, and therefore its content validity, is through systematic manipulation of those parameters. However, the content validity of an interview must also be evaluated within the context of its function. If the function of the interview is to elicit client behaviors that might allow classification along such dimensions as depressed or nondepressed or anxious or nonanxious, an interview with adequate content validity (one that maximizes the discriminant functions of the interview) might be one that is relatively stressful to the client. A stress interview, however, is likely to reduce the rapport between client and interviewer and perhaps decrease the amount of information provided by the client about historical and current maintaining factors. A stressful interview, then, might be less appropriate when the derived information is to be used for program planning.

The impact of the function of the interview upon an evaluation of its content validity is particularly evident when the divergent utilization of the interview for research and clinical purposes is considered. The function of the interview in behavioral research is frequently to elicit verbal or nonverbal behaviors that covary with some other classification scheme; an example would be Natale's research on nonverbal behaviors of depressives. In clinical behavior therapy applications, the interview is most frequently used to elicit information relevant for program implementation and evaluation and to educate and inform clients about the behavior change process. It can be assumed that the most appropriate structure and specific content of the interview would vary between these two applications. It is for the purposes of intervention design and evaluation that the interview is most useful to the behavior analyst, and it is for this function that validity research is particularly needed.

The interobserver or interrater agreement of interview data reflects on its validity but has been ascertained in only a few recently published studies. In a study by Perri, Richards, and Schultheis (1977), the responses during interviews of individuals who had attempted self-control procedures for smoking were taped and scored by independent observers, and the authors found high coefficients of interrater agreement. A similar procedure was used by Coleman, Walkind, and Ashley (1977), who found high interrater agreement on tape recordings of thirty interviews conducted with mothers of nursery school children. Interrater agreement is particularly important when more than one interviewer is utilized to collect information. In a nonbehavioral study by Rudestam (1977), for example, six different interviewers were utilized to study families of thirty-nine suicide cases, but the agreement among interviewers was not assessed. Such assessment would have facilitated interpretation of results, particularly in view of the fact that the interviewers were aware of the experimental hypotheses. Reliability may be ascertained between and within interviews. In addition to the interrater agreement previously discussed, reliability may be assessed by repetition of items within the same interview or across more than one interview with the same subject. Within-session reliability assessment is infrequently evaluated but is an efficient source of information to assess the maximum degree of confidence that can be placed in the validity of an interview.

The studies reviewed in this section suggest that data derived from interviews can be highly correlated with data derived
from other assessment instruments (criterion-related validity), can
covary with subjects' classifications on naturally occurring dimensions (discriminant validity), and can covary with manipulations of
conditions before or during interviews. It was also noted that the
content validity and interrater reliability of interviews can be indicative of the overall validity of the interview but have been infrequently reported. In view of the recent findings supporting the
applicability, utility, and validity of some interview formats, the
highly informal use of interviews in behavioral assessment is difficult to account for. This discrepancy suggests that other factors
are influencing their mode of application. As noted by Haynes
(1978), the infrequent *systematic* application of interviews in behavioral assessment may be the result of an unwarranted assumption
that the interview, compared to other assessment procedures, is
susceptible to greater or more numerous sources of error and bias.

The presumed sources of error in interviews are multiple
and include: (1) differences in race, sex, or social class between the
interviewer and client (Abramowitz and Dokecki, 1977); (2) the
retrospective nature of the interview process and error associated
with retrospective data (Ciminero and Drabman, 1977; Yarrow,
Campbell, and Burton, 1970); (3) interviewer knowledge of
hypotheses or classification of clients; (4) the social sensitivity and
type of information elicited (Ciminero and Drabman, 1977;
Haynes, 1978); (5) the age of the client; (6) the population being
interviewed (for example, college sophomores versus heroin addicts); (7) the content, format, and structure of the interview (Rosenthal and others, 1977); (8) bias in the reports of mediator-clients
(parents, psychiatric staff, and so forth); and (9) the bias presumed
to be inherent in all self-report measures. This brief review of
sources of error in the interview process illustrates the difficulty in
evaluating or controlling error sufficiently to attain a minimal degree of confidence in the derived data. Yet the studies cited in this
chapter and those noted in earlier writings suggest that the data
derived from interviews *can* be useful, reliable, and valid. It is our
assumption that interviews differ from other assessment instru-

ments in the type, rather than in the number and degree, of possible sources of error. More formalized and systematic utilization, reporting, and evaluation of interviews in behavioral intervention research would facilitate the identification and control of sources of error, in addition to facilitating the interpretation of derived information.

## Additional Issues in
## Behavioral Interviewing

Recently published research also has implications for issues of the utility, applicability, and structure of the interview. The amenability of specific populations and target behaviors to assessment by means of the interview is an important consideration. Although no recently published article has directly addressed the issue of applicability to target populations, it can be noted from Table 16 that targeted populations and behaviors have been diverse. One major determinant of applicability is probably *reactivity* as a function of the social sensitivity of the targeted behaviors. The interview is a social interaction process, and material with high social value, such as sexual behavior or behavior that significantly deviates from social mores, may be less amenable to assessment through an interview than by other means. The validity of the interview, therefore, may vary inversely with the social sensitivity of the target behaviors. The social sensitivity factor may also affect the applicability of the behavioral interview to various populations. Populations such as sex offenders, child abusers, or heroin addicts are characterized by significant deviations from important social mores, and the validity of interviews with these populations may be more suspect than with populations in which the targets have less social importance. However, it has been noted in other reviews (Haynes, 1978) that there is some evidence supporting the validity of interviews even with deviant populations, and additional investigations are needed to evaluate factors influencing validity. It should also be noted that these target populations and behaviors may demonstrate reactivity to other assessment procedures as well.

Variability has also been noted in the structure of the interview. Many of the reports reviewed in this chapter have utilized relatively structured interviews involving a fixed sequence of interactions with an invariable type and sequence of stimuli. Although no recent publication has addressed the issue of structure, we may assume that the applicability of structure varies with the function of the interview. Where the behavioral interview is utilized strictly for research purposes, a more structured format may be desirable. The functions of a preintervention assessment interview, however, demand a greater degree of flexibility because of the numerous alternative responses to interviewer-provided stimuli. Because structure will influence the content validity and degree of error in the interviewing process, additional investigation of interview structure is needed.

## Summary

The interview is a frequently applied behavioral assessment instrument. It has been utilized for a variety of functions, including diagnosis and screening, identification of cognitive events, the design of intervention strategies, and the measurement of intervention outcome. Although the behavioral interview appears to have utility for these applications, there has been insufficient investigation of its validity and factors affecting its validity. Several recently published articles bear on the validity of behavioral interviews. These studies suggest that the interview can have discriminant and criterion-related validity but that the validity of the behavioral interview is specific to particular functions and populations. Other studies have suggested that manipulating instructions to clients prior to or during interviews affects the behavior of the client and the validity of the information derived.

Haynes and Jensen (in press) summarized the assets and liabilities of interviews in behavioral assessment and offered a set of seven recommendations:

1. Report critical elements of the interview such as the identity of the interviewers and the stimuli provided to the client.
2. Specify criteria when the interview is used for diagnosis or screening.

3. Evaluate the criterion-related validity of interview-derived data.
4. Assess reliability between and within interview sessions.
5. Investigate validity and sources of error and their association with the various target problems and populations.
6. Investigate the effect of interview structure on validity.
7. Use interviews in multimodal assessment strategies.

# CHAPTER EIGHT

# *Psychophysiological Assessment*

$T$he measurement of psychophysiological variables has become an increasingly important goal of behavioral assessment. Both the absolute number and the proportion of published articles in behavioral intervention involving psychophysiological variables have dramatically increased in the last several years. This growing emphasis may be attributed to several factors: (1) an increasing emphasis on the concept of response fractionation, (2) an increasing interest by behavior analysts in psychophysiological disorders and in physiological behavior as a target for intervention, and (3) advances in psychophysiological instrumentation and measurement techniques.

Because of the role of response fractionation in facilitating the measurement of psychophysiological variables in behavioral assessment, a discussion of that concept, previously introduced in Chapter One, precedes sections of this chapter that address the application of psychophysiological methods in behavioral research, their application as outcome measures in behavior therapy, the utilization of psychophysiological variables in the diagnosis and treatment of psychophysiological disorders, and issues in psychophysiological assessment of male and female sexual arousal. Running throughout this chapter is a discussion of recent advances in instrumentation and measurement techniques. This chapter will not consider such methods and issues in psychophysiology as response specificity, law of initial values, or basic measurement technology, unless there have been recent contributions to these areas. Readers desiring greater exposure to basic psychophysiology concepts and procedures should consult Greenfield and Sternbach (1972), Venables and Christie (1975), Brown, (1967), and Venables and Martin (1967).

## Response Fractionation

The concept of response fractionation implies lack of significant covariation, nonsignificant common variance, or dysynchrony among overt behavioral, cognitive, subjective, and physiological measures. The concept is derived from the relatively reliable observation that these measures do not necessarily covary with changing environmental conditions nor do they necessarily demonstrate similar effects from behavioral intervention. This concept has been forcefully articulated by Lacey (1967) and Hodgson and Rachman (1974) and has recently been emphasized by Thomas and Rapp (1977), Bloom and Trautt (1977), Adams and Sturgis (1977), Sartory, Rachman, and Grey (1977), Haynes (1978), May (1977a, 1977b), Lang (1977), and Sersen, Clausen, and Lidsky (1978).

The assumption that behavioral syndromes or problems such as fear, sexual arousal, aggression, anxiety, or depression have multiple components that do not necessarily covary, that they may be maintained by different factors, and that they demonstrate differential reactions to behavioral intervention implies that, in many cases, psychophysiological variables are important targets of a comprehensive behavioral assessment. There is ample evidence to suggest that modification of a behavioral component does not result in the modification of a psychophysiological component as well. Fear reduction research, for example, has demonstrated that the modification of avoidance behavior or subjective feelings need not be accompanied by modification of such physiological indices of fear as elevated heart rate. In many cases, therefore, the assessment of psychophysiological functioning is important to a comprehensive evaluation of the outcome of a behavioral intervention program and to the identification of components of a behavior problem necessitating modification. Response fractionation is closely tied to the concept of *individual-response* and *stimulus-response specificity*, a relationship that suggests that reliable patterns of autonomically mediated responses tend to be associated with specific stimuli and individuals. Sersen, Clausen, and Lidsky (1978) investigated stimulus and individual stereotypy and found evidence for significant patterns across both factors. They also suggested that the method of score standardization, the selection of covariates in statistical analyses, and the choice of scoring method (such as peak versus mean response) affect estimates of stereotypy.

*Fractionation Among Psychophysiological Measures.* Response fractionation may occur among different psychophysiological measures as well as between psychophysiological and nonpsychophysiological measures. McGowan, Haynes, and Wilson (in press), for example, exposed phobic subjects to several conditions: (1) rest, (2) frontal electromyographic (EMG) biofeedback, (3) stress, and (4) poststress adaptation. Frontal EMG levels, heart rate, and peripheral temperature were monitored continuously. Significant effects of the various conditions were found for frontal EMG but not for the other cardiovascular measures. In addition, nonsignificant correlations were found among the various psychophysiological measures.

Alexander, White, and Wallace (1977) monitored frontal and forearm EMG levels, heart rate, respiration rate, and peripheral temperature while exposing subjects to various combinations of EMG feedback or no-feedback conditions. Although the authors did not report correlations among dependent measures, they noted that the effects of biofeedback were specific to the site monitored and that these effects did not generalize across measures. The results of this study were consistent with earlier work by Alexander (1975), which also noted a failure of localized EMG feedback to generalize to other muscle groups. Results consistent with these (Alexander, 1975; Alexander, White, and Wallace, 1977) were reported by Shedivy and Kleinman (1977). They assessed the generalized effects of frontal EMG feedback on sternomastoid, semispinalis and splenius muscle groups. Eight normal subjects were trained to increase and decrease frontal EMG levels for five consecutive days. Frontal EMG measures demonstrated significant changes associated with the training conditions, but sternomastoid EMG did not change during either increase or decrease conditions. Semispinalis and splenius muscle groups did not change significantly during "frontal EMG increase" conditions but significantly increased during "frontal EMG decrease" conditions.

Bloom and Trautt (1977) monitored finger pulse volume and pulse rate of sixty-four normal subjects under conditions of relaxation and threat of shock. The authors found that finger pulse volume was sensitive to the experimental conditions, while pulse rate was not. The correlation between the two was $-.17$. May (1977a) exposed thirty-six phobic subjects to externally presented and imagined phobic stimuli, while monitoring several psychophysiological variables. Electrodermal measures did not discriminate between phobic and nonphobic thoughts, but heart and respiration rates did. May also reported that heart rate and respiration rate were not significantly correlated. In a similar study, May (1977b) monitored electrodermal activity, heart rate, and respiration rate of phobic and nonphobic subjects to phobic and nonphobic thoughts. May again found that heart rate and respiration rate were sensitive to the cognitive manipulations but electrodermal activity was not. The findings from these studies are consistent with the hypothesis that electrodermal activity may be a more sensitive measure of external than of internal cues.

In a single-case study, Nolan and Sandman (1978) exposed a thirty-two-year-old pedophiliac to a series of erotic, neutral, and stressing (autopsies) slides while heart rate, peripheral vasomotor activity, skin potential, and respiration were monitored. The subject demonstrated *stimulus specificity* —that is, patterns of responses varied according to the class of slide presented and were not consistent across stimuli. Stronger relationships among psychophysiological variables were reported by Boulougouris, Rabavilas, and

Stefanis (1977). These investigators exposed twelve obsessive-compulsive patients to internally (cognitive) or externally presented anxiety-provoking stimuli and then treated them with flooding procedures. Although the results must be viewed cautiously because a large number of intercorrelations were calculated, the authors reported that heart rate was highly correlated (.61) with skin conductance during flooding. Significant correlations among measures were also reported by Rudestam and Bedrosian (1977) in a study investigating the effectiveness of desensitization and flooding with specific fears and general social fears. These authors reported that psychophysiological measures (various electrodermal measures) were significantly intercorrelated.

Other authors have also noted significant relationships among psychophysiological responses. Although inferences must be limited because EMG was treated as an independent variable and regional blood flow as a dependent variable, Noonberg, Goldberg, and Anderson (1978) found that feedback-aided increases and decreases in frontal EMG level were associated with changes in digital skin temperature. During the "decrease" EMG condition the authors noted a 2.7 degree increase in digital skin temperature but a nonsignificant (.48°F) change during the "increase" EMG condition. Similar effects were noted by Lehrer (1978), who found consistent reductions across the physiological measures—skin conductance, heart rate, and electroencephalographic pattern (EEG)—associated with relaxation training. Goldman and Lee (1978) reported a strong association between reductions in blood pressure on the one hand and decreased respiration rate but increased respiratory volume on the other. The authors found no association between blood pressure modifications and changes in frontal EMG activity. Glaus, Happ, and Kotses (1978) noted significant changes in airway resistance measures of fifty nonasthmatic subjects under "frontal EMG increase" and "frontal EMG decrease" feedback conditions but not to biofeedback-facilitated changes in the brachioradialis muscle group.

Although the studies by Noonberg, Goldberg, and Anderson (1978), Lehrer (1978), and Goldman and Lee (1978) reported significant associations among psychophysiological responses, they used manipulation designs in which one variable was modified and the effects on other psychophysiological variables were monitored. While a valid method of assessing fractionation, manipulation designs are more likely than correlational designs to result in synchronous patterns. The strength of the association among the variables will probably vary with the strength of the intervention. Although differences among studies have been noted, the recent reports on psychophysiological measures are consistent with the concept of response fractionation. The theoretical importance of psychophysiological response fractionation and patterning (Schwartz, 1976; G. E. Schwartz, 1977) has been increasingly recognized and has implications for the etiology of psychophysiological disorders, for the selection and generalized effects of biofeedback modalities, and for the generalizability of inferences from assessment procedures involving specific psychophysiological measures.

When underlying physiological bases and variability in measurement procedures of the various psychophysiological measures are considered, fractionation should be expected. Differences among physiological systems in neurological innervation would be sufficient to predict substantial fractionation (for example, strong vagal-parasympathetic influences on heart rate) and a lack of parasympathetic influences on most electrodermal responses. In addition, response systems also differ in sensitivity to hormonal or other biochemical changes, as well as in latency of response adaptation rates, degree of central nervous system (CNS) influence, and inherent variability. Because of varying CNS and biochemical influences, innervation patterns, and maintenance mechanisms, it is difficult to employ multiple psychophysiological measures without making sampling errors or errors in the temporal structure of a laboratory measurement procedure. Heart rate or EEG patterns, for example, may demonstrate significant changes within one second following a mild stimulus, while diastolic blood pressure may not demonstrate significant change until minutes or hours following the onset of intense stimulation. Similarly, poststimulation adaptation rates vary among psychophysiological measures. Because correlation coefficients are calculated by noting changes in measures at one or several points in time, low correlation coefficients among measures would be expected. This differential patterning of psychophysiological responses makes it difficult to design studies with a high degree of internal validity for all measures and necessitates cautious interpretation of indices of covariation or lack of covariation.

There are several implications of these findings for the use of psychophysiological measures in behavioral assessment: (1) it cannot be assumed that one or even several psychophysiological responses can yield an index of generalized or overall physiological functioning; (2) multiple measures should be taken when feasible; (3) psychophysiological measures should be selected after careful consideration of expected effects of the experimental or therapeutic manipulation; (4) the differential sensitivity of various measures to different manipulations (such as cognitive versus external stimuli or short-term versus long-term effects) should be taken into account when selecting measures; and (5) underlying physiological mechanisms must be understood and taken into account when selecting measures.

*Relationship Between Psychophysiological and Subjective Measures.* The concept of response fractionation has underscored the need for a closer examination of the relationship between psychophysiological measures and subjective reports, particularly self-perceptions of relaxation and tension. Alexander (Alexander, White, and Wallace, 1977; Alexander, 1975) noted that frontal EMG levels during EMG biofeedback did not correlate highly with subjective reports of tension or relaxation. Similar results were reported by Shedivy and Kleinman (1977), who obtained subjective reports of tension or relaxation during baseline, "increase frontal EMG" conditions, and "decrease frontal EMG" conditions. Although frontal EMG levels demonstrated expected effects, subjective reports increased above baseline levels in the "increase" condition but did not change during "decrease" conditions. Several other studies have noted a lack of covariation between psychophysiological and subjective measures. Boulougouris, Rabavilas, and Stefanis (1977) monitored pulse rate, electrodermal responses, and subjective ratings of anxiety of obsessive-compulsive patients under anxiety-provoking and neutral stimulation. They reported that subjective ratings of anxiety and psychophysiological measures were not significantly correlated. Rudestam and Bedrosian (1977) reported that with phobic subjects electrodermal measures were not significantly correlated with Fear Survey scores or an anxiety scale. In a study comparing the effects of frontal EMG feedback, autogenic phrases, self-relaxation, and a noncontingent tone, Jessup and Neufeld (1977) found few or no between-group differences in heart rate, forehead temperature, or hand temperature but did find significant differences between groups in questionnaire measures of anxiety and "egotism."

In the previously noted study by Nolan and Sandman (1978), a thirty-two-year-old pedophiliac male was exposed to a series of slides while various psychophysiological measures were taken. The authors noted severe discrepancies between subjective and physiological indices (heart rate) of arousal to slides of partially clothed children. Physiological indices suggested increased agitation, but this was not accompanied by subjective reports of arousal. Based on the observation that a close correspondence existed between subjective (pleasure ratings) and physiological measures of arousal on other classes of stimuli, the authors attempted to increase the congruence between these two measures of arousal for pedophiliac stimuli. Since the authors had noted that heart rate, but neither vasomotor nor electrodermal response, closely associated with pleasure ratings across stimulus classes, they focused intervention on reducing heart-rate increase to pedophiliac stimuli and increasing it to slides of adult women. While the study may make inferential errors in assuming that heart rate is indicative of "arousal," the authors present an interesting approach to increasing the congruence between subjective and physiological indices. Other studies have noted a more significant relationship between psychophysiological and subject measures. Teasdale and Rezin (1978) and Teasdale and Bancroft (1977) found that corrugator EMG was significantly related to the rate occurrence of depressive thoughts in depressed patients. Pollak (1978) had subjects record their mood in the natural environment every fifteen minutes while their blood pressure was recorded automatically. The authors noted that mood was significantly related to systolic blood pressure for fifteen of seventeen subjects, to diastolic blood pressure for thirteen of seventeen subjects, and to heart rate for thirteen of seventeen subjects.

The only recently published study to directly evaluate fractionation between subjective and self-report measures was authored by Sartory, Rachman and Grey (1977). These authors investigated Hodgson and Rachman's (1974) hypothesis that low covariation between measures would be most evident during conditions of low fear or low arousal and that under conditions of high fear or high arousal measures would be more highly correlated. In a Latin square design, seventeen subjects with specific phobias were exposed to a feared stimulus at subjective levels of 0, 50, 75, and 100 on a Fear Thermometer (the mechanism for obtaining these fear levels was not clearly explained). Heart rate and subjective fear ratings were monitored while feared stimuli were presented to subjects. Although the authors did not report correlation coefficients between measures, they suggested that the "relationship between subjective fear and heart rate can be described as positively accelerating over dimensions of fear intensity" (p. 435), a finding consistent with Hodgson and Rachman's hypothesis.

The finding in recent studies of low correlations between self-report of anxiety and relaxation and psychophysiological measures is consistent with assumptions of response desynchronization. Except, perhaps, under high arousal levels, psychophysiological events do not account for a large proportion of the variance in self-report measures of anxiety or relaxation. A self-report, evidently, is also determined by other variables, such as cognitive interpretation of environmental cues, perceptions of control or helplessness, previous experience with the stimuli, and demand and expectancy factors associated with the assessment conditions. In addition, the psychophysiological research on response fractionation cited thus far has used only group factorial designs. A side effect of the exclusive adoption of this experimental paradigm is a failure to examine individual differences in response covariation. As indicated in the study by McGowan, Haynes, and Wilson (in press), between-subject variability in the degree of response fractionation is evident. Some subjects demonstrate high correlations among measures while others evidence insignificant or inverse relationships. The significance of between-subject variability in response covariation has yet to be evaluated.

*Relationship Between Psychophysiological and Cognitive Events.*
In contrast to findings suggesting inconsistent relationships
among specific physiological measures and between psychophysiological and subjective measures, recent research supports
the hypothesis that cognitive manipulations can be associated with
significant changes in psychophysiological variables. Significant
cognitive-psychophysiological covariation has been found in
studies utilizing imagination of feared stimuli, behavior therapy
studies involving cognitive manipulation (for example, implosive
therapy or desensitization), studies involving the exposure of
subjects to nonfearful imagery, and studies assessing intellectual
functioning.

Several recently published studies have monitored
psychophysiological responses while instructing subjects to imagine
feared stimuli. Rudestam and Bedrosian (1977) noted significant
changes in electrodermal measures accompanying imagery during
flooding treatment of phobic patients. Boulougouris, Rabavilas,
and Stefanis (1977) found that exposure of obsessive-compulsive
patients to anxiety-provoking thoughts similar to those used in
flooding was associated with significant increases in heart rate and
electrodermal responses. Similar results were reported by May
(1977a, 1977b), who found that self-generated phobic thoughts
were associated with significant increases in some psychophysiological indices. In May's studies heart rate and respiration rate were,
but galvanic skin responses (GSR) were not, sensitive to the cognitive manipulation.

Several studies have investigated the effects of cognitive
tasks on psychophysiological responses. Janisse and Kuc (1977) reported research in which they manipulated several variables (such
as threatening versus nonthreatening instructions) associated with
a WAIS-type digit-span test. The authors found that pupil size but
not heart rate validly discriminated among factors of intelligence,
correctness of trials, and stress levels. Davidson and Schwartz
(1977) recorded occipital and sensorimotor EEG patterns during
visual and kinesthetic imagery. In a counterbalanced design, twenty
normal subjects were requested to imagine a flashing light and
various tapping sensations. The authors found that visual imagery

was associated with relatively greater occipital activation; this finding supported the notion that imagery of various modalities can elicit specific changes in associated cerebral sensory regions. Utilizing a correlational design, Kleinman and others (1977) found that poor performance on the Halsted-Reitan categories test was associated with blood pressure levels in essential hypertensives. Reductions in blood pressure from a blood pressure feedback program resulted in an increase in performance on the categories test.

Weerts and Lang (1978) investigated the discriminant validity of psychophysiological assessment of fear and the differences between focal and social anxieties on psychophysiological measures. Subjects who reported either spider or public speaking anxieties imagined scenes with spiders, scenes involving public speaking, and control scenes. Heart rate, skin conductance, and ocular activity were recorded, and the findings suggested that subjects tended to demonstrate higher arousal to scenes specific to their reported fear and that spider phobics demonstrated greater arousal than speech anxiety subjects to their respective imagined scenes. The authors interpreted these findings as supporting the hypothesis that specific phobias elicit more vivid imagery than do general ones and that the degree of vividness is associated with the degree of psychophysiological arousal.

Other studies also provide data on the association between cognitive activity and psychophysiological responses. As previously noted, Teasdale and Rezin (1978) and Teasdale and Bancroft (1977) found significant relationships between corrugator EMG and the occurrence or frequency of depressed thoughts. White (1978) reported four experiments using the sublingual cotton swab method of measuring salivation and noted that thoughts of food were associated with degree of salivary control (ability to increase or decrease salivation). Drummond, White, and Ashton (1978) cited references suggesting that imagination of feared stimuli is associated with increases in respiratory rate and heart rate and then proposed that imagery vividness may also be associated with the rate of habituation. In a study involving the threat of a shock (faradic stimulation), they found that habituation, as measured by electrodermal responses, was quicker for subjects with nonvivid than vivid imagery. Like Weerts and Lang (1978), Drummond,

White, and Ashton (1978) suggested that imagery vividness may be an important determinant of intervention outcome in those interventions utilizing presentation of imagery and that generalization of effects may be greater for vivid than for nonvivid imagers. This set of studies suggests that the evaluation of imagery vividness may be an important preintervention function of behavioral assessment and may have implications for the selection of intervention procedures.

The consistency of recent findings of psychophysiological covariation with cognitive manipulation can, however, be misleading. As noted by Janisse and Kuc (1977), not all psychophysiological variables are equally sensitive to cognitive manipulation; accordingly, systematic investigation of the differential sensitivity of psychophysiological measures to cognitive manipulations is needed. It is evident, however, that imagination of feared stimuli often results in indices of activation in some psychophysiological measures and that the degree of psychophysiological response may be associated with the vividness of the imagery (Weerts and Lang, 1978; White, 1978). This implies that psychophysiological variables may be valid and useful assessment targets in the preintervention assessment of phobic stimuli, in the evaluation of treatment programs designed to modify response to those stimuli, and in monitoring interventions that involve such cognitive presentations as covert sensitization or systematic desensitization. A second caution should be noted in drawing inferences about the relationship between cognitive and psychophysiological events. In previous sections of this chapter, psychophysiological and subjective measures were considered as *dependent* variables; in the studies cited in this section, cognitive factors have been treated as independent variables, and inferences have been drawn from observed modifications in psychophysiological variables accompanying cognitive manipulations. Because of the experimental paradigms utilized, assumptions of covariation between cognitive and psychophysiological variables must be made with caution.

This section has reviewed recently published research that suggests that the concept of response fractionation is having an increasing impact upon preintervention assessment, the conceptualization of behavior disorder etiologies, and the selection of intervention strategies. Fractionation has been noted among psychophysiological responses as well as between psychophysiological and other response modalities. These research findings suggest that (1) there is probably no one generally effective index of psychophysiological arousal, and thus multiple measures should be employed when feasible; (2) the selection of psychophysiological measures should be based upon expected intervention effects, underlying physiological mechanisms, and differential sensitivity of the various measures; (3) the use of nonfactorial (single-subject) designs might facilitate examination of response fractionation; (4) there is between-subject variability in the degree of covariation between responses and, as a result, factors affecting degree of response fractionation should be examined; and (5) there is a consistently significant relation between cognitive events and psychophysiological responses, although this relation must remain partially inferential because of the nature of cognition and because it is based upon manipulation designs in which cognitive events have been treated as independent variables.

## Assessment of Behavioral Intervention

Psychophysiological measures are playing an increasingly important role in the evaluation of the main effects and side-effects of behavioral intervention. Table 17 presents recently published behavioral intervention studies that utilized psychophysiological measures.

The specific psychophysiological responses selected for measurement across studies are quite consistent. Analysis of recently published articles that utilized psychophysiological measures reveals that, from the multitude of responses available, 60 percent of the studies utilized EMG (frontal EMG in most cases), 38 percent of the studies utilized heart rate, and 22 percent of the studies utilized some form of electrodermal response. The rationale for selecting a particular psychophysiological measure is seldom given, and it must be surmised that the criteria for selection are confined to availability of equipment or precedent. Selection of specific psychophysiological measures does not seem to be based on analysis of expected effects or on an understanding of the physiological mechanisms underlying the selected responses.

**Table 17. Recently Published Behavioral Intervention Studies Utilizing Psychophysiological Measures**

| Reference | Subjects | Measures | Comments |
|---|---|---|---|
| Acosta, Yamamoto, and Wilcox (1978) | Schizophrenic, neurotic, and tension headache patients | Frontal EMG[a] | Uncontrolled design involving application of frontal EMG feedback; all groups decreased EMG level |
| Beiman, Israel, and Johnson (1978) | Normal subjects | Heart rate, respiration, frontal EMG, and EDR[b] | Controlled group outcome study of effects of progressive relaxation, self-relaxation, and EMG feedback |
| Bloom and Cantrell (1978) | Thirty-five-year-old pregnant female with suspected hypertension | Blood pressure | Case study of effectiveness of behavioral anxiety management techniques in reducing blood pressure; blood pressure was sensitive to intervention |
| Boulougouris, Rabavilas, and Stefanis (1977) | Twelve obsessive-compulsive patients | Heart rate and EDR | Both measures were sensitive to anxiety-provoking stimuli and flooding effects |
| Bronwell, Hayes, and Barlow (1977) | Five cases of sexual deviation | Penile circumference | Multiple-baseline design focusing on manipulation of sexual arousal patterns; penile measure was sensitive to different stimuli and treatment effects |

Table 17. Recently Published Behavioral Intervention Studies Utilizing Psychophysiological Measures (Continued)

| Reference | Subjects | Measures | Comments |
|---|---|---|---|
| Cohen and others (1977) | Normal volunteers | Frontal EMG | Controlled group investigation of contingent and noncontingent feedback; frontal EMG was sensitive |
| Counts, Hollandsworth, and Alcorn (1978) | Test-anxious college students | Frontal EMG | Controlled group investigation of effects of EMG biofeedback and cue-controlled relaxation; used EMG as feedback modality but not as outcome measure |
| Dawson, Schell, and Catania (1977) | Twenty depressed and twenty nondepressed subjects | EDR and heart rate | Some EDRs and heart-rate measures discriminated between depressed and nondepressed subjects but were not sensitive to treatment (electroconvulsive therapy); not a behavioral study but relevant |
| Epstein and Abel (1977) | Tension headache patients | Frontal EMG | Controlled group frontal EMG was not sensitive to treatment effects |
| Epstein, Malone, and Cunningham (1978) | Two poststroke paretic patients | EMG on upper extremity | Biofeedback study; EMG feedback was associated with increased EMG activity |

| Study | Subjects | Measures | Description |
|---|---|---|---|
| Ewing and Hughes (1978) | Normal subjects | Frontal EMG | Three A-B-A-B single-subject studies suggesting that cue-controlled relaxation was effective in reducing frontal EMG levels during stress |
| Feuerstein and Adams (1977) | Four patients with migraine or tension headaches | Frontal EMG and cephalic blood volume pulse | Multiple-baseline design involving cephalic vasomotor and frontal EMG feedback; both measures were sensitive to treatment effects |
| Fey and Lindholm (1978) | Normal subjects | Blood pressure and heart rate | Controlled group study assessing effects of biofeedback and relaxation training; significant across-group, but not between-group, differences |
| Finley and others (1977) | Four children with cerebral palsy | Frontal EMG | A-B-A-B design involving frontal EMG feedback; EMG measure was sensitive to treatment effects |
| Gatchel and others (1977) | Speech-anxious volunteers | Frontal EMG, heart rate, and EDR | Controlled group design assessing heart-rate feedback and relaxation training; EMG equipment malfunction; heart rate and EDR were sensitive to treatment effects |

**Table 17. Recently Published Behavioral Intervention Studies Utilizing Psychophysiological Measures (Continued)**

| Reference | Subjects | Measures | Comments |
|---|---|---|---|
| Gatchel and others (1978) | Normal subjects | Frontal EMG, heart rate, and EDR | Controlled group study assessing generalized effects of EMG feedback and effects on response to stress |
| Gautheir and Marshall (1977) | Sixty snake-phobic undergraduates | Heart-rate variability | Parametric study on effects of flooding; heart-rate variability was sensitive to treatment effects |
| Goldfried and Goldfried (1977) | Forty-two speech-anxious subjects | Heart rate | Controlled group design assessing parameters of self-desensitization; heart rate was sensitive to treatment effects |
| Goldman and Lee (1978) | Normal subjects | Respiration, frontal EMG, and blood pressure | Assessing effects of respiration and frontal EMG as mediators of blood pressure; respiration enhanced blood pressure control while EMG was ineffective as a mediator of blood pressure |
| R. W. Green (1978) | Diabetic mental patient | Urine glucose oxidase levels (indirect measure of blood-sugar level) | Case study involving self-regulation of eating behaviors to teach control of blood-sugar levels; was effective |

| Haynes, Wilson, and Britton (in press) | Nine patients with atopic dermatitis | Frontal EMG | Series of controlled case studies; frontal EMG was not sensitive to biofeedback and relaxation treatment effects |
| Haynes and others (1975) | Twenty-four subjects with muscle-tension headaches | Frontal EMG | Controlled group design involving frontal EMG feedback; frontal EMG was sensitive to treatment effects |
| Horan and others (1977) | Six cigarette smokers | EKG[c] | Report on side effects of rapid smoking treatment; EKG abnormalities accompanying treatment in some cases |
| Hynd, Severson, and O'Neil (1976) | Cigarette smokers | Peripheral temperature, blood pressure, and heart rate | Report on side effects of rapid smoking treatment; small but significant changes in cardiovascular measures accompanied treatment |
| Jaremko (1978) | Normal subjects | EDR | Controlled group analogue study assessing prophylactic properties of systematic desensitization; desensitization was effective in preventing fear response |
| Jessup and Neufeld (1977) | Psychiatric patients | Frontal EMG, heart rate, and hand and forehead temperature | Biofeedback study in which heart rate was most sensitive measure; no effect on temperature |

**Table 17. Recently Published Behavioral Intervention Studies Utilizing Psychophysiological Measures (Continued)**

| Reference | Subjects | Measures | Comments |
|---|---|---|---|
| Kondo, Canter, and Bean (1977) | Twenty-four normal volunteers reporting "tension" | Frontal EMG | Controlled group parametric study on frontal EMG feedback; frontal EMG was sensitive to manipulations in intersession intervals |
| Lehrer (1978) | Twenty anxiety-neurotic patients, twenty nonanxious controls | EEG[d], heart rate, and EDR | Controlled group investigation of effects of relaxation training; assessed resting levels and response to loud noise |
| Levin and others (1977) | One pedophiliac male | Penile circumference | Case study involving variations of covert sensitization; penile measure was sensitive to treatment effects |
| Lick and Heffler (1977) | Forty insomniac subjects | Heart rate and EDR | Controlled group design involving relaxation training; psychophysiological measures were unrelated to treatment outcome |
| Nolan and Sandman (1978) | Thirty-two-year-old pedophiliac | Heart rate, EDR, respiration, and blood volume pulse | Single case study investigating effects of "biosyntonic" therapy; heart rate was most sensitive to stimuli and intervention |

| | | | |
|---|---|---|---|
| Noonberg, Goldberg, and Anderson (1978) | Normal subjects | Digital skin temperature and frontal EMG | Assessed effects of frontal EMG activity on digital skin temperature; temperature increases associated with biofeedback-facilitated decreases in frontal EMG |
| Patel (1977) | Essential hypertensives | EDR, blood pressure, and frontal EMG | A presentation of several studies but data from psychophysiological measures was not presented systematically; intervention with behavior therapy and biofeedback resulted in mild to moderate effects on blood pressure |
| Pearne, Zigelbaum, and Peyser (1977) | Woman with chronic urinary retention and incontinence | Frontal EMG | A case study involving EMG feedback; EMG was sensitive to treatment effects |
| Putre and others (1977) | Hyperactive children | Frontal EMG | Uncontrolled group study involving relaxation training; frontal EMG was sensitive to treatment effects |
| Rudestam and Bedrosian (1977) | Phobic subjects | EDR | Controlled group study on effects of desensitization and flooding; EDR was sensitive to treatment effects |

**Table 17. Recently Published Behavioral Intervention Studies Utilizing Psychophysiological Measures (Continued)**

| Reference | Subjects | Measures | Comments |
|---|---|---|---|
| Schroeder and others (1977) | Two retardates | Frontal EMG | Case studies involving application of EMG feedback and contingent restraint on self-injurious behavior; EMG was sensitive to treatment effects |
| Shannon, Goldman, and Lee (1978) | Normal subjects | Blood pressure | Controlled study compared three methods of biofeedback for modifying blood pressure; constant-cuff method worked better than noncontinuous methods |
| Sturgis, Tollison, and Adams (1978) | Subjects with combination of migraine and muscle-contraction headache | Temporal artery blood volume pulse and frontal EMG | Within-subject controlled investigation of differential effects of feedback modalities on various headache types |
| Surwit, Shapiro, and Good (1978) | Patients with essential hypertension | Blood pressure | Controlled group study comparing three methods of reducing blood pressure; no differences in blood pressure among groups but significant overall effects |

| Teasdale and Rezin (1978) | Depressed psychiatric patients | Corrugator EMG | Assessment of thought stopping for reducing depressive thoughts; no effect on EMG measures |
| Thomas and Rapp (1977) | One monosymptomatic phobic subject | Heart rate | Case study employing flooding; heart rate was sensitive to treatment effects |

[a]EMG: electromyography
[b]EDR: electrodermal responses
[c]EKG: electrocardiogram
[d]EEG: electroencephalogram

As noted earlier, there is substantial evidence that no single psychophysiological response is a sensitive measure of general physiological states or of the general effects of experimental or intervention manipulations. Selection of psychophysiological measures that may be inappropriate for the issues being studied decreases the content validity of the measurement process. One aspect of content validity in psychophysiological measurement is the degree to which the measure selected reflects the process of interest to the behavior analyst. Studies to be reviewed in this chapter, for example, have suggested that frontal EMG may not always be a valid measure of general physiological (particularly sympathetic-autonomic) arousal, mean heart rate may not be a sensitive measure of response to environmentally elicited stress, and some electrodermal responses may be more sensitive than others to cognitive stress. The implications of these hypotheses are that the selection of specific psychophysiological responses as dependent measures should be based on an evaluation of the issues addressed in the study and on the conclusions about physiological functioning that can be drawn.

Despite unexplained or inconsistent rationales for the selection of specific psychophysiological measures, almost all studies cited in Table 17 reported that at least one psychophysiological measure was sensitive to the treatment manipulations (demonstrated significant change associated with the intervention). The sensitivity of psychophysiological measures is evident in studies in which the target of intervention is overt behavior (Horan and others, 1977; R. W. Green, 1978; Hynd, Severson, and O'Neil, 1976), cognitions (Boulougouris, Rabavilas, and Stefanis, 1977; Gauthier and Marshall, 1977; Teasdale and Rezin, 1978), or physiological functioning (Haynes, Sides, and Lockwood, 1977; Epstein and Abel, 1977; Feuerstein and Adams, 1977; Sturgis, Tollison, and Adams, 1978). It is also interesting to note that the vast majority (82 percent) of studies utilizing psychophysiological measures also utilized intervention procedures such as biofeedback, flooding, or relaxation training that are designed to directly modify physiological functioning. Although the use of psychophysiological measures in studies that attempt to modify overt behavior (for example, avoidance behaviors or social skills) is not rare,

psychophysiological responses are apparently relegated to a role of less importance in these studies. It would appear, therefore, that the concept of response fractionation is incorporated into measurement selection procedures with greater frequency in behavior studies involving cognitive or physiological targets than in studies involving primarily overt behavioral targets. Less frequent utilization of psychophysiological measures with overt behavioral targets may also be a function of the restrictions on the activity of subjects frequently necessitated by these measurement procedures.

Many behavior therapy studies that used psychophysiological measures also failed to report measurement procedures in sufficient detail to allow for their evaluation. As indicated by Beaty and Haynes (in press), factors such as recording site, resistance levels at the recording site, integration techniques, amplification and filtering levels, conductive media, and electrode composition affect the sensitivity and validity of the resultant data. Sophistication of measurement procedures has varied from computer analysis with highly controlled recording techniques (Gatchel and others, 1977) to pulse rates taken by hand before and after treatment (Horne and Matson, 1977). It is obvious that different measurement procedures generate different levels of confidence in the resultant data.

*Individual Differences in Etiology and Response to Treatment.* A number of recently published studies involving psychophysiological measures have addressed the issue of individual differences in response to treatment and in the etiology of behavior disorders. Although sometimes underemphasized in group experimental designs, variation in subjects' responses to behavioral intervention is an expected outcome. Beaty and Haynes (in press), in reviewing behavioral intervention with muscle-contraction headache, noted variability both in treatment outcome and in frontal EMG levels associated with headache and nonheadache subjects and in headache subjects with and without headaches. These findings suggest that there are individual differences in etiological or maintaining factors of muscle-contraction headache and that the most appropriate treatment strategy might vary as a function of these factors. Preintervention assessment might help identify the relative involvement of forehead or neck muscle tension, pain tolerance,

cognitive factors, or social contingencies in the frequency or intensity of headache reports and help determine whether biofeedback,
cognitive restructuring, or family therapy would be the most promising intervention. Additional discussion of individual differences
in psychophysiological responses and of their importance for
treatment outcome can be found in reports by Lang (1977), Dawson, Schell, and Catania (1977), Boulougouris, Rabavilas, and
Stefanis (1977), Sturgis, Tollison, and Adams (1978), Valle and De-
Good (1977), Kleinman and others (1977), Haynes, Sides, and
Lockwood (1977), and Whitehead and others (1977). In a discussion article on imagery and therapy, Lang (1977) noted that there
was a significant positive relationship between the degree of
physiologically measured arousal to imagined phobic scenes and
the response to systematic desensitization. Although their results
must be interpreted with caution because of a large number of
predictor variables, Boulougouris, Rabavilas, and Stefanis (1977)
found that several psychophysiological variables (such as skin conductance responses during flooding) were associated with the outcome of flooding treatment.

   *The Evaluation of Treatment Side Effects.* Physiological side effects of behavioral intervention (effects other than those on the
main target response) have been measured or discussed in several
recently published articles. Undesirable side effects on cardiovascular functioning as a result of rapid smoking treatment programs,
which require subjects to smoke a number of cigarettes in rapid
succession (stimulus satiation paradigm), were discussed in studies
by Lichtenstein and Glasgow (1977), Horan and others (1977), and
Hynd, Severson, and O'Neil (1976). Monitoring psychophysiological responses of six subjects during rapid smoking treatment,
Horan and others (1977) noted mean heart-rate increases of 35
beats per minute (bpm) for all subjects and electrocardiogram
(EKG) abnormalities for two of the six subjects. Hynd, Severson, and
O'Neil (1976) also reported changes in psychophysiological variables (peripheral temperature, blood pressure, and pulse rate) during rapid smoking treatment, but these changes were smaller and
clinically less significant than those in the other study. In their
review of research on the side effects of rapid smoking treatment,
Lichtenstein and Glasgow (1977) emphasized the physical risks in-

volved with this intervention program, particularly in EKG abnormalities, and the importance of preintervention assessment. The authors noted that they routinely screen out approximately 8.3 percent of their applicants for medical reasons. These studies emphasize the recurring theme that evaluation of an intervention program cannot be based only on the main effects on the target behavior.

If assumptions of response fractionation and individual differences in response to intervention are valid, the evaluation of variables predicting treatment outcome and side effects becomes an important focus for basic and applied psychophysiological research. Because a specific intervention may have differential effects on the various components of a behavior disorder (such as cognitive or physiological components), it would be expected that treatment would be most beneficial to individuals manifesting disorders in the targeted components. The assessment of psychophysiological variables before, during, and following behavioral intervention may (1) assist in the selection of appropriate intervention strategies, (2) assist in the selection of intervention targets, (3) facilitate the monitoring of progress in the intervention program, and (4) provide one measure of intervention outcome and side effects.

## Measurement of
## Psychophysiological Disorders

Perhaps the most clinically relevant utilization of psychophysiological assessment procedures is in the diagnosis of psychophysiological disorders and in the evaluation of treatment outcomes with this class of disorders. Because such disorders are characterized by dysfunctions in psychophysiological responses, they are natural targets for this kind of assessment. Recently published studies have focused on the assessment of insomnia, headache, ulcers, and essential hypertension. There also have been significant advances in the technology of psychophysiological assessment—advances that have had a major impact on the evaluation of psychophysiological disorders.

*Insomnia.* Recent reviews of behavioral intervention with primary insomnia (insomnia not secondary to other psychological

or organic dysfunctions) by Nicassio and Bootzin (1978) and Ribordy and Denny (1977) emphasized the importance of individual differences in its etiology. It has been assumed that sleep-onset difficulty is partially a function of physiological arousal at bedtime that
is incompatible with sleep onset. Although differences between insomniacs and noninsomniacs in resting levels of arousal (awake but
relaxed) have been reported (Haynes and others, 1975), recently
published research (Haynes, Sides, and Lockwood, 1977) has
stressed individual variability in the role of physiological arousal in
sleep onset. The finding that some insomniacs demonstrate low
levels of physiological arousal and others demonstrate high levels
of arousal further supports the supposition that variability in
arousal is insufficient to account for variance in sleep onset and
emphasizes the need for psychophysiological and nonphysiological
assessment. Undoubtedly, excessive sleep-onset latencies may be a
function of a variety of factors, including physiological arousal at
bedtime, interfering cognitive behaviors, or misperception of sleep
states.

The desirability of utilizing psychophysiological measurement procedures to evaluate the outcome of behavior intervention
with insomnia has been stressed by Nicassio and Bootzin (1978) and
Ribordy and Denny (1977). Most studies evaluating behavioral intervention with insomnia have utilized self-report measures. Although insomnia is, in part, a disorder diagnosed through self-
report, the utilization of EEG and other physiological measures can
enhance confidence in the reported outcome. This is especially
important in view of the finding that insomniacs sometimes grossly
overestimate objectively measured sleep-onset latencies. Standard
laboratory assessment procedures (EEG, electrooculogram (EOG),
EMG, and EKG), however, are reactive and affect the sleep-onset
latencies they are designed to measure (Ribordy and Denny, 1977).
Recent findings by Coates and Thoreson (1978) have confirmed
the assumption that sleep laboratory data may not reflect sleeping
patterns at home. Coates and Thoreson developed portable sleep
laboratory equipment to record EEG patterns of subjects while they
sleep at home. The device consists of a turbanlike head cover with
a feedback system and imbedded electrodes to ensure good electrode contact with the scalp. The data is amplified by a portable

in-home unit and transferred to the main laboratory by phone hookup. Subjects who slept in both laboratory and home situations demonstrated significant differences between the two environments in measures of sleep-onset latencies and duration of sleep stages. The remote monitoring procedures developed by Coates and Thoreson offer a promising method of assessing sleep patterns in the home. At this writing, however, the approximate cost for one unit was $10,000.

The measurement of eye movements through an electrooculogram (EOG) facilitates the identification of sleep stages but has typically required two polygraph channels for appropriate interpretation. Movements from each eye are recorded, and differences between synchronous and dysynchronous eye movements assist in discriminating among sleep onset and various sleep stages. To improve the efficiency of EOG recording procedures, two methods recently have been proposed for recording eye movements on one channel without loss of artifact identification. Hord (1975) presented one system that utilizes four electrodes around the eyes as the input source for a single polygraph channel. The electrode placement and lead attachment procedures accomplish common mode rejection (rejection of artifact). Wells, Allen, and Wagman (1977) described a simpler system that apparently accomplishes the same artifact rejection as the system developed by Hord. They recommended joining leads from the outer canthus of each eye into one channel with a separate reference. They suggested that their measurement protocols were less affected by artifact than Hord's but stressed the need for further research.

The criterion and construct validity of measures of sleep onset recently has been questioned on the basis of differences between insomniacs and noninsomniacs in the degree of covariation between subjectively and physiologically determined sleep onset (West and others, 1977). Based on EEG indices of sleep onset, insomniacs, compared to noninsomniacs, have been found to greatly overestimate sleep-onset latencies. This finding has been interpreted as indicating that self-reported insomnia may be a partial function of erroneous perception of sleep-onset latencies. This hypothesis, however, is warranted only if the EEG indices of sleep onset are assumed to be valid. Although there are minor variations among sleep-research laboratories, sleep onset in most laboratories is defined as a decrease in the percentage of alpha, higher-frequency, and lower-amplitude dysynchronous brain waves, accompanied by the onset of spindles or K-complexes. However, the criterion validity of these indices of sleep onset is open to question and they must be considered arbitrary. It is possible that these physiological events are not valid indices of sleep-onset, that there is individual variation in the physiological events indicative of sleep onset or that there are differences in the physiological events or states perceived as sleep onset.

*Headaches.* Several recent publications (Epstein and Abel, 1977; Feuerstein and Adams, 1977; C. Philips, 1977; Beaty and Haynes, in press; Sturgis, Tollison, and Adams, 1978; Acosta, Yamamoto, and Wilcox, 1978) have discussed or utilized psychophysiological measurement procedures with muscle-contraction or migraine headaches. Epstein and Abel (1977) utilized frontal EMG measures as a diagnostic aid to identify subjects with muscle-contraction headache for behavioral treatment. Assuming that muscle-contraction headache should be accompanied by elevation in frontal EMG, these authors accepted for treatment those volunteers who demonstrated an integrated EMG level of at least 10 microvolts (uV) during headaches. Although the behavioral intervention (frontal EMG feedback) resulted in a diminution of self-reported headache symptoms, frontal EMG measures did not demonstrate expected reduction across treatment sessions.

Feuerstein and Adams (1977) utilized frontal EMG and cephalic vasomotor feedback in treating subjects with muscle-contraction and migraine headaches, respectively. Although significant individual differences in response to treatment were noted by the authors, biofeedback resulted in learned control of frontal EMG and cephalic vasomotor responses along with a diminution in self-reported headaches. Sturgis, Tollison, and Adams (1978) reported an interesting multiple-baseline biofeedback study with patients manifesting both migraine and muscle-contraction headaches. Subjects were exposed to a counter-balanced sequence of either temporal artery blood volume pulse or frontal EMG feedback. Control of blood volume pulse and frontal EMG was attained by both groups of subjects; decreases in migraine headaches were associated with blood volume pulse feedback, and decreases in tension headaches were associated with frontal EMG feedback. In a review of the literature on the behavioral treatment of muscle-contraction headache, Beaty and Haynes (in press) stressed the importance of monitoring nonspecific psychophysiological responses such as heart rate or vasomotor responses, as well as etiologically specific physiological responses such as frontal EMG. The authors suggested further that such data may facilitate the understanding of etiological factors in psychophysiological disorders and the mechanisms underlying treatment outcome.

*Ulcers.* Walker and Sandman (1977a) utilized multiple psychophysiological measures, including an electrogastrogram (EGG), to study the psychophysiological response of ulcer patients to various forms of stress. Because of the dearth of published reports in this area, this paper represents a significant contribution to the methodology of studying ulcers. The authors attached two specially prepared electrodes to several ulcer patients; the active electrode was attached to the navel area and the reference electrode to the left calf. Amplification was accomplished by a Grass 7P1 DC preamplifier with bucking voltage. Walker and Sandman also monitored heart rate, EMG from various sites, respiration, and skin potential while exposing ulcer, arthritic, and normal subjects to mild stress. The authors used two methods of analyzing data: (1) a conventional method focusing on wave frequency, peak amplitude (positive and negative), response time, and so forth; and (2) a power spectral analysis involving computer analysis of wave patterns from data that were digitized using a two-second sample rate. Although the degree of differentiation was not impressive, analysis of variance (ANOVA) procedures revealed that EGG measures taken during stress (slides of autopsies) differentiated ulcer patients (and arthritic patients) from healthy subjects. They reported significant deceleration of heart rate during stress for normal and arthritic but not for ulcer patients and higher EMG during stress for arthritics. The authors discuss implications of these findings for the etiology of ulcers.

*Hypertension.* Several studies have employed blood pressure measures while evaluating the effects of biofeedback on patients with essential hypertension. Kleinman and others (1977) exposed eight male hypertensives to three control sessions and nine sessions of blood pressure feedback. The authors sampled blood pressure three to five times per session by asculation to determine pretreatment and posttreatment levels and reported a small decrease following treatment (mean blood pressure levels fell from 149/93 to 143/85). The authors commendably attempted to assess situation generalization of treatment effects, and similar decreases were reported for blood pressure readings taken by patients in their homes. Patel (1977) reviewed several studies involving behavioral intervention with essential hypertension. Measures of systolic and diastolic blood pressure were taken from sitting, standing, and supine positions, and patients were exposed to a variety of intervention procedures. Pretreatment to posttreatment decrements in blood pressure were noted, with these effects tending to maintain at follow-up. The results of these studies are congruent with the findings of previously published reports that suggested that behavioral intervention can result in decrements in diastolic and systolic blood pressure, but the clinical significance of the effects must be questioned.

In more recently published research, Bloom and Cantrell (1978) provided a thirty-five-year-old pregnant female suspected to have hypertension with training in anxiety management techniques. The intervention was effective in lowering her blood pressure. In a controlled group study, Surwit, Shapiro, and Good (1978) exposed patients with essential hypertension to three methods of reducing blood pressure (cardiovascular biofeedback, neuromuscular biofeedback, and meditation) but found no differences among groups, although there were statistically significant overall reductions in blood pressure. The previously cited studies illustrate the increasing application of behavioral intervention procedures to psychophysiological disorders; a natural outgrowth has been an increasing emphasis upon psychophysiological assessment. The focus upon psychophysiological disorders has also highlighted another important application of psychophysiological measurement procedures—the diagnosis of behavioral disorders. Considered in the following section are some of the recent diagnostic uses of psychophysiological assessment procedures.

## Diagnostic Applications

Within a behavioral construct system, diagnosis refers to the identification of behavioral characteristics or syndromes, the classification of subjects and groups, and the identification of historical and current etiological factors. The hypothesized utility of diagnosis is based on assumptions that it can aid in selecting appropriate interventions, in predicting response to intervention, and in understanding the development of behavior disorders. Although diagnosis may help identify the "type" of disorder, behavioral assessment is less frequently used for this classificatory purpose. There are several areas of psychophysiological research with implications for diagnosis. These include treatment implications of different etiological factors for psychophysiological disorders, identification of fear-arousal stimuli, and discriminating between individuals who have and do not have a particular behavioral disorder.

Several authors have noted that psychophysiological disorders may be associated with multiple and complex causative factors and that the identification of those factors can facilitate the selection of appropriate treatment modalities. Beaty and Haynes (in press) noted that frontal EMG feedback, neck EMG feedback, generalized relaxation instructions, or manipulation of social and environmental factors might be selected as intervention approaches with muscle-contraction headache. Selection of the most appropriate intervention approach would be a function of the outcome of a preintervention behavioral assessment (for example, psychophysiological assessment or self-monitoring) that focused on the identification of etiological factors operating for individual subjects. Epstein and Abel (1977) stressed the importance of individual differences in the etiology of muscle-contraction headache and used a variety of behavioral assessment procedures, including monitoring of frontal EMG levels during a headache, to help identify headache type and possible causative factors. C. Philips (1977) also used EMG measures from the forehead and neck area to identify headache type and to select the site for EMG feedback. Although they did not systematically investigate this hypothesis, these authors assumed that biofeedback from the site of highest tension would result in the greatest reduction in reported muscle-contraction headaches. Norton and Nielson (1977) also discussed the importance of identifying causative factors in headaches and stressed the need for organic physical assessment (EEG, x ray) to identify possible tissue pathology.

Feuerstein and Adams (1977) monitored cephalic vasomotor and frontal EMG activity of subjects with vascular or muscle-contraction headaches. The authors found idiosyncratic patterns of physiological activity, both between and within groups, during feedback training. These authors reported that migraine patients demonstrated considerable lability in their vasomotor responses and suggested that between-subject differences in variability (rather than in mean) within the response system may have diagnostic implications. Also working with migraine patients, however, Boudewyns and Cornish (1978) found no significant differences in finger temperature between forty-one migraine patients and forty-one nonmigraine patients. Haynes, Sides, and Lockwood (1977) also noted variation in the etiology of primary sleep-onset insomnia. The authors noted significant between-subject variability in resting frontal EMG levels within a group of insomniacs. They also noted that successful biofeedback and relaxation intervention programs were not associated with reductions in frontal EMG levels. These latter findings are not consistent with the hypothesized etiological role of physiological arousal in insomnia and further suggest that the most appropriate intervention strategy might vary, depending on which of several etiological factors are operating for a particular subject.

The assessment of etiological factors in pain was discussed in a recent paper by Cairns and Pasino (1977). The authors attempted to differentiate organically determined pain from pain maintained by such nonorganic factors as social and environmental consequences, and they utilized a procedure originally reported by Walters (1959) in which the response of patients to pain stimuli (painful body manipulations) is first observed under normal conditions and later when the patient is under increasing levels of sodium pentothal. Pain maintained by nonorganic factors would not be expected to significantly decrease under sodium pentothal conditions. Although this diagnostic procedure is extremely promising, there has been insufficient evaluation of its criterion validity. In fact, in the Cairns and Pasino study, differential diagnosis through this procedure was not related to the outcome of treatment involving verbal reinforcement and feedback. Thus, the prediction that behavioral intervention procedures would be more effective for pain patients diagnosed as "psychogenic" rather than as "organic" was not substantiated.

The previously cited studies reinforce a recurring theme in this book: behavior disorders have multiple and varying determinants, and preintervention evaluation of these determinants for a particular subject is necessary for the selection of the most appropriate intervention. As discussed in Chapter One, the degree of improvement in the outcome of behavioral intervention that can be expected from an increasing focus on individual differences will be a function of the amount of variance in the disorder and in subjects' responses to treatment that are accounted for by those differences. (At the same time, it is natural to assume individual differences in etiology to be more important in some disorders than in others.) The diagnostic utility of preintervention psychophysiological assessment is also supported by the previously reviewed research (Boulougouris, Rabavilas, and Stefanis, 1977; May, 1977a, 1977b; Drummond, White, and Ashton, 1978; Weerts and Lang, 1978; White, 1978; Janisse and Kuc, 1977; Kleinman and others, 1977) that suggested that imagination of feared stimuli is associated with elevation in psychophysiological indices of arousal. These findings imply that monitoring psychophysiological events during imagination of specific stimuli may facilitate the identification of anxiety-eliciting stimuli or the ranking of stimuli on their arousal-eliciting characteristics. The diagnostic utility of this procedure, however, will be a function of the reliability of these findings and the validity of selecting target stimuli or hierarchies on the basis of psychophysiological measures.

Evaluation of differences in *general* physiological functioning between individuals with and without a particular behavior disorder is not a highly important goal of behavioral assessment (Dawson, Schell, and Catania, 1977; Wincze, Hoon, and Hoon, 1978; Walker and Sandman, 1977a). Evaluation of differences

between diagnostic groups on multiple or nonspecific psychophysiological measures can add to our understanding of the characteristics of a disorder but has little immediate impact upon the
selection of intervention modalities or targets. A demonstration
of differences between depressed and nondepressed subjects in
heart rate or EMG, for example (Dawson, Schell, and Catania,
1977; Teasdale and Bancroft, 1977; Teasdale and Rezin, 1978), cannot by itself suggest that heart-rate elevation is a causative or maintaining factor of depression. However, findings of between-group
differences on nonspecific measures can have significant impact on
treatment selection and evaluation of outcome when viewed within
the context of a broad-based assessment package.

In summary, recent research utilizing psychophysiological
measures, particularly with psychophysiological disorders, has contributed to an understanding of the multiple causation of behavior
disorders, the role of individual differences in etiology, and the
impact of these differences upon treatment selection. The importance of preintervention psychophysiological assessment and diagnosis will undoubtedly grow as a result of the increasing emphasis
upon the treatment of psychophysiological disorders, advances in
the technology of assessment and intervention, the recognition of
the role of psychophysiological variables in other behavior problems, and an increasing emphasis upon such treatment procedures
as biofeedback and relaxation training that function to directly
modify psychophysiological variables.

## Advances in Technology

As with other behavioral assessment instruments, the utility
and validity of psychophysiological assessment are influenced by
advances in the technology of measurement. The following sections will present recent advances in the measurement of specific
psychophysiological responses. Issues of sensitivity, criterion validity, construct validity, and time and event sampling, as well as new
developments in instrumentation, will be addressed.

*Electrodermal Responses (EDR).* Skin conductance and skin
resistance responses have been utilized or discussed in recent papers by Beiman and others (1978), Boulougouris, Rabavilas, and

Stefanis (1977), Burchardt and Levis (1977), Dawson, Schell, and Catania (1977), Drummond, White, and Ashton (1978), Gatchel and others (1977), Hugdahl, Fredrikson, and Ohman (1977), Jaremko (1978), Ketterer and Smith (1977), Kleinknecht and Bernstein (1978), Kotses, Glaus, and Frese (1977), Nolan and Sandman (1978), Walker and Sandman (1977a), and Weerts and Lang (1978).

Findings on the sensitivity of EDRs to treatment effects and on the association between EDRs and other psychophysiological measures have varied. Interpretation of research in this area is complicated because the sensitivity of EDRs is influenced by the specific components selected for measurement (spontaneous fluctuation versus absolute levels). Several authors (Beiman and others, 1978; Burchardt and Levis, 1977; Drummond, White, and Ashton, 1978; Gatchel and others, 1977; Jaremko, 1978; Kotses, Glaus, and Frese, 1977; Rudestam, 1977; Weerts and Lang, 1978) found that EDRs were sensitive to the effects of various interventions or stimulus presentations, but in two papers May (1977a, 1977b) found that skin resistance responses and skin conductance levels were not sensitive to the presentation of phobic stimuli. May suggested that EDRs may be more sensitive to external than to internal (cognitive) stimuli. Similarly, Nolan and Sandman (1978) found that electrodermal responses were not sensitive to various classes of stimuli (arousing, neutral, and stressful) presented to a pedophiliac but that heart rate was. As noted earlier in the chapter, low levels of correlation among psychophysiological measures is a common finding. Boulougouris, Rabavilas, and Stefanis (1977), however, reported a correlation of .61 between maximum skin conductance level and heart rate during flooding scenes. Rudestam and Bedrosian (1977) also found significant correlations between EDRs and other psychophysiological measures.

Several authors have noted that the sensitivity and validity of EDRs may be related to the components that are sampled, the time-sampling parameters utilized, and the specific measurement sites and procedures used. Laterality differences in EDRs recorded on finger or palmar areas have been noted by Ketterer and Smith (1977) and Varni (1975). Ketterer and Smith reported a higher frequency of skin conductance responses in the left than in the right hand of individuals with a family history of left-handed dominance but no laterality differences in individuals with entirely dextral families. These authors also reported an interaction between laterality and the sex of the subject; females more frequently demonstrated higher skin conductance levels in the right hand and males in the left hand.

Hugdahl, Fredrikson, and Ohman (1977), Lockhart and Lieberman (1977), and Kotses, Glaus, and Frese (1977) have suggested that the interval in which EDRs are sampled following stimulus presentation will affect the sensitivity of the measure. Utilizing a classical conditioning paradigm, Hugdahl and others found that EDRs measured one to four seconds, compared to four to nine seconds, following stimulus presentation provided a more sensitive measure of arousal. In contrast, Kotses and associates monitored electrodermal responses to visual stimuli and noted that significant differences among various classes of stimuli were found only when measured four to ten seconds following stimulus presentation. Although these findings have important implications for sampling EDRs, they are difficult to integrate. Evidently variation in sampling procedures will affect the sensitivity and validity of the resultant measures of EDRs. The sampling interval of optimal sensitivity, however, will be a function of the experimental paradigm and type of stimuli utilized and requires further study.

The importance of sampling in determining the validity and sensitivity of EDRs also extends to the selection of target components. As indicated in standard reference books on psychophysiology, there are many components of EDRs (such as conductance, fluctuations, latency, and wave forms) that often do not exhibit a high degree of covariance. Lockhart and Lieberman (1977) provided additional support for the assumption of fractionation by performing factor analyses on the different elements of the electrodermal response. The authors found tentative support for four general factors—latency, rise time, half-time recovery, and amplitude—and noted that these factors varied in degree of sensitivity to behavioral phenomena. The findings that sensitivity and validity vary as a function of which components of an EDR are sampled and that they are also influenced by the temporal characteristics of the sampling complicate the task of the behavior analyst who wishes to utilize EDRs in behavioral assessment. Since there is insufficient data on the validity of the multitude of components involved in EDRs, and on the basis of previous research, the behavior analyst should probably utilitize the frequency of skin conductance responses as a measure of EDR.

We located only one recently published article addressing instrumentation in electrodermal responses. Lowry (1977) noted that the passive voltage-divider instrumentation that is utilized to measure skin resistance and conductance provides only indirect measures of these phenomena and, under some circumstances, results in nonlinear data, particularly in the higher ranges of skin conductance. Presenting circuitry for direct measurement of skin resistance and conductance to eliminate error due to nonlinearity, Lowry described two circuits that involve a variable-gain voltage amplifier for direct measurement of skin resistance and a current-to-voltage transducer for direct measurement of skin conductance. A combined working circuit has thus been made available for application in behavioral assessment.

Kleinknecht and Bernstein (1978) and Slutsky and Allen (1978) used the palmar sweat index as one measure of sympathetic arousal. In the palmar sweat index, a print of the palmar area is made, and the number of open sweat pores in a given area is counted. Although this is not a new measure and is only grossly related to EDRs, it provides one relatively unobtrusive index of sympathetic activation applicable in the natural environment. In their study on dental fear, Kleinknecht and Bernstein took palmar sweat index measures from high- and low-fearful dental subjects while they were waiting in the dentist's office, just prior to injection of a local anesthetic, and just before they left the office. The authors found nonsignificant effects for fear level or the sex of the patient but significant effects over time. Male and female subjects with low fear levels adapted over time; the sweat index of high-fear males increased over time. Thus, Kleinknecht and Bernstein's study illustrated the potential application of this measure in the natural environment but did not support its discriminant validity (no significant differences were found between high- and low-fear subjects).

In summary, the differential sensitivity of EDRs, resulting

from variation in temporal and component sampling and measurement procedures, has been noted in several recently published
reports and has direct implications for the measurement of EDR in
behavioral assessment. In addition, as indicated by Hodgson and
Rachman (1974), Hugdahl, Fredrikson, and Ohman (1977), Christie and Venables (1972), and Stern and Walrath (1977), EDRs have
complex and poorly understood physiological and psychological
determinants. Indications that EDR is affected by sympathetic but
not by parasympathetic innervation, that sympathetic post-
ganglionic fibers are cholinergic rather than adrenergic, and that
there are individual differences in responsivity further suggest that
EDR is a multifaceted response system associated with psychological phenomena other than simply anxiety or fear. The obvious
implication of all this is that care must be exercised in the utilization
and interpretation of electrodermal measures.

*Heart Rate.* This continues to be a popular target response
in both behavioral and nonbehavioral psychophysiological assessment. Its popularity is probably due to the ease with which this
response can be measured and analyzed. Recent publications have
provided further support for the utilization of heart rate as a predictor and sensitive indicator of treatment outcome (Lang, 1977;
Lehrer, 1978; Horne and Matson, 1977; Nolan and Sandman,
1978; Hynd, Severson, and O'Neil, 1976; Goldfried and Goldfried,
1977; Fey and Lindholm, 1978; Gatchel and others, 1977; Thomas
and Rapp, 1977), as a measure of treatment side effects (Horan and
others, 1977; Hynd, Severson, and O'Neil, 1976), as a response
system discriminating between phobic and nonphobic stimuli
(Boulougouris, Rabavilas, and Stefanis, 1977; Burchardt and Levis,
1977; Thomas and Rapp, 1977; May, 1977a, 1977b; Weerts and
Lang, 1978), as a measure discriminating between subjects with and
without specific behavior disorders (Dawson, Schell, and Catania,
1977; Lehrer, 1978; Walker and Sandman, 1977a), as a measure
discriminating stressful from nonstressful conditions ( Janisse and
Kuc, 1977; Obrist, Langer, and Grignolo, 1977; Hersen, Bellack,
and Turner, 1978), and as a measure differentiating among specific
cognitive events ( Janisse and Kuc, 1977; May, 1977a, 1977b; Weerts
and Lang, 1978). Of the recently published studies in which heart
rate was monitored, only in a study by Peck (1977) was heart rate
insensitive to the experimental manipulations.

Bloom and Trautt (1977) directly evaluated the validity of heart rate (pulse rate) in discriminating between varying levels of experimentally induced anxiety. Heart rate and finger pulse volume (or blood volume pulse) were monitored for thirty-two male and thirty-two female subjects under conditions of relaxation and threat of shock. Both measures were found to discriminate between conditions, although their intercorrelation was low ($-.17$), and finger pulse volume responded with shorter latency to threat of shock and removal of threat than did heart rate. Two other recently published studies have implications for the discriminant validity of heart-rate measures. Weerts and Lang (1978) found higher heart rates associated with stressful than with nonstressful imagery. Nolan and Sandman (1978) found that, of several psychophysiological measures monitored, heart rate was the most sensitive indicator of various classes of slide presentations (arousing and stressful) to a pedophiliac male. Although the previously cited literature suggests that heart rate is a sensitive index of experimentally manipulated stress, Gautheir and Marshall (1977) noted that heart-rate mean may be a less sensitive measure than heart-rate variability. The authors monitored heart activity of sixty snake-phobic subjects during exposure to a live caged snake as part of a behavior avoidance test (see Chapter Four) and presented data that suggested that a measure of variability in rate was a more sensitive indicator of the experimental manipulations than was mean rate. This finding is consistent with that of Prigatano and Johnson (1974) and serves to emphasize that different methods of sampling and analysis of psychophysiological data affect the validity of resultant inferences. Another problem with using heart rate is the directional fractionation associated with "intake" and "rejection" and the heart-rate response to novel and threatening stimuli. The fear or anxiety that a stimulus may provoke interacts with other qualities of the stimulus to produce the response (Gannon, personal communication, 1979).

Heslegrave, Ogilvie, and Furedy (1978) suggested that nonrandom trends in heart rate attributable to sinus arrhythmia and the gradual nature of the heart-rate response to intervention make normal estimates of variance invalid. They suggested that the procedure called "successive difference mean square" would be a more appropriate method of estimating variance. They presented data from fifty subjects to illustrate their point and further emphasized the idea that different methods of analyzing heart-rate data lead to different interpretations about heart-rate variability. They also suggested that interbeat intervals are better measures than mean rate or beats per minute. Further evaluation of the relative sensitivity and validity of heart-rate mean and variability is needed, with particular attention directed to the factors affecting the sensitivity of each, their latency of response, and adaptation rates following stress termination.

*Blood Flow and Temperature.* Measures of blood flow (blood volume pulse, blood volume, and peripheral temperature) have been utilized frequently as indices of sympathetic activation. Although peripheral blood flow is influenced by such transient environmental and historical factors as ambient temperature, exercise, diet, and hormonal levels, peripheral vasoconstriction has commonly been observed to follow presentation of stressful stimuli and has been assumed to provide one index of psychophysiological response to stress. Several recently published studies have also noted that peripheral blood flow measures were sensitive to environmental stress manipulations (Hynd, Severson, and O'Neil, 1976; Jessup and Neufeld, 1977; Bloom and Trautt, 1977; Feuerstein and Adams, 1977; Hersen, Bellack, and Turner, 1978), and Noonberg, Goldberg, and Anderson (1978), noted significant increases in digital skin temperature associated with EMG-facilitated relaxation. Bloom and Trautt (1977) monitored the finger pulse volume of sixty-four male and female subjects under conditions of relaxation and threat of shock. The authors reported that finger pulse volume was sensitive to the experimental manipulations and was more sensitive to these conditions than was heart rate. Therefore, this study provided support for the utilization of blood volume pulse as a measure of experimentally induced anxiety. The low correlation between finger pulse volume and pulse rate ($-.17$) was hypothesized to be a function of the differential temporal responsivity of the two response systems. The authors pointed out that changes in finger pulse volume occurred more quickly than changes in heart rate and that low intercorrelations at a given time period would therefore be expected.

Feuerstein and Adams (1977) monitored the cephalic vasomotor responses (blood volume pulse) of migraine patients as part of a biofeedback study. The authors positioned a Grass reflectance plethysmograph over the zygomaticofacial branch of the superficial temporal artery and provided subjects with feedback about the amplitude of their blood volume pressure. Cephalic vasomotor feedback was associated with reports of reduced headache frequency. The authors also noted apparent changes in the wave form of recorded blood volume pulses prior to and during migraine headaches and that blood volume pressure from the temporal artery was modified with treatment. Similar effects were reported by Sturgis, Tollison, and Adams (1978) in treating two subjects with both migraine and muscle-contraction headaches. Another measure of blood flow, namely, peripheral hand temperature, was found to be insensitive to intervention in a study by Jessup and Neufeld (1977). The authors employed four relaxation techniques—frontal EMG, autogenic phrases, self-relaxation, and noncontingent tone—with psychiatric patients. There were no differences among the four treatment groups on measures of forehead and hand temperature, although questionnaire and heart-rate measures discriminated among the four interventions. Nonsignificant differences in hand temperature between migraine and nonmigraine patients were also reported by Boudewyns and Cornish (1978).

Several recently published articles have discussed instrumentation or procedures in temperature and blood flow measurement. Tahmoush and Sullivan (1977) conducted a laboratory analogue analysis of the physiological foundations of photoplethysmography. The authors studied photoplethysmographically measured pulsatile blood flow in a glass cylinder and noted that, as expected, pulse amplitude varied with changes in flow but also with hematocrit (volume of erythrocytes) and with the orientation of the blood cells during flow. The authors noted that the magnitude of nonpulsatile backscattered light (analagous to blood volume measures) depended upon hematocrit and the optical properties of the cutaneous tissue. The authors are continuing their work with the aim of approaching quantification of physiological variables through photoplethysmography. One instrumentation difficulty that has plagued photoplethysmography research is the light-history effect. Because photoplethysmography involves a light source and sensor, the recorded signal can sometimes be influenced by previous exposure to light (Tahmoush and others, 1976). One proposed solution is to use infrared transducers to reduce light-history effects. Spaiser (1977) describes a coupling circuit for an infrared transducer. This particular circuit was designed for use with a Bechman Type-R polygraph, but the author suggested that suitable modifications in design can be incorporated to make it usable with most research-quality polygraphs.

Romanczyk and others (1977) noted that recent attention to circadian ryhthms and to individual differences in physiological activity has necessitated the development of methods to monitor deep body temperature (core temperature, as opposed to peripheral temperature) over long periods of time. Romanczyk and associates described a temperature-measuring instrument designed to be accurate, inexpensive, comfortable, and safe to use with disturbed patients. The procedure utilizes a Yellow Springs thermistor, connecting wires, heat-shrinkable tubing held in place in the armpit by layers of micropore tape, gauze pads, and a large square Band-Aid. The authors furnish a diagram for placement and construction. In a criterion validity evaluation, temperatures from their apparatus were found to correlate .96 with rectal temperatures across one day. In summary, recent research involving blood flow and temperature measures has tended to support their sensitivity to experimental "anxiety" manipulations and their accuracy as measures of treatment effects in biofeedback research. As with other psychophysiological measures, however, peripheral blood flow is complexly determined, and care must be exercised in interpreting data.

*Cardiovascular Rate-Pressure Product.* Although this measure is used primarily in direct medical research (Amsterdam and others, 1974; Bruce, 1974; Monroe, 1964; Redwood and others, 1971; Robinson, 1967), Goldstein, Ross, and Brady (1977) have suggested that the rate-pressure product may have utility as an index of cardiovascular functioning in behavioral intervention research. Rate-pressure product is an arithmetic derivation of heart rate and blood pressure and is reflected in the formula: rate-pressure product = blood pressure (mm Hg) × heart rate (beats/minute) × $10^3$. This product is assumed to be indicative of overall cardiovascular functioning, and Goldstein, Ross, and Brady (1977) found it to be sensitive to the effects of biofeedback training. Rate-pressure product is a promising measure of cardiovascular functioning but has been used in an insufficient number of behavioral studies to allow for evaluation.

*Cardiac Stroke Volume.* Another measure of cardiovascular functioning that has been infrequently utilized by behavior analysts but that has potential utility is cardiac stroke volume (Baker, 1971; Denninston and others, 1976; Gliner, Browe, and Horvath, 1977; Kinnen, 1970; Kubicek and others, 1966; Labadidi and others, 1971; Naggar and others, 1975). Cardiac stroke volume (output at systole) can provide a sensitive index of general cardiovascular functioning, but its utilization has been hampered by the invasiveness of the commonly utilized measurement procedures (dye dilution techniques—Gliner, Browe, and Horvath, 1977). Gliner, Browe, and Horvath (1977) raised the issue of invasiveness in psychophysiology research and discussed impedance cardiography as a noninvasive method of measuring stroke volume. They utilized an IFM/Minnesota impedance cardiograph that involves the detection of impedance changes from electrical current impressed at two points on the body. The authors also cited criterion validity research that suggests that impedance cardiography is highly correlated ($+/-$ 8 percent difference) with the more commonly used methods. Cardiac output can be calculated from measures of stroke volume and heart rate.

Miller and Horvath (1978) presented an excellent review of the basis, accuracy, and limitations of impedance cardiography as a measure of cardiac output. These authors noted that significant controversy has surrounded use of impedance cardiography but suggested that it may be a useful and noninvasive, although relative, measure of cardiac output if the limitations of the method are acknowledged. Specifically, the authors noted that (1) variations among individuals in thoracic resistivity and thoracic cross-section affect the resultant measures and invalidate between-subject comparisons; (2) impedance cardiography usually results in an overestimate of cardiac output (by a factor of 1.3); (3) impedance cardiography is highly correlated with other estimates of cardiac output, and error factors may be relatively constant within subjects; and (4) impedance cardiography is invalid for measurement in certain conditions (such as valvular insufficiency), and the phase of the respiratory cycle in which measurements are made must be controlled. Cardiac output and stroke volume might be useful measures when the target of behavioral intervention is general cardiac functioning. Although complexly determined, stroke volume and cardiac output may serve as general indicators of cardiovascular activation. These measures are particularly relevant when cardiovascular events are targeted for intervention, as in the treatment of essential hypertension or cardiac arrhythmias, but may also be useful indicators of the generalized physiological effects of behavioral interventions such as relaxation training or biofeedback.

*Blood Pressure.* This has been discussed in many recently published studies. Its importance in behavioral assessment is the result of an increasing recognition of nonorganic determinants of essential hypertension and an increasing examination of behavioral interventions for reducing elevated blood pressure. Assessment of blood pressure and intervention with essential hypertension have been aided by advances in the technology of blood pressure measurement in the last several years. This section will review recent applications of blood pressure measurement in behavioral intervention and summarize such recent technological advances in the measurement of blood pressure as constant-cuff procedures, continuous monitoring procedures, pulse-wave velocity measures, and cuff oscillations.

Blood pressure traditionally has been measured with an occlusion cuff and a device for sensing Korotkoff sounds (Tursky, 1974). The pressure in the occlusion cuff is increased above systole (pressure at heart systole) and slowly decreased until Korotkoff sounds or wave forms are identified. The point on the decreasing pressure gradient at which a full Korotkoff wave form or sound is detected is assumed to indicate systolic blood pressure. The point on the decreasing pressure gradient at which the wave form disappears is assumed to indicate diastolic blood pressure. For research purposes, pressure gradients and superimposed Korotkoff wave forms from a microphone are permanently recorded on polygraph paper. Significant problems with this method of measuring blood pressure, including unreliability and suspect criterion validity, have been noted elsewhere (Haynes, 1978) and have served as an incentive for the development of more reliable and valid measurement procedures. Despite its drawbacks, however, indirect measurement of blood pressure utilizing occlusion procedures continues to be utilized frequently in behavioral and psychophysiological research (Bloom and Cantrell, 1978; Hynd, Severson, and O'Neil, 1976; Patel, 1977; Kleinman and others, 1977; Surwit, Shapiro, and Good, 1978). Patel (1977) reviewed several studies involving behavioral and biofeedback treatment of hypertension, and the occlusion cuff was employed to evaluate the diastolic and systolic blood pressure of subjects before, during, and following treatment. Readings were taken from sitting, standing, and supine positions, and the blood pressure recordings were sensitive to treatment effects.

Blood pressure was the major dependent variable in a study by Fey and Lindholm (1978) that compared the effects of biofeedback and progressive relaxation procedures on systolic and diastolic blood pressure. Two groups of subjects received relaxation training and then were instructed to lower their blood pressure during either blood pressure feedback or no-feedback conditions; subjects in a third group received a control procedure and were also instructed to lower their blood pressure with the aid of feedback. Although all groups demonstrated significant decreases in blood pressure, the group receiving relaxation training first demonstrated the most pronounced effect. The authors utilized standard occlusion cuff methods of assessing blood pressure but utilized a constant-cuff procedure (see below) to provide blood pressure feedback. Blood pressure was also monitored through occlusion procedures in a study by Kleinman and others (1977) in which subjects with essential hypertension were evaluated and provided with nine sessions of blood pressure feedback. The authors reported that within-session changes in blood pressure were significantly greater for feedback sessions than for control (no-feedback) sessions. In a commendable effort to assess situation generalization, the investigators also requested that patients monitor their blood pressure five times per day with portable equipment at home. Statistically significant reductions in blood pressure across sessions were reported, although their clinical significance is questionable (systolic blood pressure was reduced from 155 to 147; diastolic from 97 to 89).

One of the difficulties with the standard occlusion cuff method of recording blood pressure is that it provides only intermittent measures with a minimum interval of approximately thirty seconds between measures. Because of this temporal restriction, its sensitivity to transient or rapid changes in blood pressure is reduced. One method of providing a continuous recording of blood pressure for brief periods of time is a constant-cuff procedure (Miller and others, 1970; Fey and Lindholm, 1978; Brener and Kleinman, 1970; Shannon, Goldman, and Lee, 1978). In the system described by Brener and Kleinman (1970), the pressure in a finger cuff is inflated above systole and then slowly allowed to decrease until Korotkoff sounds are detected. At this point the pressure of the cuff is increased 5 mm Hg and then slowly decreased again. Such a system provides a measure of systolic pressure every several seconds until discomfort of the subject necessitates deflation of the cuff (usually within 30 to 120 seconds). A similar procedure was discussed by Miller and others (1970) in which the presence or absence of Korotkoff sounds again served as the controlling stimulus for cuff pressure. Modification in the characteristics of the Korotkoff sounds indicated changes in blood pressure, and an automated tracking system modified cuff pressure accordingly (for measuring systolic pressure, increase cuff pressure with detection of Korotkoff sounds; decrease it in absence of sounds).

A similar system for continuous monitoring of blood pressure utilizing an occlusion cuff on each arm has been described by Elder and others (1977a). As in the systems described by Brener and Kleinman, and Miller and others, cuff pressure in the method decribed by Elder and others was controlled by electronic monitoring of Korotkoff sounds, and each cuff was inflated alternately for 100 seconds. They found that the blood pressure measures derived from their constant-cuff procedures correlated .94 with standard sphygmomanometer methods. The authors provide schematics and cost estimates for the components. Two systems utilizing an occlusion cuff and microphone for tracking blood pressure were described by Lee, Caldwell, and Lee (1977). For one system, inflation and deflation occur in alternate forty-five-second periods. Small modifications are made in the cuff pressure during inflation on the basis of Korotkoff sounds during the previous inflation. In the second system, the cuff is alternately inflated to approximately the blood pressure level for five seconds and then deflated for five seconds. Modifications in inflation pressure are determined by monitoring the number of Korotkoff sounds during the previous inflation. The authors suggest that, compared to the first system, the second is slower (less sensitive) but capable of more continuous measurement. Both systems have been used successfully to provide feedback to subjects about their blood pressure.

In an abstract of a paper, Pollak (1978) reported on the use of a portable and automatic blood pressure recording device. The instrument was programmed to monitor blood pressure automatically every fifteen minutes, and it recorded pressure gradients and Korotkoff sounds on magnetic tape. The author used this instrument to evaluate the relationship between blood pressure and mood and found significant relationships between blood pressure and affect for most subjects.

A recently developed method of indirect measurement of blood pressure utilizes pulse-wave velocity or pulse propagation time (Obrist, Langer, and Grignolo, 1977; Pollak, Koss, and Zeiner, 1977; Steptoe, 1976, 1977). This procedure is based on the observation that the speed of an arterial pulse generated by heart systole will vary inversely with blood pressure (Pollak, Koss, and Zeiner, 1977). Standard measurement procedures involve electronic timing and computer analysis of the time between the onset of an R-wave and the detection of the pulse at a designated peripheral point such as a foot, femoral artery, or brachial artery. Initial enthusiasm for this measurement procedure, however, has been replaced by a more careful appraisal of its reliability, validity, sources of error, and determinants. For example, Pollak, Koss, and Zeiner (1977) investigated the relationship between pulse propagation time (PPT) and direct arterial measures of blood pressure in anesthetized cats. These researchers investigated the covariance between the two measures during common carotid occlusion and intravenous injection of norepinephrine. Although the authors indicated significant ($-.5$ to $-.9$) correlations between the two measures, PPT and direct arterial measures were not linearly related under some conditions. Additional research is being conducted by the authors to determine the conditions affecting linearity.

Obrist, Langer, and Grignolo (1977) monitored PPT, systolic blood pressure, diastolic blood pressure, and heart rate of three groups of subjects, including hypertensives, who were exposed to several experimental conditions (cold pressure, pornography, and shock avoidance). PPT was monitored utilizing either the carotid pulse wave or temporal pulse wave; it correlated $-.74$ with systolic blood pressure, $-.57$ with heart rate, $-.65$ with carotid dP/dt, and $-.01$ with diastolic blood pressure. In a separate group of subjects, beta-adrenergic pharmacological blockade was utilized to investigate influences on PPT. PPT significantly increased during the three stimulus conditions but was only minimally correlated with other cardiovascular measures. The authors interpreted these findings as supporting the hypothesis that PPT reflects sympathetic influences on the myocardium as well as changes in systolic blood pressure. In a blood pressure biofeedback study, Steptoe (1977) utilized PPT as a feedback modality by providing feedback to subjects about the pulse transit time from the R wave of the EKG to the foot. With feedback, subjects were able to modify pulse-wave velocities. Correlations between PPT and postsession sphygmomanometer measures were $-.71$ for systolic blood pressure, and $-.70$ for mean arterial pressure, but only $-.39$ for diastolic blood pressure. In summary, measures of PPT offer a potentially reliable, valid, noninvasive, continuous, and indirect measure of blood pressure, particularly systolic blood pressure. Issues that must be addressed prior to confident adoption of this procedure include the relationship between PPT and direct arterial pressure measures, physiological determinants and covariates, sources of measurement error, and standardization of measurement sites.

Geddes and Newberg (1977) reported another method of indirect measurement of mean blood pressure. Their procedures are based on the observation that changes in blood pressure of a partially inflated occlusion cuff will be reflected in changes in the baseline or amplitude of cuff-pressure oscillations on a polygraph. If cuff pressure is slightly less than the pressure that results in maximum cuff oscillations, increases in blood pressure will result in a decrease in the amplitude of oscillations. Because maximum oscillations are associated with mean blood pressure, the mean blood pressure can be continuously monitored for short intervals of time.

The authors provided data from one subject to demonstrate their measurement techniques.

In summary, some of the most significant advances in the technology of psychophysiological assessment are occurring in the measurement of blood pressure. Although standard occlusion methods have been successfully applied in assessment and intervention, difficulties with these procedures have spurred investigation of alternative measurement procedures. Several recently developed procedures, particularly pulse propogation time, have the potential for providing less invasive and less reactive, as well as more reliable, more sensitive, longer, and more valid, measures of blood pressure than those used previously. A substantial amount of investigation is required, however, before these measurement procedures can be applied with a sufficient degree of confidence.

*Electromyography (EMG).* The measurement of electrical potentials generated by the contraction of muscle fibers continues to be one of the most frequently used psychophysiological measures in behavioral assessment. Several recently published studies have utilized EMG as one measure of the outcome of behavioral intervention. Putre and others (1977) monitored frontal EMG in hyperactive children before, during, and following relaxation training and noted decreases associated with relaxation training. Gatchel and others (1977) monitored frontal EMG along with other psychophysiological and subjective responses in a behavior therapy program with speech-anxious subjects. Participants in the therapy program received heart-rate feedback or relaxation training, but because of equipment malfunction EMG data were not reported. Walker and Sandman (1977a) monitored EMG from various sites with ulcer, arthritic, and nonpsychosomatic subjects. The authors reported that the arthritics, compared to the other two groups, demonstrated significantly higher EMG levels from involved sites during exposure to stressful slides. C. Philips (1977) monitored frontal and neck EMG for diagnostic and treatment evaluation purposes with muscle-contraction headache patients. Acosta, Yamamoto, and Wilcox (1978) monitored frontal EMG levels of schizophrenic, neurotic, and tension headache subjects and noted significant differences in resting levels among these groups and significant reductions in EMG level associated with frontal EMG feedback. Ewing and Hughes (1978) reported three single-case studies that suggested that cue-controlled relaxation was effective in reducing and maintaining low frontal EMG during aversive stimulation. Teasdale and Rezin (1978) found that thought stopping applied to depressed thoughts had no effect on corrugator EMG, which had previously been shown to be correlated with frequency of depressive thoughts. Glaus, Happ, and Kotses (1978) reported that response-contingent feedback of frontal and brachioradiali EMG was effective in modifying those responses and that generalized effects on airway resistance were noted for frontal EMG changes.

Because frontal EMG has been presumed to have etiological significance for a number of psychophysiological disorders, to mediate physiological arousal, and to covary with other indices of physiological activation (Beaty and Haynes, in press), it has been used as a feedback modality in a number of biofeedback studies. Cohen and others (1977) provided EMG feedback to addicts in a double-blind study. There was no difference between contingent and noncontingent feedback in effect on addictive disorders, although the contingent-feedback group demonstrated greater control over frontal EMG levels. Feuerstein and Adams (1977) monitored frontal EMG in a cephalic vasomotor feedback study with patients manifesting migraine or muscle-contraction headache and found frontal EMG to be sensitive to treatment effects. In a single-subject design study by Finley and others (1977), frontal EMG feedback and child-selected contingencies were found to be useful in the treatment of children with cerebral palsy. Haynes, Sides, and Lockwood (1977) utilized frontal EMG feedback as one treatment modality with insomniacs and found that, although treatment was effective, frontal EMG levels were not sensitive to treatment effects and were not associated with treatment outcome. Kondo, Canter, and Bean (1977) manipulated intersession intervals in a frontal EMG feedback study with normal student subjects. They found that greater reductions in frontal EMG levels were associated with shorter intersession intervals. Patel (1977) monitored frontal EMG of hypertensive patients receiving biofeedback and relaxation training, but insufficient data were provided to allow for interpretation of results. Pearne, Zigelbaum, and Peyser (1977) utilized frontal EMG feedback to successfully treat a twenty-seven-year-old woman with urinary retention and incontinence. EMG measures were sensitive to treatment effects. C. Philips (1977) found significant decreases in frontal EMG levels for muscle-contraction headache subjects receiving frontal EMG feedback but not for those receiving pseudofeedback. Frontal EMG feedback was also utilized in the successful treatment of two cases of self-injurious behavior in a study by Schroeder and others (1977). Other recently published studies utilizing EMG feedback include Epstein, Malone, and Cunningham (1978) with poststroke paretic patients, Gatchel and others (1978), who assessed the generalized effects of frontal EMG feedback, Counts, Hollandsworth, and Alcorn (1978), who used EMG feedback in the treatment of test-anxious college students, Acosta, Yamamoto, and Wilcox (1978), who applied EMG feedback to schizophrenic, neurotic, and tension headache patients, Ewing and Hughes (1978), who utilized a single-subject design to assess the stress-reduction properties of frontal EMG feedback, Beiman, Israel, and Johnson (1978), who compared the effects of progressive relaxation, self-relaxation, and EMG feedback, and Noonberg, Goldberg, and Anderson (1978), who assessed the effects of frontal EMG activity on digital skin temperature.

The increasing use of EMG measures in psychophysiology and behavioral assessment underscores the need for careful scrutiny of the characteristics of the measurement and recording instruments. As Rugh and Schwitzgebel (1977b) point out, there is tremendous variation among measurement instruments in their physical and functional characteristics. These authors surveyed eleven EMG biofeedback devices (biofeedback instruments also function as measurement instruments in most cases) and noted extreme variability in such important variables as input impedance, filter band width, and sensitivity. The authors constructed a table describing the functional characteristics of the various instruments. The implication of variability in functional characteristics among instruments is that EMG data from different studies may not be comparable. Although insufficient research has been devoted, at this point, to determining the optimal characteristics of EMG mea-

surement instruments, standardization of instrument functions
and characteristics would increase confidence in inferences involving EMG measures.

Several recent investigations have studied the covariance of
frontal EMG measures with measures from other muscle groups
and with cardiovascular measures. Alexander, White, and Wallace
(1977) extended earlier reasearch (Alexander, 1975) on the response generalization of frontal EMG feedback. In the 1977 study,
subjects in one group received frontal and then forearm feedback;
another group received forearm and then frontal feedback; two
control groups received only instructions to relax. On measures of
frontal and forearm EMG, heart rate, respiration, and peripheral
temperature, all groups demonstrated significant reductions, but
there were no significant differences among groups. There were
no generalized effects across measurement sites associated with the
EMG feedback conditions. Shedivy and Kleinman (1977) monitored frontal EMG, sternomastoid EMG, splenius capitus EMG,
and self-report of tension in subjects who were trained through
EMG feedback to increase and decrease frontal EMG levels. The
authors reported: (1) significant changes in frontal EMG with varying conditions; (2) no significant changes for the sternomastoid
EMG; (3) splenius capitus/semisplinalis EMG did not change during "increase frontal" conditions but increased during "decrease
frontal" conditions; and (4) subjective estimates of tension increased during "increase frontal" conditions but did not change
during "decrease frontal" conditions. These findings are generally
consistent with those reported by Alexander (1975) and Alexander,
White, and Wallace (1977).

McGowan, Haynes, and Wilson (in press) also investigated
the generalized effects of feedback-aided frontal EMG manipulations. Heart rate, blood flow, peripheral temperature, and frontal
EMG were monitored under conditions of rest, frontal EMG feedback, stress (visualizations of fear-producing stimuli), and post-
stress adaptation. Significant changes among conditions were
noted on measures of frontal EMG but not for the other cardiovascular measures. Gatchel and others (1978) evaluated the effects of
frontal EMG feedback on other physiological modalities and on
response to stress. Twelve subjects were randomly assigned to

either a frontal EMG feedback or a false feedback condition. Reductions in frontal EMG during feedback sessions were associated with concomitant decreases in heart rate and respiration rate but with an increase in skin conductance level. Subjects receiving feedback were also able to maintain lower frontal EMG levels during stress (anticipation of shock) than those not receiving feedback, but this effect did not generalize to other physiological measures. Additional evidence on cardiovascular correlates of frontal EMG activity comes from a study by Noonberg, Goldberg, and Anderson (1978). Each of eight subjects was exposed to frontal EMG feedback designed to facilitate increases and decreases in EMG activity. Increases in frontal EMG were not associated with significant peripheral temperature changes, but decreases in frontal EMG were associated with a 2.7°F increase in digital skin temperature.

These results, in conjunction with the results of previously noted studies, further support the contention that caution should be exercised in interpreting the physiological significance of frontal EMG measures. Except for some of the results of Gatchel and others (1978) and Noonberg, Goldberg, and Anderson (1978), most of the evidence accumulated thus far suggests that changes in frontal EMG, in most cases, are not indicative of changes in other psychophysiological measures. If the behavior analyst desires indices of general physiological changes, measures in addition to frontal EMG should be monitored. Frontal EMG, however, would appear to have utility as a measure of specific response with disorders such as muscle-contraction headache or arthritis.

As noted, most studies utilizing EMG measures monitor frontal EMG, and all involve a standard placement in which electrodes are placed approximately 2.5 centimeters above the eyebrows and 5 centimeters apart. Davis and others (1978) have suggested that this placement is illogical given the anatomy of the frontal muscle groups. They noted that the frontales are actually two muscles, each of which extends from the eye area vertically to the top of the skull. The conventional method of EMG measurement actually combines both frontales. There are two main disadvantages to this method. First, because only differences in potential between the two sites are recorded, simultaneous EMG activity will not be recorded. Second, standard measurement procedures are vulnerable to contamination from other sources of electrical activity, such as surrounding muscle groups. These authors suggested that electrodes be placed vertically on the forehead and that the pupil be used as the reference point.

*Electrogastrogram.* The previously described study by Walker and Sandman (1977a) is significant because it presents one of the few applications of the electrogastrogram (EGG) in the assessment of ulcer patients. To reiterate, their study involved monitoring EGG, EMG, and heart rate of patients with arthritis, patients with ulcers, and normal subjects during exposure to stressful and nonstressful stimuli. The authors analyzed the resultant EGG response curves by conventional methods and by power spectral analysis and thereby identified components that discriminated among groups. The authors suggested that the EGG may be bidimensional because tonic components (basal resting levels and displacement) differentiated among subject groups, and phasic components (frequency and amplitude) differentiated among stimuli (arithmetic problems and autopsy slides). Although additional research is necessary to further evaluate measurement procedures, methods of analysis, criterion validity, sensitivity, and sources of error, the study by Walker and Sandman (1977a) provides strong support for the applicability of the EGG as a noninvasive assessment procedure with ulcers. The sensitivity of the EGG to various stimulus conditions as well as to subject groups also suggests that the EGG may be useful in identifying stressful stimuli for ulcer patients.

*Recent Applications of Other Psychophysiological Assessment Procedures.* In addition to EDR, EMG, EGG, and the cardiovascular measures reviewed in previous sections, there are several other recently published studies that utilized psychophysiological measures for assessment. These have been summarized in Table 18. Of special interest to behavior analysts are reports by White (1977a, 1977b, 1978) concerning the measurement of salivation. In the first article, White (1977a) noted the infrequent use of salivary measures in present research and reviewed a number of techniques for measuring salivation: having subjects chew dry foods and then measuring increases in the weight of the expectorated food, measuring secretion through pathologically produced fistulae or

**Table 18. Additional Recent Studies Utilizing Psychophysiological Measures**

| Reference | Subjects | Measures | Comments |
|---|---|---|---|
| Brabyn and Strelow (1977) | Case study of normal subject | Locomotion | Describes mechanism to monitor locomotion of subject in enclosed room; utilizes attached lines, take-up drums, and computer-analyzed digital data |
| Brockway (1978) | Cigarette smokers and nonsmokers | Thiocyanate levels in blood | Discusses the use of serum thiocyanate as a measure of frequency and recentness of cigarette smoking |
| Davidson and Schwartz (1977) | Twenty normal subjects | EEG[a] from occipital and sensorimotor regions | Controlled group study in which imagination of sensorimotor or visual stimuli was associated with EEG activation from associated area |
| Denninston and others (1976) | Ten normal males | Impedance cardiography for measurement of cardiac output | A basic physiology study but provides excellent description of method of impedance cardiography for measuring cardiac output |

**Table 18. Additional Recent Studies Utilizing Psychophysiological Measures (Continued)**

| Reference | Subjects | Measures | Comments |
|---|---|---|---|
| Janisse and Kuc (1977) | Normal subjects of varying IQ levels | Pupil size and heart rate | Controlled study in which pupil size discriminated factors of IQ, performance on digit-span test, and stress manipulation; heart rate was more sensitive to stress factors |
| Knapp and Wells (1978) | Asthmatics | Several measures of breathing function | Discussed the use of several measures with asthmatics, including peak forced expiratory flow and forced expiratory volume; recommended total respiratory resistance |
| Lansky, Nathan, and Lawson (1978) | Alcoholics | Blood-alcohol levels; Gas Chromatograph Intoximeter | Used blood-alcohol levels taken by Gas Chromatograph (similar to Breathalyzer) |
| Maisto and Adesso (1977) | Nonalcoholic drinkers | Breathalyzer; blood-alcohol levels | Example of monitoring blood-alcohol levels of subjects undergoing discrimination training for blood-alcohol level |

| | | General instrumentation | |
|---|---|---|---|
| Milligan (1977) | Discussion paper | | Describes instrumentation for automatic switching of input leads for research involving multiple measures |
| Valle and DeGood (1977) | Normal subjects with high and low trait anxiety | EEG | Controlled study in which subjects were exposed to biofeedback to enhance or suppress alpha level; ability to modify alpha level was related to level of trait and state anxiety |
| White (1977a) | Review and experiment with salivation | Salivation | Reviews salivation measurement technique on issues of reliability and validity; presents data from experiment utilizing different measurement techniques |

[a]EEG: electroencephalogram

through cannulae inserted directly into salivary ducts, collecting saliva with Lashley capsules (double-chambered collection discs), weighting amount of saliva following voiding, using a saliva ejector, removing saliva by pipette or hypodermic syringe, and weighing absorption by cotton swabs. White noted that studies have also differed in how the resultant saliva is measured (volume, displacement, or weight). White reviewed the reliability (test-retest) data from eleven studies and noted that eighteen of twenty-five correlations were above .70. In a multimethod measurement study involving ten male and ten female college students, the author also reported that frequently used measurement techniques (whole mouth, parotid capsule, and cotton swabs) were significantly intercorrelated. He also found nonsignificant sex differences but no consistent laterality effects. In his second article, White (1977b) reviewed nine studies pertaining to the applicability of the law of initial value and suggested that the law does not consistently operate for salivation. The range of correlations between change values and prestimulus levels varied between .67 and −.67. White (1978) also investigated the effects of imagery on salivation. Using a cotton swab technique, White had subjects imagine food and found that vividness of imagery was highly related to degree of salivation control—that is, to the subject's ability to increase or decrease salivation. White suggested, and we agree, that salivation has potential utility in psychophysiological assessment. Although insufficient research has been conducted on its psychological and physiological determinants, as well as on its reliability and validity, it may provide a useful, if nonspecific, index of parasympathetic activity and may be particularly useful in the assessment of gastrointestinal disorders. The principal drawback at this time lies in its cumbersome measurement procedures and the high degree of error inherent in their use.

Several other recently published studies have addressed measurement techniques not considered in previous sections. R. W. Green (1978) successfully utilized a glucose oxidase test to measure the amount of sugar in a diabetic patient's urine. Although this procedure was used in a behavioral intervention program to facilitate eating control, it could as easily function as a dependent variable in research in which blood-sugar levels or sugar intake are an important target. Brockway (1978) discussed the use of serum thiocyanate as a measure of smoking. Thiocyanate is a salt byproduct of the body's transformation of chemicals (cyanide compounds) in cigarette smoke. The author suggested that serum thiocyanate (1) can discriminate between smokers and nonsmokers; (2) is the most reliable indirect measure of smoking behavior; (3) results in few false positive and false negative classifications; (4) can discriminate between light, moderate, and heavy smokers; and (5) involves a technique that is efficient and easy to learn.

In a review of twenty-four studies on behavior therapy for asthma, Knapp and Wells (1978) reviewed commonly used procedures for measuring the respiration efficiency of asthmatics. They noted that seven of ten controlled experiments used peak forced expiratory flow rates and the others used forced expiratory volume. Both procedures require the subject to breathe into a flow meter as forcefully as possible. Forced expiratory volume is the volume of air expired during the first second, and peak forced expiratory flow rate is a measure of maximum expiration rate. Knapp and Wells noted that both procedures are dependent upon the effort expended by the subject (motivation variables), that the excessive effort required over several trials may have undesirable consequences on the subject, and that the procedures require extensive cooperation by the subject. As an alternative, the authors recommend measuring total respiratory resistance by the forced oscillation technique. They noted research suggesting a high correlation (.81 to .93) between this measure and whole body plethysmography during baseline and bronchodilatory trials.

## Additional Issues

In addition to response fractionation, the issues of individual differences in psychophysiological responses, content validity of the assessment situation, and temporal and component sampling have been addressed in recently published research. As noted in Chapter One, the importance of behavioral assessment procedures and concepts in behavioral intervention is based upon assumptions of individual differences in response topography, etiological factors, maintaining variables, and response to intervention. Individual differences in psychophysiological responses have implications for the etiology of psychophysiological disorders and therefore for the design of intervention programs. Differences among individuals in resting levels, response to stress, and post-stress adaptation rates, as well as differences in the reactivity of individual physiological response systems, have been documented for many years, yet the importance of individual differences in psychophysiological responsiveness has perhaps been underestimated. Thus, significant individual differences in physiological response patterns have been noted recently by Walker and Sandman (1977a) with ulcer, arthritic, and normal subjects; by McGowan, Haynes, and Wilson (in press) with normal subjects exposed to cognitive stress and biofeedback; by Haynes, Sides, and Lockwood (1977) with insomniacs; by Barrell and Price (1977) with normal subjects exposed to threat of shock; by Haynes, Wilson, and Britton (in press) with atopic dermatitis patients undergoing behavioral treatment; by Ketterer and Smith (1977) in a study assessing laterality and sex differences in skin conductance measures; and by Kleinman and others (1977) with essential hypertensives.

Because of the time and complex equipment necessary for psychophysiological measurement, the most efficient approach to the assessment of individual differences in psychophysiological responsivity would be to develop questionnaire measures that can accurately predict those responses. Recent efforts in this area have met with varying degrees of success. D. Carroll (1977) reviewed several articles that utilized the Autonomic Perception Questionnaire (Mandler, Mandler, and Uviller, 1958) and concluded that this questionnaire was not significantly correlated with the ability to control heart rate. Carroll's conclusion is congruent with recent findings by Whitehead and others (1977) that scores on the Autonomic Perception Questionnaire were not related to the ability to control or acquire control of heart rate. A significant correlation between a questionnaire measure and physiological control or responsivity might facilitate the selection of individuals for whom biofeedback or other intervention strategies would be appropriate. In a 1977 paper, for example, Lang suggested that heightened psychophysiological responsivity to stressful stimuli, such as fear imagery, might be associated positively with the outcome of systematic desensitization. Barrell and Price (1977) noted that individual differences in psychophysiological responsivity to a particular stimulus might be predicted from an analysis of the individual subject's experience with that stimulus. Valle and DeGood (1977) suggested that measures of state and trait anxiety might account for some of the individual variance noted in the response to biofeedback.

The heterogeneous findings cited above confirm the importance of individual differences in psychophysiological assessment but do not advance our understanding or predictive abilities. While the implications of between-subject variability for behavioral assessment and for the conceptualization of behavior disorders are clear, the utilization of this concept in applied behavioral assessment and our ability to measure or predict individual variability are minimal. Research on individual differences in psychophysiological responsivity should focus on (1) the relationship between the responsivity of various physiological systems (such as muscle tension and cardiac systems) and the utility of those systems for assessment and intervention, and (2) the relationship between the psychophysiological responsivity of the various systems and the development of specific psychosomatic disorders.

The issue of content validity in psychophysiological assessment usually refers to the selection of appropriate response systems for measurement (Haynes, 1978). As noted earlier in this chapter, the response systems selected for measurement must be those that reflect the physiological events of interest, that are congruent with predicted effects of the manipulations, and that are consistent with consideration of physiological determinants of the targeted disorder. However, the validity of inferences drawn from psychophysiological assessment is also affected by the environmental context and stimulus conditions within which the assessment occurs. For example, the discriminant validity of heart rate as a measure of response to stress will vary with the type of stimuli utilized (overt or covert), the duration of stimulus presentation, the duration between stimulus presentations, the preexperimental instructions, and ambient conditions in the assessment environment.

In a study with implications for the content validity of psychophysiological measurement, Sartory, Rachman, and Grey

(1977) exposed seventeen subjects to a specific feared stimulus while monitoring subjective discomfort and heart rate. The authors employed a Latin square design in which subjects were exposed to the feared stimulus at Fear Thermometer levels of 0, 50, 75, and 100. The authors noted higher correlations (criterion validity) between subjective and psychophysiological measures at higher fear levels. These findings suggest that the discriminant validity of psychophysiological or subjective measures may vary with the type and level of stressful stimuli. The issue of the content validity of psychophysiological measures in fear assessment has also been addressed by Burchardt and Levis (1977). These authors monitored heart rate, EDR, and self-report measures of anxiety and found that in vivo presentation of feared stimuli (rats) resulted in greater discriminant validity (discriminating between subjects who could and those who could not touch a rat) than slide presentation of the same stimulus.

The assessment and treatment of pain has been of interest to psychophysiologists and behavior analysts for a number of years. The findings reported in several recently published articles addressing the issue of pain assessment may have relevance for the assessment of psychophysiological disorders such as headache. The pentothal pain study developed by Walters (1959) and utilized by Cairns and Pasino (1977) and Mooney, Cairns, and Robertson (1975) has already been described. Weisenberg (1977) published a review article on pain and its measurement and stressed that both threshold and tolerance were important assessment targets. Weisenberg also noted that pain treatment often involves the reduction of "anxiety," a finding that suggests that the assessment of anxiety might be a useful component of preintervention assessment of pain disorders. The author noted that such cognitive factors as attribution or perception of control over the painful stimulus are significant determinants of pain response and threshold. These informal observations imply that assessment of cognitive factors might be an important part of the behavioral assessment of disorders involving pain. A pain survey schedule that may be of assistance in the assessment of pain was recently published by Cautela (1977). The instrument evidently can be utilized in either a questionnaire or an interview format.

As indicated in the sections on individual response systems, the elements of a psychophysiological response that are selected for sampling, along with the temporal parameters of sampling, affect the sensitivity and validity of the derived measures. For example, whether mean heart rate, peak heart rate, or heart-rate variability is sampled (Sartory, Rachman, and Grey 1977), whether skin conductance or skin conductance response is sampled, the duration after stimulus onset of sampling (Hugdahl, Fredrikson, and Ohman, 1977; Kotses, Glaus, and Frese, 1977), and the element of the EGG selected for sampling (Walker and Sandman, 1977a) all have significant effects on the sensitivity and validity of derived data. In addition, data points may be derived from point-time sampling, from averaging a number of responses, or from arithmetic derivations of raw data. All these factors affect indices of the physiological system being measured and are differentially applicable as a function of the experimental parameters involved. Unfortunately, research on various sampling procedures is at an early stage and does not allow for definitive conclusions. It is evident, however, that selection of appropriate target responses, method of sampling, temporal parameters of sampling, and manipulation of data prior to analysis affect the validity and sensitivity of derived data and should be based upon a thorough evaluation of the experimental paradigm and the physiological basis of the responses under study.

### Sexual Arousal and Functioning

Sexual arousal and functioning have become frequent targets of psychophysiological assessment. Impetus for research in this area has come from recent advances in measurement techniques (Henson and others, 1977), an increasing concern with the assessment and treatment of sexual dysfunctions (Hoon, Hoon, and Wincze, 1976; Geer, 1975; Heiman, 1976), and the publicity surrounding the work of researcher-clinicians such as Masters and Johnson and Kaplan and LoPiccolo. Because basic issues in psychophysiological measurement of sexual arousal and functioning have been reviewed elsewhere (Haynes, 1978), the following sections will focus on recent contributions to the area, including advances in measurement of female and male sexual arousal, the technology of psychophysiological measurement, the validity of psychophysiological measures, and the application of psychophysiological assessment procedures to sexual dysfunctions and disorders.

*Measurement of Female Sexual Arousal.* Early efforts in the psychophysiological assessment of female sexual arousal focused on such nonspecific indices of arousal as heart rate and blood pressure (Colson, 1974) and on the development of sensitive and valid measures of specific psychophysiological responses, including vaginal lubrication, vaginal pH, vaginal temperature, vaginal contraction, and clitoral temperature. Although nonspecific indices of sexual arousal have been shown to discriminate between aroused and nonaroused states, the interpretation and utility of these data are diminished because of their covariance with other states such as anxiety. The results of several recently published studies have also questioned the utility of general psychophysiological responses as indices of sexual arousal. Henson and others (1977) found that peripheral temperature from the sternum did not demonstrate differential levels during subjects' exposure to erotic and nonerotic films, although a more specific measure (labial temperature) did. Heiman (1977) found small but nonsignificant differences in finger pulse volume and heart rate when male and female subjects were exposed to erotic and nonerotic tapes, although specific measures (vaginal photoplythsmograph and penile tumescence) did demonstrate significant differences between these classes of stimuli. Wilson (1976) monitored frontal EMG level but found that it was not associated with subjective reports of sexual arousal and did not discriminate between viewing erotic and nonerotic films. Hoon, Wincze, and Hoon (1977b) monitored blood pressure, heart rate, skin conductance, and blood volume pulse, along with specific indicators of sexual arousal, and found that the nonspecific measures did not evidence significant change as a function of the manipulations (erotic and nonerotic fantasies, biofeedback).

Two recent articles reported significant changes in nonspecific physiological measures as a function of sexual arousal. Boudewyns (1978) reexamined the relationship between finger temperature and sexual arousal. Earlier studies had found a decrease in finger temperature associated with sexual arousal.

Boudewyns suggested that this is inconsistent with expected physiological effects of sexual arousal and that it might be an artifact of sampling parameters. Utilizing longer presentations of erotic stimuli, Boudewyns found a bidirectional response (an increase followed by a decrease) in finger temperature. Wincze, Hoon, and Hoon (1978) monitored several nonspecific psychophysiological responses of five women undergoing behavioral intervention for low sexual arousal. With an erotic film as a test stimulus, systolic and diastolic blood pressure were the only two measures to demonstrate significant changes across sessions; there were no significant differences in finger blood volume pulse, heart rate, skin conductance, or several measures of vaginal blood volume. These studies further suggest that caution should be exercised in utilizing nonspecific psychophysiological responses as indices of sexual arousal. The effects of sexual stimuli are not confined to the genital area, however, and monitoring general physiological responses to erotic stimuli can enhance our understanding of human sexual behavior and physiology. Still, although changes in nonspecific psychophysiological responses during exposure to erotic stimuli have important implications, care should be exercised in interpreting these responses as indicative of sexual arousal.

Henson and others (1977) noted difficulties with many of the traditionally utilized specific measures of female sexual arousal: (1) vaginal lubrication and pH changes occur with the onset of erotic stimuli but are not sensitive to termination of erotic stimuli, nor do they demonstrate high correlations with subjective reports of decreased sexual arousal; (2) uterine contractions occur only at high levels of arousal; (3) vaginal temperature is a more accurate measure of core temperature than of blood flow changes in the vaginal wall accompanying sexual arousal; and (4) vaginal contractions and clitoral temperature are promising indicators of sexual arousal but have not been sufficiently validated. Up to now, however, photoplethysmography has been the most frequently employed specific measure of female sexual arousal. Vaginal plethysmographs consist of a light source and sensor. The amount of light received is primarily determined by the amount of blood in the vaginal wall arterioles (Sintchak and Geer, 1975). Two measures can be derived from vaginal plethysmography: (1) vaginal blood volume (VBV), a measure of the AC component reflecting transient fluctuations in blood flow; and (2) vaginal blood volume pulse (VBVP), a measure of the AC component reflecting transient fluctuations in blood flow. Recent research involving vaginal plethysmography has implications for the sensitivity and validity of these measures, their correlation with subjective reports, and their comparative utility.

Several recently published studies have assessed the changes in VBV accompanying erotic stimulation and the correlation between VBV and subjective reports of arousal. Wincze, Hoon, and Hoon (1976) reported that VBV demonstrated significant changes when women viewed erotic films but that the correlation coefficient between VBV and subjective reports of arousal only approached significance. In a later study, Wincze, Hoon, and Hoon (1977) also monitored subjective measures of arousal and VBV while women viewed erotic films. In that study, subjective arousal was found to be significantly correlated with VBV, with correlation coefficients for individuals ranging from .12 to .78. A continuous measure of sexual arousal was obtained by having subjects continuously change the position of a lever. The authors reported that there was no significant correlation between subjective and psychophysiological measures following film termination and suggested that this may have been due to the failure of VBV to return to prestimulus levels after termination of the erotic stimulus. Similar results were reported by Geer (1975), who found no significant relationship between VBV and subjective reports of arousal, although both were sensitive to the presentation of erotic films. In a later study, Geer and Quartararo (1976) reported that VBV demonstrated significant changes when female subjects masturbated. Van Dam and others (1976) also exposed female subjects to erotic films and found significant changes in VBV and subjective reports of arousal but no significant correlation between the two. Heiman (1977) exposed 59 female undergraduate students to a variety of erotic and nonerotic tape recordings and found that VBV was sensitive to the tape manipulations but less so than was VBVP. Hoon, Wincze, and Hoon (1977b) found that vaginal blood volume demonstrated significant changes to erotic fantasies but not to biofeedback. When Henson, Rubin, and Henson (in press) compared VBV to their newly developed method of clitoral temperature measurement, vaginal blood volume demonstrated significant changes during exposure to erotic films but was not significantly correlated with subjective reports of arousal.

The studies reviewed above have been fairly consistent in indicating the VBV significantly discriminates between erotic and nonerotic stimuli but that it is not significantly correlated with subjective reports of arousal. The lack of significant covariance between VBV and subjective report is disconcerting in view of the finding that both measures typically discriminate between erotic and nonerotic stimuli. Several factors may account for such a discrepancy. First, the temporal characteristics (latency) of the two measures may be dysynchronous, and, as indicated earlier, correlating dysynchronous measures at identical points in time will generate only small coefficients of association. Second, covariation between the two responses does not necessarily mean that subjective report is based upon perception of changes in blood flow in the vaginal wall. A third possibility is that the two measures are significantly correlated during part of the arousal cycle, such as during initial exposure to erotic stimuli, but that subjective reports of arousal during other parts of the cycle are influenced by factors in addition to, or other than, vaginal blood flow. In such a case, correlation coefficients generated from data throughout the cycle would be expected to be small.

Vaginal blood volume pulse (VBVP) has also been utilized in several recently published studies. Heiman (1977) found that VBVP was more sensitive to erotic stimuli than VBV. Furthermore, subjective reports of high arousal were correctly associated with high pulse amplitude measures in 89 percent of the female subjects. In other studies, Gillan (1976) found that VBVP was sensitive to female masturbation, and Wilson and Lawson (1976) reported that measures of VBVP were sensitive to the presentation of erotic stimuli and also to alcohol dosage. Advances in instrumentation in the measurement of VBV and VBVP have centered around the light-history effects on photoplythsmography. As noted earlier, use of an infrared light source and sensor decreases the error attributable to light history (Tahmoush and others, 1976). An infrared

light source for the measurement of VBV was utilized in studies by
Hoon, Wincze, and Hoon (1977b) and Henson, Rubin, and Henson
(in press).

Perhaps the most significant recent advance in the
psychophysiological assessment of female sexual arousal involves
the measurement of labial temperature. The apparatus for measurement of labial temperature consists of a small adjustable "roach
clip" with an attached thermistor. (This apparatus was developed in
the laboratory of Harry Rubin at Southern Illinois University at
Carbondale.) In two recently published studies, labial temperature
was found to be a valid measure of female sexual arousal. Henson
and others (1977) discussed difficulties with standard methods of
psychophysiological assessment of sexual arousal in the female and
introduced the method of measuring temperature changes at the
labia minora. In their first study, the authors exposed undergraduate women to erotic and nonerotic films while monitoring
labial temperature and subjective reports of arousal. Labial temperature was found to discriminate between stimuli and also to be
correlated highly with subjective reports of arousal. The authors
noted that preexisting sexual states may affect the measure and
cause a labial temperatures in some subjects to fail to return to
baseline levels following termination of erotic stimuli.

Additional data on the sensitivity and validity of labial temperature measures were presented by these investigators in a more
recent publication (Henson, Rubin, and Henson, in press). The
function of this study was to compare labial temperature and VBV
as psychophysiological measures of sexual arousal. Subjects (eight
female undergraduates) were instructed in the placement of the
measurement device and then allowed to become acclimated to the
experimental situation until variability in labial temperature was
minimized. Subjects were then exposed to an erotic film while subjective arousal, VBV, and labial temperature were measured during the film and for fifteen minutes following its termination. The
authors noted big changes in labial temperature to erotic stimuli
(1.38 degrees, Celius) and high correlations with self-reported sexual arousal. More specifically, Henson, Rubin, and Henson reported: (1) responses to the erotic stimuli were greater for labial

temperature than for VBV; (2) the two measures were highly correlated during the film for most subjects; (3) there were no significant correlations between the two measures for pooled subjects; (4) the two measures were significantly correlated for only three of the eight subjects for the postfilm adaptation period; (5) latency-to-peak responses were not significantly different between the two, although VBV response to film onset appeared to be quicker than labial temperature; (6) there was no difference at the end of the session in level of arousal as measured by the two instruments; (7) during the film, subjective ratings of arousal correlated .83 with labial temperature but only .39 with VBV; and (8) subjective ratings following the film did not significantly correlate with either of the two psychophysiological measures. In comparing VBV and labial temperature, the investigators concluded that both labial temperature and VBV were valid measures of arousal to an erotic stimulus. Labial temperature was more highly correlated than VBV with subjective reports of arousal during the film but also demonstrated slower return to baseline following termination of the erotic stimulus. While the two studies from Rubin's laboratory highly suggest that labia minora temperature may be a sensitive and valid psychophysiological measure of sexual arousal, the clinical utility of this measure in diagnostic and therapeutic applications remains to be assessed.

In summary, recent research on the psychophysiological assessment of female sexual arousal has provided additional data on the validity and sensitivity of vaginal blood volume and vaginal blood volume pulse measures, on the use of infrared techniques in photoplythsmography, and on the development of labial temperature as a measure of sexual arousal. Although VBV has been shown to discriminate between erotic and nonerotic stimuli, several studies have recently found it to be less sensitive than other measures. In one study (Heiman, 1977) VBV was found to be less sensitive than VBVP, and in another (Henson, Rubin, and Henson, in press) it was found to be less sensitive than measures of labial temperature. The results of these studies suggest that measures of VBVP of labial temperature may be preferable to VBV, but such inferences are still tentative and will require further examination.

Additional research is particularly needed on the sensitivity, reliability, determinants, and sources of error of labial temperature
measures.

   *Measurement of Male Sexual Arousal.* The measurement procedures most frequently employed in the psychophysiological assessment of male sexual arousal involve monitoring nonspecific
physiological responses such as heart rate and penile tumescence.
We located two recently published studies (Briddell and Wilson,
1976; Kotses, Glaus, and Frese, 1977) that monitored nonspecific
physiological responses while exposing males to erotic stimuli. As in
the measurement of female sexual arousal, nonspecific measures of
male sexual arousal are generally unsatisfactory because of insufficient sensitivity and their inability to discriminate between sexual
and other types of arousal (Bancroft, and Matthews, 1971; Heiman,
1977). Briddell and Wilson (1976) found that frontal EMG readings
were not significantly correlated with manipulations of sexual
arousal or alcohol level. Kotses, Glaus, and Frese (1977), however,
noted that slides of sexual stimuli elicited greater electrodermal
responses than slides of violent stimuli when the four-to-ten-second
latency range was sampled. The latter study suggests that the discriminant validity of nonspecific measures may be enhanced with
the use of appropriate temporal sampling techniques. Nolan and
Sandman (1978) found that peripheral vasomotor activity or electrodermal responses were not sensitive to the presentation of erotic
stimuli to a pedophiliac but that heart rate was.

   The strain gauge measure of penile circumference has been
the most popular specific measure of male sexual arousal. In a
number of recent studies, strain gauge measures have been shown
to discriminate between sexual and nonsexual stimuli (Heiman,
1977; Laws and Rubin, 1969; Bronwell, Hayes, and Barlow, 1977;
Wilson and Lawson, 1976; Levin and others, 1977; Rosen and
Kopel, 1977) and to correlate significantly with subjective reports of
sexual arousal (Heiman, 1977). Penile tumescence has also been
used as a diagnostic and outcome measure in recent studies on the
modification of sexual preferences. Table 19 summarizes several
studies that utilized specific measures of male sexual arousal as
outcome measures in the behavioral intervention of sexual prefer-

**Table 19. Recent Psychophysiological Assessment of Males' Erective Response in Evaluation of Behavioral Treatment Outcome**

| Reference | Subjects | Assessment Situation | Comments |
|---|---|---|---|
| Bronwell, Hayes, and Barlow (1977) | Five cases of multiple sexual deviations | Exposure to deviant and nondeviant stimuli, to treated and nontreated stimuli, and to slides and actual fetish stimuli | A-B-A-B replication design and multiple-assessment measures; high correlation between erections and self-report |
| Levin and others (1977) | Thirty-nine-year-old pedophiliac male | Slides of deviant and nondeviant stimuli | Case study with multiple-assessment measures |
| Rosen and Kopel (1977) | Transvestite-exhibitionist | Erotic film and in vivo exposure to deviant stimuli | Case study with multiple-assessment measures |

ence. It is notable that all recent studies are of a case-study format. In a review of behavioral sexual reorientation methods with homosexuals, Adams and Sturgis (1977) noted that 43 percent of the 37 studies reviewed utilized specific and/or nonspecific psychophysiological measures, although penile tumescence has become the most popular target response in recent years. In most cases, measures of erective response have been useful and valid indicators of sexual preference and treatment outcome.

One promising diagnostic application of penile plethysmography is in the differential diagnosis of organic and functional impotence by using measures of nocturnal erections (Fisher and others, 1975; Karacan, 1970). This assessment procedure is based on the observation (Karacan, Hursch, and Williams, 1972; Fisher, Gross, and Zurch, 1965) that penile erections normally accompany rapid-eye-movement (REM) sleep (sleep assumed to be highly correlated with dreaming). Approximately 20 to 25 percent of sleep time is spent in REM, and twenty to twenty-five-minute durations of REM sleep are noted approximately every ninety minutes. Penile erections typically occur during 24 to 32 percent of REM periods, depending upon the age of the male. It has been hypothesized that REM-associated erections are indicative of maximum possible erections while awake, in the absence of functional impairment. If this hypothesis is valid, functional impotence (impotence due to nonorganic causes) would be expected to be associated with little or no impairment in REM erections; impotence caused by organic factors should be associated with impairment of the REM erections, particularly in the degree of erective response. Support for these hypotheses has come from a recent study by Fisher and others (1975), who monitored nocturnal erections for several subjects with independent diagnoses of organic or functional erective impairment. Although the results were presented in a case-study format, subjects with an organic diagnosis demonstrated significant impairment of nocturnal erective responses while those with a functional diagnosis evidenced little impairment. Measurement of nocturnal REM-associated erections offers exciting diagnostic possibilities and may also be useful in evaluating the effectiveness of medical intervention with organically based erective impairment. Prior to clinical use, however, several issues need to be addressed: (1) more controlled investigations are needed on the criterion and discriminant validity of this procedure, (2) the reliability and stability of nocturnal erective measures need to be further assessed, (3) the validity of independent diagnoses should be evaluated, and (4) sources of variance and error need to be identified.

*Issues in the Psychophysiological Assessment of Sexual Arousal.* The issue of content validity of the assessment environment was raised in a previous section and is particularly relevant to the assessment of sexual arousal. It was noted that the validity of resultant measures may be a function of the characteristics of the assessment environment and stimuli as well as a function of the measures selected. Because of variability among subjects as to what is considered arousing, care must be exercised in selecting erotic stimuli and in generalizing results among subjects and stimuli. A lack of sexual arousal during exposure of a sexually aberrant individual (for example, a pedophiliac) to a film depicting heterosexual intercourse may indicate that that class of stimuli is unarousing, or the lack of arousal may be specific to the particular stimuli utilized. Care must be exercised in selecting "erotic" stimuli, and it is important to avoid inferences that what is arousing to the behavior analyst will be arousing to others.

Examples of the importance of content validity are provided by several recently published studies. Rosen and Kopel (1977), in assessing a transvestite-exhibitionist, noted that the subject exhibited a full erection to a standard erotic film but not to in vivo handling of women's undergarments (a reported sexual fetish) and that this finding was inconsistent with predictions based on the subject's history. The patient achieved full erection, however, when he cross-dressed in front of a full-length mirror while masturbating. This episode was videotaped and later replayed to the subject while erective responses were monitored as a method of assessing treatment progress across the program phases. In this particular case, the addition of a mirror, masturbation, and cross-dressing behavior enhanced the content and, therefore, discriminant validity of the assessment situation. A similar assessment situation involving in vivo stimulus presentation was utilized in a case study by Bronwell, Hayes, and Barlow (1977). Erective responses of a transvestite subject were monitored while he was instructed to open a briefcase filled with women's undergarments. In a case study involving behavioral intervention with a pedophiliac, Levin and others (1977) exposed a subject to slides of women or young girls. To increase the validity of the assessment situation, they instructed the subject to imagine involvement with the female on the slide.

The implication of these studies is that care must be exercised in selecting stimuli for the assessment of sexual arousal or preference. Stimuli might best be selected on the basis of interviews with the subjects or some other method of assessment. More importantly, care must be exercised in assuming that the responses of a subject to a particular stimulus are indicative of that subject's response to a class of stimuli to which the assessment stimulus is presumed to belong. The studies reviewed underscore the diagnostic possibilities of specific measures of sexual arousal. If situations of appropriate content validity can be constructed, specific psychophysiological measurement procedures may facilitate the diagnosis of sexual preference. Valid identification of sexually arousing stimuli would be a significant contribution to the planning and evaluation of behavioral intervention programs. Freund (1977), however, has reiterated some difficulties with diagnostic applications of penile plethysmography. He noted that the ability of some subjects to suppress and/or enhance erective responses, along with an unacceptable number of false classifications, makes it difficult to rely solely on specific measures as diagnostic criteria. Freund also noted that apparent erection curves on protocols may be a function of artifact and that methods of detecting artifact and other sources of error currently are limited. Accordingly, he suggested that concurrent monitoring of other psychophysiological measures, such as EMG or heart rate, may facilitate the development of technology for identifying error factors in the diagnostic use of penile plethysmography. These findings indicate that penile plethysmography, used alone, may not be sufficiently discriminating to be used as an indicator of sexual preference, particularly when the consequences or legal ramifications could be severe, as in the treatment of incarcerated sexual offenders.

In addition to the research needed with nocturnal measures of erective responses, research is needed in several areas in the field of specific measures of sexual arousal. These include:

1. Evaluation of the most sensitive and valid response measures, such as latency of response, latency to maximum response, percent of full response, and percent increase
2. Evaluation of the role of state factors such as immediate sexual history and personal values regarding sex
3. Evaluation of the content validity of stimulus materials
4. Assessment of the mechanisms of and individual differences in voluntary control over sexual arousal
5. Evaluation of sources of error and artifact
6. Identification of the determinants and characteristics of post-stimulus adaptation curves
7. Determinants of subjective reports of arousal
8. Evaluation of the applicability of psychophysiological assessment procedures with cases of sexual dysfunctions
9. The amenability of specific measures as treatment outcome measures with dysfunctional subjects

## Summary

This chapter presented recent advances in the application, concepts, and instrumentation of psychophysiological assessment. The impetus for the application of psychophysiological measures to behavioral assessment derives from the increasing importance of behavioral approaches to psychophysiological disorders, the increasing cognizance of the importance of physiological components in behavior problems, advances in instrumentation that facilitate the measurement of these components, and fractionation between psychophysiological and nonpsychophysiological responses. Response fractionation, or the lack of covariation between responses, has been evidenced in many recently published studies. The lack of strong covariation among psychophysiological responses might be expected because of differences among measures in their characteristics and physiological determinants. Because of dysynchrony among responses, no single physiological response can be presumed to be indicative of other physiological responses or of general physiological arousal. Dissimilarities were also noted between psychophysiological and subjective measures, suggesting that subjective estimates of arousal or relaxation may be based upon factors other than, or in addition to, perceptions of physiological responses. Stronger relationships were noted between cognitive manipulations and physiological changes than between psychophysiological and subjective measures.

Psychophysiological assessment has been applied to a wide range of target problems and populations and for a wide range of purposes. Psychophysiological measures are frequently used as one measure of behavioral intervention outcome or side effects but are primarily confined to behavioral interventions involving psychophysiological disorders or anxiety. They have also been frequently applied as diagnostic instruments and for the assessment of intervention outcomes of psychophysiological disorders such as insomnia, headaches, hypertension, and ulcers. Issues of discriminant validity, criterion-related validity, content validity, and sources of error are important issues that deserve continued appraisal. Several technological advances were noted, including assessment of individual differences in EDR responses, the effect of varying sampling periods and intervals, the differences in sensitivity between heart-rate mean and heart-rate variability, advances in the measurement of blood flow and temperature, the use of rate-pressure products and cardiac stroke volume as measures of cardiac activity, the measurement of blood pressure through such indirect methods as constant-cuff procedures, pulse-wave velocity measures, the lack of generalization of electromyographic measures, and the application of electrogastrogram measures with ulcer patients. Recent advances in the measurement of male and female sexual arousal were also noted. Particular emphasis was placed on the labial temperature measures of female sexual arousal and the use of nocturnal REM-associated erections as measures of organic versus functional erective impairment.

# References

Abikoff, H., Gittelman-Klein, R., and Klein, D. F. "Validation of a Classroom Observation Code for Hyperactive Children." *Journal of Consulting and Clinical Psychology*, 1977, *45*, 772–783.

Abramowitz, C. V., and Dokecki, P. R. "The Politics of Clinical Judgment: Early Empirical Returns." *Psychological Bulletin*, 1977, *84*, 460–476.

Abramson, P. R., and Mosher, D. L. "Development of a Measure of Negative Attitudes Toward Masturbation." *Journal of Clinical and Consulting Psychology*, 1975, *43*, 485–490.

Achenbach, T. M. *Developmental Psychopathology*. New York: Ronald Press, 1974.

Achenbach, T. M. "The Child Behavior Profile: I. Boys Aged 6–11." *Journal of Consulting and Clinical Psychology*, 1978, *46*, 478–488.

Achenbach, T. M., and Edelbrock, C. S. "The Classification of Child Psychopathology: A Review and Analysis of Empirical Efforts." *Psychological Bulletin*, 1978, *85*, 1275–1301.

Acosta, F. X., Yamamoto, J., and Wilcox, S. A. "Application of Electromyographic Biofeedback to the Relaxation Training of

Schizophrenic, Neurotic, and Tension Headache Patients." *Journal of Consulting and Clinical Psychology*, 1978, *46*, 383–384.

Adams, H. E., and Sturgis, E. T. "Status of Behavioral Reorientation Techniques in the Modification of Homosexuality: A Review." *Psychological Bulletin*, 1977, *84*, 1171–1188.

Adams, N., and others. "The Eating Behavior of Obese and Nonobese Women." *Behavior Research and Therapy*, 1978, *16*, 225–232.

Ainsworth, M. D. S., Bell, S. M., and Stayton, D. J. "Individual Differences in Strange Situation Behavior of One-Year-Olds." In H. R. Schaffer (Ed.), *The Origins of Human Social Relations*. New York: Academic Press, 1971.

Alevizos, P., and others. "The Behavior Observation Instrument: A Method of Direct Observation for Program Evaluation." *Journal of Applied Behavior Analysis*, 1978, *11*, 243–257.

Alexander, A. B. "An Experimental Test of Assumptions Relating to the Use of Electromyographic Biofeedback as a General Relaxation Training Technique." *Psychophysiology*, 1975, *12*, 656–662.

Alexander, A. B., White, P. D., and Wallace, H. M. "Training and Transfer of Training Effects in EMG Biofeedback-Assisted Muscular Relaxation." *Psychophysiology*, 1977, *14*, 551–559.

Algozzine, B. "The Emotionally Disturbed Child: Disturbed or Disturbing?" *Journal of Abnormal Child Psychology*, 1977, *5*, 205–211.

Alpert, R., and Haber, R. N. "Anxiety in Academic Achievement Situations." *Journal of Abnormal and Social Psychology*, 1960, *61*, 207–215.

Amsterdam, E. A., and others. "Indirect Assessment of Myocardial Oxygen Consumption in the Evaluation of Mechanisms and Therapy of Angina Pectoris." *American Journal of Cardiology*, 1974, *33*, 737–743.

Anderson, B. J., and Standley, K. "Manual for Naturalistic Observation of the Childbirth Environment." *Catalog of Selected Documents in Psychology*, 1977, *7*, 6.

Anderson, B. J., Vietze, P., and Dokecki, P. R. "Reciprocity in Vocal Interactions of Mothers and Infants." *Child Development*, 1977, *48*, 1676–1681.

Andrasik, F., and McNamara, J. R. "Optimizing Staff Performance in an Institutional Behavior Change System: A Pilot Study." *Behavior Modification*, 1977, *1*, 235–248.

Angle, H. V., and others. "Computer-Aided Interviewing in Comprehensive Behavioral Assessment." *Behavior Therapy*, 1977, *8*, 747–754.

Arkowitz, H., and others. "The Behavioral Assessment of Social Competence in Males." *Behavior Therapy*, 1975, *6*, 3–13.

Arnold, S., Sturgis, E., and Forehand, R. "Training a Parent to Teach Communication Skills: A Case Study." *Behavior Modification*, 1977, *1*, 259–276.

Ashby, W. A., and Wilson, G. T. "Behavior Therapy for Obesity: Booster Sessions and Long-Term Maintenance of Weight Loss." *Behavior Research and Therapy*, 1977, *15*, 451–463.

Atsaides, J. P., Neuringer, C., and Davis, K. L. "Development of an Institutionalized Chronic Alcoholic Scale." *Journal of Consulting and Clinical Psychology*, 1977, *45*, 609–611.

Auerbach, R., and Kilmann, P. R. "The Effects of Group Systematic Desensitization on a Secondary Erectile Failure." *Behavior Therapy*, 1977, *8*, 330–339.

Ayllon, P., and Azrin, N. H. *The Token Economy: A Motivational System for Therapy and Rehabilitation*. New York: Appleton-Century-Crafts, 1968.

Ayllon, T., and Haughton, E. "Modification of Symptomatic Verbal Behavior of Mental Patients." *Behavior Research and Therapy*, 1964, *2*, 87–97.

Azrin, N. H., Naster, B. J., and Jones, R. "Reciprocity Counseling: A Rapid Learning-Based Procedure for Marital Counseling." *Behavior Research and Therapy*, 1973, *11*, 365–382.

Azrin, V. B., Azrin, N. H., and Armstrong, P. M. "The Student-Oriented Classroom: A Method of Improving Student Conduct and Satisfaction." *Behavior Therapy*, 1977, *8*, 193–204.

Baer, D. M. "Perhaps It Would Be Better Not to Know Everything." *Journal of Applied Behavior Analysis*, 1977a, *10*, 167–172.

Baer, D. M. "Reviewer's Comment: Just Because It's Reliable Doesn't Mean That You Can Use it." *Journal of Applied Behavior Analysis*, 1977b, *10*, 117–119.

Baer, R., Ascione, F., and Casto, G. "Relative Efficacy of Two Token Economy Procedures for Decreasing the Disruptive Classroom

Behavior of Retarded Children." *Journal of Abnormal Child Psychology*, 1977, *5*, 135–146.

Bailey, K. G., Deardorff, P., and Nay, W. R. "Students Play Therapist: Relative Effects of Role Playing, Videotape Feedback, and Modeling in a Simulated Interview." *Journal of Consulting and Clinical Psychology*, 1977, *45*, 257–266.

Bakeman, R., and Brown, J. V. "Behavioral Dialogues: An Approach to the Assessment of Mother-Infant Interaction." *Child Development*, 1977, *48*, 195–203.

Baker, B. L., Cohen, D. C., and Saunders, J. T. "Self-Directed Desensitization for Acrophobia." *Behavior Research and Therapy*, 1973, *11*, 79–89.

Baker, L. E., and others. "The Measurement of Cardiac Output by Means of Electrical Impedence." *Cardiovascular Research Center Bulletin*, 1971, *9*, 135–145.

Baker, R. P., and Dreger, R. M. "The Preschool Behavioral Classification Project: A Follow-Up Report." *Journal of Abnormal Child Psychology*, 1977, *5*, 241–248.

Bancroft, J. H. J. *Deviant Sexual Behavior Modification and Assessment.* Oxford, England: Clarendon Press, 1974.

Bancroft, J., and Mathews, A. "Autonomic Correlates of Penile Erection." *Journal of Psychosomatic Research*, 1971, *15*, 159–167.

Bandura, A. *Principles of Behavior Modification.* New York: Holt, Rinehart and Winston, 1969.

Bandura, A. "Self-Efficacy: Toward a Unifying Theory of Behavioral Change." *Psychological Review*, 1977, *84*, 191–215.

Barber, R. M., and Kagey, J. R. "Modification of School Attendance for an Elementary Population." *Journal of Applied Behavior Analysis*, 1977, *10*, 41–48.

Barber, T. *The Pitfalls of Human Research.* Elmsford, N. Y.: Pergamon Press, 1976.

Barkley, R. A. "Review of Stimulant Drug Research with Hyperactive Children." *Journal of Child Psychology and Psychiatry and Allied Disciplines.*" 1977a, *18*, 137–165.

Barkley, R. A. "The Effects of Methylphenidate on Various Types of Activity Level and Attention in Hyperkinetic Children." *Journal of Abnormal Child Psychology*, 1977b, *5*, 351–370.

Barkley, R. A., and Jackson, T. L. "Hyperkinesis, Autonomic Nervous System Activity, and Stimulant Drug Effects." *Journal of Child Psychology and Psychiatry and Allied Disciplines,* 1977, *18,* 347–357.

Barlow, D. H., and others. "A Heterosocial Skills Behavior Checklist for Males." *Behavior Therapy,* 1977a, *8,* 229–239.

Barlow, D. H., and others. "Single-Case Designs and Clinical Biofeedback Experimentation." *Biofeedback and Self-Regulation,* 1977b, *3,* 221–239.

Barnard, J. D., Christophersen, E. R., and Wolf, M. M. "Teaching Children Appropriate Shopping Behavior Through Parent Training in the Supermarket Setting." *Journal of Applied Behavior Analysis,* 1977, *10,* 49–59.

Barrell, J. J., and Price, D. D. "Two Experiential Orientations Toward a Stressful Situation and Their Related Somatic and Visceral Responses." *Psychophysiology,* 1977, *14,* 517–521.

Barrera, M., Jr., and Rosen, G. M. "Detrimental Effects of a Self-Reward Contracting Program on Subjects' Involvement in Self-Administered Desensitization." *Journal of Consulting and Clinical Psychology,* 1977, *45,* 1180–1181.

Barrett, D. E., and Yarrow, M. R. "Prosocial Behavior, Social Inferential Ability, and Assertiveness in Children." *Child Development,* 1977, *48,* 475–481.

Barton, E. J., and Osborne, J. G. "The Development of Classroom Sharing by a Teacher Using Positive Practice." *Behavior Modification,* 1978, *2,* 231–250.

Bassett, J. E., and Blanchard, E. B. "The Effect of the Absence of Close Supervision on the Use of Response Cost in a Prison Token Economy." *Journal of Applied Behavioral Analysis,* 1977, *10,* 375–379.

Bassett, J. E., Blanchard, E. G., and Koshland, E. "On Determining Reinforcing Stimuli: Armchair Versus Empirical Procedures." *Behavior Therapy,* 1977, *8,* 205–212.

Bates, H., and Zimmerman, S. F. "Toward the Development of a Screening Scale for Assertive Training." *Psychological Reports,* 1971, *28,* 99–107.

Bauman, K. E., and Iwata, B. A. "Maintenance of Independent Housekeeping Skills Using Scheduling Plus Self-Recording Procedures." *Behavior Therapy,* 1977, *8,* 554–560.

Beaty, E. T., and Haynes, S. N. "Behavioral Treatment of Muscle-Contraction Headache." *Psychosomatic Medicine,* in press.

Beck, A. T. *Depression: Clinical, Experimental, and Therapeutic Aspects.* New York: Harper & Row, 1967.

Beck, A. T., Laude, R., and Bohnert, M. "Ideational Components of Anxiety Neurosis." *Archives of General Psychiatry,* 1974, *31,* 319-325.

Beck, A. T., Schuyler, D., and Herman, I. "Development of Suicidal Intent Scales." In A. T. Beck, H. L. P. Resnik, and D. J. Lettieri (Eds.), *The Prediction of Suicide.* Bowie, Md.: Charles Press, 1974.

Beck, R., Morris, J., and Beck, A. T. "Cross-Validation of the Suicidal Intent Scale." *Psychological Reports,* 1974, *34,* 445-446.

Beck, R., Morris, J., and Lester, D. "Suicide Notes and Risk of Future Suicide." *Journal of the American Medical Association,* 1974, *228,* 495-496.

Becker, J. M. T. "A Learning Analysis of the Development of Peer-Oriented Behavior in Nine-Month-Old Infants." *Developmental Psychology,* 1977, *13,* 481-491.

Becker, J. V., Turner, S. M., and Sajwaj, T. E. "Multiple Behavioral Effects of the Use of Lemon Juice with a Ruminating Toddler-Age Child." *Behavior Modification,* 1978, *2,* 267-278.

Becker, W. C., and others. "The Contingent Use of Teacher Attention and Praise in Reducing Classroom Behavior Problems." *Journal of Specific Education,* 1967, *1,* 287-307.

Behar, L. B. "The Preschool Behavior Questionaire." *Journal of Abnormal Child Psychology,* 1977, *5,* 265-276.

Beiman, I., Graham, L. E., and Ciminero, A. R. "Self-Control Progressive Relaxation Training as an Alternative Nonpharmacological Treatment for Essential Hypertension: Therapeutic Effects in the Natural Environment." *Behavior Research and Therapy,* 1978, *16,* 371-375.

Beiman, J., Israel, E., and Johnson, S. A. "During Training and Posttraining Effects of Live and Taped Extended Progressive Relaxation, Self-Relaxation, and Electromyogram Biofeedback." *Journal of Consulting and Clinical Psychology,* 1978, *46,* 314-321.

Beiman, J., and others. "Validation of a Self-Report/Behavioral Subject Selection Procedure for Analogue Fear Research." *Behavior Therapy,* 1978, *9,* 169-177.

Bellack, A. S., and Hersen, M. "Self-Report Inventories in Behavioral Assessment." In J. D. Cone and R. P. Hawkins (Eds.), *Behavioral Assessment: New Directions in Clinical Psychology*. New York: Brunner/Mazel, 1977.

Bellack, A. S., Hersen, M., and Turner, S. M. "Role-Play Tests for Assessing Social Skills: Are They Valid?" *Behavior Therapy*, 1978, *9*, 448–461.

Bellack, A. S., Rozensky, R., and Schwartz, J. "A Comparison of the Two Forms of Self-Monitoring in a Behavioral Weight Reduction Program." *Behavior Therapy*, 1974, *5*, 523–530.

Bem, S. L. "The Measurement of Psychological Androgyny." *Journal of Consulting and Clinical Psychology*, 1974, *42*, 155–162.

Bentler, P. M. "Heterosexual Behavior Assessments: I. Males." *Behavioral Research and Therapy*, 1968, *6*, 21.

Berman, P. W., Monda, L. C., and Myerscough, R. P. "Sex Differences in Young Children's Responses to an Infant: An Observation Within a Daycare Setting." *Child Development*, 1977, *48*, 711–715.

Bernal, M. E., and others. "Comparison of Boys' Behaviors in Homes and Schools." In E. J. Mash, L. A. Hamerlynck, and L. C. Handy (Eds.), *Behavior Modification and Families*. New York: Brunner/Mazel, 1976.

Bernstein, D. A. "Situation Factors in Behavioral Fear Assessment: A Progress Report." *Behavior Therapy*, 1973, *4*, 41–48.

Bernstein, D. A., and Allen, G. J. "Fear Survey Schedule (II): Normative Data and Factor Analysis Based upon a Large College Sample." *Behavior Research and Therapy*, 1969, *7*, 403–408.

Bernstein, G. S. "Time-Series Analysis and Research in Behavior Modification: Some Unanswered Questions." *Behavior Therapy*, 1977, *8*, 503–504.

Bersoff, D. N., and Moyer, D. "Positive Reinforcement Observation Schedule (PROS): Development and Use." Paper presented at 81st annual meeting of the American Psychological Association, Montreal, August 1973.

Best, J. A. "Tailoring Smoking Withdrawal Procedures to Personality and Motivational Differences." *Journal of Consulting and Clinical Psychology*, 1975, *43*, 1–8.

Birchler, G. R., and Webb, L. J. "Discriminating Interaction Behaviors in Happy and Unhappy Marriages." *Journal of Consulting and Clinical Psychology*, 1977, *45*, 494–495.

Bittle, R., and Hake, D. F. "A Multielement Design Model for Component Analysis and Cross-Setting Assessment of a Treatment Package." *Behavior Therapy,* 1977, *8,* 906–914.

Blatt, S. J., D'Afflitti, J. P., and Quinlan, D. M. "Experiences of Depression in Normal Young Adults." *Journal of Abnormal Psychology,* 1976, *85,* 383–389.

Blehar, M. C., Lieberman, A. F., and Ainsworth, M. D. S. "Early Face-to-Face Interaction and Its Relation to Later Infant-Mother Attachment." *Child Development,* 1977, *48,* 182–194.

Blittner, M., Goldberg, J., and Merbaum, M. "Cognitive Self-Control Factors in the Reduction of Smoking Behavior." *Behavior Therapy,* 1978, *9,* 553–561.

Bloom, L. J., and Cantrell, D. "Anxiety Management Training for Essential Hypertension in Pregnancy." *Behavior Therapy,* 1978, *9,* 377–382.

Bloom, L. J., and Trautt, G. M. "Finger Pulse Volume as a Measure of Anxiety: Further Evaluation." *Psychophysiology,* 1977, *14,* 541–544.

Blum, J. D. "On Changes in Psychiatric Diagnosis over Time." *American Psychologist,* 1978, *33,* 1017–1031.

Bollard, R. J., and Woodroffe, P. "The Effect of Parent-Administered Dry-Bed Training on Nocturnal Enuresis in Children." *Behavior Research and Therapy,* 1977, *15,* 159–165.

Bolstad, O. D., and Johnson, S. M. "The Relationship Between Teachers' Assessments of Students and the Students' Actual Behavior in the Classroom." *Child Development,* 1977, *48,* 570–578.

Bootzin, R., and Kazdin, A. "A Comparison of Systematic Desensitization with Systematic Habituation for Fear of Heights." Paper presented at annual meeting of the Midwestern Psychological Association, Cleveland, 1972.

Borkovec, T. D., and Hennings, B. L. "The Role of Physiological Attention Focusing in the Relaxation Treatment of Sleep Disturbance, General Tension, and Specific Stress Reaction." *Behavior and Therapy,* 1978, *16,* 7–19.

Borkovec, T. D., and others. "Identification and Measurement of a Clinically Relevant Target Behavior for Analogue Outcome Research." *Behavior Therapy,* 1974, *5,* 503–513.

Bornstein, M. R., Bellack, A. S., and Hersen, M. "Social Skills

Training for Unassertive Children: A Multiple-Baseline Analysis." *Journal of Applied Behavior Analysis*, 1977, *10*, 183–195.

Bornstein, P. H., Hamilton, S. B., and Quevillon, R. P. "Behavior Modification by Long Distance: Demonstration of Functional Control over Disruptive Behavior in a Rural Classroom Setting." *Behavior Modification*, 1977, *1*, 369–380.

Bornstein, P. H., and others. "Reliability Enhancement: Increasing the Accuracy of Self-Report through Mediation-Based Procedures." *Cognitive Therapy and Research*, 1977a, *1*, 85–98.

Bornstein, P. H., and others. "Reliability and Validity Enhancement: A Treatment Package for Increasing Fidelity of Self-Report." *Journal of Clinical Psychology*, 1977b, *33*, 861–866.

Bornstein, P. H., and others. "Self-Monitoring Training: Effects on Reactivity and Accuracy of Self-Observation." *Behavior Therapy*, 1978, *9*, 545–552.

Boudewyns, P. A. "Finger Temperature Response to Sexual Stimulation." *Behavior Therapy*, 1978, *9*, 618–621.

Boudewyns, P. A., and Cornish, R. D. "Finger Temperature Norms For Migraine Sufferers." *Behavior Therapy*, 1978, *9*, 689.

Boulougouris, J. C., Rabavilas, A. D., and Stefanis, C. "Psychophysiological Responses in Obsessive-Compulsive Patients." *Behavior Research and Therapy*, 1977, *15*, 221–230.

Brabyn, J. A., and Strelow, E. R. "Computer-Analyzed Measures of Characteristics of Human Locomotion and Mobility." *Behavior Research Methods and Instrumentation*, 1977, *9*, 456–462.

Brady, J. P. "An Empirical Study of Behavioral Marital Therapy in Groups." *Behavior Therapy*, 1977, *8*, 512–513.

Braun, P., and Reynolds, D. "A Factor Analysis of a 100-Item Fear Survey Inventory." *Behavior Research and Therapy*, 1969, *7*, 399–402.

Brener, J., and Kleinman, R. A. "Learned Control of Decreases in Systolic Blood Pressure." *Nature*, 1970, *226*, 1063–1064.

Briddell, D. W., and Wilson, G. T. "The Effects of Alcohol and Expectancy Set on Male Sexual Arousal." *Journal of Abnormal Psychology*, 1976, *85*, 225–234.

Brockway, B. S. "Chemical Validation of Self-Reported Smoking Rates." *Behavior Therapy*, 1978, *9*, 685–686.

Broden, M., Beasley, A., and Hall, R. V. "In-Class Spelling Performance: Effects of Home Tutoring by a Parent." *Behavior Modification,* 1978, *2,* 511–530.

Broden, M., and others. "Altering Student Responses Through Changes in Teacher Verbal Behavior." *Journal of Applied Behavior Analysis,* 1977, *10,* 479–487.

Brody, G. H., Lahey, B. B., and Combs, M. L. "Effects of Intermittent Modeling on Observational Learning." *Journal of Applied Behavior Analysis,* 1978, *11,* 87–90.

Brodzinsky, D. M. "Children's Comprehension and Appreciation of Verbal Jokes in Relation to Conceptual Tempo." *Child Development,* 1977, *48,* 960–967.

Bronson, G. W., and Pankey, W. B. "On the Distinction Between Fear and Wariness." *Child Development,* 1977, *48,* 1167–1183.

Bronwell, K. D., Hayes, S. C., and Barlow, D. H. "Patterns of Appropriate and Deviant Sexual Arousal: The Behavioral Treatment of Multiple Sexual Deviations." *Journal of Consulting and Clinical Psychology,* 1977, *45,* 1144–1155.

Brown, C. C. *Methods in Psychophysiology.* Baltimore: Williams & Wilkins, 1967.

Browning, R. M. "Treatment Effects of a Total Behavior Modification Program with Five Autistic Children." *Behavior Research and Therapy,* 1971, *9,* 319–327.

Bruce, R. A. "Methods of Exercise Testing." *American Journal of Cardiology,* 1974, *33,* 715–720.

Buell, J., and others. "Collateral Social Development Accompanying Reinforcement of Outdoor Play in a Preschool Child" *Journal of Applied Behavior Analysis,* 1968, *1,* 167–175.

Bugental, D. B., Whalen, C. K., and Henker, B. "Causal Attributions of Hyperactive Children and Motivational Assumptions of Two Behavior-Change Approaches: Evidence for an Interactionist Position." *Child Development,* 1977, *48,* 874–884.

Bumberry, W., Oliver, J. M., and McClure, J. N. "Validation of the Beck Depression Inventory in a University Population Using Psychiatric Estimate as the Criterion." *Journal of Consulting and Clinical Psychology,* 1978, *46,* 150–155.

Burchardt, C. J., and Levis, D. J. "The Utility of Presenting Slides of a Phobic Stimulus in the Context of a Behavioral Avoidance Procedure." *Behavior Therapy,* 1977, *8,* 340–346.

Burleigh, R. A., and Marholin, D., II. "Don't Shoot Until You See the Whites of His Eyes: An Analysis of the Adverse Side Effects of Verbal Prompts." *Behavior Modification*, 1977, *1*, 109–122.

Buskirk, S. S. V. "A Two-Phase Perspective on the Treatment of Anorexia Nervosa." *Psychological Bulletin*, 1977, *84*, 529–538.

Buss, A. H. *The Psychology of Aggression.* New York: Wiley, 1961.

Cahalan, D., Cisin, I. H., and Crossley, H. M. *American Drinking Practices.* Monograph No. 6. New Brunswick, N.J.: Rutgers Center of Alcohol Studies, 1969.

Cairns, D., and Pasino, J. A. "Comparison of Verbal Reinforcement and Feedback in the Operant Treatment of Disability Due to Chronic Low-Back Pain." *Behavior Therapy*, 1977, *8*, 621–630.

Camp, B. W., and others. "'Think Aloud': A Program for Developing Self-Control in Young Aggressive Boys." *Journal of Abnormal Child Psychology*, 1977, *5*, 157–170.

Campbell, D. T., and Fiske, D. W. "Convergent and Discriminant Validation by the Mutitrait-Multimethod Matrix." *Psychological Bulletin*, 1959, *56*, 81–105.

Campbell, S. B., Endman, M. W., and Bernfeld, G. "A Three-Year Follow-Up of Hyperactive Preschoolers into Elementary School." *Journal of Child Psychology and Psychiatry and Allied Disciplines*, 1977, *18*, 239–249.

Camras, L. A. "Facial Expressions Used by Children in a Conflict Situation." *Child Development*, 1977, *48*, 1431–1435.

Cantor, N. L., and Gelfand, D. M. "Effects of Responsiveness and Sex of Children on Adults' Behavior." *Child Development*, 1977, *48*, 232–238.

Carlin, A. S., and Stauss, F. F. "Descriptive and Functional Classifications of Drug Abusers." *Journal of Consulting and Clinical Psychology*, 1977, *45*, 222–227.

Carr, E. G. "The Motivation of Self-Injurious Behavior: A Review of Some Hypotheses." *Psychological Bulletin*, 1977, *84*, 800–816.

Carr, E. G., and others. "Acquisition of Sign Language by Autistic Children." *Journal of Applied Behavior Analysis*, 1978, *11*, 489–501.

Carroll, D. "Cardiac Perception and Cardiac Control." *Biofeedback and Self-Regulation*, 1977, *2*, 349–370.

Carroll, P. J. "A Durable Recording and Feedback System." *Journal of Applied Behavior Analysis*, 1977, *10*, 339–340.

Carter, R. D., and Thomas, E. J. "A Case Application of a Signal System (SGM) to the Assessment and Modification of Selected Problems of Marital Communication." *Behavior Therapy*, 1973a, *4*, 629–645.

Carter, R. D., and Thomas, E. J. "Modification of Problematic Marital Communication Using Corrective Feedback and Instruction." *Behavior Therapy*, 1973b, *4*, 100–109.

Caster, D. U., and Parsons, O. A. "Relationship of Depression, Sociopathy, and Locus of Control to Treatment Outcome in Alcoholics." *Journal of Consulting and Clinical Psychology*, 1977, *45*, 751–756.

Cattell, R. B., and Cattell, M. D. *Handbook for the Junior/Senior High School Personality Questionnaire "HSPQ."* Champaign, Ill.: Institute for Personality and Ability Testing, 1969.

Cautela, J. R. "The Use of Covert Conditioning in Modifying Pain Behavior." *Journal of Behavior Therapy and Experimental Psychiatry*, 1977, *8*, 45–52.

Cautela, J. R., and Kastenbaum, R. A. "A Reinforcement Survey Schedule for Use in Therapy, Training, and Research." *Psychological Reports*, 1967, *20*, 1115–1130.

Cautela, J. R., and Upper, D. "The Process of Individual Behavior Therapy." In M. Hersen, R. M. Eisler, and P. M. Miller (Eds.), *Progress in Behavior Modification*. Vol. 1. New York: Academic Press, 1975.

Cavior, N., and Marabotto, C. M. "Monitoring Verbal Behaviors in a Dyadic Interaction." *Journal of Consulting and Clinical Psychology*, 1976, *44*, 68–76.

Cawson, P., and Perry, J. "Environmental Correlates of Attitudes Among Residential Staff." *British Journal of Criminology*, 1977, *17*, 141–156.

Celhoffer, L., Boukydis, C., and Minde, K. "The DCR-II Event Recorder: A Portable High-Speed Digital Cassette System with Direct Computer Access." *Behavior Research Methods and Instrumentation*, 1977, *9*, 442–446.

Chesney, M. A., and Tasto, D. L. "The Effectiveness of Behavior Modification with Spasmodic and Congestive Dysmenorrhea." *Behavior Research and Therapy*, 1975, *13*, 237–244.

Christie, M. J., and Venables, P. H. "Site, State, and Subject Characteristics of Palmar Skin Potential Levels." *Psychophysiology*, 1972, *9*, 645–649.

Ciminero, A. R., Calhoun, K. S., and Adams, H. E. (Eds.). *Handbook of Behavioral Assessment*. New York: Wiley, 1977.

Ciminero, A. R., and Drabman, R. S. "Current Developments in the Behavioral Assessment of Children." In B. Lahey and A. Kazdin (Eds.), *Advances in Clinical Child Psychology*. New York: Plenum, 1977.

Clark, H. B., and others. "A Parent Advice Package for Family Shopping Trips: Development and Evaluation." *Journal of Applied Behavior Analysis*, 1977, *10*, 605–624.

Clavelle, P. R., and Butcher, J. N. "An Adaptive Typological Approach to Psychiatric Screening." *Journal of Consulting and Clinical Psychology*, 1977, *45*, 851–859.

Clement, P. G. "A Formula for Computing Interobserver Agreement." *Psychological Reports*, 1976, *39*, 257–258.

Coan, R. W., and Cattell, R. B. *Manual for the Early School Personality Questionnaire "ESPQ."* Champaign, Ill.: Institute for Personality and Ability Testing, 1972.

Coates, T. J., Rosekind, M. R., and Thoresen, C. E. "All-Night Sleep Recordings in Clients' Homes by Telephone." *Journal of Behavior Therapy and Experimental Psychiatry*, 1978, *9*, 157–162.

Coates, T. J., and Thoresen, C. E. "Using Generalizability Theory in Behavioral Observation." *Behavior Therapy*, 1978, *9*, 605–613.

Cochran, M. M. "A Comparison of Group-Day and Family Child-Rearing Patterns in Sweden." *Child Development*, 1977, *48*, 702–707.

Cohen, D. C. "Comparison of Self-Report and Overt-Behavioral Procedures for Assessing Acrophobia." *Behavior Therapy*, 1977, *8*, 17–23.

Cohen, H. D., and others. "A Double-Bind Methodology for Biofeedback Research." *Psychophysiology*, 1977, *14*, 603–608.

Cohen, J. "A Coefficient of Agreement for Nominal Scales." *Educational and Psychological Measurement*, 1960, *20*, 27–46.

Cohen, S. E., and Beckwith, S. "Caregiving Behavior and Early Cognitive Development as Related to Ordinal Position in Preterm Infants." *Child Development*, 1977, *48*, 152–157.

Coleman, J., Walkind, S., and Ashley, L. "Symptoms of Behavior

Disturbance and Adjustment to School." *Journal of Child Psychology and Psychiatry and Allied Disciplines,* 1977, *18,* 201–209.

Colletti, G., and Harris, S. L. "Behavior Modification in the Home: Siblings as Behavior Modifiers, Parents as Observers." *Journal of Abnormal Child Psychology,* 1977, *5,* 21–30.

Colligan, R. C. "The Minnesota Child Development Inventory as an Aid in the Assessment of Developmental Disability." *Journal of Clinical Psychology,* 1977, *33,* 162–163.

Collis, G. M., and Sharp, N. J. "Simple Optical Methods for Adding Time and Other Signals to Video Recordings." *Behavior Research Methods and Instrumentation,* 1977, *9,* 57–58.

Colson, C. E. "The Evaluation of Pornography: Effects of Attitude and Perceived Physiological Reaction." *Archives of Sexual Behavior,* 1974, *3,* 307–323.

Cone, J. D. "The Relevance of Reliability and Validity for Behavioral Assessment." *Behavior Therapy,* 1977, *8,* 411–426.

Cone, J. D., and Hawkins, R. P. (Eds.). *Behavioral Assessment: New Directions in Clinical Psychology.* New York: Brunner/Mazel, 1977.

Conger, J. C., Conger, A. J., and Brehm, S. S. "Fear Level as a Moderator of False Feedback Effects in Snake Phobics." *Journal of Consulting and Clinical Psychology,* 1976, *40,* 135–141.

Conners, C. K. "A Teacher Rating Scale for Use in Drug Studies with Children." *American Journal of Psychiatry,* 1969, *126,* 884–889.

Conners, C. K. "Rating Scales for Use in Drug Studies with Children." *Psychopharmacology Bulletin (Special Issue: Pharmacotherapy of Children),* 1973, 24–42.

Conners, G. J., Maisto, S. A., and Sobell, M. B. "Extension of the Taste-Test Analogue as an Unobtrusive Measure of Preference for Alcohol." *Behavior Research and Therapy,* 1978, *16,* 289–291.

Connor, J. M., and Serbin, L. A. "Behaviorally Based Masculine- and Feminine-Activity-Preference Scales for Preschoolers: Correlates with Other Classroom Behaviors and Cognitive Tests." *Child Development,* 1977, *48,* 1411–1416.

Conway, J. B. "Behavioral Self-Control of Smoking Through Aversive Conditioning and Self-Management." *Journal of Consulting and Clinical Psychology,* 1977, *45,* 348–357.

Cooper, J. E. "The Leyton Obsessional Inventory." *Psychological Medicine,* 1970, *1,* 48–64.

Cooper, J. E., and Kelleher, M. "The Leyton Obsessional Inventory: A Principal Components Analysis on Normal Subjects." *Psychological Medicine*, 1973, *3*, 204–208.

Counts, D. K., Hollandsworth, J. G., Jr., and Alcorn, J. D. "Use of Electromyographic Biofeedback and Cue-Controlled Relaxation in the Treatment of Test Anxiety." *Journal of Consulting and Clinical Psychology*, 1978, *46*, 990–996.

Cowen, E. L., and others. "Parental Perceptions of Young Children and Their Relation to Indexes of Adjustment." *Journal of Consulting and Clinical Psychology*, 1970, *34*, 97–103.

Cox, D. J. "Menstrual Symptom Questionnaire: Further Psychometric Evaluation." *Behavior Research and Therapy*, 1977, *15*, 506–508.

Craig, K. D., Best, H., and Best, J. A. "Self-Regulatory Effects of Monitoring Sensory and Affective Dimensions of Pain." *Journal of Consulting and Clinical Psychology*, 1978, *46*, 573–574.

Cronbach, L. J., and others. *The Dependability of Behavioral Measures.* New York: Wiley, 1972.

Crowne, D. P., and Marlowe, D. *The Approval Motive: Studies in Evaluative Dependence.* New York: Wiley, 1964.

Curran, J. P. "Skills Training as an Approach to the Treatment of Heterosexual Social Anxiety: A Review." *Psychological Bulletin*, 1977, *84*, 140–157.

Curran, J. P., and Gilbert, F. S. "A Test of the Relative Effectiveness of a Systematic Desensitization Program and an Interpersonal Skills Training Program with Date-Anxious Subjects." *Behavior Therapy*, 1975, *6*, 510–552.

Curran, J. P., Gilbert, F. S., and Little, L. M. "A Comparison Between Behavioral Training and Sensitivity Training Approaches to Heterosexual Dating Anxiety." *Journal of Consulting Psychology*, in press.

Cuvo, A. J., Leaf, R. B., and Borakove, L. S. "Teaching Janitorial Skills to the Mentally Retarded: Acquisition, Generalization, and Maintenance." *Journal of Applied Behavior Analysis*, 1978, *11*, 345–355.

Dahlkoetter, J., and Foster, S. L. "Enhancing the Reactivity of Self-Monitoring in Training for Competitive Athletics." Paper presented at annual meeting of the Association for Advancement of Behavior Therapy, Chicago, December 1978.

Darlington, R. B. "Reduced-Variance Regression." *Psychological Bulletin*, 1978, *85*, 1238–1255.

Dash, J. D., and Brown, R. A. "The Development of a Rating Scale for the Prediction of Success in Weight Reduction." *Journal of Clinical Psychology*, 1977, *33*, 748–752.

David, O. J., and others. "Lead and Hyperactivity: Lead Levels Among Hyperactive Children." *Journal of Abnormal Child Psychology*, 1977, *5*, 405–416.

Davidson, R. J., and Schwartz, G. E. "Brain Mechanisms Subserving Self-Generated Imagery: Electrophysiological Specificity and Patterning." *Psychophysiology*, 1977, *14*, 598–602.

Davidson, R. S., and Bremser, R. F. "Case Studies in Controlled Alcoholic Drinking: Differential Reinforcement of Low Rates of Drinking." *Behavior Modification*, 1977, *1*, 221–234.

Davis, C. M., and others. "Tension in the Two Frontales: Electrode Placement and Artifact in the Recording of Forehead EMG." *Psychophysiology*, 1978, *15*, 591–593.

Dawley, H. H., and Sardenga, P. B. "Aversive Cigarette Smoking as a Smoking Cessation Procedure." *Journal of Clinical Psychology*, 1977, *33*, 234–239.

Dawson, M. E., Schell, A. M., and Catania, J. J. "Autonomic Correlates of Depression and Clinical Improvement Following Electroconvulsive Shock Therapy." *Psychophysiology*, 1977, *14*, 569–578.

DeGiovanni, I. S., and Epstein, N. "Unbinding Assertion and Aggression in Research and Clinical Practice." *Behavior Modification*, 1978, *2*, 173–192.

Deitz, S. M. "Current Status of Applied Behavior Analysis: Science Versus Technology." *American Psychologist*, 1978, *33*, 805–814.

Dietz, S. M., and others. "Reducing Inappropriate Behavior in Special Classrooms by Reinforcing Average Interresponse Times: Interval DRL." *Behavior Therapy*, 1978, *9*, 37–46.

Denninston, J. C., and others. "Measurement of Cardiac Output by Electrical Impedance at Rest and During Exercise." *Journal of Applied Physiology*, 1976, *40*, 91–95.

Denny, D. R., and Sullivan, B. J. "Desensitization and Modeling Treatments of Spider Fears Using Two Types of Scenes." *Journal of Consulting and Clinical Psychology*, 1976, *44*, 573–579.

Dericco, D. A., Brigham, T. A., and Garlington, W. K. "Development and Evaluation of Treatment Paradigms for the Suppression of Smoking Behavior." *Journal of Applied Behavior Analysis,* 1977, *10,* 173–181.

Dericco, D. A., and Garlington, W. K. "An Operant Treatment Procedure for Alcoholics." *Behavior Research and Therapy,* 1977, *15,* 497–499.

Deysach, R. E., Ross, A. W., and Hiers, T. G. "Locus of Control in Prediction of Counselor Effectiveness Within a Therapeutic Camp Setting." *Journal of Clinical Psychology,* 1977, *33,* 273–278.

Diament, D., and Wilson, G. T. "An Experimental Investigation of the Effects of Covert Sensitization in an Analogue Eating Situation." *Behavior Therapy,* 1975, *6,* 499–509.

Doke, L. A., Geaster, C. A., and Predmore, D. L. "Managing the 'Eat-and-Run' Behavior of Adolescents via Family-Style Dining." *Behavior Modification,* 1977, *1,* 73–92.

Dolan, M. P., and Norton, J. C. "A Programmed Training Technique That Uses Reinforcement to Facilitate Acquisition and Retention in Brain-Damaged Patients." *Journal of Clinical Psychology,* 1977, *33,* 496–501.

Doleys, D. M., and others. "Dry-Bed Training and Retention Control Training: A Comparison." *Behavior Therapy,* 1977a, *8,* 541–548.

Doleys, D. M., and others. "Responding by Alcoholics During Aversive Conditioning." *Behavior Modification,* 1977b, *1,* 205–220.

Drabman, R. S., and others. "Retarded Children as Observers, Mediators, and Generalization Programmers Using an Icing Procedure." *Behavior Modification,* 1978, *2,* 371–385.

Dreger, R. M. "The Children's Behavioral Classification Project: An Interim Report." *Journal of Abnormal Child Psychology,* 1977, *5,* 289–298.

Drummond, P., White, K., and Ashton, R. "Imagery Vividness Affects Habituation Rate." *Psychophysiology,* 1978, *15,* 193–195.

Dubey, D. R., and others. "Reactions of Children and Teachers to Classroom Observers: A Series of Controlled Investigations." *Behavior Therapy,* 1977, *8,* 887–897.

Dubno, P., and others. "An Attitude Toward Behavior Modification Scale." *Behavior Therapy,* 1978, *9,* 99–108.

Durfee, J. T., and others. "Infant Social Behavior Manual." *Catalog of Selected Documents in Psychology,* 1977, *7,* 38.

Eckerman, C. O., and Whatley, J. L. "Toys and Social Interaction Between Infant Peers." *Child Development,* 1977, *48,* 1645–1656.

Edinberg, M. A., Karoly, P., and Gleser, G. C. "Assessing Assertion in the Elderly: An Application of the Behavioral-Analytic Model of Competence." *Journal of Clinical Psychology,* 1977, *33,* 869–874.

Edleson, J. L. "An Inexpensive Instrument for Rapid Recording of 'In Vivo' Observations." *Journal of Applied Behavior Analysis,* 1978, *11,* 502.

Efran, J. S., and others. "Should Fearful Individuals Be Instructed to Proceed Quickly or Cautiously?" *Journal of Clinical Psychology,* 1977, *33,* 535–539.

Eisler, R. M., Frederiksen, L. W., and Peterson, G. L. "The Relationship of Cognitive Variables to the Expression of Assertiveness." *Behavior Therapy,* 1978, *9,* 419–427.

Eisler, R. M., and others. "Social Skill Training with and Without Modeling for Schizophrenic and Nonpsychotic Hospitalized Psychiatric Patients." *Behavior Modification,* 1978, *2,* 147–172.

Elardo, R., Bradley, R., and Caldwell, B. M. "A Longitudinal Study of the Relation of Infants' Home Environments to Language Development at Age Three." *Child Development,* 1977, *48,* 595–603.

Elder, S. T., and others. "Apparatus and Procedure for Training Subjects to Control Their Blood Pressure." *Psychophysiology,* 1977a, *14,* 68–72.

Elder, S. T., and others. "Acquisition, Discriminative Stimulus Control, and Retention of Increases/Decreases in Blood Pressure of Normotensive Human Subjects." *Journal of Applied Behavior Analysis,* 1977b, *10,* 381–390.

Elliott, C. H., and Denny, D. R. "A Multiple-Component Treatment Approach to Smoking Reduction." *Journal of Consulting and Clinical Psychology,* 1978, *46,* 1330–1339.

Emery, R. E., and Marholin, D., II. "An Applied Behavior Analysis of Delinquency: The Irrelevancy of Relevant Behavior." *American Psychologist,* 1977, *32,* 860–873.

Emmelkamp, P. M. G., and Kraanen, J. "Therapist-Controlled Exposure In Vivo Versus Self-Controlled Exposure In Vivo: A

Comparison with Obsessive-Compulsive Patients." *Behavior Research and Therapy,* 1977, *15,* 491–495.

Emmelkamp, P. M. G., Kuipers, A. C. M., and Eggeraat, J. B. "Cognitive Modification Versus Prolonged Explosure In Vivo: A Comparison with Agoraphobics as Subjects." *Behavior Research and Therapy,* 1978, *16,* 33–41.

Emmelkamp, P. M. G., and Kwee, K. G. "Obsessional Ruminations: A Comparison Between Thought Stopping and Prolonged Exposure in Imagination." *Behavior Research and Therapy,* 1977, *15,* 441–444.

Emmelkamp, P. M. G., and Walta, C. "Effects of Therapy Set on Electrical Aversion Therapy and Covert Sensitization." *Behavior Therapy,* 1978, *9,* 185–188.

Endler, N. S., Hunt, J. M., and Rosenstein, A. J. "An S-R Inventory of Anxiousness." *Psychological Monographs,* 1962, *76* (entire issue).

Epstein, L. H., and Abel, G. G. "An Analysis of Biofeedback Training Effects for Tension Headaches." *Behavior Therapy,* 1977, *8,* 37–47.

Epstein, L. H., Malone, D. R., and Cunningham, J. "Feedback-Influenced EMG Changes in Stroke Patients." *Behavior Modification,* 1978, *2,* 387–402.

Epstein, L. H., and Martin, J. E. "Compliance and Side Effects of Weight Regulation Groups." *Behavior Modification,* 1977, *1,* 551–558.

Epstein, R., and Goss, C. M. "A Self-Control Procedure for the Maintenance of Nondisruptive Behavior in an Elementary School Child." *Behavior Therapy,* 1978, *9,* 109–117.

Evans, D. R., and Kazarian, S. S. "Development of a State Measure of Obsessive-Compulsive Behavior." *Journal of Clinical Psychology,* 1977, *33,* 436–439.

Evans, M. B. "Biofeedback Training: Some Clinical Considerations." *Behavior Therapy,* 1977, *8,* 101–103.

Ewing, J. W., and Hughes, H. H. "Cue-Controlled Relaxation: Its Effect on EMG Levels During Aversive Stimulation." *Journal of Behavior Therapy and Experimental Psychiatry,* 1978, *9,* 39–44.

Eysenck, H. J. "Personality and Factor Analysis: A Reply to Guilford." *Psychological Bulletin,* 1977, *84,* 405–411.

Eysenck, H. J., and Eysenck, B. G. *Manual for the Eysenck Personality Inventory*. San Diego, Calif.: Educational and Industrial Testing Service, 1968.

Fabry, P. L., and Reid, D. H. "Teaching Foster Grandparents to Train Severely Handicapped Persons." *Journal of Applied Behavior Analysis*, 1978, *11*, 111–123.

Fagot, B. I. "Consequences of Moderate Cross-Gender Behavior in Preschool Children." *Child Development*, 1977a, *48*, 902–907.

Fagot, B. I. "Variations in Density: Effect on Task and Social Behaviors of Preschool Children." *Developmental Psychology*, 1977b, *13*, 166–167.

Fagot, B. I. "Reinforcing Contingencies for Sex-Role Behaviors: Effect of Experience with Children." *Child Development*, 1978, *49*, 30–36.

Farb, J., and Throne, J. M. "Improving the Generalized Mnemonic Performance of a Down's Syndrome Child." *Journal of Applied Behavior Analysis*, 1978, *11*, 413–419.

Farley, F. H., and Mealiea, W. L. "Dissimulation and Social Desirability in the Assessment of Fears." *Behavior Therapy*, 1971, *2*, 101–102.

Farran, D. C., and Ramey, C. T. "Infant Daycare and Attachment Behaviors Toward Mothers and Teachers." *Child Development*, 1977, *48*, 1112–1116.

Farrell, A. D., Wallander, J. L., and Mariotto, M. J. "A Preliminary Evaluation of the Survey of Heterosexual Interactions as a Screening Instrument for Heterosexual Anxiety Research." Paper presented at the 12th annual meeting of the Association for Advancement of Behavior Therapy, December 1978.

Fawcett, S. B., and Fletcher, R. K. "Community Applications of Instructional Technology: Teaching Writers of Instructional Packages." *Journal of Applied Behavior Analysis*, 1977, *10*, 739–746.

Fazio, A. F. "Verbal and Overt-Behavioral Assessment of a Specific Fear." *Journal of Consulting and Clinical Psychology*, 1969, *33*, 703–709.

Feldman, M. P., and MacCulloch, M. J. *Homosexual Behavior: Therapy and Assessment*. Oxford, England: Pergamon Press, 1971.

Feldman, M. P., and others. "The Application of Anticipatory Avoidance Learning to the Treatment of Homosexuality: III.

The Sexual Orientation Method." *Behavior Research and Therapy,* 1966, *4,* 289–299.

Ferguson, L. W. "Public Service Drug Use Scales." *Psychological Reports,* 1974, *34,* 871–876.

Feuerstein, M., and Adams, H. E. "Cephalic Vasomotor Feedback in the Modification of Migraine Headache." *Biofeedback and Self-Regulation,* 1977, *3,* 241–254.

Fey, G. S., and Lindholm, E. "Biofeedback and Progressive Relaxation: Effects on Systolic and Diastolic Blood Pressure and Heart Rate." *Psychophysiology,* 1978, *15,* 239–247.

Fidler, D. S., and Kleinknecht, R. E. "Randomized Response Versus Direct Questioning: Two Data Collection Methods for Sensitive Information." *Psychological Bulletin,* 1977, *84,* 1045–1049.

Fiedler, D., and Beach, L. R. "On the Decision to be Assertive." *Journal of Consulting and Clinical Psychology,* 1978, *46,* 537–546.

Field, T. M. "Effects of Early Separation, Interactive Deficits, and Experimental Manipulations on Infant-Mother Face-to-Face Interaction." *Child Development,* 1977, *48,* 763–771.

Finch, B. E., and Wallace, C. J. "Successful Interpersonal Skills Training with Schizophrenic Inpatients." *Journal of Consulting and Clinical Psychology,* 1977, *45,* 885–890.

Finley, W. W., and Wansley, R. A. "Auditory Intensity as a Variable in the Conditioning Treatment of Enuresis Nocturna." *Behavior Research and Therapy,* 1977, *15,* 181–185.

Finley, W. W., Wansley, R. A., and Blenkarn, M. M. "Conditioning Treatment of Enuresis Using a 70 Percent Intermittent Reinforcement Schedule." *Behavior Research and Therapy,* 1977, *15,* 419–427.

Finley, W. W., and others. "Electrophysiological Behavior Modification of Frontal EMG in Cerebral-Palsied Children." *Biofeedback and Self-Regulation,* 1977, *2,* 59–79.

Fischetti, M., Curran, J. P., and Wessberg, H. W. "Sense of Timing: A Skill Deficit in Heterosexual Socially Anxious Males." *Behavior Modification,* 1977, *1,* 179–194.

Fisher, C., Gross, J., and Zurch, J. "A Cycle of Penile Erection Synchronous with Dreaming (REM) Sleep." *Archives of General Psychiatry,* 1965, *12,* 29–45.

Fisher, C., and others. "The Assessment of Nocturnal REM Erection in the Differential Diagnosis of Sexual Response." *Journal of Sex and Marital Therapy*, 1975, *1*, 277–289.

Fitzpatrick, L. J. "Automated Data Collection for Observed Events." *Behavior Research Methods and Instrumentation*, 1977a, *9*, 447–451.

Fitzpatrick, L. J. "BEHAVE—An Automated Data Analysis System for Observed Events." *Behavior Research Methods and Instrumentation*, 1977b, *9*, 452–455.

Foa, E. B., and others. "Is Horror a Necessary Component of Flooding (Implosion)?" *Behavior Research and Therapy*, 1977, *15*, 397–402.

Forehand, R., and Atkeson, B. M. "Generality of Treatment Effects with Parents as Therapists: A Review of Assessment and Implementation Procedures." *Behavior Therapy*, 1977, *8*, 575–593.

Forehand, R., and King, H. E. "Noncompliant Children: Effects of Parent Training on Behavior and Attitude Change." *Behavior Modification*, 1977, *1*, 93–108.

Forrest, M. S., and Hokanson, J. E. "Depression and Autonomic Arousal Reduction Accompanying Self-Punitive Behavior." *Journal of Abnormal Psychology*, 1975, *84*, 346–357.

Foster, A. L. "The Sexual Compatibility Test." *Journal of Consulting and Clinical Psychology*, 1977, *45*, 332–333.

Foster, W. F. "Adjunctive Behavior: An Underreported Phenomenon in Applied Behavior Analysis." *Journal of Applied Behavior Analysis*, 1978, *11*, 545–547.

Foxx, R. M. "Attention Training: The Use of Overcorrection Avoidance to Increase the Eye Contact of Autistic and Retarded Children." *Journal of Applied Behavior Analysis*, 1977, *10*, 489–499.

Foxx, R. M., and Hake, D. F. "Gasoline Conservation: A Procedure for Measuring and Reducing the Driving of College Students." *Journal of Applied Behavior Analysis*, 1977, *10*, 61–74.

Foxx, R. M., and Jones, J. R. "A Remediation Program for Increasing the Spelling Achievement of Elementary and Junior High School Students." *Behavior Modification*, 1978, *2*, 211–230.

Foxx, R. M., and Shapiro, S. T. "The Time-out Ribbon: A Nonexclusionary Time-out Procedure." *Journal of Applied Behavior Analysis*, 1978, *11*, 125–136.

Frankel, F., and Weber, D. "A Portable Low-Cost Multichannel

Timing Apparatus for Collection of Observational Duration Data." *Journal of Applied Behavior Analysis*, 1978, *11*, 522.

Frankosky, R. J., and Sulzer-Azaroff, B. "Individual and Group Contingencies and Collateral Social Behaviors." *Behavior Therapy*, 1978, *9*, 313–327.

Frederiksen, L.W., Epstein, L. H., and Kosevsky, B. P. "Reliability and Controlling Effects of Three Procedures for Self-Monitoring Smoking." *Psychological Record*, 1975, *25*, 255–264.

Free, S. M. "Statistical Problems in the Measurement of Change. Neuropsychopharmacology." *Excerpta Medica International Congress Series*, 1974, *359*, 223–228.

Free, S. M., Jr., and Overall, J. E. "The Brief Outpatient Psychopathology Scale (BOPS)." *Journal of Clinical Psychology*, 1977, *33*, 677–688.

Fremouw, W. J., and Zitter, R. E. "A Comparison of Skills Training and Cognitive Restructuring—Relaxation for the Treatment of Speech Anxiety." *Behavior Therapy*, 1978, *9*, 248–259.

Freund, K. "Psychophysiological Assessment of Change in Erotic Preferences." *Behavior Research and Therapy*, 1977, *15*, 297–301.

Friedman, P. H. "The Effects of Modeling and Role Playing on Assertive Behavior." In R. D. Rubin and others (Eds.), *Advances in Behavior Therapy*. New York: Academic Press, 1971.

Frisch, H. L. "Sex Stereotypes in Adult-Infant Play." *Child Development*, 1977, *48*, 1671–1675.

Galassi, J. P., and Galassi, M. D. "Validity of a Measure of Assertiveness." *Journal of Counseling Psychology*, 1974, *21*, 248–250.

Galassi, J. P., and Galassi, M. D. "The Relationship Between Assertiveness and Aggressiveness." *Psychological Reports*, 1975, *36*, 352–354.

Galassi, J. P., and others. "The College Self-Expression Scale: A Measure of Assertiveness." *Behavior Therapy*, 1974, *5*, 164–171.

Galassi, J. P., and others. "Behavioral Performance in the Validation of an Assertiveness Scale." *Behavior Therapy*, 1976, *7*, 447–452.

Gallagher, J. W., and Arkowitz, H. "Weak Effects of Covert Modeling Treatment of Test Anxiety." *Journal of Behavior Therapy and Experimental Psychiatry*, 1978, *9*, 23–26.

Gambrill, E. D., and Richey, C. A. "An Assertion Inventory for

Use in Assessment and Research." *Behavior Therapy*, 1975, *6*, 550–561.

Garcia, E. E., and Batista-Wallace, M. "Parental Training of the Plural Morpheme in Normal Toddlers." *Journal of Applied Behavior Analysis*, 1977, *10*, 505.

Garcia, E. E., Bullet, J., and Rust, F. P. "An Experimental Analysis of Language Training Generalization Across Classroom and Home." *Behavior Modification*, 1977, *1*, 531–550.

Garlington, W. K., and Dericco, D. A. "The Effect of Modeling on Drinking Rate." *Journal of Applied Behavior Analysis*, 1977, *10*, 207–211.

Gatchel, R. J., and others. "Comparative Effectiveness of Voluntary Rate Control and Muscular Relaxation as Active Coping Skills for Reducing Speech Anxiety." *Journal of Consulting and Clinical Psychology*, 1977, *45*, 1093–1100.

Gatchel, R. J., and others. "A Multiple-Response Evaluation of EMG Biofeedback Performance During Training and Stress-Induction Conditions." *Psychophysiology*, 1978, *15*, 253–258.

Gautheir, J., and Marshall, W. L. "The Determination of Optimal Exposure to Phobic Stimuli in Flooding Therapy." *Behavior Research and Therapy*, 1977, *15*, 403–410.

Gay, M. L., Hollandsworth, J. R., Jr., and Galassi, J. P. "An Assertiveness Inventory for Adults." *Journal of Counseling Psychology*, 1975, *22*, 340–344.

Geddes, L. A., and Newberg, D. C. "Cuff Pressure Oscillations in the Measurement of Relative Blood Pressure." *Psychophysiology*, 1977, *14*, 198–202.

Geer, J. H. "The Development of a Scale to Measure Fear." *Behavior Research and Therapy*, 1965, *3*, 45–53.

Geer, J. H. "Direct Measurement of Genital Responding." *American Psychologist*, 1975, *30*, 415–418.

Geer, J. H., and Quartararo, J. D. "Vaginal Blood Volume Responses During Masturbation." *Archives of Sexual Behavior*, 1976, *5*, 403–413.

Giannetti, R. A., and others. "The Potential for Dynamic Assessment Systems Using On-Line Computer Technology." *Behavior Research Methods and Instrumentation*, 1976, *8*, 101–103.

Giesen, J. M., and McGlynn, F. D. "Skin Conductance and Heart-Rate Responsivity to Public Speaking Imagery Among Students with High and Low Self-Reported Fear: A Comparative Analysis of 'Response' Definitions." *Journal of Clinical Psychology,* 1977, *33,* 68–76.

Gillan, P. "Objective Measures of Female Sexual Arousal." *Journal of Physiology,* 1976, *260,* 64P–65P.

Ginsburg, H. J., Pollman, V. A., and Wauson, M. S. "An Ethological Analysis of Nonverbal Inhibitors of Aggressive Behavior in Male Elementary School Children." *Developmental Psychology,* 1977, *13,* 417–418.

Gladstone, B. W., and Spencer, C. J. "The Effects of Modeling on the Contingent Praise of Mental Retardation Counselors." *Journal of Applied Behavior Analysis,* 1977, *10,* 75–84.

Glasgow, R. E., and Arkowitz, H. "The Behavioral Assessment of Male and Female Social Competence in Dyadic Heterosexual Interactions." *Behavior Therapy,* 1975, *6,* 488–499.

Glass, G. V., Wilson, V. L., and Gottman, J. M. *Design and Analysis of Time-Series Experiments.* Boulder: Colorado Associated University Press, 1975.

Glaus, K. D., Happ, A., and Kotses, H. "Airway Resistance Changes Associated with Conditioned Frontalis and Brachioradialis EMG." Abstract of paper presented at 17th annual meeting of the Society for Psychophysiological Research. *Psychophysiology,* 1978, *15,* 264–265.

Glennon, B., and Weisz, J. R. "An Observational Approach to the Assessment of Anxiety in Young Children." *Journal of Consulting and Clinical Psychology,* 1978, *46,* 1246–1257.

Gliner, J. A., Browe, A. C., and Horvath, S. M. "Hemodynamic Changes as a Function of Classical Aversive Conditioning in Human Subjects." *Psychophysiology,* 1977, *14,* 281–286.

Glogower, R., and Sloop, E. W. "Two Strategies of Group Training of Parents as Effective Behavior Modifiers." *Behavior Therapy,* 1976, *7,* 177–184.

Goldberg, J., and Yinon, Y. "Fear in Periods of Stress and Calm Among Israeli Students." *Journal of Behavior Therapy and Experimental Psychiatry,* 1977, *8,* 5–9.

Goldberg, J., Yinon, Y., and Cohen, A. "A Cross-Cultural Comparison Between the Israeli and American Fear Survey Inventory." *Journal of Social Psychology,* in press.

Goldfried, M. R., and Goldfried, A. P. "Importance of Hierarchy

Content in the Self-Control of Anxiety." *Journal of Consulting and Clinical Psychology,* 1977, *45,* 124–134.

Goldfried, M. R., Lineham, M. M., and Smith, J. L. "Reduction of Test Anxiety Through Cognitive Restructuring." *Journal of Consulting and Clinical Psychology,* 1978, *46* (1), 32–39.

Goldman, M. S., and Lee, R. M. "Operant Conditioning of Blood Pressure: Effects of Mediators." *Psychophysiology,* 1978, *15,* 531–537.

Goldstein, D. S., Ross, R. S., and Brady, J. V. "Biofeedback Heart-Rate Training During Exercise." *Biofeedback and Self-Regulation,* 1977, *2,* 107–125.

Goren, E. R., Romanczyk, R. G., and Harris, S. L. "A Functional Analysis of Echolalic Speech: The Effects of Antecedent and Consequent Events." *Behavior Modification,* 1977, *1,* 481–498.

Gottman, J. M. "The Effects of a Modeling Film on Social Isolation in Preschool Children: A Methodological Investigation." *Journal of Abnormal Child Psychology,* 1977a, *5,* 69–78.

Gottman, J. M. "Toward a Definition of Social Isolation in Children." *Child Development,* 1977b, *48,* 513–517.

Gough, H. G., and Heilbrun, A. B. *The Adjective Check List Manual.* Palo Alto, Calif.: Consulting Psychologists Press, 1965.

Grant, R. L., and Maletsky, B. M. "Application of the Weed System to Psychiatric Records." *Psychiatry in Medicine,* 1972, *3,* 119–129.

Green, B. F. "In Defense of Measurement." *American Psychologist,* 1978, *33,* 664–670.

Green, L. "Temporal and Stimulus Factors in Self-Monitoring by Obese Persons." *Behavior Therapy,* 1978, *9,* 328–341.

Green, R. W. "Self-Regulated Eating Behaviors in a Diabetic Mental Patient." *Behavior Therapy,* 1978, *9,* 521–525.

Green, S. B., and Alverson, L. G. "A Comparison of Indirect Measures for Long-Duration Behavior." *Journal of Applied Behavior Analysis,* 1978, *11,* 530.

Greene, B. F., and others. "Measuring Client Gains from Staff-Implemented Programs." *Journal of Applied Behavior Analysis,* 1978, *11,* 395–412.

Greenfield, N. S., and Sternbach, R. A. *Handbook of Psychophysiology.* New York: Holt, Rinehart and Winston, 1972.

Greenwald, D. P. "The Behavioral Assessment of Differences in

Social Skill and Social Anxiety in Female College Students." *Behavior Therapy*, 1977, *8*, 925–937.

Greenwald, D. P. "Self-Report Assessment in High- and Low-Dating College Women." *Behavior Therapy*, 1978, *9*, 297–299.

Greenwald, M. "Communication: Audiotaping Social Skills Responses." *Journal of Applied Behavior Analysis*, 1977, *10*, 254.

Greenwood, C. R., Hops, H., and Walker, H. M. "The Durability of Student Behavior Change: A Comparative Analysis at Follow-Up." *Behavior Therapy*, 1977, *8*, 631–638.

Greenwood, G. E., Breivogel, W. F., and Olmsted, P. P. "Study of Changes in Parents Employed as Paraprofessionals in a Home Intervention Follow-Through Program." *Catalog of Selected Documents in Psychology*, 1977, *7*, 15.

Griffiths, R. R., Bigelow, G., and Liebson, I. "Comparison of Social Time-Out and Activity Time-Out Procedures in Suppressing Ethanol Self-Administration in Alcoholics." *Behavior Research and Therapy*, 1977, *15*, 329–336.

Guilford, J. P. "Factors and Factors of Personality." *Psychological Bulletin*, 1975, *82*, 802–814.

Guitar, B., and Andrews, G. "Communication: An Inexpensive Cumulative Counter." *Journal of Applied Behavior Analysis*, 1977, *10*, 530.

Hake, D. F., and Foxx, R. M. "Promoting Gasoline Conservation: The Effects of Reinforcement Schedule, A Leader, and Self-Recording." *Behavior Modification*, 1978, *2*, 339–370.

Hall, J. N., Baker, R. D., and Hutchinson, K. "A Controlled Evaluation of Token Economy Procedures with Chronic Schizophrenic Patients." *Behavior Research and Therapy*, 1977, *15*, 261–283.

Hall, S. M., and others. "Contingency Contracting as a Therapeutic Tool with Methadone Maintenance Clients: Six Single-Subject Studies." *Behavior Research and Therapy*, 1977a, *15*, 438–441.

Hall, S. M., and others. "Self- and External-Management Compared with Psychotherapy in the Control of Obesity." *Behavior Research and Therapy*. 1977b, *15*, 89–95.

Hallman, N. "On the Ability of Enuretic Children to Hold Urine." *Acta Pediatrica*, 1950, *39*, 87–93.

Hamilton, S. B., and Bornstein, P. H. "Increasing the Accuracy of Self-Recording in Speech-Anxious Undergraduates Through the Use of Self-Monitoring Training and Reliability Enhancement Procedures." *Journal of Consulting and Clinical Psychology,* 1977a, *45,* 1076–1085.

Hamilton, S. B., and Bornstein, P. H. "Modified Induced Anxiety: A Generalized Anxiety Reduction Procedure." *Journal of Consulting and Clinical Psychology,* 1977b, *45,* 1200–1201.

Hanf, C., and Kling, J. "Facilitating Parent-Child Interaction: A Two Stage Training Model." Unpublished paper, University of Oregon Medical School, 1973.

Hansen, G. D. "A Simple Interval Timer for Nonclockwatchers." *Behavior Therapy,* 1977, *8,* 487–488.

Hanson, S. A., and Deysach, R. E. "Effects of Positive Reinforcement on Physical Complaints at a Therapeutic Summer Camp." *Journal of Clinical Psychology,* 1977, *33,* 1107–1112.

Harris, F. C., and Ciminero, A. R. "The Effect of Witnessing Consequences on the Behavioral Recordings of Experimental Observers." *Journal of Applied Behavior Analysis,* 1978, *11,* 513–521.

Harris, F. C., and Lahey, B. B. "A Method for Combining Occurrence and Nonoccurrence Interobserver Agreement Scores." *Journal of Applied Behavior Analysis,* 1978, *11,* 523–527.

Harris, L. S., and Purohit, A. P. "Bladder Training and Enuresis: A Controlled Trial." *Behavior Research and Therapy,* 1977, *15,* 485–490.

Harris, S. L., and Ersner-Hershfield, R. "Behavioral Suppression of Seriously Disruptive Behavior in Psychotic and Retarded Patients: A Review of Punishment and its Alternatives." *Psychological Bulletin,* 1978, *85,* 1352–1375.

Harris, W. J., Drummond, R. J., and Schultz, E. W. "An Investigation of Relationships Between Teachers' Ratings of Behavior and Children's Personality Traits." *Journal of Abnormal Child Psychology,* 1977, *5,* 43–52.

Hartmann, D. P. "Considerations in the Choice of Interobserver Reliability Estimates." *Journal of Applied Behavior Analysis,* 1977a, *10,* 103–116.

Hartmann, D. P. "Notes on Methodology: On Choosing an Interobserver Reliability Estimate." *Journal of Applied Behavior Analysis,* 1977b, *10,* 103–116.

Hartmann, D. P., Roper, B. L., and Gelfand, D. M. "An Evaluation of Alternative Modes of Child Psychotherapy." In B. Lahey and A. E. Kazdin (Eds.), *Advances in Clinical Child Psychology.* New York: Plenum, 1977.

Hay, D. F. "Following Their Companions as a Form of Exploration for Human Infants." *Child Development,* 1977, *48,* 1624–1632.

Hay, L. R., Hay, W. M., and Angle, H. V. "The Reactivity of Self-Recording: A Case Report of a Drug Abuser." *Behavior Therapy,* 1977, *8,* 1004–1007.

Hay, L. R., Nelson, R. O., and Hay, W. M. "The Use of Teachers as Behavioral Observers." *Journal of Applied Behavior Analysis,* 1977, *10,* 345–348.

Hay, W. M., Hay, L. R., and Nelson, R. O. "Direct and Collateral Changes in On-Task and Academic Behavior Resulting from On-Task Versus Academic Contingencies." *Behavior Therapy,* 1977a, *8,* 431–441.

Hay, W. M., Hay, L. R., and Nelson, R. O. "The Adaptation of Covert Modeling Procedures to the Treatment of Chronic Alcoholism and Obsessive-Compulsive Behavior: Two Case Reports." *Behavior Therapy,* 1977b, *8,* 70–76.

Hayes, S. C., and Barlow, D. H. "Flooding Relief in a Case of Public Transportation Phobia." *Behavior Therapy,* 1977, *8,* 742–746.

Hayes, S. C., and Cone, J. D. "Reducing Residential Electrical Energy Use: Payments, Information, and Feedback." *Journal of Applied Behavior Analysis,* 1977, *10,* 425–435.

Haynes, S. N. "Principles and Methods of Behavioral Self-Control." Paper presented at 18th annual meeting of Southeastern Psychological Association, New Orleans, April 1972.

Haynes, S. N. *Principles of Behavioral Assessment.* New York: Halstead Press, 1978.

Haynes, S. N., and Follingstad, D. R. "Behavioral Assessment of Marital Dysfunction." *Journal of Consulting and Clinical Psychology,* in press.

Haynes, S. N., Follingstad, D. R., and McGowan, W. T. "Insomnia: Sleep Patterns and Anxiety Level." *Journal of Psychosomatic Research,* 1975, *18,* 69–74.

Haynes, S. N., and Jensen, B. "The Behavioral Interview." In press.

Haynes, S. N., and Kerns, R. D. "Validation of a Behavioral Observation System: A Comment." *Journal of Consulting and Clinical Psychology*, in press.

Haynes, S. N., Sides, H., and Lockwood, G. "Relaxation Instructions and Frontalis Electromyographic Feedback Intervention with Sleep-Onset Insomnia." *Behavior Therapy*, 1977, *8*, 644–652.

Haynes, S. N., Wilson, C. C., and Britton, B. T. "Behavioral Intervention with Atopic Dermatitis." *Biofeedback and Self-Regulation*, in press.

Haynes, S. N., and others. "Electromyographic Biofeedback and Relaxation Instructions in the Treatment of Muscle-Contraction Headaches." *Behavior Therapy*, 1975, *6*, 672–678.

Heilbrun, A. B., Jr., and Landauer, S. P. "Stereotypic and Specific Attributions of Parental Characteristics by Late-Adolescent Siblings." *Child Development*, 1977, *48*, 1748–1751.

Heiman, J. R. "Issues in the Use of Psychophysiology to Assess Female Sexual Dysfunction." *Journal of Sex and Marital Therapy*, 1976, *2*, 197–204.

Heiman, J. R. "A Psychophysiological Exploration of Sexual Arousal Patterns in Females and Males." *Psychophysiology*, 1977, *14*, 266–274.

Heimberg, R. G., and others. "Assertion Training: A Review of the Literature." *Behavior Therapy*, 1977, *8*, 953–971.

Hekmat, H. "Semantic Behavior Therapy: Unidimensional or Multidimensional?" *Behavior Therapy*, 1977, *8*, 805–809.

Helwig, J. J., and others. "The Measurement of Manuscript Letter Strokes." *Journal of Applied Behavior Analysis*, 1976, *9*, 231–236.

Henson, D. E., Rubin, H. B., and Henson, C. "Consistency of the Labial Temperature Change Measure of Human Female Eroticism." *Behavior Research and Therapy*, in press.

Henson, D. E., and others. "Temperature Change of the Labia Minora as an Objective Measure of Human Female Eroticism." *Journal of Behavior Therapy and Experimental Psychiatry*, 1977, *8*, 401–410.

Herbert-Jackson, E., and Risley, T. R. "Behavioral Nutrition: Consumption of Foods of the Future by Toddlers." *Journal of Applied Behavior Analysis*, 1977, *10*, 407–413.

Herjanic, B., and Campbell, W. "Differentiating Psychiatrically Disturbed Children on the Basis of a Structured Interview." *Journal of Abnormal Child Psychology,* 1977, *5,* 127–134.

Herr, D. E., Eaves, R. C., and Algozzine, B. "Use of the Behavior Problem Checklist with Psychotic Adolescents." *Journal of Consulting and Clinical Psychology,* 1977, *45,* 1176–1177.

Hersen, M. "Fear Scale Norms for an Inpatient Population." *Journal of Clinical Psychology,* 1971, *27,* 375–378.

Hersen, M. "Self-Assessment of Fear." *Behavior Therapy,* 1973, *4,* 241–257.

Hersen, M., and Barlow, D. H. *Single Case Experimental Designs: Strategies for Studying Behavior Change in the Individual.* Elmsford, N.Y.: Pergamon Press, 1976.

Hersen, M., and Bellack, A. S. (Eds.). *Behavioral Assessment: A Practical Handbook.* Elmsford, N.Y.: Pergamon Press, 1976a.

Hersen, M., and Bellack, A. S. "Social Skills Training for Chronic Psychiatric Patients: Rationale, Research Findings, and Future Directions." *Comprehensive Psychiatry,* 1976b, *17,* 559–580.

Hersen, M., Bellack, A. S., and Turner, S. M. "Assessment of Assertiveness in Female Psychiatric Patients: Motor and Autonomic Measures." *Journal of Behavior Therapy and Experimental Psychiatry,* 1978, *9,* 11–16.

Heslegrave, R. J., Ogilvie, J. C., and Furedy, J. J. "Measuring Baseline Treatment Differences in Heart-Rate Variability: Variance Versus Successive Difference Mean Square, and Beats per Minute Versus Interbeat Intervals." Abstract of paper presented at 17th annual meeting of Society for Psychophysiological Research. *Psychophysiology,* 1978, *15,* 260.

Higgins, R. L., and Marlatt, G. A. "Fear of Interpersonal Evaluation as a Determinant of Alcohol Consumption in Male Social Drinkers." *Journal of Abnormal Psychology,* 1975, *84,* 644–651.

Hobbs, N. (Ed.). *Issues in the Classification of Children: A Sourcebook on Categories, Labels, and Their Consequences.* Vol. 1. San Francisco: Jossey-Bass, 1975a.

Hobbs, N. (Ed.). *Issues in the Classification of Children: A Sourcebook on Categories, Labels, and Their Consequences.* Vol. 2. San Francisco: Jossey-Bass, 1975b.

Hobbs, N. *The Futures of Children: Categories, Labels, and Their Consequences.* San Francisco: Jossey-Bass, 1975c.

Hobbs, S. A., Forehand, R., and Murray, R. G. "Effects of Various Durations of Time-Out on the Noncompliant Behavior of Children." *Behavior Therapy,* 1978, *9,* 652–656.

Hodges, P. M., and Deich, R. F. "Teaching an Artificial Language to Nonverbal Retardates." *Behavior Modification,* 1978, *2,* 489–509.

Hodgson, R., and Rachman, S. "Dysynchrony in Measures of Fear." *Behavior Research and Therapy,* 1974, *12,* 319–326.

Hodgson, R., and Rachman, S. "Obsessional-Compulsive Complaints." *Behavior Research and Therapy,* 1977, *15,* 389–395.

Hoffman, N. G., and Overall, P. B. "Factor Structure of the SCL-90 in a Psychiatric Population." *Journal of Consulting and Clinical Psychology,* 1978, *46,* 1187–1191.

Hogan, R., DeSoto, C. B., and Solano, C. "Traits, Tests, and Personality Research." *American Psychologist,* 1977, *81,* 255–264.

Hollandsworth, J. G., Jr., and Cooley, M. L. "Provoking Anger and Gaining Compliance with Assertive Versus Aggressive Responses." *Behavior Therapy,* 1978, *9,* 640–646.

Hollandsworth, J. G., Jr., Galassi, J. P., and Gay, M. L. "The Adult Self-Expression Scale: Validation by the Multitrait-Multimethod Procedure." *Journal of Clinical Psychology,* 1977, *33,* 407–415.

Holroyd, K. A. "Effectiveness of an 'Attribution Therapy' Manipulation with Test Anxiety." *Behavior Therapy,* 1978, *9,* 526–534.

Homme, L. E., and others. *How to Use Contingency Contracting in the Classroom.* Champaign, Ill.: Research Press, 1969.

Honigfeld, G., Gillis, R. C., and Klett, C. J. "NOSIE-30: A Treatment-Sensitive Ward Behavior Scale." *Psychological Reports,* 1966, *19,* 180–192.

Hoon, E. F., Hoon, P. W., and Wincze, J. P. "An Inventory for the Measurement of Female Sexual Arousability: The SAI." *Archives of Sexual Behavior,* 1976, *5,* 291.

Hoon, P. W., Wincze, J. P., and Hoon, E. F. "Physiological Assessment of Sexual Arousal in Women." *Psychophysiology,* 1976, *13,* 196–204.

Hoon, P. W., Wincze, J. P., and Hoon, E. F. "A Test of Reciprocal Inhibition: Are Anxiety and Sexual Arousal in Women Mutually

Inhibitory?" *Journal of Abnormal Psychology,* 1977a, *86,* 65–74.

Hoon, P. W., Wincze, J. P., and Hoon, E. F. "The Effects of Biofeedback and Cognitive Mediation upon Vaginal Blood Volume." *Behavior Therapy,* 1977b, *8,* 694–702.

Hopkins, B. L., and Hermann, J. A. "Evaluating Interobserver Reliability of Interval Data." *Journal of Applied Behavior Analysis,* 1977, *10,* 121–126.

Hops, H., and others. "Marital Interaction Coding System." Unpublished paper, Oregon Research Institute, 1972.

Horan, J. J., and others. "Rapid Smoking: A Cautionary Note." *Journal of Consulting and Clinical Psychology,* 1977, *45,* 341–343.

Hord, D. "Common Mode Rejection Techniques in Conjugate Eye Movement Recording During Sleep." *Psychophysiology,* 1975, *12,* 354–355.

Horn, W. F. "Sex of the Observer and Sex of the Observed as a Source of Observer Bias in Systematic Observation Data." Unpublished Master's Thesis, Southern Illinois University, 1978.

Horne, A. M., and Matson, J. L. "A Comparison of Modeling, Desensitization, Flooding, Study Skills, and Control Groups for Reducing Test Anxiety." *Behavior Therapy,* 1977, *8,* 1–8.

Horne, D. J. L. "Behavior Therapy for Trichotillomania." *Behavior Research and Therapy,* 1977, *15,* 192–196.

Hugdahl, K., Fredrikson, M., and Ohman, A. "'Preparedness' and 'Arousability' as Determinants of Electrodermal Conditioning." *Behavior Research and Therapy,* 1977, *15,* 345–353.

Hughes, H. M., and Haynes, S. N. "Structured Laboratory Observation in the Behavioral Assessment of Parent-Child Interactions: A Methodological Critique." *Behavior Therapy,* 1978, *9,* 428–447.

Hull, D. B., and Hull, J. H. "Rathus Assertiveness Schedule: Normative and Factor-Analytic Data." *Behavior Therapy,* 1978, *9,* 673.

Humphrey, L. L., Karoly, P., and Kirschenbaum, D. S. "Self-Management in the Classroom: Self-Imposed Response Cost Versus Self-Reward." *Behavior Therapy,* 1978, *9,* 592–601.

Hundert, J., and Batstone, D. "A Practical Procedure to Maintain Pupils' Accurate Self-Rating in a Classroom Token Program." *Behavior Modification,* 1978, *2,* 93–111.

Hundert, J., and Bucher, B. "Pupils' Self-Scored Arithmetic Performance: A Practical Procedure for Maintaining Accuracy." *Journal of Applied Behavior Analysis*, 1978, *11*, 304.

Huntwork, D., and Ferguson, L. W. "Drug Use and Deviation from Self-Concept Norms." *Journal of Abnormal Child Psychology*, 1977, *5*, 53–60.

Husek, T. R., and Alexander, S. "The Effectiveness of the Anxiety Differential in Examination Stress Situations." *Educational and Psychological Measurement*, 1963, *23*, 309–318.

Huston-Stein, A., Friedrick-Cofer, L., and Susman, E. J. "The Relation of Classroom Structure to Social Behavior, Imaginative Play, and Self-Regulation of Economically Disadvantaged Children." *Child Development*, 1977, *48*, 908–916.

Hynd, G. W., Severson, H. H., and O'Neil, M. "Cardiovascular Stress During the Rapid Smoking Procedure." *Psychological Reports*, 1976, *39*, 371–375.

Inoff, G. E., and Galverson, C. F., Jr. "Behavioral Disposition of Child and Caretaker-Child Interaction." *Developmental Psychology*, 1977, *13*, 274–281.

Israel, E., and Beiman, I. "Live Versus Recorded Relaxation Training: A Controlled Investigation." *Behavior Therapy*, 1977, *8*, 251–254.

Jacklin, C. N., and Maccoby, E. E. "Social Behavior at Thirty-Three Months in Same-Sex and Mixed-Sex Dyads." *Child Development*, 1978, *49*, 557–569.

Jacobson, N. S. "Problem Solving and Contingency Contracting in the Treatment of Marital Discord." *Journal of Consulting and Clinical Psychology*, 1977, *45*, 92–100.

James, S. "Treatment of Homosexuality II. Superiority of Desensitization-Arousal as Compared with Anticipatory Avoidance Conditioning: Results of a Controlled Trial." *Behavior Therapy*, 1978, *9*, 28–36.

Janisse, M. P., and Kuc, S. G. "The Cognitive-Emotional Arousal Distinction as Assessed by Pupil Size and Heart Rate." Abstract of paper presented at 16th annual meeting of Society for Psychophysiological Research. *Psychophysiology*, 1977, *14*, 79–80.

Jaremko, M. E. "Prophylactic Systematic Desensitization: An

Analogue Test." *Journal of Behavior Therapy and Experimental Psychiatry,* 1978, *9,* 5–9.

Jeffrey, R. W., Wing, R. R., and Stunkard, A. J. "Behavioral Treatment of Obesity: The State of the Art 1976." *Behavior Therapy,* 1978, *9,* 189–199.

Jeger, A. M., and Goldfried, M. R. "A Comparison of Situation Tests of Speech Anxiety." *Behavior Therapy,* 1976, *7,* 252–255.

Jehu, D., and others. "A Controlled Trial of the Treatment of Nocturnal Enuresis in Residential Homes for Children." *Behavior Research and Therapy,* 1977, *15,* 1–16.

Jenkins, J., and others. "Increasing Engagement in Activity of Residents in Old People's Homes by Providing Recreational Materials." *Behavior Research and Therapy,* 1977, *15,* 429–434.

Jessup, B. A., and Neufeld, R. W. J. "Effects of Biofeedback and 'Autogenic Relaxation' Techniques on Physiological and Subjective Responses in Psychiatric Patients: A Preliminary Analysis." *Behavior Therapy,* 1977, *8,* 160–167.

Johnson, J. H., Giannetti, R. A., and Williams, T. A. "Computers in Mental Health Care Delivery: A Review of the Evolution Toward Interventionally Relevant On-Line Processing." *Behavior Research Methods and Instrumentation,* 1976, *8,* 83–91.

Johnson, M. S., and Bailey, J. S. "The Modification of Leisure Behavior in a Halfway House for Retarded Women." *Journal of Applied Behavior Analysis,* 1977, *10,* 273–282.

Johnson, S. M., and Bolstad, O. D. "Methodological Issues in Naturalistic Observation: Some Problems and Solutions for Field Research." In L. A. Hamerlynck, L. C. Handy, and E. J. Mash (Eds.), *Behavior Change: Methodology, Concepts, and Practice.* Champaign, Ill.: Research Press, 1973.

Johnson, S. M., and Bolstad, O. D. "Reactivity to Home Observations: A Comparison of Audio-Recorded Behavior with Observers Present or Absent." *Journal of Applied Behavior Analysis,* 1975, *8,* 181–185.

Johnson, S. M., and Christensen, A. "Multiple-Criteria Follow-Up of Behavior Modification with Families." *Journal of Abnormal Child Psychology,* 1975, *3,* 135–154.

Johnson, S. M., and Sechrest, L. "Comparison of Desensitization and Progressive Relaxation in Treating Text Anxiety." *Journal of Consulting and Clinical Psychology,* 1968, *32,* 380–386.

Johnston, A., and others. "Validation of a Laboratory Play Measure of Child Aggression." *Child Development,* 1977, *48,* 324–327.

Jones, F. H., Fremouw, W., and Carples, S. "Pyramid Training of Elementary School Teachers to Use a Classroom Management 'Skill Package.'" *Journal of Applied Behavior Analysis,* 1977, *10,* 239–253.

Jones, J. C., Trap, J., and Cooper, J. O. "Technical Report: Students' Self-Recording of Manuscript Letter Strokes." *Journal of Applied Behavior Analysis,* 1977, *10,* 509–514.

Jones, R. G. "A Factored Measure of Ellis' Irrational Belief System with Personality and Maladjustment Correlates." Unpublished doctoral dissertation, Texas Technological College, 1968.

Jones, R. R., Reid, J. B., and Patterson, G. R. "Naturalistic Observation in Clinical Assessment." In P. McReynolds (Ed.), *Advances in Psychological Assessment.* Vol. 3. San Francisco: Jossey-Bass, 1975.

Jones, R. R., Vaught, R. S., and Weinrott, M. "Time-Series Analysis in Operant Research." *Journal of Applied Behavior Analysis,* 1977, *10,* 151–166.

Jones, R. R., Weinrott, M., and Vaught, R. S. "Visual Versus Statistical Inference in Operant Research." Paper presented at symposium on use of statistics in $N = 1$ research at 83rd annual meeting of American Psychological Association, Chicago, September 1975.

Jones, R. R., Weinrott, M., and Vaught, R. S. "Effects of Serial Dependency on the Agreement Between Visual and Statistical Inference." *Journal of Applied Behavior Analysis,* 1978, *11,* 277–283.

Kandel, H. J., Ayllon, T., and Rosenbaum, S. "Flooding or Systematic Exposure in the Treatment of Extreme Social Withdrawal in Children." *Journal of Behavior Therapy and Experimental Psychiatry,* 1977, *8,* 75–81.

Kanfer, F. H. "Self-Monitoring: Methodological Limitations and Clinical Applications." *Journal of Consulting and Clinical Psychology,* 1970, *35,* 148–152.

Kanfer, F. H., and Grimm, L. G. "Behavioral Analysis: Selecting

Target Behaviors in the Interview." *Behavior Modification,* 1977, *1,* 7–28.

Kantorowitz, D. A. "An Experimental Investigation of Preorgasmic Reconditioning and Postorgasmic Deconditioning." *Journal of Applied Behavior Analysis,* 1978, *11,* 23–34.

Kaplan, R. M., and Litrownik, A. J. "Some Statistical Methods for the Assessment of Multiple-Outcome Criteria in Behavioral Research." *Behavior Therapy,* 1977, *8,* 383–392.

Kaplan, R. M., and Litrownik, A. J. "Further Comments on Multivariate Methods in Behavioral Research." *Behavior Therapy,* 1978, *9,* 474–476.

Karacan, I. "Clinical Value of Nocturnal Erection in the Prognosis and Diagnosis of Impotence." *Medical Aspects of Human Sexuality,* April 1970, pp. 27–34.

Karacan, I., Hursch, C. J., and Williams, R. L. "Some Characteristics of Nocturnal Penile Tumescence in Young Adults." *Archives of General Psychiatry,* 1972, *26,* 351–356.

Karoly, P., and Dirks, M. J. "Developing Self-Control in Preschool Children Through Correspondence Training." *Behavior Therapy,* 1977, *8,* 398–405.

Karoly, P., and Rosenthal, M. "Training Parents in Behavior Modification: Effects on Perceptions of Family Interaction and Deviant Child Behavior." *Behavior Therapy,* 1977, *8,* 405–410.

Kauffman, J., Hallahan, D. P., and Ianna, S. "Suppression of a Retardate's Tongue Protrusion by Contingent Imitation: A Case Study." *Behavior Research and Therapy,* 1977, *15,* 196–198.

Kaufman, K. F., and O'Leary, K. D. "Reward, Cost, and Self-Evaluation Procedures for Disruptive Adolescents in a Psychiatric Hospital School." *Journal of Applied Behavior Analysis,* 1972, *5,* 293–309.

Kazarian, S. S., Evans, D. R., and Lefave, K. "Modification and Factorial Analysis of the Leyton Obsessional Inventory." *Journal of Clinical Psychology,* 1977, *33,* 422–425.

Kazdin, A. E. "Reactive Self-Monitoring: The Effects of Response Desirability, Goal Setting, and Feedback." *Journal of Consulting and Clinical Psychology,* 1974, *42,* 704–716.

Kazdin, A. E. "Statistical Analyses for Single-Case Experimental

Designs." In M. Hersen and D. H. Barlow (Eds.), *Single-Case Experimental Designs: Strategies for Studying Behavior Change.* Oxford,. England: Pergamon Press, 1976.

Kazdin, A. E. "Artifact, Bias, and Complexity of Assessment: The ABC's of Reliability." *Journal of Applied Behavior Analysis,* 1977a, *10,* 141–150.

Kazdin, A. E. "Assessing the Clinical or Applied Importance of Behavior Change Through Social Validation." *Behavior Modification,* 1977b, *1,* 427–452.

Kazdin, A. E. "The Influence of Behavior Preceding a Reinforced Response on Behavior Change in the Classroom." *Journal of Applied Behavior Analysis,* 1977c, *10,* 299–310.

Kazdin, A. E. "Vicarious Reinforcement and the Direction of Behavior Change in the Classroom." *Behavior Therapy,* 1977d, *8,* 57–63.

Kazdin, A. E. "Evaluating the Generality of Findings in Analogue Therapy Research." *Journal of Consulting and Clinical Psychology,* 1978a, *46,* 673–686.

Kazdin, A. E. "Methodological and Interpretive Problems of Single-Case Experimental Designs." *Journal of Consulting and Clinical Psychology,* 1978b, *46,* 629–642.

Kazdin, A. E. "Methodology of Applied Behavior Analysis." In A. C. Catania and T. A. Brigham (Eds.), *Handbook of Applied Behavior Analysis: Social and Instructional Processes.* New York: Irvington, in press.

Kazdin, A. E., and Geesey, S. "Simultaneous-Treatment Design Comparisons of the Effects of Earning Reinforcers for One's Peers Versus for Oneself." *Behavior Therapy,* 1977, *8,* 682–693.

Kelly, J. A., and Drabman, R. S. "Generalizing Response Suppression of Self-Injurious Behavior Through an Overcorrection Punishment Procedure: A Case Study." *Behavior Therapy,* 1977a, *8,* 468–472.

Kelly, J. A., and Drabman, R. S. "The Modification of Socially Detrimental Behavior." *Journal of Behavior Therapy and Experimental Psychiatry,* 1977b, *8,* 101–104.

Kelly, J. A., and others. "Training and Generalization of Commendatory Assertiveness: A Controlled Single-Subject Experiment."

*Journal of Behavior Therapy and Experimental Psychiatry,* 1978, *9,* 17–21.

Kelly, M. B. "A Review of the Observational Data Collection and Reliability Procedures Reported in the Journal of Applied Behavior Analysis." *Journal of Applied Behavior Analysis,* 1977, *10,* 97–101.

Kendall, P. C., and Finch, A. J., Jr. "A Cognitive-Behavioral Treatment for Impulsivity: A Group Comparison Study." *Journal of Consulting and Clinical Psychology,* 1978, *46,* 110–118.

Kendall, P. C., and others. "The State-Trait Anxiety Inventory: A Systematic Evaluation." *Journal of Consulting and Clinical Psychology,* 1976, *44,* 406–412.

Kenny, F. T., Mowbray, R. M., and Lalani, S. "Faradic Disruption of Obsessive Ideation in the Treatment of Obsessive Neurosis: A Controlled Study." *Behavior Therapy,* 1978, *9,* 209–221.

Kent, R. N., and O'Leary, K. D. "Treatment of Conduct Problem Children: B.A. and/or Ph.D. Therapists." *Behavior Therapy,* 1977, *8,* 653–658.

Kent, R. N., and others. "Observer Reliability as a Function of Circumstances of Assessment." *Journal of Applied Behavior Analysis,* 1977a, *10,* 317–324.

Kent, R. N., and others. "An Approach to Teaching Parents and Adolescents Problem-Solving Communications Skills: A Preliminary Report." *Behavior Therapy,* 1977b, *8,* 639–643.

Ketterer, M. W., and Smith, B. D. "Bilateral Electrodermal Activity, Lateralized Cerebral Processing, and Sex." *Psychophysiology,* 1977, *14,* 513–516.

Kilbride, H. W., Johnson, D. L., and Streissguth, A. P. "Social Class, Birth Order, and Newborn Experience." *Child Development,* 1977, *48,* 1686–1688.

Kilmann, P. R., Wagner, M. K., and Sotile, W. M. "The Differential Impact of Self-Monitoring on Smoking Behavior: An Exploratory Study." *Journal of Clinical Psychology,* 1977, *33,* 912–914.

Kimmel, D. C., and Van der Veen, F. "Factors of Marital Adjustment in Locke's Marital Adjustment Test." *Journal of Marriage and the Family,* 1974, *36,* 57–63.

Kingsley, R. G., and Wilson, G. T. "Behavior Therapy for Obesity:

A Comparative Investigation of Long-Term Efficacy." *Journal of Consulting and Clinical Psychology,* 1977, *45,* 288–298.

Kinnen, E. "Cardiac Output from Transthoracic Impedance Variations." *Annals of the New York Academy of Sciences,* 1970, *170,* 747–756.

Kinsey, N., Pomeroy, W. B., and Martin, C. E. *Sexual Behavior in the Human Male.* Philadelphia: Saunders, 1948.

Kirby, F. D., and Toler, H. C., Jr. "Modification of Preschool Isolate Behavior: A Case Study." *Journal of Applied Behavior Analysis,* 1970, *3,* 309–314.

Kirsch, I., and Henry, D. "Extinction Versus Credibility in the Desensitization of Speech Anxiety." *Journal of Consulting and Clinical Psychology,* 1977, *45,* 1052–1059.

Kirschenbaum, D. S., and Karoly, P. "When Self-Regulation Fails: Tests of Some Preliminary Hypotheses." *Journal of Consulting and Clinical Psychology,* 1977, *45,* 1116–1125.

Klaus, D., Hersen, M., and Bellack, A. S. "Survey of Dating Habits of Male and Female Students: A Necessary Precursor to Measurement and Modification." *Journal of Clinical Psychology,* 1977, *33,* 369–375.

Klein, D. C., and Seligman, E. P. "Reversal of Performance Deficits and Perceptual Deficits in Learned Helplessness and Depression." *Journal of Abnormal Psychology,* 1976, *85,* 11–26.

Kleinknecht, R. A., and Bernstein, D. A. "The Assessment of Dental Fear." *Behavior Therapy,* 1978, *9,* 626–634.

Kleinknecht, R. A., McCormick, C. E., and Thorndike, R. M. "Stability of Stated Reinforcers as Measured by the Reinforcement Survey Schedule." *Behavior Therapy,* 1973, *4,* 407–413.

Kleinman, K. M., and others. "Relationship Between Essential Hypertension and Cognitive Functioning: II. Effects of Biofeedback Training Generalize to Nonlaboratory Environment." *Psychophysiology,* 1977, *14,* 192–197.

Klingler, D. E., and others. "Process Evaluation of an On-Line Computer-Assisted Unit for Intake Assessment of Mental Health Patients." *Behavior Research Methods and Instrumentation,* 1977, *9,* 110–116.

Klorman, R., and others. "Psychometric Description of Some

Specific Fear Questionnaires." *Behavior Therapy*, 1974, *5*, 401–409.

Klorman, R., Weissberg, R. P., and Wiesenfeld, A. R. "Individual Differences in Fear and Autonomic Reactions to Affective Stimulation." *Psychophysiology*, 1977, *14*, 51.

Knapp, C. W. "A Portable One-Way Observation Screen." *Journal of Applied Behavior Analysis*, 1978, *11*, 284.

Knapp, T. J., and Wells, L. A. "Behavior Therapy for Asthma: A Review." *Behavior Research*, 1978, *16*, 103–115.

Knight, G. P., and Kagan, S. "Development of Prosocial and Competitive Behaviors in Anglo-American and Mexican-American Children." *Child Development*, 1977, *48*, 1385–1394.

Knight, R. A., and Blaney, P. H. "Interrater Reliability of the Psychotic Inpatient Profile." *Journal of Clinical Psychology*, 1977, *33*, 647–653.

Knox, D. *Marriage Happiness: A Behavioral Approach to Counseling.* Champaign, Ill.: Research Press, 1971.

Koegel, R. L., Clahn, T. J., and Nieminen, G. S. "Generalization of Parent-Training Results." *Journal of Applied Behavior Analysis*, 1978, *11*, 95–109.

Koegel, R. L., and Rincover, A. "Treatment of Psychotic Children in classroom Environments: Learning in a Large Group." *Journal of Applied Behavior Analysis*, 1974, *7*, 45–59.

Koegel, R. L., and Rincover, A. "Research on the Difference Between Generalization and Maintenance in Extra-Therapy Responding." *Journal of Applied Behavior Analysis*, 1977, *10*, 1–12.

Koegel, R. L., Russo, D. C., and Rincover, A. "Assessing and Training Teachers in the Generalized Use of Behavior Modification with Autistic Children." *Journal of Applied Behavior Analysis*, 1977, *10*, 199–205.

Kohn, M. "The Kohn Social Competence Scale and Kohn Symptom Checklist for the Preschool Child: A Follow-Up Report." *Journal of Abnormal Child Psychology*, 1977, *5*, 249–264.

Kogen, K. L., Wimberger, H. C., and Bobbitt, R. A. "Analysis of Mother-Child Interaction in Young Mental Retardates." *Child Development*, 1969, *40*, 799–812.

Komaki, J., and Barnett, F. T. "A Behavioral Approach to Coaching

Football: Improving the Play Execution of the Offensive Backfield on a Youth Football Team." *Journal of Applied Behavior Analysis,* 1977, *10,* 657–664.

Kondo, C. Y., Canter, A., and Bean, J. A. "Intersession Interval and Reductions in Frontalis EMG During Biofeedback Training." *Psychophysiology,* 1977, *14,* 15–17.

Kotses, H., Glaus, K. D., and Frese, F. J. "Skin Conductance Responses to Complex Visual Stimuli." Abstract of paper presented at 16th annual meeting of Society for Psychophysiological Research. *Psychophysiology,* 1977, *14,* 100–101.

Kovacs, M., and Beck, A. T. "The Wish to Die and the Wish to Live in Attempted Suicides." *Journal of Clinical Psychology,* 1977, *33,* 361–365.

Kratochwill, T. R., and Brody, G. H. "Single-Subject Designs: A Perspective on the Controversy over Employing Statistical Inference and Implications for Research and Training in Behavior Modification." *Behavior Modification,* 1978, *2,* 291–307.

Kratochwill, T. R., and Wetzel, R. J. "Observer Agreement, Credibility, and Judgment: Some Considerations in Presenting Observer Agreement Data." *Journal of Applied Behavior Analysis,* 1977, *10,* 133–139.

Kubicek, W. G., and others. "Development and Evaluation of an Impedance Cardiac Output System." *Aerospace Medicine,* 1966, *37,* 1208–1212.

Labadidi, A., and others. "Evaluation of Impedance Cardiac Output in Children." *Pediatrics,* 1971, *47,* 870–879.

Lacey, J. I. "Somatic Response Patterning and Stress: Some Revisions of Activation Theory." In M. H. Appley and R. Trumbull (Eds.), *Psychological Stress: Issues in Research.* New York: Appleton-Century-Crofts, 1967.

Lahey, B. B., and others. "Treatment of Severe Perceptual-Motor Disorders in Children Diagnosed as Learning Disabled." *Behavior Modification,* 1977a, *1,* 123–140.

Lahey, B. B., and others. "An Evaluation of Daily Report Cards with Minimal Teacher and Parent Contacts as an Efficient Method of Classroom Intervention." *Behavior Modification,* 1977b, *1,* 381–394.

Lamb, M. E. "Father-Infant and Mother-Infant Interaction in the First Year of Life." *Child Development,* 1977a, *48,* 167–181.

Lamb, M. E. "The Development of Mother-Infant and Father-Infant Attachments in the Second Year of Life." *Developmental Psychology,* 1977b, *13,* 456–459.

Lamb, M. E. "Interaction Between Eighteen-Month-Olds and Their Preschool-Aged Siblings." *Child Development,* 1978, *49,* 51–59.

Lambert, L., Essen, J., and Gead, J. "Variations in Behavior Ratings of Children Who Have Been in Care." *Journal of Child Psychology and Psychiatry and Allied Disciplines,* 1977, *18,* 335–346.

Lando, H. A. "Successful Treatment of Smokers with a Broad-Spectrum Behavioral Approach." *Journal of Consulting and Clinical Psychology,* 1977, *45,* 361–366.

Lang, P. J. "The Application of Psychophysiological Methods to the Study of Psychotherapy and Behavior Modification." In A. E. Bergin and S. L. Garfield (Eds.), *Handbook of Psychotherapy and Behavior Change.* New York: Wiley, 1971.

Lang, P. J. "Imagery in Therapy: An Information-Processing Analysis of Fear." *Behavior Therapy,* 1977, *8,* 862–886.

Lang, P. J., and Lazovik, A. P. "Experimental Desensitization of a Phobia." *Journal of Abnormal and Social Psychology,* 1963, *66,* 519–525.

Lang, P. J., Melamed, B. G., and Hart, J. "A Psychophysiological Analysis of Fear Modification Using an Automated Desensitization Procedure." *Journal of Abnormal Psychology,* 1970, *76,* 220–234.

Lansky, D., Nathan, P. E., and Lawson, D. M. "Blood-Alcohol-Level Discrimination by Alcoholics: The Role of Internal and External Cues." *Journal of Consulting and Clinical Psychology,* 1978, *46,* 953–960.

Lanyon, R. I. "Measurement of Social Competence in College Males." *Journal of Consulting Psychology,* 1967, *31,* 493–498.

Lanyon, R. I. "Effect of Biofeedback-Based Relaxation on Stuttering During Reading and Spontaneous Speech." *Journal of Consulting and Clinical Psychology,* 1977, *45,* 860–866.

Lasky, R. E. "The Effect of Visual Feedback of the Hand on the

Reaching and Retrieval Behavior of Young Infants." *Child Development,* 1977, *48,* 112–117.

Laws, D. R., and Rubin, H. B. "Instrumental Control of an Automatic Sexual Response." *Journal of Applied Behavioral Analysis,* 1969, *2,* 93–99.

Lawson, K., Daum, C., and Turkewitz, G. "Environmental Characteristics of a Neonatal Intensive Care Unit." *Child Development,* 1977, *48,* 1633–1639.

Lazarus, A. A. *Multimodal Behavior Therapy.* New York: Springer-Verlag, 1976.

LeBow, M. D., Goldberg, P. A., and Collins, A. "A Methodology for Investigating Differences in Eating Between Obese and Nonobese Persons." *Behavior Therapy,* 1976, *5,* 707–709.

LeBow, M. D., Goldberg, P. A., and Collins, A. "Eating Behavior of Overweight and Nonoverweight Persons in the Natural Environment." *Journal of Consulting and Clinical Psychology,* 1977, *45,* 1204–1205.

Lee, R. M., Caldwell, J. R., and Lee, J. A. "Blood Pressure Tracking Systems and Their Application to Biofeedback." *Biofeedback and Self-Regulation,* 1977, *2,* 435–447.

Lehrer, P. M. "Psychophysiological Effects of Progressive Relaxation in Anxiety-Neurotic Patients and of Progressive Relaxation and Alpha Feedback in Nonpatients." *Journal of Consulting and Clinical Psychology,* 1978, *46,* 389–404.

Leiblum, S. R., and Kopel, S. A. "Screening and Prognosis in Sex Therapy: To Treat or Not to Treat." *Behavior Therapy,* 1977, *8,* 480–486.

Leitenberg, H. L. *Handbook of Behavior Modification and Behavior Therapy.* Englewood Cliffs, N.J.: Prentice-Hall, 1976.

Leitenberg, H., and others. "Using Positive Reinforcement to Suppress Behavior: Some Experimental Comparisons with Sibling Conflict." *Behavior Therapy,* 1977, *8,* 168–182.

Leiter, M. P. "A Study of Reciprocity in Preschool Play Groups." *Child Development,* 1977, *48,* 1288–1295.

Lester, D., and Beck, A. T. "Suicidal Wishes and Depression in Suicidal Ideators: A Comparison with Attempted Suicides." *Journal of Clinical Psychology,* 1977, *33,* 92–94.

Levin, S. M., and others. "Variations of Covert Sensitization in the

Treatment of Pedophiliac Behavior: A Case Study." *Journal of Consulting and Clinical Psychology*, 1977, *45*, 896–907.

Levitt, E. E., and Lubin, B. *Depression: Concepts, Controversies, and Some New Facts.* New York: Springer-Verlag, 1975.

Levy, S. M. "Schizophrenic Symptomatology: Reaction or Strategy? A Study of Contextual Antecedents." *Journal of Abnormal Psychology*, 1976, *85*, 435–445.

Lewinsohn, P. M., and Shaffer, M. "Use of Home Observations as an Integral Part of the Treatment of Depression: Preliminary Report and Case Studies." *Journal of Consulting and Clinical Psychology*, 1971, *39*, 87–94.

Liberman, R. P., and others. "Behavioral Measurement in a Community Mental Health Center." In P. D. Davidson, F. W. Clark, and L. A. Hamerlynck (Eds.), *Evaluation of Behavioral Progress in Community and School Settings.* Champaign, Ill. Research Press, 1974.

Lichtenstein, E., and Glasgow, R. E. "Rapid Smoking: Side Effects and Safeguards." *Journal of Consulting and Clinical Psychology*, 1977, *45*, 815–821.

Lick, J. R. "The Effects of Pretreatment Demand Characteristics on Verbally Reported Fear." *Behavior Therapy*, 1977, *8*, 727–730.

Lick, J. R., and Heffler, D. "Relaxation Training and Attention Placebo in the Treatment of Severe Insomnia." *Journal of Consulting and Clinical Psychology*, 1977, *45*, 153–161.

Lick, J. R., Sushinsky, L. W., and Malow, R. "Specificity of Fear Survey Schedule Items and the Prediction of Avoidance Behavior." *Behavior Modification*, 1977, *1*, 195–204.

Lick, J. R., and Unger, T. E. "The External Validity of Behavioral Fear Assessment: The Problem of Generalizing from the Laboratory to the Natural Environment." *Behavior Modification*, 1977, *1*, 283–306.

Lieberman, A. F. "Preschoolers' Competence with a Peer: Relations with Attachment and Peer Experience." *Child Development*, 1977, *48*, 1277–1287.

Lineham, K. S., and others. "Homogeneity and Heterogeneity of Problem Class in Modeling Treatment of Fears." *Behavior Research and Therapy*, 1977, *15*, 211–215.

Lipinski, D., and Nelson, R. "The Reactivity and Unreliability of

Self-Recording." *Journal of Consulting and Clinical Psychology,* 1974, *42,* 111–123.

Litow, L. "Glossary of Classroom Behaviors." *Catalog of Selected Documents in Psychology,* 1977, *7,* 53.

Little, L. M., Curran, J. P., and Gilbert, F. S. "The Importance of Subject Recruitment Procedures in Therapy Analogue Studies of Heterosexual Social Anxiety." *Behavior Therapy,* 1977, *8,* 24–29.

Lobitz, G. K., and Johnson, S. M. "Normal Versus Deviant Children: A Multimethod Comparison." Unpublished paper, University of Oregon, 1973.

Locke, H. J., and Wallace, K. M. "Short Marital Adjustment and Prediction Tests: Their Reliability and Validity." *Marriage and Family Living,* 1959, *21,* 251–255.

Lockhart, R. A., and Lieberman, W. "Factor Structure of the Electrodermal Response." Abstract of paper presented at 16th annual meeting of Society for Psychophysiological Research. *Psychophysiology,* 1977, *14,* 80.

Loos, F. M., Williams, K. P., and Bailey, J. S. "A Multielement Analysis of the Effect of Teacher Aides in an 'Open'-Style Classroom." *Journal of Applied Behavior Analysis,* 1977, *10,* 437–448.

LoPiccolo, J., and Steger, J. C. "The Sexual Interaction Inventory: A New Instrument for Assessment of Sexual Dysfunction." *Archives of Sexual Behavior,* 1974, *3,* 585–595.

Lorr, M., and Vestre, N. D. *Psychotic Inpatient Profile Manual.* Los Angeles: Western Psychological Services, 1968.

Lorr, M., and Vestre, N. D. "The Psychotic Inpatient Profile: A Nurses' Observation Scale." *Journal of Clinical Psychology,* 1969, *25,* 137–140.

Lougee, M. D., Grueneich, R., and Hartup, W. W. "Social Interaction in Same- and Mixed-Age Dyads of Preschool Children." *Child Development,* 1977, *48,* 1353–1361.

Lovaas, O. I., and others. "Some Observations on the Nonextinguishability of Children's Speech." *Child Development,* 1977, *48,* 1121–1127.

Lowe, M. R., and Cautela, J. R. "A Self-Report Measure of Social Skill." *Behavior Therapy,* 1978, *9,* 535–544.

Lowry, R. "Active Circuits for Direct Linear Measurement of Skin

Resistance and Conductance." *Psychophysiology*, 1977, *14*, 329–331.

Lubar, J. F., and Shouse, M. N. "Use of Biofeedback in the Treatment of Seizure Disorders and Hyperactivity." In B. Lahey and A. Kazdin (Eds.), *Advances in Clinical Child Psychology*. New York: Plenum, 1977.

Lubin, B. *Manual for the Depression Adjective Check List*. San Diego: Educational and Industrial Testing Service, 1967.

Lubin, B., Marone, J. G., and Nathan, R. G. "Comparison of Self-Administered and Examiner-Administered Depression Adjective Check Lists." *Journal of Consulting and Clinical Psychology*, 1978, *46*, 584–585.

Lucas, R. W., and others. "Psychiatrists and a Computer as Interrogators of Patients with Alcohol-Related Illnesses: A Comparison." *British Journal of Psychiatry*, 1977, *131*, 160–167.

Lytton, H. "Do Parents Create, or Respond to, Differences in Twins?" *Developmental Psychology*, 1977, *13*, 456–459.

McClannahan, L. E., and Risley, T. R. "Design of Living Environments for Nursing Home Residents: Increasing Participation in Recreation Activities." *Journal of Applied Behavior Analysis*, 1975, *8*, 261–268.

MacDonough, T. S. "A Critique of the First Feldman and MacCulloch Avoidance Conditioning Treatment of Homosexuals." *Behavior Therapy*, 1972, *3*, 104–111.

McFall, R. M., and Lillesand, D. V. "Behavior Rehearsal with Modeling and Coaching in Assertive Training." *Journal of Abnormal Psychology*, 1971, *77*, 313–323.

McGowan, W. T., Haynes, S. N., and Wilson, C. C. "Frontal EMG Feedback: Stress Attenuation and Generalization." *Biofeedback and Self-Regulation*, in press.

McGullough, J. P., Huntsinger, G. M., and Nay, R. W. "Self-Control Treatment of Aggression in a 16-Year-Old Male." *Journal of Consulting and Clinical Psychology*, 1977, *45*, 323–331.

McLaughlin, J. G., and Nay, W. R. "Treatment of Trichotillomania Using Positive Coverants and Response Cost: A Case Report." *Behavior Research and Therapy*, 1977, *15*, 192–195.

MacWhinney, B., and Osser, H. "Verbal Planning Functions in Children's Speech." *Child Development*, 1977, *48*, 978–985.

Magrab, P. R., and Papadopoulou, Z. L. "The Effect of a Token Economy on Dietary Compliance for Children on Hemodialysis." *Journal of Applied Behavior Analysis*, 1977, *10*, 573–578.

Mahoney, M. J. "Self-Reward and Self-Monitoring Techniques for Weight Control." *Behavior Therapy*, 1974, *5*, 48–57.

Mahoney, M. J. "Reflections on the Cognitive-Learning Trend in Psychotherapy." *American Psychologist*, 1977, *32*, 5–13.

Mahoney, M. J., Moura, N. G., and Wade, T. C. "Relative Efficacy of Self-Reward, Self-Punishment, and Self-Monitoring Techniques for Weight Loss." *Journal of Consulting and Clinical Psychology*, 1973, *40*, 404–407.

Mahoney, M. J., and others. "Effects of Continuous and Intermittent Self-Monitoring on Academic Behavior." *Journal of Consulting and Clinical Psychology*, 1974, *42*, 118–123.

Maisto, S. A., and Adesso, V. J. "Effect of Instructions and Feedback on Blood-Alcohol-Level Discrimination Training in Nonalcoholic Drinkers." *Journal of Consulting and Clinical Psychology*, 1977, *45*, 625–636.

Maletzky, B. M. "'Assisted' Covert Sensitization in the Treatment of Exhibitionism." *Journal of Consulting and Clinical Psychology*, 1974, *42*, 34–40.

Maletzky, B. M. "'Booster' Sessions in Aversion Therapy: The Permanency of Treatment." *Behavior Therapy*, 1977, *8*, 460–463.

Maloney, M. P., and Ward, M. P. *Psychological Assessment: A Conceptual Approach.* New York: Oxford University Press, 1976.

Mandler, G., and Kremen, I. "Autonomic Feedback: A Correlation Study." *Journal of Personality*, 1958, *26*, 388–399.

Mandler, G., Mandler, J. M., and Uviller, E. T. "Autonomic Feedback: The Perception of Autonomic Activity." *Journal of Abnormal and Social Psychology*, 1958, *56*, 367–373.

Marchetti, A., McGlynn, F. D., and Patterson, A. S. "Effects of Cue-Controlled Relaxation, a Placebo Treatment, and No Treatment on Changes in Self-Reported and Psychophysiological Indices of Test Anxiety Among College Students." *Behavior Modification*, 1977, *1*, 47–72.

Margolies, P. J., and Weintraub, S. "The Revised 56-Item CRPBI as a Research Instrument: Reliability and Factor Structure." *Journal of Clinical Psychology*, 1977, *33*, 472–476.

Margolin, G., and Weiss, R. L. "Communication Training and Assessment: A Case of Behavioral Marital Enrichment." *Behavior Therapy*, 1978, *9*, 508–520.

Marholin, D., II, and Steinman, W. M. "Stimulus Control in the Classroom as a Function of the Behavior Reinforced." *Journal of Applied Behavior Analysis*, 1977, *10*, 465–478.

Marholin, D., II, and Townsend, N. M. "An Experimental Analysis of Side Effects and Response Maintenance of a Modified Overcorrection Procedure." *Behavior Therapy*, 1978, *9*, 383–390.

Mariotto, M. H., and Paul, G. L. "A Multimethod Validation of the Inpatient Multidimensional Psychiatric Scale with Chronically Institutionalized Patients." *Journal of Consulting and Clinical Psychology*, 1974, *42*, 497–508.

Marks, I., and Sartorius, N. "A Contribution to the Measurement of Sexual Attitude." *Journal of Nervous and Mental Diseases*, 1968, *145*, 441–451.

Marlatt, G. A. "Behavioral Assessment of Social Drinking and Alcoholism." In G. A. Marlatt and P. E. Nathan (Eds.), *Behavioral Approaches to the Assessment and Treatment of Alcoholism*. New Brunswick, N.J.: Center of Alcohol Studies, Rutgers University, in press.

Marlowe, R. H., and others. "Severe Classroom Behavior Problems: Teachers or Counselors." *Journal of Applied Behavior Analysis*, 1978, *11*, 53–66.

Marshall, W. L., Presse, L., and Andrews, W. R. "A Self-Administered Program for Public Speaking Anxiety." *Behavior Research and Therapy*, 1977, *14*, 33–39.

Marshall, W. L., Stoian, M., and Andrews, W. R. "Skills Training and Self-Administered Desensitization in the Reduction of Public Speaking Anxiety." *Behavior Research and Therapy*, 1977, *15*, 115–117.

Marshall, W. L., and others. "Flooding Therapy: Effectiveness, Stimulus Characteristics, and the Value of Brief In Vivo Exposure." *Behavior Research and Therapy*, 1977, *15*, 79–87.

Marston, A., and others. "In Vivo Observation of the Eating Behavior of Obese and Nonobese Subjects." *Journal of Consulting and Clinical Psychology*, 1977, *45*, 335–336.

Martin, B. "Brief Family Intervention: Effectiveness and the Importance of Including the Father." *Journal of Consulting and Clinical Psychology*, 1977, *6*, 1002–1010.

Martin, D. N. "Disruptive Behavior and Staff Attitudes at the St. Charles Youth Treatment Center." *Journal of Child Psychology and Psychiatry and Allied Disciplines*, 1977, *18*, 221–228.

Martin, R. B., and Moltmann, M. L. "Extraversion and Neuroticism in Chronic Residents of a State Hospital." *Journal of Behavior Therapy and Experimental Psychiatry*, 1977, *8*, 11–14.

Marziller, J. S., and Winter, K. "Success and Failure in Social Skills Training: Individual Differences." *Behavior Research and Therapy*, 1978, *16*, 67–84.

Mathews, A., and Rezin, V. "Treatment of Dental Fears by Imaginal Flooding and Rehearsal of Coping Behavior." *Behavior Research and Therapy*, 1977, *15*, 321–328.

Mathews, A., and Shaw, P. "Cognitions Related to Anxiety: A Pilot Study of Treatment." *Behavior Research and Therapy*, 1977, *15*, 503–505.

Mathews, R. M., and Fawcett, S. B. "Community Applications of Instructional Technology: Training Low-Income Proctors." *Journal of Applied Behavior Analysis*, 1977, *10*, 747–754.

Matson, J. L., and Ollendick, T. H. "Issues in Toilet Training Normal Children." *Behavior Therapy*, 1977, *8*, 549–553.

Matson, J. L., and Stephens, R. M. "Overcorrection of Aggressive Behavior in a Chronic Psychiatric Patient." *Behavior Modification*, 1977, *1*, 559–564.

Matson, J. L., and Stephens, R. M. "Increasing Appropriate Behavior of Explosive Chronic Psychiatric Patients with a Social Skills Training Package." *Behavior Modification*, 1978, *2*, 61–76.

May, J. R. "A Psychophysiological Study of Self- and Externally Regulated Phobic Thoughts." *Behavior Therapy*, 1977a, *8*, 849–861.

May, J. R. "Psychophysiology of Self-Regulated Phobic Thoughts." *Behavior Therapy*, 1977b, *8*, 150–159.

Mayne, J. G., Weksel, W., and Sholtz, P. N. "Toward Automating the Medical History." *Mayo Clinic Proceedings,* 1968, *43,* 1–25.

Meighan, M. "Communication: Confidence Intervals and Reliability Coefficients." *Journal of Applied Behavior Analysis,* 1977, *10,* 530.

Melahan, C. L., and O'Donnell, C. R. "Norm-Based Behavioral Consulting." *Behavior Modification,* 1978, *2,* 309–338.

Mellstrom, M., Jr., Zuckerman, M., and Cicala, G. A. "General Versus Specific Traits in the Assessment of Anxiety." *Journal of Consulting and Clinical Psychology,* 1978, *46,* 423–431.

Melnick, J., and Stocker, R. B. "An Experimental Analysis of the Behavioral Rehearsal with Feedback Technique in Assertiveness Training." *Behavior Therapy,* 1977, *8,* 222–228.

Meyers, H., Nathan, P. E., and Kopel, S. A. "Effects of a Token Reinforcement System on Journal Reshelving." *Journal of Applied Behavior Analysis,* 1977, *10,* 213–218.

Milby, J. B., and others. "Token Economy Process Variables: Effects of Increasing and Decreasing the Critical Range of Savings." *Behavior Therapy,* 1977, *8,* 137–145.

Miller, A. G. (Ed.). *The Social Psychology of Psychological Research.* New York: Free Press, 1972.

Miller, J. C., and Horvath, S. M. "Impedance Cardiography." *Psychophysiology,* 1978, *15,* 80–91.

Miller, L. C. "Louisville Behavior Checklist for Males 6-12 Years of Age." *Psychological Reports,* 1967, *21,* 885–896.

Miller, L. C. "School Behavior Checklist: An Inventory of Deviant Behavior for Elementary School Children." *Journal of Consulting and Clinical Psychology,* 1972, *38,* 134–144.

Miller, L. C., and others. "Children's Deviant Behavior Within the General Population." *Journal of Consulting and Clinical Psychology,* 1971, *37,* 16–22.

Miller, N. E., and others. "Learned Modification of Autonomic Functions: A Review and Some New Data." Supplement 1 to *Circulation Research,* 1970, *26* and *27,* 3–111.

Miller, W. R. "Behavioral Treatment of Problem Drinkers: A Comparative Outcome Study of Three Controlled Drinking

Therapies." *Journal of Consulting and Clinical Psychology*, 1978, *46*, 74–86.

Milligan, W. L. "Electromechanical Switching of Preamplifier Input Leads: A Method of Increasing the Usefulness of Electrophysiological Recording Instruments." *Psychophysiology*, 1977, *14*, 507–508.

Minde, K. K. "Children in Uganda: Rates of Behavioral Deviations and Psychiatric Disorders in Various School and Clinic Populations." *Journal of Child Psychology and Psychiatry and Allied Disciplines*, 1977, *18*, 23–37.

Minkoff, K., and others. "Hopelessness, Depression, and Attempted Suicide." *American Journal of Psychiatry*, 1973, *130*, 455–459.

Mintz, J. "What is 'Success' in Psychotherapy?" *Journal of Abnormal Psychology*, 1972, *80*, 11–19.

Mintz, J., and others. "Patients', Therapists', and Observers' Views of Psychotherapy: A Rashoman Experience or a Reasonable Consensus." *British Journal of Medical Psychology*, 1973, *46*, 83–89.

Mischel, W. "On the Future of Personality Measurement." *American Psychologist*, 1977, *32*, 246–264.

Mitchell, K. R., and White, R. G. "Behavioral Self-Management: An Application to the Problem of Migraine Headaches." *Behavior Therapy*, 1977a, *8*, 213–221.

Mitchell, K. R., and White, R. G. "Self-Management of Severe Predormital Insomnia." *Journal of Behavior Therapy and Experimental Psychiatry*, 1977b, *8*, 57–63.

Monroe, R. G. "Myocardial Oxygen Consumption During Ventricular Contraction and Relaxation." *Circulation Research*, 1964, *14*, 294.

Montegar, C. A., and others. "Increasing Institutional Staff to Resident Interactions Through In-Service Training and Supervisor Approval." *Behavior Therapy*, 1977, *8*, 533–540.

Mooney, V., Cairns, D., and Robertson, J. "The Psychological Evaluation and Treatment of the Chronic Back Pain Patient—A New Approach." *Official Journal of the Orthopedic Nurses Association*, 1975, *2*, 163–165.

Moore, B. K., and Bailey, J. S. "Social Punishment in the Modification of a Preschool Child's 'Autistic-Like' Behavior with Mother as Therapist." *Journal of Applied Behavior Analysis,* 1973, *6,* 497–507.

Moore, S. F., and Stern, S. L. "A Group Demonstration of the Reinforcement Effects of Social Attention." *Behavior Therapy,* 1978, *9,* 614–617.

Morf, M., Syrotuik, J., and Krznaric, S. "Real Data Simulation of a Two-Stage Statistical Diagnostic System." *Journal of Consulting and Clinical Psychology,* 1977, *45,* 822–828.

Mosher, D. L. "The Development and Multitrait-Multimethod Matrix Analysis of Three Measures of Three Aspects of Guilt." *Journal of Consulting Psychology,* 1966, *30,* 25–29.

Mosher, D. L. "Measurement of Guilt in Females by Self-Report Inventories." *Journal of Consulting and Clinical Psychology,* 1968, *32,* 690–695.

Moskowitz, D. S., Schwarz, J. C., and Corsini, D. A. "Initiating Daycare at Three Years of Age: Effects on Attachment." *Child Development,* 1977, *48,* 1271–1276.

Moss, M. K., and Arend, R. A. "Self-Directed Contact Densensitization." *Journal of Consulting and Clinical Psychology,* 1977, *45,* 730–738.

Mueller, E., and Brenner, J. "The Origins of Social Skills and Interaction Among Play Group Toddlers." *Child Development,* 1977, *48,* 854–861.

Mueller, E., and others. "The Development of Peer Verbal Interaction Among Two-Year-Old Boys." *Child Development,* 1977, *48,* 284–287.

Murdock, J. Y., Garcia, E. E., and Hardman, M. L. "Generalizing Articulation Training with Trainable Mentally Retarded Subjects." *Journal of Applied Behavior Analysis,* 1977, *10,* 717–733.

Murphy, M. J., and Zahm, D. "Effect of Improved Physical and Social Environment on Self-Help and Problem Behaviors of Institutionalized Retarded Males." *Behavior Modification,* 1978, *2,* 193–210.

Murphy, R. J., and Doughty, N. R. "Communication: A Device to Facilitate Correct Head Position." *Journal of Applied Behavior Analysis,* 1977, *10,* 120.

Naggar, C. Z., and others. "Accuracy of the Stroke Index as Determined by the Transthoracic Electrical Impedance Method." *Anesthesiology*, 1975, *42*, 201–205.

Natale, M. "Effects of Induced Elation-Depression on Speech in the Initial Interview." *Journal of Consulting and Clinical Psychology*, 1977, *45*, 45–52.

Neef, N. A., Iwata, B. A., and Page, T. J. "Public Transportation Training: In Vivo Versus Classroom Instruction." *Journal of Applied Behavior Analysis*, 1978, *11*, 331–344.

Nelson, R. O. "Assessment and Therapeutic Functions of Self-Monitoring." In M. Hersen, R. Eisler, and P. Miller (Eds.), *Progress in Behavior Modification*. Vol. 5. New York: Academic Press, 1977.

Nelson, R. O., Hay, L. R., and Hay, W. M. "Comments on Cone's 'The Relevance of Reliability and Validity for Behavioral Assessment.'" *Behavior Therapy*, 1977, *8*, 427–430.

Nelson, R. O., Lipinski, D. P., and Boykin, R. A. "The Effects of Self-Recorders' Training and the Obtrusiveness of the Self-Recording Device on the Accuracy and Reactivity of Self-Monitoring." *Behavior Therapy*, 1978, *9*, 200–208.

Nelson, R. O., and others. "The Reactivity and Accuracy of Teachers' Self-Monitoring of Positive and Negative Classroom Verbalizations." *Behavior Therapy*, 1977, *8*, 972–985.

Nevid, J. S., and Rathus, S. A. "Multivariate and Normative Data Pertaining to the RAS with the College Population." *Behavior Therapy*, 1978, *9*, 675.

Neville, K. G., and Shemberg, K. M. "Establishing the Use of Color-Noun Combinations in the Spontaneous Speech of Disadvantaged Children." *Behavior Therapy*, 1978, *9*, 235–242.

Newmark, C. S., and others. "Comparing Traditional Clinical Procedures with Four Systems to Diagnose Schizophrenia." *Journal of Abnormal Psychology*, 1976, *85*, 66–72.

Newmark, C. S., Woody, G., and Ziff, D. "Understanding and Similarity in Relation to Marital Satisfaction." *Journal of Clinical Psychology*, 1977, *33*, 83–86.

Newsom, C. D., and Simon, K. M. "A Simultaneous Discrimination Procedure for the Measurement of Vision in Nonverbal Children." *Journal of Applied Behavior Analysis*, 1977, *10*, 633–644.

Nicassio, P., and Bootzin, R. "A Comparison of Progressive Relaxation and Autogenic Training as Treatments for Insomnia." *Journal of Abnormal Psychology*, 1974, *83*, 253–260.

Nicassio, P., and Bootzin, R. "Behavioral Treatment of Insomnia." In M. Hersen, R. M. Eisler, and P. M. Miller (Eds.), *Progress in Behavior Modification*. New York: Academic Press, 1978.

Nietzel, M. T., Martorano, R. D., and Melnick, J. "The Effects of Covert Modeling with and Without Reply Training on the Development and Generalization of Assertive Responses." *Behavior Therapy*, 1977, 138–192.

Nisbett, R. E., and Wilson, T. D. "Telling More Than We Can Know: Verbal Reports on Mental Processes." *Psychological Review*, 1977, *84*, 231–259.

Nolan, J. D., and Sandman, C. "'Biosyntonic' Therapy: Modification of an Operant Conditioning Approach to Pedophilia." *Journal of Consulting and Clinical Psychology*, 1978, *46*, 1133–1140.

Noonberg, A., Goldberg, J., and Anderson, D. E. "Digital Skin Temperature Responses to Self-Regulation of Frontal EMG Activity." Abstract of paper presented at 17th annual meeting of Society for Psychophysiological Research. *Psychophysiology*, 1978, *15*, 268–269.

Norton, G. R., and Nielson, W. R. "Headaches: The Importance of Consequent Events." *Behavior Therapy*, 1977, *8*, 504–506.

Novaco, R. W. *Anger Control: The Development and Evaluation of an Experimental Treatment*. Lexington, Mass.: Lexington Books, 1975.

Novaco, R. W. "Stress Inoculation: A Cognitive Therapy for Anger and Its Application to a Case of Depression." *Journal of Consulting and Clinical Psychology*, 1977, *45*, 600–608.

Nucci, L. P., and Turiel, E. "Social Interactions and the Development of Social Concepts in Preschool Children." *Child Development*, 1978, *49*, 400–407.

Nunes, D. L., Murphy, R. J., and Ruprecht, M. L. "Reducing Self-Injurious Behavior of Severely Retarded Individuals Through Withdrawal of Reinforcement Procedures." *Behavior Modification*, 1977, *1*, 499–516.

Nutter, D., and Reid, D. H. "Teaching Retarded Women a Clothing Selection Skill Using Community Norms." *Journal of Applied Behavior Analysis*, 1978, *11*, 475–487.

Obler, M. "Systematic Desensitization in Sexual Disorders." *Journal of Behavior Therapy and Experimental Psychiatry*, 1973, *4*, 93–101.

Obrist, P. A., Langer, A. W., and Grignolo, A. "Pulse Propagation Time: Relationship in Humans to Systolic and Diastolic Blood Pressure, Heart Rate, and Carotid dP/dt with and Without Beat-Adrenergic Blockage." Abstract of paper presented at 16th annual meeting of Society for Psychophysiological Research. *Psychophysiology*, 1977, *14*, 80–81.

Oden, S., and Asher, S. R. "Coaching Children in Social Skills for Friendship Making." *Child Development*, 1977, *48*, 495–506.

O'Farrell, T. J., and Upper, D. "The Interjudge Reliability of Cautela and Upper's Behavioral Coding System." *Journal of Behavior Therapy and Experimental Psychiatry*, 1977, *8*, 39–43.

O'Grady, K. "Comments on 'Some Statistical Methods for the Assessment of Multiple-Outcome Criteria in Behavioral Research.'" *Behavior Therapy*, 1978, *9*, 471–473.

O'Leary, K. D., and Becker, W. C. "Behavior Modification of an Adjustment Class: A Token Reinforcement Program." *Exceptional Children*, 1967, *33*, 637–642.

O'Leary, K. D., and Kent, R. "Behavior Modification for Social Action: Research Tactics and Problems." In L. A. Hamerlynck, L. C. Handy, and E. J. Mash (Eds.), *Behavior Change: Methodology, Concepts, and Practice*. Champaign, Ill.: Research Press, 1973.

O'Leary, K. D., and O'Leary, S. G. (Eds.). *Classroom Management*. Elmsford, N.Y.: Pergamon Press, 1972.

O'Leary, K. D., and Turkewitz, H. "Methodological Errors in Marital and Child Treatment Research." *Journal of Consulting and Clinical Psychology*, 1978, *46*, 747–758.

O'Leary, M. R., and others. "Perceived Locus of Control, Experienced Control, and Depression: A Trait Description of the Learned Helplessness Model of Depression." *Journal of Clinical Psychology*, 1977, *33*, 164–168.

Oliveus, D. "Aggression and Peer Acceptance in Adolescent Boys: Two Short-Term Longitudinal Studies of Ratings." *Child Development*, 1977, *48*, 1301–1313.

Ollendick, T. H., and Nettle, M. D. "An Evaluation of the Relaxation Component of Induced Anxiety." *Behavior Therapy*, 1977, *8*, 561–566.

Oltmans, T. F., Broderick, J. E., and O'Leary, K. D. "Marital Adjustment and the Efficacy of Behavior Therapy with Children." *Journal of Consulting and Clinical Psychology,* 1977, *45,* 724–729.

Palmer, M. H., Lloyd, M. E., and Lloyd, K. E. "An Experimental Analysis of Electricity Conservation Procedures." *Journal of Applied Behavior Analysis,* 1977, *10,* 665–671.

Parsonson, B. S., and Baer, D. M. "Training Generalized Improvisation of Tools by Preschool Children." *Journal of Applied Behavior Analysis,* 1978, *11,* 363–380.

Patel, C. H. "Biofeedback-Aided Relaxation and Meditation in the Management of Hypertension." *Biofeedback and Self-Regulation,* 1977, *2,* 1–41.

Patterson, G. R. "Interventions for Boys with Conduct Problems: Multiple Settings, Treatments, and Criteria." *Journal of Consulting and Clinical Psychology,* 1974, *42,* 471–481.

Patterson, G. R. "Accelerating Stimuli for Two Classes of Coercive Behaviors." *Journal of Abnormal Child Psychology,* 1977a, *5,* 335–350.

Patterson, G. R. "Naturalistic Observation in Clinical Assessment." *Journal of Abnormal Child Psychology,* 1977b, *5,* 309–322.

Patterson, G. R., and others. *Manual for Coding of Family Interactions* (rev. ed.). (NAPS document 01234.) New York: Microfiche Publications, 1969.

Patterson, G. R., and others. *A Social Learning Approach to Family Intervention.* Vol. 1.: *Families with Aggressive Children.* Eugene, Ore.: Castalia, 1975.

Paul, G. L. *Insight Versus Desensitization in Psychotherapy.* Stanford, Calif.: Stanford University Press, 1966.

Paulsen, K., and others. "A Self-Control Approach to Inefficient Spending." *Journal of Consulting and Clinical Psychology,* 1977, *45,* 433–435.

Peacock, R., Lyman, R. D., and Rickard, C. "Correspondence Between Self-Report and Observer-Report as a Function of Task Difficulty." *Behavior Therapy,* 1978, *9,* 578–583.

Pearne, D. H., Zigelbaum, S. D., and Peyser, W. P. "Biofeedback-Assisted EMG Relaxation for Urinary Retention and Incontinence." *Biofeedback and Self-Regulation,* 1977, *2,* 213–217.

Peck, C. L. "Desensitization for the Treatment of Fear in the

High-Level Adult Retardate." *Behavior Research and Therapy*, 1977, *15*, 137–148.

Peed, S., Roberts, M., and Forehand, R. "Evaluation of the Effectiveness of a Standardized Parent Training Program in Altering the Interaction of Mothers and Their Noncompliant Children." *Behavior Modification*, 1977, *1*, 323–350.

Pelham, W. E. "Withdrawal of a Stimulant Drug and Concurrent Behavioral Intervention in the Treatment of a Hyperactive Child." *Behavior Therapy*, 1977, *8*, 473–479.

Perri, M. G., Richards, C. S., and Schultheis, K. R. "Behavioral Self-Control and Smoking Reduction: A Study of Self-Initiated Attempts to Reduce Smoking." *Behavior Therapy*, 1977, *8*, 360–365.

Peterson, P. R., and Quay, H. C. *Factor-Analyzed Problem Checklist.* Urbana: Children's Research Center, University of Illinois, 1967.

Peterson, R. F., and others. "The Effects of Furniture Arrangements on the Behavior of Geriatric Patients." *Behavior Therapy*, 1977, *8*, 464–467.

Philip, A. E. "Cross-Cultural Study of the Factorial Dimensions of the NOSIE." *Journal of Clinical Psychology*, 1977, *33*, 467–468.

Philips, C. "The Modification of Tension Headache Pain Using EMG Biofeedback." *Behavior Research and Therapy*, 1977, *15*, 119–129.

Philips, J. P. N. "A Note on the Scoring of the Sexual Orientation Method." *Behavior Research and Therapy*, 1968, *6*, 121–123.

Philips, J. P. N. "A Simple Method of Obtaining a Ratio Scaling of a Hierarchy." *Behavior Research and Therapy*, 1977, *15*, 285–295.

Philips, L, and Draguns, J. G. "Classification of the Behavior Disorders." *Annual Review of Psychology*, 1971, *22*, 447–482.

Piersel, W. C., Brody, G. H., and Kratochwill, T. R. "A Further Examination of Motivational Influences on Disadvantaged Minority Group Children's Intelligence Test Performance." *Child Development*, 1977, *48*, 1142–1145.

Pipp, S. L., and Gaith, M. M. "Infant Visual Scanning of Two- and Three-Dimensional Forms." *Child Development*, 1977, *48*, 1640–1644.

Pishkin, V., and Thorne, F. C. "A Factorial Structure of the Dimensions of Femininity in Alcoholic, Schizophrenic, and Normal Populations." *Journal of Clinical Psychology*, 1977, *33*, 10–17.

Plummer, S., Baer, D. M., and Leblanc, J. M. "Functional Considerations in the Use of Procedural Time-Out and an Effective Alternative." *Journal of Applied Behavior Analysis,* 1977, *10,* 689–705.

Polirstok, S. R., and Greer, R. D. "Remediation of Mutually Aversive Interactions Between a Problem Student and Four Teachers by Training the Student in Reinforcement Techniques." *Journal of Applied Behavior Analysis,* 1977, *10,* 707–716.

Pollak, M. H. "Relationship Between Ambulatory Blood Pressure in Unrestricted Humans and Self-Ratings of Mood and Behavior." Abstract of paper presented at 17th annual meeting of Society for Psychophysiological Research. *Psychophysiology,* 1978, *15,* 264–265.

Pollak, M. H., Koss, M. C., and Zeiner, A. R. "The Relationship of Beat-by-Beat Changes in Arterial Pulse Propagation Time and Arterial BP in Anesthetized Cats." Abstract of paper presented at 16th annual meeting of Society for Psychophysiological Research. *Psychophysiology,* 1977, *14,* 104.

Pope, B., and others. "Anxiety and Depression in Speech." *Journal of Consulting and Clinical Psychology,* 1970, *35,* 128–133.

Pope, B., and others. "Some Effects of Discrepant Role Expectations on Interviewee Verbal Behavior in the Initial Interview." *Journal of Consulting and Clinical Psychology,* 1972, *39,* 210–215.

Porter, R. B., and Cattell, R. B. *Handbook for the Children's Personality Questionnaire (The CPQ).* Champaign, Ill.: Institute for Personality and Ability Testing, 1972.

Posavac, E. J., and others. "Further Factor-Analytic Investigation of the Thorne Femininity Study." *Journal of Clinical Psychology,* 1977, *33,* 24–31.

Powell, J., Martindale, A., and Kulp, S. "An Evaluation of Time-Sampling Measures of Behavior." *Journal of Applied Behavior Analysis,* 1975, *8,* 463–469.

Powell, J., and Rockinson, R. "On the Inability of Interval Time Sampling to Reflect Frequency-of-Occurrence Data." *Journal of Applied Behavior Analysis,* 1978, *11,* 531–532.

Powell, J., and others. "Taking a Closer Look: Time Sampling and Measurement Error." *Journal of Applied Behavior Analysis,* 1977, *10,* 325–332.

Prigatano, G. P., and Johnson, H. J. "Autonomic Nervous System

Changes Associated with a Spider-Phobic Reaction." *Journal of Abnormal Psychology*, 1974, *83*, 169–177.

Prinz, R. J., and Kent, R. N. "Recording Parent-Adolescent Interactions Without the Use of Frequency or Interval-by-Interval Coding." *Behavior Therapy*, 1978, *9*, 602–604.

Putre, W., and others. "An Effectiveness Study of a Relaxation Training Tape with Hyperactive Children." *Behavior Therapy*, 1977, *8*, 355–359.

Quay, H. C. "Patterns of Aggression, Withdrawal, and Immaturity." In H. C. Quay and J. S. Werry (Eds.), *Psychopathological Disorders of Children*. New York: Wiley, 1972.

Quay, H. C. "Measuring Dimensions of Deviant Behavior: The Behavior Problem Checklist." *Journal of Abnormal Child Psychology*, 1977, *5*, 277–288.

Quay, H. C., and Peterson, D. R. *Manual for the Behavior Problem Checklist*. Champaign: University of Illinois Child Research Center, 1967.

Quay, H. C., and Peterson, D. R. *The Behavior Problem Checklist Manual*. Unpublished paper, University of Miami, 1975.

Quereshi, M. Y. "Psychosocial Correlates of Obesity Control." *Journal of Clinical Psychology*, 1977, *33*, 343–350.

Quilitch, H. R., Christophersen, E. R., and Risley, T. R. "The Evaluation of Children's Play Materials." *Journal of Applied Behavior Analysis*, 1977, *10*, 501–502.

Quillin, J., Besing, S., and Dinning, D. "Standardization of the Rathus Assertiveness Schedule." *Journal of Clinical Psychology*, 1977, *33*, 418–422.

Rachman, S. "The Passing of the Two-Stage Theory of Fear and Avoidance: Fresh Possibilities." *Behavior Research and Therapy*, 1976, *14*, 125–131.

Rathus, S. A. "A 30-Item Schedule for Assessing Assertive Behavior." *Behavior Therapy*, 1973, *4*, 398–406.

Rathus, S. A., and Nevid, J. S. "Concurrent Validity of the 30-Item Assertiveness Schedule with a Psychiatric Population." *Behavior Therapy*, 1977, *8*, 393–397.

Redwood, D. R., and others. "Importance of the Design of an Exercise Protocol in the Evaluation of Patients with Angina Pectoris." *Circulation*, 1971, *43*, 618–628.

Reid, D. H., and Hurlbut, B. "Teaching Nonvocal Communication

Skills to Multihandicapped Retarded Adults." *Journal of Applied Behavior Analysis,* 1977, *10,* 591–603.

Reid, J. B. (Ed.). *A Social Learning Approach to the Treatment and Study of Families: II. Observation Manual and Observer Training Procedures.* Eugene, Ore.: Castalia, 1977.

Reidy, T. J. "The Aggressive Characteristics of Abused and Neglected Children." *Journal of Clinical Psychology,* 1977, *33,* 1140–1145.

Reisinger, J. J., and Ora, J. P. "Parent-Child Clinic and Home Interaction During Toddler Management Training." *Behavior Therapy,* 1977, *8,* 771–786.

Rekers, G. A. "Stimulus Control over Sex-Typed Play in Cross-Gender-Identified Boys." *Journal of Experimental Child Psychology,* 1975, *20,* 136–148.

Rekers, G. A. "Assessment and Treatment of Childhood Gender Problems." In B. Lahey and A. Kazdin (Eds.), *Advances in Clinical Child Psychology.* New York: Plenum, 1977a.

Rekers, G. A. "Atypical Gender Development and Psychosocial Adjustment." *Journal of Applied Behavior Analysis,* 1977b, *10,* 559–571.

Rekers, G. A., Amaro-Plotkin, H. D., and Low, B. P. "Sex-Typed Mannerisms in Normal Boys and Girls as a Function of Sex and Age." *Child Development,* 1977, *48,* 275–278.

Rekers, G. A., and Varni, J. W. "Self-Monitoring and Self-Reinforcement Processes in a Pretranssexual Boy." *Behavior Research and Therapy,* 1977, *15,* 177–180.

Rekers, G. A., and others. "Assessment of Childhood Gender Behavior Change." *Journal of Child Psychology and Psychiatry and Allied Disciplines,* 1977, *18,* 53–65.

Resick, P. A., Forehand, R., and McWhorter, A. "The Effect of Parent Treatment with One Child on an Untreated Sibling." *Behavior Therapy,* 1976, *7,* 544–548.

Resick, P. A., and others. "Systematic Slowed Speech: A New Treatment for Stuttering." *Behavior Research and Therapy,* 1978, *16,* 161–167.

Reynolds, B. S. "Psychological Treatment Models and Outcome Results for Erectile Dysfunction: A Critical Review." *Psychological Bulletin,* 1977, *84,* 1218–1238.

Ribordy, S. C., and Denny, D. R. "The Behavioral Treatment of

Insomnia: An Alternative to Drug Therapy." *Behavior Research and Therapy*, 1977, *15*, 39–50.

Richards, C. S., Anderson, D. C., and Baker, R. B. "The Role of Information Feedback in the Relative Reactivity of Self-Monitoring and External Observations." *Behavior Therapy*, 1978, *9*, 687.

Richardson, F. C., and Suinn, R. M. "The Mathematics Anxiety Rating Scale: Normative Data." *Journal of Counseling Psychology*, 1973, *80*, 252–283.

Richardson, F. C., and Tasto, D. L. "Development of Factor Analysis of a Social Anxiety Inventory." *Behavior Therapy*, 1969, *1*, 69–73.

Richardson, F. C., and others. "Factor Analysis of the Test Anxiety Scale and Evidence Concerning the Components of Test Anxiety." *Journal of Consulting and Clinical Psychology*, 1977, *45*, 704–705.

Rimm, D. C., and others. "An Exploratory Investigation of the Origin and Maintenance of Phobias." *Behavior Research and Therapy*, 1977, *15*, 231–238.

Rincover, A., and Koegel, R. L. "Classroom Treatment of Autistic Children: II. Individualized Instruction in a Group." *Journal of Abnormal Child Psychology*, 1977, *5*, 113–126.

Rippere, V. "Antidepressive Behavior: A Preliminary Report." *Behavior Research and Therapy*, 1976, *14*, 289–299.

Robinson, B. F. "Relation of Heart Rate and Systolic Blood Pressure to the Onset of Pain in Angina Pectoris." *Circulation*, 1967, *35*, 1073–1083.

Rogers-Warren, A., Warren, S. F., and Baer, D. M. "A Component Analysis: Modeling, Self-Reporting, and Reinforcement of Self-Reporting in the Development of Sharing." *Behavior Modification*, 1977, *1*, 307–322.

Rollings, J. P., Baumeister, A. A., and Baumeister, A. A. "The Use of Overcorrection Procedures to Eliminate the Stereotyped Behaviors of Retarded Individuals: An Analysis of Collateral Behaviors and Generalization of Suppressive Effects." *Behavior Modification*, 1977, *1*, 29–46.

Romanczyk, R. G. "Self-Monitoring in the Treatment of Obesity: Parameters of Reactivity." *Behavior Therapy*, 1974, *5*, 531–540.

Romanczyk, R. G. "Intermittent Punishment of Self-Stimulation: Effectiveness During Application and Extinction." *Journal of Consulting and Clinical Psychology,* 1977, *45,* 53–60.

Romanczyk, R. G., and others. "Measuring Circadian Cycles: A Simple Temperature-Recording Preparation." *Behavior Research Methods and Instrumentation,* 1977, *9,* 393–394.

Roper, R., and Hinde, R. A. "Social Behavior in a Play Group: Consistency and Complexity." *Child Development,* 1978, *49,* 570–579.

Rose, T. L. "The Functional Relationship Between Artificial Food Colors and Hyperactivity." *Journal of Applied Behavior Analysis,* 1978, *11,* 439–446.

Rosen, A. C., Rekers, G. A., and Friar, L. R. "Theoretical and Diagnostic Issues in Child Gender Disturbances." *Journal of Sex Research,* in press.

Rosen, G. M., Glasgow, R. E., and Barrera, M., Jr. "A Controlled Study to Assess the Clinical Efficacy of Totally Self-Administered Systematic Desensitization." *Journal of Consulting and Clinical Psychology,* 1976, *44,* 208–217.

Rosen, G. M., Glasgow, R. E., and Barrera, J. M., Jr. "A Two-Year Follow-Up on Systematic Desensitization with Data Pertaining to the External Validity of Laboratory Fear Assessment." *Journal of Consulting and Clinical Psychology,* 1977, *45,* 1188–1189.

Rosen, R. C., and Kopel, S. A. "Penile Plethysmography and Biofeedback in the Treatment of a Transvestite-Exhibitionist." *Journal of Consulting and Clinical Psychology,* 1977, *45,* 908–916.

Rosenthal, T. L., Hung, J. H., and Kelley, J. E. "Therapeutic Social Influence: Sternly Strike While the Iron is Hot." *Behavior Research and Therapy,* 1977, *15,* 253–259.

Ross, A. O. *Psychological Disorders of Children: A Behavioral Approach to Theory, Research, and Therapy.* New York: McGraw-Hill, 1974.

Ross, A. O., Lacey, H. M., and Parton, D. A. "The Development of a Behavior Checklist for Boys." *Child Development,* 1965, *36,* 1013–1027.

Rotter, J. B. "Generalized Expectancies for Internal Versus External Control of Reinforcement." *Psychological Monograph,* 1966, *80* (entire issue).

Royce, W. S., and Arkowitz, H. "Multimodal Evaluation of Practive

Interactions as Treatment for Social Isolation." *Journal of Consulting and Clinical Psychology*, 1978, *46*, 239–245.

Rozensky, R. H. "The Effect of Timing of Self-Monitoring Behavior on Reducing Cigarette Consumption." *Journal of Behavior Therapy and Experimental Psychiatry*, 1974, *5*, 301–303.

Rozensky, R. H., and Rehm, L. P. "Depression and Self-Reinforcement Behavior in Hospitalized Patients." *Journal Behavior Therapy and Experimental Psychiatry*, 1977, *8*, 35–38.

Rubin, B., and others. "Factor Analysis of a Fear Schedule." *Behavior Research and Therapy*, 1968, *6*, 65–75.

Rubin, S. E., and others. "Factor Analysis of the 122-Item Fear Survey Schedule." *Behavior Research and Therapy*, 1969, *7*, 381–386.

Rudestam, K. E. "Physician and Psychological Responses to Suicide in the Family." *Journal of Consulting and Clinical Psychology*, 1977, *45*, 162–170.

Rudestam, K. E., and Bedrosian, R. "An Investigation of the Effectiveness of Desensitization and Flooding with Two Types of Phobias." *Behavior Research and Therapy*, 1977, *15*, 23–30.

Rugh, J. D., and Schwitzgebel, R. L. "Instrumentation for Behavioral Assessment." In A. R. Ciminero, K. S. Calhoun, and H. E. Adams (Eds.), *Handbook of Behavioral Assessment*. New York: Wiley-Interscience, 1977a.

Rugh, J. D., and Schwitzgebel, R. L. "Variability in Commercial Electromyographic Biofeedback Devices." *Behavior Research Methods and Instruments*, 1977b, *9*, 281–285.

Runyan, W. M. "How Should Treatment Recommendations Be Made? Three Studies in the Logical and Empirical Bases of Clinical Decision Making." *Journal of Consulting and Clinical Psychology*, 1977, *45*, 552–558.

Russell, A., and Winkler, R. "Evaluation of Assertive Training and Homosexual Guidance Service Groups to Improve Homosexual Functioning." *Journal of Consulting and Clinical Psychology*, 1977, *45*, 1–13.

Russell, M. B., and Bernal, M. E. "Temporal and Climatic Variables in Naturalistic Observation." *Journal of Applied Behavior Analysis*, 1977, *10*, 399–405.

Russo, D. C., and Koegel, R. L. "A Method for Integrating an Autistic Child into a Normal Public School Classroom." *Journal of Applied Behavior Analysis*, 1977, *10*, 579–590.

Rutter, M. "A Children's Behavior Questionnaire for Completion by Teachers." *Journal of Child Psychology and Psychiatry and Allied Disciplines*, 1967, *8*, 1–11.

Ryan, V. L., Krall, C. A., and Hodges, W. F. "Self-Concept Change in Behavior Modification." *Journal of Consulting and Clinical Psychology*, 1976, *44*, 638–645.

Sacks, S., and De Leon, G. "Training the Disturbed Enuretic." *Behavior Research and Therapy*, 1978, *16*, 296–299.

Sarason, I. G. "Experimental Approaches to Test Anxiety: Attention and the Uses of Information." In C. D. Spielberger (Ed.), *Anxiety: Current Trends in Theory and Research*. Vol. 2. New York: Academic Press, 1972.

Sartory, G., Rachman, S., and Grey, S. "An Investigation of the Relation Between Reported Fear and Heart Rate." *Behavior Research and Therapy*, 1977, *15*, 435–538.

Saudargas, R. S., Madsen, C. H., Jr., and Scott, J. W. "Differential Effects of Fixed- and Variable-Time Feedback on Production Rates of Elementary School Children." *Journal of Applied Behavior Analysis*, 1977, *10*, 673–678.

Sawin, D. B., Langlois, J. H., and Leitner, E. F. "What Do You Do After You Say Hello? Observing, Coding, and Analyzing Parent-Infant Interactions." *Behavior Research Methods and Instrumentation*, 1977, *9*, 425–428.

Schaefer, E. S. "Children's Reports of Parental Behavior: An Inventory." *Child Development*, 1965, *36*, 413–424.

Schiederer, E. G. "Effects of Instructions and Modeling in Producing Self-Disclosure in the Initial Clinical Interview." *Journal of Consulting and Clinical Psychology*, 1977, *45*, 378–384.

Schleifer, M., and others. "Hyperactivity in Preschoolers and the Effect of Methylphenidate." *American Journal of Orthopsychiatry*, 1975, *45*, 38–50.

Schnelle, J. F. "A Brief Report on Invalidity of Parent Evaluations of Behavior Change." *Journal of Applied Behavior Analysis*, 1974, *7*, 341–343.

Schnelle, J. F., and others. "Patrol Evaluation Research: A Multiple-Baseline Analysis of Saturation Police Patrolling During Day and Night Hours." *Journal of Applied Behavior Analysis,* 1977, *10,* 33–40.

Schrader, S. L., Craighead, W. E., and Schrader, R. M. "Reinforcement Patterns in Depression." *Behavior Therapy,* 1978, *9,* 1–14.

Schroeder, H., and Craine, L. "Relationships Among Measures of Fear and Anxiety for Snake Phobics." *Journal of Consulting and Clinical Psychology,* 1971, *36,* 443.

Schroeder, H. E., and Rich, A. R. "The Process of Fear Reduction Through Systematic Desensitization." *Journal of Consulting and Clinical Psychology,* 1976, *44,* 191–199.

Schroeder, S. R., and others. "EMG Feedback and the Contingent Restraint of Self-Injurious Behavior Among the Severely Retarded: Two Case Illustrations." *Behavior Therapy,* 1977, *8,* 738–741.

Schulman, J. L., Stevens, T. M. and Kupst, M. J. "The Biomotometer: A New Device for the Measurement and Remediation of Hyperactivity." *Child Development,* 1977, *48,* 1152–1154.

Schulman, J. L., and others. "Modification of Activity Level Through Biofeedback and Operant Conditioning." *Journal of Applied Behavior Analysis,* 1978, *11,* 145–152.

Schumaker, J. B., Hovell, M. F., and Sherman, J. A. "A Home-Based School Achievement Program." Lawrence, Kans.: H & H Enterprises, 1977a.

Schumaker, J. B., Hovell, M. F., and Sherman, J. A. "An Analysis of Daily Report Cards and Parent-Managed Privileges in the Improvement of Adolescents' Classroom Performance." *Journal of Applied Behavior Analysis,* 1977b, *10,* 449–464.

Schwartz, G. E. "Self-Regulation of Response Patterning: Implications for Psychophysiological Research and Therapy." *Biofeedback and Self-Regulation,* 1976, *1,* 7–30.

Schwartz, G. E. "Biofeedback and Patterning of Autonomic and Central Processes: CNS-Cardiovascular Interactions." In G. E. Schwartz and J. Beatty (Eds.), *Biofeedback: Theory and Research.* New York: Academic Press, 1977.

Schwartz, G. J. "College Students as Contingency Managers for

Adolescents in a Program to Develop Reading Skills." *Journal of Applied Behavior Analysis*, 1977, *10*, 645–655.

Serbin, L. A., Tonick, I. J., and Sternglanz, S. H. "Shaping Cooperative Cross-Sex Play." *Child Development*, 1977, *48*, 924–929.

Serralde de Scholz, H. C., and McDougall, D. "Comparison of Potential Reinforcer Ratings Between Slow Learners and Regular Students." *Behavior Therapy*, 1978. *9*, 60–64.

Sersen, E. A., Clausen, J., and Lidsky, A. "Autonomic Specificity and Stereotopy Revisited." *Psychophysiology*, 1978, *15*, 60–67.

Shafto, F., and Sulzbacher, S. "Comparing Treatment Tactics with a Hyperactive Preschool Child: Stimulant Medication and Programmed Teacher Intervention." *Journal of Applied Behavior Analysis*, 1977, *10*, 13–20.

Shannon, B. J., Goldman, M. S., and Lee, R. M. "Biofeedback Training of Blood Pressure: A Comparison of Three Feedback Techniques." *Psychophysiology*, 1978, *15*, 53–59.

Shaw, B. "Comparison of Cognitive Therapy and Behavior Therapy in the Treatment of Depression." *Journal of Consulting and Clinical Psychology*, 1977, *45*, 543–551.

Shedivy, D. I., and Kleinman, K. M. "Lack of Correlation Between Frontalis EMG and Either Neck EMG or Verbal Ratings of Tension." *Psychophysiology*, 1977, *14*, 182–186.

Sherman, T. M., and Cormier, W. H. "An Investigation of the Influence of Student Behavior on Teacher Behavior." *Journal of Applied Behavior Analysis*, 1974, *7*, 11–21.

Shure, G. H., and Meeker, R. J. "A Minicomputer System for Multiperson Computer-Assisted Telephone Interviewing." *Behavior Research Methods and Instrumentation*, 1978, *10*, 196–202.

Siegel, R. K. "Stimulus Selection and Tracking During Urination: Autoshaping Directed Behavior with Toilet Targets." *Journal of Applied Behavior Analysis*, 1977, *10*, 255–265.

Silvestri, R. "Implosive Therapy Treatment of Emotionally Disturbed Retardates." *Journal of Consulting and Clinical Psychology*, 1977, *45*, 14–22.

Simonton, D. K. "Cross-Sectional Time-Series Experiments: Some Suggested Statistical Analyses." *Psychological Bulletin*, 1977, *84*, 489–502.

Sintchak, G., and Geer, J. "A Vaginal Plethysmography System." *Psychophysiology*, 1975, *12*, 113–115.

Skarin, K. "Cognitive and Contextual Determinants of Stranger Fears in Six- and Eleven-Month-Old Infants." *Child Development*, 1977, *48*, 537–544.

Slack, W. V., and Van Cura, L. J. "Patient Reaction to Computer-Based Medical Interviewing." *Computers and Biomedical Research*, 1968, *1*, 527–531.

Sleator, E. K., and von Neumann, A. W. "Methylphenidate in the Treatment of Hyperkinetic Children." *Clinical Pediatrics*, 1974, *13*, 19–24.

Sluckin, A. M., and Smith, P. K. "Two Approaches to the Concept of Dominance in Preschool Children." *Child Development*, 1977, *48*, 917–923.

Slutsky, J. M., and Allen, G. J. "Influence of Contextual Cues on the Efficacy of Desensitization and a Credible Placebo in Alleviating Public Speaking Anxiety." *Journal of Consulting and Clinical Psychology*, 1978, *46*, 119–125.

Smith, G. P., and Coleman, R. E. "Processes Underlying Generalization Through Participant Modeling with Self-Directed Practice." *Behavior Research and Therapy*, 1977, *15*, 204–206.

Smith, P. K., and Daglish, L. "Sex Differences in Parent and Infant Behavior in the Home." *Child Development*, 1977, *48*, 1250–1254.

Smith, R. E., Smoll, F. L., and Hunt, E. B. "Training Manual for the Coaching Behavior Assessment System (CBAS)." *Catalog of Selected Documents in Psychology*, 1977, *7*, 2.

Snyder, A. L., and Deffenbacher, J. L. "Comparison of Relaxation as Self-Control and Systematic Desensitization in the Treatment of Test Anxiety." *Journal of Consulting and Clinical Psychology*, 1977, *45*, 1202–1203.

Snyder, J. J. "Reinforcement Analysis of Interaction in Problem and Nonproblem Families." *Journal of Abnormal Psychology*, 1977, *86*, 528–535.

Sobell, L. C., and Sobell, M. B. "Validity of Self-Reports in Three Populations of Alcoholics." *Journal of Consulting and Clinical Psychology*, 1978, *46*, 901–907.

Solnick, J. V., Rincover, A., and Peterson, C. R. "Some Determinants of the Reinforcing and Punishing Effects of Time-Out." *Journal of Applied Behavior Analysis,* 1977, *10,* 415–424.

Spaiser, L. H. "An Infrared Photoplethysmograph Coupler." *Psychophysiology,* 1977, *14,* 75–76.

Spanier, G. B. "Measuring Dyadic Adjustment: New Scales for Assessing the Quality of Marriage and Similar Dyads." *Journal of Marriage and the Family,* 1976, *38,* 15–28.

Spielberger, C. D., Gorsuch, R. L., and Lushene, R. E. *STAI Manual.* Palo Alto, Calif.: Consulting Psychologists Press, 1970.

Spilton, D., and Lee, L. C. "Some Determinants of Effective Communication in Four-Year-Olds." *Child Development,* 1977, *48,* 968–977.

Spitzer, R. L., and Fleiss, J. L. "A Reanalysis of the Reliability of Psychiatric Diagnosis." *British Journal of Psychiatry,* 1974, *125,* 341–347.

Spring, C., Greenberg, L. M., and Yellin, A. M. "Agreement of Mothers' and Teachers' Hyperactivity Ratings with Scores on Drug-Sensitive Psychological Tests." *Journal of Abnormal Child Psychology,* 1977, *5,* 199–204.

Spring, C., and others. "Validity and Norms of a Hyperactivity Rating Scale." *Journal of Special Education,* in press.

Steffen, J. J., and Myszak, K. A. "Influence of Pretherapy Induction upon the Outcome of a Self-Control Weight Reduction Program." *Behavior Therapy,* 1978, *9,* 404–409.

Stephenson, G. R., and Roberts, T. W. "The SSR System 7: A General Encoding System with Computerized Transcription." *Behavior Research Methods and Instrumentation,* 1977, *9,* 434–441.

Steptoe, A. "Blood Pressure Control: A Comparison of Feedback and Instructions Using Pulse-Wave Velocity Measurements." *Psychophysiology,* 1976, *13,* 528–535.

Steptoe, A. "Voluntary Blood Pressure Reductions Measured with Pulse Transit Time: Training Conditions and Reactions to Mental Work." *Psychophysiology,* 1977, *14,* 492–498.

Stern, J. A., and Walrath, L. C. "Orienting Responses and Conditioning of Electrodermal Responses." *Psychophysiology,* 1977, *14,* 334–342.

Stimbert, V. E., Minor, J. W., and McCoy, J. F. "Intensive Feeding

Training with Retarded Children." *Behavior Modification,* 1977, *1,* 517–530.

Stokes, T. F., and Fawcett, S. B. "Evaluating Municipal Policy: An Analysis of a Refuse-Packaging Program." *Journal of Applied Behavior Analysis,* 1977, *10,* 391–398.

Strain, P. S. "An Experimental Analysis of Peer Social Initiations on the Behavior of Withdrawn Preschool Children: Some Training and Generalization Effects." *Journal of Abnormal Child Psychology,* 1977, *5,* 445–456.

Strain, P. S., and Ezzell, D. "The Sequence and Distribution of Behavioral Disordered Adolescents' Disruptive/Inappropriate Behaviors: An Observational Study in a Residential Setting." *Behavior Modification,* 1978, *2,* 403–425.

Strain, P. S., Shores, R. E., and Kerr, M. M. "An Experimental Analysis of 'Spillover' Effects on the Social Interaction of Behaviorally Handicapped Preschool Children." *Journal of Applied Behavior Analysis,* 1976, *9,* 31–40.

Strain, P. S., Shores, R. E., and Timm, M. A. "Effects of Peer Social Initiations on the Behavior of Withdrawn Preschool Children." *Journal of Applied Behavior Analysis,* 1977, *10,* 289–298.

Strasburger, E. I., and Jackson, D. N. "Improving Accuracy in a Clinical Judgmental Task." *Journal of Consulting and Clinical Psychology,* 1977, *45,* 303–309.

Stuart, R. B. *"Trick or Treatment: How and When Psychotherapy Fails."* Champaign, Ill.: Research Press, 1970.

Stuart, R. B., and Stuart, F., *Marital Precounseling Inventory.* Champaign, Ill.: Research Press, 1972.

Stunkard, A., and Kaplan, D. "Eating in Public Places: A Review of Reports of the Direct Observation of Eating Behavior." *International Journal of Obesity,* 1977, *1,* 89–101.

Sturgis, E. T., Tollison, C. D., and Adams, H. E. "Modification of Combined Migraine-Muscle Contraction Headaches Using BVP and EMG Feedback." *Journal of Applied Behavior Analysis,* 1978, *11,* 215–223.

Suarez, Y., Crowe, M. J., and Adams, H. E. "Depression: Avoidance Learning and Physiological Correlates in Clinical and Analogue Populations." *Behavior Research and Therapy,* 1978, *16,* 21–31.

Suedfeld, P., and Hare, R. D. "Sensory Deprivation in the Treatment of Snake Phobia: Behavioral, Self-Report, and Physiological Effects." *Behavior Therapy*, 1977, *8*, 240–250.

Suinn, R. "The STABS, A Measure of Test Anxiety for Behavior Therapy: Normative Data." *Behavior Research and Therapy*, 1969, *7*, 335–339.

Sullivan, G. J., and Denny, D. R. "Expectancy and Phobic Level: Effects on Desensitization." *Journal of Consulting and Clinical Psychology*, 1977, *45*, 763–771.

Surwit, R. S., Shapiro, D., and Good, M. I. "Comparison of Cardiovascular Biofeedback, Neuromuscular Biofeedback, and Meditation in the Treatment of Borderline Essential Hypertension." *Journal of Consulting and Clinical Psychology*, 1978, *46*, 252–263.

Switzer, E. B., Deal, T. E., and Bailey, J. S. "The Reduction of Stealing in Second Graders Using a Group Contingency." *Journal of Applied Behavior Analysis*, 1977, *10*, 267–272.

Sykes, R. E. "Techniques of Data Collection and Reduction in Systematic Field Observation." *Behavior Research Methods and Instrumentation*, 1977, *9*, 407–417.

Tahmoush, A. J., and Sullivan, M. C. "A Physiological Basis for the Photoplethysmograph Signal." Abstract of paper presented at 16th annual meeting of Society for Psychophysiological Research." *Psychophysiology*, 1977, *14*, 110.

Tahmoush, A. J., and others. "Characteristics of a Light-Emitting Diode — Transistor Photoplethysmograph." *Psychophysiology*, 1976, *13*, 357–362.

Taplin, P. S., and Reid, J. B. "Changes in Parent Consequences as a Function of Family Intervention." *Journal of Consulting and Clinical Psychology*, 1977, *45*, 973–981.

Teasdale, J. D., and Bancroft, J. "Manipulation of Thought Content as a Determinant of Mood and Corrugator Electromyographic Activity in Depressed Patients." *Journal of Abnormal Psychology*, 1977, *86*, 235–241.

Teasdale, J. D., and Rezin, V. "Effect of Thought-Stopping on Thoughts, Mood, and Corrugator EMG in Depressed Patients." *Behavior Research and Therapy*, 1978, *16*, 97–102.

Thomas, J. D., and others. "Natural Rates of Teacher Approval and Disapproval in Grade-7 Classrooms." *Journal of Applied Behavior Analysis*, 1978, *11*, 91–94.

Thomas, M. R., and Rapp, M. S. "Physiological, Behavioral, and Cognitive Changes Resulting from Flooding in a Monosymptomatic Phobia." *Behavior Research and Therapy*, 1977, *15*, 304–306.

Thompson, M. S., and Conrad, P. L. "Multifaceted Behavioral Treatment of Drug Dependence: A Case Study." *Behavior Therapy*, 1977, *8*, 731–737.

Thorndike, R. M., and Kleinknecht, R. A. "Reliability of Homogeneous Scales of Reinforcers: A Cluster Analysis of the Reinforcement Survey Schedule." *Behavior Therapy*, 1974, *5*, 58–63.

Thorne, F. C. *The Femininity Study*. Brandon, Vt.: Clinical Psychology, 1965.

Thorne, F. C. "The Sex Inventory." *Journal of Clinical Psychology*, 1966, *22*, 367–374.

Thorne, F. C. "The Measurement of Femininity." *Journal of Clinical Psychology*, 1977, *33*, 5–10.

Thorne, F. C., and Pishkin, V. "Comparative Study of the Factorial Composition of Femininity in Alcoholic, Schizophrenic, and Normal Populations." *Journal of Clinical Psychology*, 1977, *33*, 18–23.

Tobias, L. L., and MacDonald, M. L. "Internal Locus of Control and Weight Loss: An Insufficient Condition." *Journal of Consulting and Clinical Psychology*, 1977, *45*, 647–653.

Tonick, I., Friehling, J., and Warhit, J. "Classroom Observation Code." Unpublished paper, Point of Woods Laboratory School, State University of New York at Stony Brook, 1973.

Torgerson, L. "Datamyte 900." *Behavior Research Methods and Instrumentation*, 1977, *9*, 405–406.

Trap, J. J., and others. "The Effects of Feedback and Consequences on Transitional Cursive Letter Formation." *Journal of Applied Behavior Analysis*, 1978, *11*, 381–393.

Trause, M. A. "Stranger Responses: Effects of Familiarity, Stranger's Approach, and Sex of Infant." *Child Development*, 1977, *48*, 1657–1661.

Trower, P., and others. "The Treatment of Social Failure: A Comparison of Anxiety-Reduction and Skills-Acquisition Procedures on Two Social Problems." *Behavior Modification,* 1978, *2,* 41–60.

Tunnell, G. B. "Three Dimensions of Naturalness: An Expanded Definition of Field Research." *Psychological Bulletin,* 1977, *84,* 425–437.

Turner, R. K., James, S. R. N., and Orwin, A. "A Note on the Internal Consistency of the Sexual Orientation Method." *Behavior Research and Therapy,* 1974, *12,* 273–278.

Turner, S. M., and Adams, H. E. "Effects of Assertive Training on Three Dimensions of Assertiveness." *Behavior Research and Therapy,* 1977, *15,* 475–483.

Turner, S. M., Hersen, M., and Bellack, A. S. "Effects of Social Disruption, Stimulus Interference, and Aversive Conditioning on Auditory Hallucinations." *Behavior Modification,* 1977, *1,* 249–258.

Tursky, B. "The Indirect Recording of Human Blood Pressure." In P. A. Obrist and others (Eds.), *Cardiovascular Psychophysiology: Current Issues in Response Mechanisms, Biofeedback, and Methodology.* Chicago: Aldine, 1974.

Twardosz, S., Cataldo, M. F., and Risley, T. R. "Menus for Toddler Daycare: Food Preference and Spoon Use." *Young Children,* 1975, *30,* 129–144.

Twentyman, C. T., and McFall, R. M. "Behavioral Training of Social Skills in Shy Males." *Journal of Consulting and Clinical Psychology,* 1975, *43,* 384–395.

Upper, D., Lochman, J. E., and Aveni, C. A. "Using Contingency Contracting to Modify the Problematic Behaviors of Foster Home Residents." *Behavior Modification,* 1977, *1,* 405–416.

Vaal, J. J. "The Rathus Assertiveness Schedule: Reliability at the Junior High School Level." *Behavior Therapy,* 1975, *6,* 566–567.

Valle, R. S., and DeGood, D. E. "Effects of State-Trait Anxiety on the Ability to Enhance and Suppress EEG Alpha." *Psychophysiology,* 1977, *14,* 1–7.

van Dam, F. S. A. M., and others. "Sexual Arousal Measured by Photoplethysmography." *Behavioral Engineering,* 1976, *3,* 97–101.

Van Houten, R., and Van Houten, J. V. "The Performance Feedback System in the Special Education Classroom: An Analysis of Public Posting and Peer Comments." *Behavior Therapy,* 1977, *8,* 366–376.

Varni, J. G. "Learned Asymmetry of Localized Electrodermal Responses." *Psychophysiology,* 1975, *12,* 41–45.

Venables, P. H., and Christie, M. J. *Research in Psychophysiology.* New York: Wiley, 1975.

Venables, P. H., and Martin, I. *A Manual of Psychophysiological Methods.* New York: Wiley, 1967.

Vogler, R. E., Weissbach, T. A., and Compton, J. V. "Learning Techniques for Alcohol Abuse." *Behavior Research and Therapy,* 1977, *15,* 31–38.

Vogler, R. E., and others. "Integrated Behavior Change Techniques for Problem Drinkers in the Community." *Journal of Consulting and Clinical Psychology,* 1977, *45,* 267–279.

Wade, T. C., Malloy, T. E., and Proctor, S. "Imaginal Correlates of Self-Reported Fear and Avoidance Behavior." *Behavior Research and Therapy,* 1977, *15,* 17–22.

Wahler, R. G. "Setting Generality: Some Specific and General Effects of Child Behavior Therapy." *Journal of Applied Behavior Analysis,* 1969, *2,* 239–246.

Wahler, R. G. "Some Structural Aspects of Deviant Child Behavior." *Journal of Applied Behavior Analysis,* 1975, *8,* 27–42.

Wahler, R. G., House, A. E., and Stambaugh, E. E. *Ecological Assessment of Child Problem Behavior: A Clinical Package for Home, School, and Institutional Settings.* Elmsford, N.Y.: Pergamon Press, 1976.

Walk, R. D. "Self-Ratings of Fear in a Fear-Invoking Situation." *Journal of Abnormal and Social Psychology,* 1956, *52,* 171–178.

Walker, B. B., and Sandman, C. A. "Physiological Response Patterns in Ulcer Patients: Phasic and Tonic Components of the Electrogastrogram." *Psychophysiology,* 1977a, *14,* 393–400.

Walker, B. B., and Sandman, C. A. "The Bidimensionality of the Electrogastrogram." Abstract of paper presented at 16th annual meeting of Society for Psychophysiological Research. *Psychophysiology,* 1977b, *14,* 81.

Walls, R. T., and others. "Behavior Checklists." In J. D. Cone and

R. P. Hawkins (Eds.), *Behavioral Assessment: New Directions in Clinical Psychology*. New York: Brunner/Mazel, 1977.

Walters, A. "The Differentiation of Causalgia and Hyperpathia." *Canadian Medical Association Journal*, 1959, *80*, 105–109.

Warren, N. J., and Gilner, F. H. "Measurement of Positive Assertive Behaviors: The Behavioral Test of Tenderness Expression." *Behavior Therapy*, 1978, *9*, 178–184.

Waters, E., Matas, L., and Sroufe, L. A. "Infants' Reactions to an Approaching Stranger: Description, Validation, and Functional Significance of Wariness." *Child Development*, 1975, *46*, 348–356.

Watson, D., and Friend, R. "Measurement of Social-Evaluative Anxiety." *Journal of Consulting and Clinical Psychology*, 1969, *33*, 448–457.

Waxer, P. H. "Nonverbal Cues for Depression." *Journal of Abnormal Psychology*, 1974, *83*, 319–322.

Waxer, P. H. "Nonverbal Cues for Depth of Depression: Set Versus No Set." *Journal of Consulting and Clinical Psychology*, 1976, *44*, 493.

Waxer, P. H. "Nonverbal Cues for Anxiety: An Examination of Emotional Leakage." *Journal of Abnormal Psychology*, 1977, *86*, 306–314.

Weed, L. L. *Medical Records, Medical Education, and Patient Care.* Chicago: Year Book Medical, 1970.

Weerts, T. C., and Lang, P. J. "Psychophysiology of Fear Imagery: Differences Between Focal Phobia and Social Performance Anxiety." *Journal of Consulting and Clinical Psychology*, 1978, *46*, 1157–1159.

Wein, K. S., Nelson, R. O., and Odom, J. V. "The Relative Contributions of Reattribution and Verbal Extinction to the Effectiveness of Cognitive Restructuring." *Behavior Therapy*, 1975, *6*, 459–474.

Weisenberg, M. "Pain and Pain Control." *Psychological Bulletin*, 1977, *84*, 1008–1044.

Weiss, A. R. "A Behavioral Approach to the Treatment of Adolescent Obesity." *Behavior Therapy*, 1977, *8*, 720–726.

Weiss, R. L., Hops, H., and Patterson, G. R. "A Framework for Conceptualizing Marital Conflict, A Technology for Altering It,

Some Data for Evaluating It." In F. W. Clark and L. A. Hamer-lynck (Eds.), *Critical Issues on Research and Practice: Proceedings of the Fourth Banff International Conference on Behavior Modification.* Champaign, Ill.: Research Press, 1973.

Weiss, R. L., and Margolin, G. "Marital Conflict and Accord." In A. R. Ciminero, K. S. Calhoun, and H. E. Adams (Eds.), *Handbook for Behavioral Assessment.* New York: Wiley, 1977.

Weissberg, M. "A Comparison of Direct and Vicarious Treatments of Speech Anxiety: Desensitization, Desensitization with Coping Imagery, and Cognitive Modification." *Behavior Therapy,* 1977, *8,* 606–620.

Wellman, H. M., and Lempers, J. D. "The Naturalistic Communicative Abilities of Two-Year-Olds." *Child Development,* 1977, *48,* 1052–1057.

Wells, D. T., Allen, R. P., and Wagman, A. M. I. "A Single-Channel System for Recording Eye Movements." *Psychophysiology,* 1977, *14,* 73–74.

Wells, K. C., Forehand, R., and Hickey, K. "Effects of a Verbal Warning and Overcorrection on Stereotyped and Appropriate Behaviors." *Journal of Abnormal Child Psychology,* 1977, *5,* 387–404.

Wells, K. C., and others. "Effects of a Procedure Derived from the Overcorrection Principle on Manipulated and Nonmanipulated Behaviors." *Journal of Applied Behavior Analysis,* 1977, *10,* 679–687.

Wener, A. E., and Rehm, L. "Depressive Affect: A Test of Behavioral Hypotheses." *Journal of Abnormal Psychology,* 1975, *84,* 221–227.

Werry, J. S. "Developmental Hyperactivity." *Pediatric Clinics of North America,* 1968, *15,* 581–600.

Werry, J. S., Sprague, R. L., and Cohen, M. N. "Conners' Teacher Rating Scale for Use in Drug Studies with Children—An Empirical Study." *Journal of Abnormal Child Psychology,* 1975, *3,* 217–229.

Werry, J. S., and others. "Studies on the Hyperactive Child: III. The Effect of Chlorpromazine upon Behavior and Learning." *Journal of the American Academy of Child Psychiatry,* 1966, *5,* 292–312.

West, S. M., and others. "Behavioral and Physiological Correlates of Insomnia." Paper presented at meeting of the Southeastern

Psychological Association, Miami, April 1977.

White, G. D. "The Effects of Observer Presence on the Activity Level of Families." *Journal of Applied Behavior Analysis,* 1977, *10,* 734.

White, K. D. "Salivation: A Review and Experimental Investigation of Major Techniques." *Psychophysiology,* 1977a, *14,* 203–212.

White, K. D. "Salivation and the Law of Initial Value." *Psychophysiology,* 1977b, *14,* 560–562.

White, K. D. "Salivation: The Significance of Imagery in Its Voluntary Control." *Psychophysiology,* 1978, *15,* 196–204.

Whitehead, W. E., Drescher, V. M., and Hanenson, I. B. "Communication: Reflex Decreases in Human Diastolic Blood Pressure." *Journal of Applied Behavior Analysis,* 1977, *10,* 526.

Whitehead, W. E., and others. "Relation of Heart-Rate Control to Heartbeat Perception." *Biofeedback and Self-Regulation,* 1977, *2,* 371–392.

Wicker, A. W. "Attitudes Versus Actions: The Relationship of Verbal and Overt Behavioral Responses to Attitudinal Objects." *Journal of Social Issues,* 1969, *25,* 41–78.

Wiggins, J. S., Wiggins, N., and Conger, J. C. "Correlates of Heterosexual Somatic Preferences." *Journal of Personality and Social Psychology,* 1968, *10,* 83–90.

Wildman, B. G., and Erickson, M. T. "Methodological Problems in Behavioral Observation." In J. D. Cone and R. P. Hawkins (Eds.), *Behavioral Assessment: New Directions in Clinical Psychology.* New York: Brunner/Mazel, 1977.

Williams, C. L., and Ciminero, A. R. "Development and Validation of a Heterosexual Skills Inventory: The Survey of Heterosexual Interactions for Females." *Journal of Consulting and Clinical Psychology,* 1978, *46,* 1547–1548.

Williams, R. L., and Workman, E. A. "The Development of a Behavioral Self-Concept Scale." *Behavior Therapy,* 1978, *9,* 680–681.

Willner, A. G., and others. "The Training and Validation of Youth-Preferred Social Behaviors of Child Care Personnel." *Journal of Applied Behavior Analysis,* 1977, *10,* 219–230.

Wilson, G. T. "Alcohol and Human Sexual Behavior." *Behavior Research and Therapy,* 1977, *15,* 239–252.

Wilson, G. T., and Lawson, D. M. "The Effects of Alcohol on Sexual Arousal in Women." *Journal of Abnormal Psychology*, 1976, *85*, 489–497.

Wincze, J. P., Hoon, E. F., and Hoon, P. W. "Physiological Responsivity of Normal and Sexually Dysfunctional Women During Erotic Stimulus Exposure." *Journal of Psychosomatic Research*, 1976, *20*, 445–457.

Wincze, J. P., Hoon, E. F., and Hoon, P. W. "Multiple-Measure Analysis of Women Experiencing Low Sexual Arousal." *Behavior Research and Therapy*, 1978, *16*, 43–49.

Wincze, J. P., Hoon, P. W., and Hoon, E. F. "Sexual Arousal in Women: A Comparison of Cognitive and Physiological Responses by Continuous Measurement." *Archives of Sexual Behavior*, 1977, *6*, 121–133.

Wing, L., Gould, J., and Yeates, S. R. "Symbolic Play in Severely Mentally Retarded and in Autistic Children." *Journal of Child Psychology and Psychiatry and Allied Disciplines*, 1977, *18*, 167–178.

Winkler, R. C. "What Types of Sex-Role Behavior Should Behavior Modifiers Promote?" *Journal of Applied Behavior Analysis*, 1977, *10*, 549–552.

Wolfe, J. L., and Fodor, I. G. "Modifying Assertive Behavior in Women: A Comparison of Three Approaches." *Behavior Therapy*, 1977, *8*, 567–574.

Wolfe, M. M. "Social Validity: The Case for Subjective Measurement, or How Applied Behavior Analysis is Finding Its Heart." *Journal of Applied Behavior Analysis*, 1978, *11*, 203–214.

Wolff, E., and Epstein, L. H. "A Procedure for Implementing the Problem-Oriented Medical Record in Open Settings." *Behavior Therapy*, 1977, *8*, 506–507.

Wollersheim, J. P. "Effectiveness of Group Therapy Based upon Learning Principles in the Treatment of Overweight Women." *Journal of Abnormal Psychology*, 1970, *76*, 462–474.

Wolpe, J. *The Practice of Behavior Therapy*. Elmsford, N.Y.: Pergamon Press, 1969.

Wolpe, J. "Inadequate Behavior Analysis: The Achilles Heel of Outcome Research in Behavior Therapy." *Journal of Behavior Therapy and Experimental Psychiatry*, 1977, *8*, 1–3.

Wolpe, J., and Lang, P. J. "A Fear Survey Schedule for Use in

Behavior Therapy." *Behavior Research and Therapy*, 1964, *2*, 27–30.

Wolpe, J., and Lazarus, A. A. *Behavior Therapy Techniques: A Guide to the Treatment of Neuroses.* Oxford, England: Pergamon Press, 1966.

Wood, D. D., and others. "Communication: A Behaviorally Based Logbook." *Journal of Applied Behavior Analysis*, 1977, *10*, 706.

Wood, R., and Flynn, J. M. "A Self-Evaluation Token System Versus an External Evaluation Token System Alone in a Residential Setting with Predelinquent Youth." *Journal of Applied Behavior Analysis*, 1978, *11*, 503–512.

Wright, D. F., and Bunch, G. "Parental Intervention in the Treatment of Chronic Constipation." *Journal of Behavior Therapy and Experimental Psychiatry*, 1977, *8*, 93–95.

Wroblewski, P. F., Jacob, T., and Rehm, L. P. "The Contribution of Relaxation to Symbolic Modeling in the Modification of Dental Fears." *Behavior Research and Therapy*, 1977, *15*, 113–117.

Wulbert, M., and Dries, R. "The Relative Efficacy of Methylphenidate (Ritalin) and Behavior Modification Techniques in the Treatment of a Hyperactive Child." *Journal of Applied Behavior Analysis*, 1977, *10*, 21–31.

Yarrow, M. R., Campbell, J. D., and Burton, R. V. "Recollections of Childhood: A Study of the Retrospective Method." *Monographs of the Society for Research in Child Development*, 1970, *35* (5), 1–83.

Yeaton, W. H., and Bailey, J. S. "Teaching Pedestrian Safety Skills to Young Children: An Analysis and One-Year Follow-Up." *Journal of Applied Behavior Analysis*, 1978, *11*, 315–329.

Yelton, A. R., Wildman, B. G., and Erickson, M. T. "A Probability-Based Formula for Calculating Interobserver Agreement." *Journal of Applied Behavior Analysis*, 1977, *10*, 127–131.

Yepes, L. E., and others. "Amitriptyline and Methylphenidate Treatment of Behaviorally Disordered Children." *Journal of Child Psychology and Psychiatry and Allied Disciplines*, 1977, *18*, 39–52.

Young-Browne, G., Rosenfeld, H. M., and Horowitz, F. D. "Infant Discrimination of Facial Expressions." *Child Development*, 1977, *48*, 555–562.

Zegiob, L. E., and Forehand, R. "Parent-Child Interactions: Observer Effects and Social Class Differences." *Behavior Therapy,* 1978, *9,* 118–123.

Zeichner, A., Pihl, R. O., and Wright, J. C. "A Comparison Between Volunteer Drug Abusers and Nondrug Abusers on Measures of Social Skills." *Journal of Clinical Psychology,* 1977, *33,* 585–590.

Zeiss, A. M., Rosen, G. M., and Zeiss, R. A. "Orgasm During Intercourse: A Treatment Strategy for Women." *Journal of Consulting and Clinical Psychology,* 1977, *45,* 891–895.

Zeiss, R. A. "Self-Directed Treatment of Premature Ejaculation: Preliminary Case Reports." *Journal of Behavior Therapy and Experimental Psychiatry,* 1977, *8,* 87–91.

Zeiss, R. A. "Self-Directed Treatment for Premature Ejaculation." *Journal of Consulting and Clinical Psychology,* 1978, *46,* 1234–1241.

Zemore, R. "Systematic Desensitization as a Method of Teaching a General Anxiety-Reducing Skill." *Journal of Consulting and Clinical Psychology,* 1975, *43,* 157–161.

Zivin, G. "On Becoming Subtle: Age and Social Rank Changes in the Use of a Facial Gesture." *Child Development,* 1977, *48,* 1314–1321.

Zuckerman, M. "Development of a Situation-Specific Trait-State Test for the Prediction and Measurement of Affective Responses." *Journal of Consulting and Clinical Psychology,* 1977, *45,* 513–523.

# Name Index

# Subject Index